POCKET

ENGLISH - TAGALOG

VISAYAN

CEBUANO — ILONGO

Vocabulary

By

M. JACOBO ENRIQUEZ
JOSE A. BAUTISTA

and

FRANCIS J. JAMOLANGUE, Jr.

EDITION - 1999

Publisher & Distributor

**MARREN
PUBLISHING
HOUSE
INC.**

Ground Floor, Marren Bldg.
1157 Quezon Ave., Quezon City
Tel. Nos. 372-89-40 / 372-89-41
415-31-16 / 415-31-17

BILANG PANGUNA

Ang pagtukib, sa isá ka Kapulongan (bokabularyo ukón diksyonaryo) amó ang isá ka buluhatón nga mauti kag nagakinahanglan sing nagakaigó nga kahulogán sunó sa naandan niya nga militlangon. Indi ini patarasak katulad sang pagsulát, sanglit ang Kapulongan amo'ng salandigan sang tanán nga hambal. Agúd nga hatagan sing sabát ang madamó nga bumalasa sa hinilagaynon sang madugay na nila ginapangayó nga Diksyonaryo ukón Kapulongan, sa maalwan nga kabubut-on sang Marren Publishing House, Inc. natigayon namon ang paghumán, dili lamang sa isá ka pulong kondi sa apat ka pulong. Ini nga pagtigayon, nagakahulogán nga umuswag kitá sa aton panulatan kag bilang pagsakdag sang pungsodnon nga pulong.

Pananglit may mgá tinaga nga nagahilibag sa ila kahulogán, butáng iná nga ginapauna sang tagbuhat sini nga pasaylohón lamang nila, bangód ang hiniligaynon, kutob sadto, walá pa sing nabantalá nga de awtoridad nga pulong. Sa mga tinaga nga gingamit sa Bokabularyo nga ini sang Iningles-Tinagalog (Binisaya) Cebuano-Inilonggo, gintuyó namon ang labing mahapós hangpon nga tinagá kag hambal sang bug-os nga Kabisay-an. Indi mahimutig nga may sakút nga kinatsilá kag iningles, sanglit sa pagpamanggad sang pulong, kinahanglan manghulám kitá sa ibán subong sang ginbuhat sang kinatsilá kag iningles nga nanghulám sa latin.

FRANCIS J. JAMOLANGUE, Jr.

Ilongo - Cebuano

ENGLISH - TAGALOG - VISAYAN
Vocabulary

— Tagalog-English-Visayan Vocabulary —

ABBREVIATIONS USED

adj. — Adjective — Pang-urì — Adhetibo — Panarî

adv. — Adverb — Pang-abay — Adberbiyo — Pang-ubáy

art. — Article — Pantukoy — Panudlo — Panuyò

conj. — Conjunction — Pangatníg — Panugtong — Panabíd

interj. — Interjection — Pandamdám — Pabatyag

n. — Noun — Pangngalan — Pangalan (nombre)—Pangalan

prep. — Preposition — Pang-ukol — Preposisyon — Patungód

pron. — Pronoun — Panghalíp — Pronombre — Pang-ilis

rw. — Root Word—Salitáng ugát—Ugat-pulong—Panghambal-ugát

v. — Verb — Pandiwà — Berbo — Panglihok

PASIUNA

Ang paghikay usa ka Kapulongnan (bokabularyo kun diksiyonaryo) maoy usa ka buluhaton nga makuti ug nagkinahanglan dakung pagbantay, pailub ug pangduki-duki sa iyang Tagsulat kun Taghikay. Kining basahon nga naglangkob sa mga pulong-kahulogan sa upat ka lain-laing pinulongan (Iningles-Tinagalog-Binisayang Cebuano-Binisayang Inilonggo) among idulot sa katilingban uban ang tumang panghinaut nga makatuman unta sa iyang tuyo ug tinguha nga mao ang pagtampo alang sa kalamboan ug kauamaran sa mga pinulongang Pilipinhon tupad sa pinulongang Iningles nga gihimong gabayan kun panukaran ning atong Bakabularyo.

Ang mga taghikay niini nga basahon nanghinaut usab nga kining bunga sa ilang mga pagtukaw ug paningkamut makahatag untag igong kapuslanan alang niadtong mga tawo nga nagkinahanglan diyutayng kahayag sa natad sa mga pinulongan. Kini nga aklat dili matawag nga hingpit sa iyang pagkamao, apan among paningkamutan ang paghikay sa ulahing mga higayon usa ka bokabularyo nga labi pang haduol sa kahingpitan, ken dili man ugaling hingpit gayud sa iyang kinatibuk-an.

—JOSE A. BAUTISTA
(Sa Binisayang Cebuano)

ENGLISH-TAGALOG-VISAYAN

(Cebuano-Ilongo)

— A —

A, art.—isá, unang titik ng Abakada—usá, unang titik sa Aba-
kadhan—isá, unang tinaga sang
Abakada

ABANDON, v.—pabayaan, iwan—
pagbiyá, biyaan—pabayaan

ABDOMEN, n.—tiyán—tiyan—tiyán

ABDUCT, v.—itakas, agawin —
Pagtaban, Pagdagít — ipalagyo,
agawon

ABEYANCE, n.—paghihíntay —
ang paghulát—paghulát

ABIDE, v.—manirahan—pagpuyo,
pagpahiuyon—pagpuyô

ABILITY, n.—kakayahán — kata-
kús—pagkabatíd

ABLE, adj.—maykaya, maylakás
—takús, saráng — makasaráng,
makasangkul

ABNORMAL, adj.—naiibá sa karaniwan—lahi sa naandan — tuhay sa kinaandan

ABOLISH, v.—alisin, pawalán ng
bisà—paghanaw, pagwagtang —
kuhaon, kuhaan sing gahúm

ABOARD, adv.—nakalulan, lulan
—sakáy, anaa sa itaás—sumakáy, nakalulan

ABORTIVE, n. — panganganak
nang walâ sa panahón—panga-
nák nga wala sa panahon—na-
hulogan, pagpanganák nga walâ sa panahón

ABOUT, prep. adv.—tungkól sa,
halos—sa ibabaw, labaw sa —
pa ibabaw, kapín sa

ABOVE, adv.—sa ibabaw, higít sa
—sa ibabaw, labaw sa—tungód
sa, halos

ABRUPT, a.—biglâ — kalit, hinanali—hinali

ABRIDGE, v.—igsián, paikliín —
pagputól, pagmubó—lip-utón

ABSENT, adj.—walâ, dî pumasok
—paghiwala, wala sa dapit—
walâ

ABSORB, v.—sipsipín, tangayín—
pagsuyop—supsupón

ABSURD, adj.—katawá-tawâ, waláng katuturán — makapatawâ,
walay-pasikaran—siháy

ABSOLUTE, adj.—makapangyari-
hán, ganáp—tinud-anon, mapig-
uton—minatuód, madaúgdaugon

ABUNDANCE, n.—kasaganaan —
ang pagkadaghan, abunda—ka-
dagayan

ABUSE, n.—paslangín, pagmalabi-
sán—pasipala, palabi-labi, patu-
yang—aboso, kakapinán

1

ACCENT, n.—tuldík, diín—tulbok, litók—asento

ACCEPT, v.—tanggapín—pagdawat—pagbaton

ACCIDENTALLY, adv.—nang disinásadyâ, di-sinásadyâ—sa dili tinuyo—dî-hungód

ACCOMPANY, v.—saliwán, samahan—pagkuyog, pagduyog—pagbuylog

ACCOMPLISH, v.—tùpdín, gawín —paghumán, pagtapus—pagtuman

ACCOUNT, v.—ipagsulit, panagután—pagsayud, asoy—kasayuran

ACCOUNTANT, n.—tagaayos ng kuwenta — mangingîhap, tagkwenta—tagkwenta

ACCUSE, v.—pagbintángán—pagsumbong—pagsumbong

ACCUSTOM, v.—igawî, hiratihin —pag-anad—paghianad

ACHE, v.—sumakít—sakit, ngutngot, pagsakit—sakít, alay

ACIDITY, n.—asim, pangangasim —kaaslum, kakisum—aslum, asluman

ACKNOWLEDGE, v. — kilalanin, tanggapín—pag-ila, pagdawat—kilalahon, batonon

ACQUAINT, v.—ipabatíd, ipaalám —pagpaila, pagsinati—ipasayud

ACQUIRE, v.—bilhín, kamtán — pagbatón, pagkab-ut—baklon

ACROSS, prep.—sa ibayo, sa kabilâ—sa tabok, sa pikas—sa tabúk

ACT, v.—gumawâ, gumanáp, kumilos—buhat, yugto, pagbuhat —magbuhat

ACTION, n.—kilos—lihok—hulag

ACTIVE, adj.—maliksí, buháy na loób—abtik, buhi, liksi—maabtik

ACTRESS, n.—artistang babac—artistang babaye—artistang babáe

ACTUAL, adv.—tunay—buhainon, lihoknon—tunay

ADD, v.—idagdág, pagsamahin. — pagdugang, pagsuma—idugang, tingbon

ADDITION, n.—pagsasama, pagdaragdag — ang pagsuma, ang pagpunó — pagtilingob, pagdugang

ADDRESS, n.—direksyón, tinítirhán—pinuy-anan, direksiyon — direksyon, puluy-an.

ADEQUATE, adj.—hustó, karampatan—igo, husto—husto, nagakaigò

ADJECTIVE, n.—pang-urì—adhetibo, pangmatang—pangsarî

ADJUST, v.—itumpák, itamà—isibu, pagsibu—isibù, itamà

ADMIRAL, n.—almirante—almirante—almirante

2

ADMIRATION, n. — paghangà — dalayeg, pagdayo -- admirasyon, paghangád

ADMIRE, v.—purihin, hangaan — pagdayeg, malbugong pagbati — hangarón

ADMISSION, n. — pagtanggáp. pagpasok — pagtugot, pag-ang-kon—batonon

ADMIT, v. — tanggapín, aminin, papasukin—pag-amin, pagdawat —akuon, pasudlon

ADOPT, v.—pagtibayin, kalingain —pagsagop—sapupohon, sagurón

ADORE, v. — hangaan, purihin, sambahín—paghigugma, simbahon—higugmaón

ADULT, n.—matandâ, magulang, may-edád—hamtong, edaran — may-edád

ADVANCE, n.—pagsulong, páuná —sulong, pag-una — pag-uswag, manguna

ADVANTAGE, n. — kalamangán, kahigitán, kapakinabangán—labaw, bintaha—kaayohán, kapuslanan

ADVENTURE, n.—pakikipagsápalarán — pamagdoy, asanyas — pagpasimpalád

ADVENTUROUS, adj.—mapagsápalarán — mabagdoyon — magpasimpalád

ADVERB, n.—pang-abay—adberbiyo, pangbulok—pang-ubáy, adberbyo

ADVERTISE, v.—ianunsiyo, ibabalâ, mag-anunsiyo — pagpamantala, imantala — ianunsyo. ipabantalà

ADVERTISEMENT, n.—anunsiyo. palathalà—pamantala — anunsyo, pabantala

ADVICE, n.—payo, turò—tambag, sambag—lugpay, laygay, tudlò

ADVISE, v.—pagpayuhan, turuan. pahiwatigan—pagpahibalo, pagsayud—tudluán, laygayán. pahibaloan

AFFAIR, n.—kabagayán, gáwain. kapakanán—butang — katuyoán, pagkabutáng

AFFIDAVIT, n.—pahayag na pinasumpaán—sinumpaang pahayag—apidabit

AFFILIATE, v.—umanib, sumapi —pagpasakop, kaanib—makigbuylog,. makigsimpon

AFFORD, v.—makaya, magbigáy, matiís—maghatag, makahatag—masarangán, maghatag

AFRAID, adj.—natátakot, nangángambá—nahadlok, nalisang — nahadlok

AFTER, prep., adv. — pagkaraán, pagkatapos — human, tapus— pagkatapos

AFTERNOON, n.—tanghalì, hapon —hapon—hapon, ugtó

AFTERWARDS, adv. — pagkatapos, pagkaraán — pagkahuman, pagkatapus—kahingapusán

AGAIN, adv.—mulî, ulî — usab, upod—liwát

AGAINST, prep.—laban sa, labág sa—batok—batok sa

AGE, n.—gulang, katandaán, edád —panuigon, kapanahonan—kagulangón, edád

AGENCY, n.—ahensiya, sangáy—ahensiya, sanga—ahensya

AGENT, n.—kinatawán, ahente —tinugyanan, ahente—ahente, tinogyanán

AGREE, v. — pumayag, sumangayon—pag-uyon — pumasugót, pumaayón

AGREEABLE, adj.—nakalúlugód, sang-ayon—mauyonan — makapahalipay

AGREEMENT, n. — kásunduan, kontrato—kauyonan — kasugtanan, kontrato

AGRICULTURE, n. — pagsasaka, pagbubungkál ng lupà—pangyuta, panguma — pagpanguma, agrikultura

AHEAD, adv.—náuuná, una—nanguna, sa unahan—nagapanguna

AID, n.—tulong—tabang, pagtabang—tabang, bulig

AIM, n.—pakay, layon—tinguha, pagpaninguha—handum, tilinguhaón

AIR, n.—hangin—hangin—hangin

AIRMAIL, n.—pahatirang-sulat sa himpapawíd—koreyo sa ayroplano—airmail

AIRPLANE, n.—eroplano — ayroplano, salakhangin—eroplano

AISLE, n.—eskinita, maliít na daán, pasilyo—sigpit agianan—eskinita, pasilyo

ALARM, n.—hudyát—pahibalo sa kalisang—patundà

ALAS, conj.—nakú—ayay ko! — abáw

ALCOHOL, n.—alkohól—al;rohol alkohól

ALIEN, n.—dayuhan, taga-ibáng bansá—langyaw, lumalangyaw—dumuluong

ALIENATE, v.—ilayô ang kalooban—pagpahilayo—ipahilayô ang buót

ALIGHT, v.—dumapò, bumabâ—pagkanaug—lumusad

ALIGNMENT, n.—pagkakáhanay, pakikipanig — pakig-abyanay—pagkulubay

4

ALIKE, adj.—magkamukhâ, magkahawíg, magkatulad — sama, maingon-ingon, may-ong—magkanawóng, magkaanggid

ALIVE, adj.—buháy, maliksí—buhi—buhî

ALL, pron.—lahát—tanan—tanán

ALLEGIANCE, n. — pagtatapát, pagkatig—pagpakig-anib — pagpakighangup

ALLIGATOR, n.--buwaya—buaya—buaya

ALLOW, v.—payagan, pahintulutan—pagtugot—tugotan

ALLY, n.—kakampí, kasama—kaabin, kaanib—kakampi, kaupod

ALMIGHTY, n. — Makapangyarihan sa láhát—Makagagahum—Makagagahum

ALMOST, adv.—halos—hapit — halos

ALONE, adj.—nag-íisá — usa ra, nag-musara—isahanon

ALOUD, adv.—malakás — makusog—mabaskug

ALPHABET, n.—abakada—akakadhan, alpabeto—alpabeto

ALREADY, adv.—na—na—na

ALSO, adv.—rin, patí, man—usab, upod, gihapon — patí, man

ALTAR, n. — dambanà, altár — alampoanan, altar—altar

ALTHOUGH, conj.—kahit na, káhiman—bisan, bisan pa—bisán, bisán pa

ALTOGETHER, adv. — lahát-lahát, ganap—tanan-tanan — tanán-tanán

ALTITUDE, n.—kataasan—kahabugon—kataasan

ALWAYS, adv.—lagì na, parati—sa kanunay—gihapon

AM, v.—(akó) ay—ako—akó

AMAZE, v.—gulatin, papagtakhín—paghibulong — patingalahon kibutón

AMBASSADOR, n.—sugò, kinata wán—embahador—embahador

AMBITION, n.—lunggatî, hángarin—tingusbawan—handum

AMEND, v.—ibahín, susugan, baguhin—pag-usab, pagbalhin ligwatón

AMONG, prep.—kahalubilò, kasama, sa gitnâ—apil, uban sa panon—sa ibán (nga)

AMOUNT, v.—umabot, magkaha lagá—bili, kantidad—bilí, kantidád

AMPLE, adj.—sapát, malakí—daku, daghan—sangkad, halúg

AMULET, n.—antíng-antíng—anting-anting—anting-anting

AMUSEMENT, n.—katuwaan, áliwan, líbangan — kalingawan — kalingawan

ANCESTOR, n.—ninunò—katigulangan—kaliwatan

ANCHOR, v.—dumaóng—angkla—angkla, sinipit

ANCIENT, adj.—matandâ—karaan—katigulangan

AND, conj.—at, sakâ—ug—kag

ANGELUS, n.—orasyón—orasyon—orasyon

ANGER, n.—galit, poót—kasuko, kapikal—akíg

ANGUISH, n.—sakít, hirap—kasakit, kaguol—kamingaw, kalisúd

ANIMAL, n.—hayop—mananap—hayop

ANKLE, n.—bukung-bukong—tuhod, buol-buol—bukóbuko

ANNIVERSARY, n. — kaarawán, anibersaryo — kaadlawan, anibersaryo—kaadlawan, anibersaryo

ANNOUNCE, v.—ihayag, sabihin, ipatalastás—pagpahibalo, ipahayag—ipahibaló, ipasayud

ANNOY, v.—yamutín, abalahin—pagsamok—tublagón, awatón

ANNUAL, adj.—táunan—tinuig—tuigtuig

ANOTHER, n.—ibá, isá pa—lain—ibán, isá pa

ANSWER, n.—sagót, tugón — tubag, balus—sabát

ANT, n.—langgám — hulmigas — subáy

ANUS, n.—puwít—samput, kotipot—bulî, aliputan

ANXIETY, n.—pag-aalaala, pananabík, pagkabalisa—paghigwaos—pahanumdum

ANXIOUS, adj.—sabík, balisâ —

ANYBODY, pron. — sínumán—bisan kinsa—bisán sin-o

ANYTHING, n.—anumán, kahit ano—bisan unsa—bisán anó

ANYWAY, adv.—kahit paano, sa paano't paánumán—bisan pa—bisán pa

ANYWHERE, adv.—kahit saán, saanmán—bisan asa, bisan diin—bisán diín

APART, adv.—hiwaláy, bukód — lain, himulag—tuhay, putáputá

APARTMENT, n.—silíd, bahay-páupahán—lawak, puluy-anan — baláy-hinakayan

APIECE, adv —bawa't isá—tagsatagsa—tagsatagsa

APPARITION, n.—multó—multo, kalag—murto

APPARATUS, adj. — aparato — aparatu, makina—aparatus

APPARENTLY, adv.—sa malas—sa dayag—kahimutaran

APPEAL, n.—paghahabol—tutol, apelasyon—pag-apelár, pagsungkà

APPEAL, v.—mamanhík, maghabol—pagdangop, pagtutol—magapelár, magpasungkà

APPEAR, v.—pakita; lumitáw — pagpakita—pagpakità

APPEARANCE, n. — paglabás, ayos—panagway, pagula—dagway

APPETITE, n.—gana, kagustuhan —gana—gana, gaman

APPLICATION, n. — kahílingan, paglalapat — kagamitan, solisitud—aplikasyon

APPLY, v.—lapatan, humilíng, dumulóg—pagsulod (sa buhat) — tuyò sa pagsulód

APPOINT, v.—hirangin, humirang —pagtudlo—lawagon

APPOINTMENT, n. — pagkahirang, tiyapan—pagkatudlo, kasabutan sa pakigkita—lawag

APPRECIATE, v.—ikaligaya, ikalugód, pahalagahán, pasalamatan — pagtamud, paghiayon — pagtamúd, higugmaón

APPRECIATION, n.—pagbibigáyhalagá, pagkalugód—paghatagbili—pagkamahigugmaon, pagtinamdanay

APPRENTICE, n.—aprendis, katulong—aprendis—aprendis, kabulig

APPROACH, v.—lumapit, lapitan —pagduol—palapitán

APPROVE, v.—pasiyahán, mabutihin—pagdason, pagtugot—pakamaayohon

APRICOT, n.—melokotón—melokoton—melokotón

APRON, n.—tapî, tapis—tapis — tampis

ARBOR, n.—balag—bahin sa kahoy—arbor, handongan

ARCH, n.—arkó, balantók—arko—arko

ARCHIPELAGO, n.—kapuluán — kapupud-an—kapuloán

ARCHITECT, n.—árkitekto—arkitekto—arkitekto

ARE, v.—ay (marami)—timaan sa daghan—sanday, nanday

AREA, n.—lapad, sukat, kalakhán —gidak-on, gilapdon—kalapad, kadakuón

ARDOR, n.—init, alab, kataimtiman—kainit, dilaab sa pagbati —kainit, kaalabaab

ARGUE, v.—makipagtalo—paglantugi, paglalis—magpakigbais

ARGUMENT, n.—pagtatalo, katuwiran—lantugi, lalis—pagbaisáy

7

ARISE, v.—tumindíg, bumangon, bumalikwás— pagbangon, pagtindog — tumindog, bumangon, bumungkalas

ARITHMETIC, n.—aritmetika — aritmetika — aritmetika

ARMOR, n. — kalasag, baluti — puthaw'ng kalasag kung saput— taming

ARMS, n.—mga sandata, mga bisig—mga bukton, hinagiban — butkon, armas

ARMY, n.—sundalo — kasundalohan—armada, kasoldadohan

AROUND, adv.—sa paligid—libut, anaa sa duol—sa palibot

ARRANGE, v.—ayusin, husayin— paghusay—husayon

ARRANGEMENT, n. — pagkakaayòs—husay—pagkahusay

ARREST, n.—pagkadakíp, pagkahuli, pagdakíp—pagdakop, ang pagsikop—pagkadakúp

ARREST, v.—dakipín—dakpon — dakpon

ARRIVAL, n.—pagdatíng, pagsapit—ang paghiabut—pag-abót

ARRIVE, v.—dumatíng, sumapit— pag-abut—umabót

ARROW, n.—palasô—gapasan, udyong—panâ

ART, n.—sining—arte, siampat — arte, taliambong

ARTICLE, n.—pantukoy (grammar) — (patungod sa gramatika)—patungód

ARTICLE, n.—panindá, tuntunin —butang, sinulat—tinda, artikuló

AS, adv.—gaya ng, tulad ng — ingon sa — subong sang, tulad sang

ASCEND, v.—umakyát, pumaitaàs —pagsaka, pagpatoas—sumakà, pumaibabaw

ASCENDANCY, n.—pag-akyát — ang paghitaas—pagsakà

ASH, n.—abó—abu—abó

ASHAMED, adj.—nahíhiyâ, nakí kimî—naulaw—nahuyâ

ASHORE, adv.—nasa lupà, nasa pampáng—sa yuta—sa dutà, sa takas

ASIDE, adv.—bukód—sa laing bahin—luás sa ibán nga butáng

ASK, v.—itanóng, hingín, usisain —pagpangayo, pagpangutana — ipamangkut, pangayuon, usisaon

ASLEEP, adj.—natútulog, tulóg— natulog—nagkatulóg

ASSAIL, v.—daluhungin, tuligsaín —pagsaway, pagsukmag—dalasáón

ASSAULT, v.—awayin, salakayín, halayin — paghasmag, pagsukmag—awayon, gubaton

ASSEMBLE, v.—ipunin, magtipon —pagtipon—tiponon, tiliponon

ASSEMBLY, n.—kapulungan, pagtitipon—tigum, katiguman, dalam—pagtililipon

ASSEMBLYMAN. n.—kinatawán, representante—magbabalaod — tiglawás, representante

ASSIGN, v.—ipagawâ, itakdâ — pagtudlo, ipabuhat — idestino, ipaatipán

ASSIGNMENT, n.—takdáng gáwain, takdáng aralín—tinugyan nga buluhaton — idestino, alatipanón

ASSIMILATE, v.—isama — pagipon-ipon—itabíd

ASSIST, v.—tulungan, dumaló — pagtabang—buligan

ASSISTANCE, n.—tulóng—panabang, hinabang—bulig

ASSOCIATE, n.—kasamä — käuban, tambayayong—kaupod

ASSOCIATION, n. — kapisanan, samahán—kapunongan, pundok —talapoanan

ASSUME, v.—ipalagáy, gampanán —pagdawat—ibutáng naton, ipaakò

ASSURE, v.—tiyakín—pagseguro, pagmatuod—pat-urón

ASTRAY, adv.—ligáw—libud—tumalang

ASTONISH, v.—magitlâ, magtaká, magulat—pagkatingala, pagpakurat—matingala

ASTONISHMENT, n.—pagkagulat, pagtataká, pagkabiglâ—ang katingala, kahikurat—pagkatingala

ASYLUM, n.—ampunan—asilo — alaypan, asilo

AT, prep.—sa, nasa—sa, anaa sa —sa

ATTACH, v.—ikabít, isanib—paglakip, pagpadikit—iapíd

ATTACHMENT, n.—pagkakákabít, pagkálapít ng loób — ang pagbating kadug-ol—pagkaapíd

ATTACK, v.—atakihin, salakayin, daluhungín, paslangín — dasdas, pagsulong, paghasmag — atakehon, salakayon

ATTAIN, v.—tamuhín, abutín — pagkab-ut—agumon

ATTAINMENT, n.—naabot, natapos, nátamó—ang nakab-ut — naagum, natapos, naangkon

ATTEMPT, v.—subukin, pagpilitan—pagsulay, sulay—tilawán, tinguhaán

ATTEND, v.—dumaló, alagaan, asikasuhin—pagtambong, pagtagad—dumugok, alagarán, asikasohon

ATTENDANT, n.—tagapag-alagà, taga-asikaso, katulong—ang tigtagad, tig-alima—tagtatap, enpermera

ATTENTION, n.—pansín, pakikiníg, pag-aasikaso — ang pagtagad, pagpatalinghog—patalupangod

ATTIRE, n.—damít, kasúutan — saput, besti, sinina—sapút, panapton

ATTORNEY, n. — mánananggól, abugado—manlalaban, abogado —mananabang, abogado

ATTRACT, v.—akitin, ganyakín, bighaniin—pagbihag, pagdani — bihagon, lumayón

ATTRACTION, n.—palabás, panghalina—dulogokon, atraksiyon— dulugokan, atraksyon

ATTRACTIVE, adj. — nakaháhalina, nakatátawag pansín — madanihon—makabibihag

AUDACIOUS, adj.—waláng-gulat, matapang—mapangahason, maalig-aligon—walá'y kahadlok, isganán

AUDIENCE, n. — mga nakikiníg, mga nanónoód, taga-pakiníg, tagapanoód—tigpaminaw — dumulugok, manogpamatî

AUTHOR, n.—awtor, may-gawâ, may-kathâ, may-akdâ—tagsulat, tagbuhat—tagsulát

AUTHORITY, n.—kapangyarihan —gahum, kagamhanan—punoan

AUTHORIZE, v. — bigyán ng kapangyarihan o pamamahalà — hatagan ug gahum—pahanugotan

AUNT, n.—ale, tiyá—iyaán—tiyà

AVERAGE, v.—karaniwan—kapin kun kulang, kasarangan—kapín ukón kulang

AVID, adj.—masigasig, matakaw, —dawo, mahakogon — matakaw, aresgado

AVOID, v.—iwasan, luyuán, ilagan—paglikay, pagpalayo—likawan

AWAIT, v.—hintayín — hulaton, paghulat—hulatón

AWAKE, a.—gisíng—nagmata — bugtaw

AWAY, adv.—malayò, nasa malayò—halayo, sa layo—sa unhan, sa malayô

AWE, n.—pangimì, sindák — kahadlok—hadlok, pagkahadlok

AWHILE, adj.—sandalî—makadiyut lamang—madalî lang

AWL, n.—pambutas — iglulungag —barina

AWNING, n.—tabing, habong—bayungbong, atop-atop—panglipón (kanbas ukón trapál)

AX, n.—palakól, palatáw — atsa, wasay, pakol—wasay

— B —

BABY, n.—sanggól — masuso — lapsag, batà nga diótay pa

BACK, n.—likód—likod, buko-buko—likód

BACKWARD, adj.—napag-íiwan, atrasado—albog, iwit—sa ulihan

BACON, n.—tosino, karnéng baboy na inasnán at pinaasuhan—tosino, baboy nga hinudno—tosino, karne sang baboy nga pinaasohan

BAD, adj.—masamâ — mangil-ad, malaksot—malain

BADGE, n.—sagisag, tandâ, tsapa —tsapa—syapa

BADLY, adv.—nápakasamâ—nangil-ad—tuman kalain

BAFFLE, v.—lituhín— paglibug, pagsango—libangón

BAG, n.—supot, balutan, bayóng—sako, baluyot, puyo — may-ong, sako

BAGGAGE, n. — dala-dalahan — ekipahe, mga dala—bagahe

BAGGASSE, n.—pınagkatasán ng tubó, bagaso, pinagpangusán, sapal ng tubó—bagaso, tinupsan sa tubo—bagaso

BAIL, n.—lagak, piyansa—pasalig, piyansa—pyansa

BAKE, v.—lutuin sa hurnó—pagluto sa hudnohan—hurnohón

BAKER, n.—magtitinapáy, manggagawà ng tinapay—maghuhudno sa tinapay—manogtinapáy

BAKERY, n.—panaderya, gáwaan ng tinapay — hudnohan, lutoan sa pan—panaderya

BALANCE, n.—nátitirá, timbangan—timbangan, nahabilin — nabilín, timbangan

BALANCE, v.—magtuós, timbangín, pagtamain—pagtimbang—timbangón

BALL, n.—bola, sáyawan — bola, sayaw—bola

BALLOT, n.—balota—balota—balota

BALLROOM, n.—bulwagan, sáyawan—sayawan—salautár, salón

BAMBOO, n.—kawayan — kawayan—kawayan

BANK, n.—bangko—bangko, tipiganan sa salapi—banko

BANQUET, n.—bangkete, káinan —kumbira, piging, bahug-bahug—bangkite

BARGAIN, n.—mura, baratilyo — baratilyo, hangyo—baratilyo

BARGAIN, v.—tumawad, makipag-ayos—paghangyo — ibaratilyo

BARK, n.—tahol, balát ng kahoy —paghot, usig, hulhol, panit sa kahoy—panit sang kahoy

BARKER, n.—taga-sigáw—tigyagaw—tagsinggit, taghol

BARN, n.—bangán, kamalig—kamalig—kamalig

BARREL, n.—bariles — bariles— bariles

BARREN, adj.—baóg, hindî magbunga, payát — landay, yutang hupas, panas—baúg, lamgod

BARRICADE, n.—tanggulan, hadláng—salipod, barakada — kutà, trinsera

BASE, n.—patungán, hanggahan —sukaranan—tungtongan

BASE, adj.—hamak, imbí—ipasikad—nalupyakán, baho (sa musiká)

BASEMENT, n.—silong, ilalim* — silong, ilalum sa balay—silong, idalum

BASIN, n.—palanggana, batyáng maliít — palanggana, dulang — palanggana labadór

BASKET, n. — buslô, sisidlán, pangnán—bukag, baskit—alát

BAT, n.—pánikì, pamalò ng bola— kabugkuwaknit, hapak sa bola— kabúg

BATH, n.—paliligò, páliguán — pagkaligo, kaligo—ligosán

BATHROOM, n.—páliguán o silíd na páliguán—kaligoanan — paligoán ukón hulót paligosán

BATTLE, n.—labanán, digmaan— away, gubat—inaway

BAWL, v.—sigawán—pagnga-ab— singgitan

BAY, n.—loók — lo-ok, diyutayng dagat—linaw, sapásapà

BE, v.—maging—pagkamao—nangín

BEACH, n.—aplaya, baybáy-dagat —lapyahan, baybayon—hunasan

BEACON, n.—sinyál—banwag sa sumasakay—sinyalan

BEAD, n.—butil ng kuwintás, abaloryo—lusok, lobitos—abaloryo, uyás sang kolintas

BEAK, n.—tukâ—sungo—tuktok

BEAM, n.—kilo ng bahay, kisláp, sinag—silaw sa adlaw, sagbayan —pasamano, badlak, igpat

BEAR, n., v.—oso batahín, tiisin, (bear fruit) magbunga — usa; kugoson, antuson—oso, antusón, bumuga

BEARD, n.—balbás—balbas, bungot—barbas, bungot

BEAT, v.—paluin, hambalusin — pagmakmak, paglatus, pagpuspos—pukpukón, bakulon

BEAUTIFUL, adj.—marikít, magandá—maanyag, matahum — matahúm, maanyag

BEAUTY, n.—gandá, kariktán — kaanyag, katahum — katahúm, kaanyag

BECAUSE, conj.—pagká't, sapag-ká't, mangyari — tungod kay, sanglit kay—tungod kay

BECOME, v.—magíng, bumagay—pagkahimo—mangín

BECOMING, adj.—bagay, magan-dá—bagay, angayan—mangín

BED, n.—kama, hígaan — higda-anan, katre—kama, higdaan

BEDROOM, n.—silíd-hígaan—si-bay, lawak-higdaan—hulót-tulu-gán

BEDBUG, n.—surot — dugho, ku-ting—baksat

BEE, n.—bubuyog, putaktí — bu-yog, putyokan — libog, buyóg, putyokan

BEEF, n.—karné ng baka—kar-neng baka—karne sang baka

BEEFSTEAK, n.—bistík — linu-tong unod sa baka—bistik

BEER, n.—serbesa—serbesa—ser-bisa

BEFORE, adv.—datí, bago—kan-ladto, kanhi, sa atubangan—sa walâ pa; buót

BEG, v.—manghingî, magpalimós, mamanhík—pagpangayo, pagpa-kiluoy—pakilimós

BEGGARLINESS, ·n.—kahirapan, karamutan—kapaitan — kaimo-lón

BEGGAR, n.—pulubi, nagpápali-mós—nagapakilimos — nagapa-kilimós, bulág

BEGIN, v.—magsimulâ, mag-um-pisá — magsugod, pagsugod — magsugod

BEGINNER, n.—baguhan—sumo-sugod—bag-ohan

BEGINNING, n.—pasimulâ — si-nugdanan, sugod—sugod

BEHAVE, v.—magpakatao, mag-pakaayos—paghinatarung, pag-pakabuotan—magpakatarung

BEHAVIOR, n.—asal, ayos—gawi, pamatasan—katarung

BEHIND, prep.—sa likód, hulí — sa luyo, iwit—sa luyó, sa likód

BEHOLD, v. — tingnán, malasin, masdán—pagtan-aw, pagsid-ing-—talupangdi

BELIEF, n. — paniniwalâ, pana-nampalataya—ang pagtuo, tinu-hoan—pagtuo

BELIEVABLE, adj.—mapaníniwa-laan—katuhoan—matinuohon

BELIEVE, v.—maniwalà, sumam-palataya—pagtuo, tuhoan—mag-pati, magtuo

BELL, n.—kampanà, batingáw — lingganay, kampana—lingganay.

BELONG, v.—náuukol — paghisa-kop, kaugalingon—natungód

BELOVED, n.—minámahál, giliw, irog—minahal, hinigugma—hini-gugma

BELOW, prep.—sa ibabâ, sa ilalim—sa ubos, silong — sa ubós, sa idalum

BELT, n.—sinturón—bakus, sinturon—paha, wagkus

BEND v.—baluktutín, iyukô — pagyuko, pagbawog — patikuón, pakurbahón

BENEATH, prep.—sa ilalim, mababà—sa ubos, sa ilalum — sa idalum

BENEFIT, v. — kapakinabangán, bigay-palà—kaayohan, benepisyo —kapuslanan

BENT, adj.—baluktót, hukót—yuko, bawog—tikû, kubóng

BESEECH, v.—magmakaamò, pakiusapan—mangamuyo, mangilaba—magpaubós

BESIDE, prep.—sa tabí—abay, tupad sa—sa luyó

BESIEGE, v.—kulungín, kubkubín —likosan, libutan—bukuton, kibonon

BESMEAR, v.—bahiran, dumihán —pagmansa, pagdaut-daut, bulingan—pahirán

BESTOW, v.—ipagkaloób, ibigáy —paghatag, pagtanyag — itugyan, ihatag

BESPEAK, v. — nagpápatunay, nagpápakilala—nagmatuod, nagpaila — nagpamatuod, nagpakilala

BEST, adj.—pinakamabuti, pinakamahusay—ang labíng maayo, hawod—labíng maayo

BET, n.—pustá—pusta, kasado — pusta

BETRAY, v.—ipagkánuló — pagbudhi, pagliput—liputón

BETTER, adj.—lalong mabuti, higít na mainam—labawng maayo, maarang-arang—labíng maayo, kapín kaayo

BETROTHAL, n. — kasunduang pakasal—sayud sa kasal—kaugyonan sa pagpakasál

BETWEEN, prep.—sa pagitan — tunga-tunga sa, taliwala sa—sa gintung-an

BEVERAGE, n.—ínumin—ilimnon —ilimnon

BEWARE, v.—mag-ingat — pagbantay — magbantay, mag-andam

BEYOND, prep.—sa dako pa roron—sa halayo pa, sa unahan kaayo—didto nayon

BIBLE, n.—Bíbliyá, Banái na Kasulatan—Bibliya, balaang kasulatan—Biblia, Balaan nga Kasulatan

BICYCLE, n.—bisikleta—bisikleta —bisikleta

BID, n.—turing, tawad — puhal, hangyo—tukós

BIDDER, n.—mámimili, mánanawad—magpupuhal—tagtukós

BIER, n.—ataúl—lungow, andas— lungón, langkapan

BIG, adj.—malakí, tanyág—daku —dakû, lutáw

BIGWIG, n.—tanyág, o kilaláng tao—dakung tawo—lutáw dungganon.

BILL, n. — katibayan, tálaan ng utang, panukalang batás, tukâ—sungo, balaoron, talaan—tuktok, resibo, layí

BILLBOARD, n.—lathalaan, anunsyuhan—anunsiyohan, kartil — bantalaan, anunsyohan

BIMONTHLY, adv.—tuwíng ikalawáng buwán—kaduha sa usa ka bulan—kinsenal

BIND, v.—talian, bigkisín — bugkos, pagbugkos, baatan—higtan, bugkosón

BIRD, n.—ibon—langgam—pispis

BIRTH, n.—kapanganakan, kaarawán—pagkatawo, pagpanganak —kapanganakán, pagkatáo

BIRTHDAY, n.—araw ng pagsilang, kaarawán, kapanganakan —kaadlawan, adlaw ng natawhan—kaadlawan, kapanganakán

BISCUIT, n.—biskwít—biskwit — biskwít

BISHOP, n.—obispo—obispo, sunat—obispo

BIT, n.—kapyangót, maliit—diyutay kaayong bahin—tipík, momho

BITE, n.—kapiraso, kagát — pahít, ingkib, paak—pidaso, kagát, angkab

BITE, v. — kagatín, kumagát — pagpahit, pagpaak—kadton, angkabón

BITTER, v.—mapaít — mapait — mapaít

BLACK, adj.—maitím, itím—maitum—itúm

BLACKBOARD, n.—pisára—pisara—pisara

BLADDER, n.—pantóg—pantog—barukhan

BLACKSMITH, n.—pandáy—panday sa puthaw—panday sa salsalon

BLACKMAIL, n.—takutin upáng kuwaltahán — panghulga aron makasapi—pahugon agúd kuartahán

BLADE, n.—talím, dahon—suwab, sulab—talúm, suláb

BLAME, v.—sisihin—pakasad-on, basulon—basulon

BLANK, adj.—walang sulat, waláng lamán—walay sulod, way sulat—blanko

BLANKET, n.—kumot—habol — habul

BLASPHEMY, n. — di-paggalang. pagkutyâ sa Diyos — pasipala, tampalas—pamuyayaw

BLAST, n.—ihip, sigáw—budyong, buto, unos—huypon, tumusngaw

15

BLAZE, n.—ningas, lagabláb—siga, dilaab—dabadaba

BLEACH, v.—ikulá, paputiín — pagladlad—ilatag, paputión

BLEED, v.—dumugô, kuwaltahán —pagdugo—dumugô

BLEMISH, n.—dumí, batík—apan, panghimaraut—higkò, pintok

BLEND, v.—pagsamahin — pagtipon, pagsambog—sakuton, salakuton

BLESS, v. — biyayaan, purihin, basbasán—pagpanalangin — bugayán

BLESSING, n.—biyayà, pagpapalà —panalangin, kabulahan—bugáy

BLIGHT, n. — pagkatuyô, pagkasirà — pagkadaut, dangan— pagkakigás

BLIND, n.—bulág, takíp, tabing— buta, halap — bulág, takúp sa matá, butábuta

BLISS, n.—kaligayahan—himaya —kalipayan

BLOCK, v.—kalô, hulmahan, hanay—kaulangan, hulmahan sa kalo—kaulangán, hurmahan sa kalú, bioke, mutón

BLOCKHEAD, n. — waláng muwáng—pulpol, way kaisipan wala'y puwáng

BLOOD, n.—dugô—dugo—dugô

BLOODY, adj.—marugô, duguán— dugoon—duguón

BLOOM, v.—bumukád, mamulaklák — paglimbukad — bumukád, namulak

BLOSSOM, n. — bulaklák—bulak, pagpamulak—bulak

BLOT, n.—dungis, katkatin, dumí —buling, ipahunob sa sekante— pintok, higkò

BLOUSE, n.—blusa, pang-itaás ng saya — blusa, sinina — blusa, pangibabaw sang saya

BLOW, n.—hampás, ihip, dagok— huyop, paghuyop, sumbag—haplit, huyóp

BLOW-OUT, n.—káinan, putók, sirà—pagbuto na goma, pangaon —paudak, lupók

BLUE, n.—asúl, bugháw—pughaw, asul—asúl, tagum

BLUFF, n.—mataás at matarík na pampáng, pagpapakunwàrî — pangpang, paglingla — tindogon nga pangpang, hambog

BLUFF, v.—magkunwarî—paglansis — paghambog

BLUNT, adj.—pulpól, biglâ, malabò — amol, habolan, pundol — umál, malubóg

BLUSH, v.—mamulá, bumukád — pamula sa nawong, manglipaghong—magpalamulá, magbusaag

BOARD, v.—mangasera, sumakáy —tabla, - pagsakay—mangasera, tapì, sumakáy

BOARDING HOUSE, n.—káserahán, tírahan — balay kaserahan —kaserahán

BOAST, v.—mangalandakan, maghambóg, magyabáng — pagpangandak, pagpagawal, panghambug—magpakahambog

BOAT, n.—bapór, sasakyáng-dagat, bangkâ—sakayan sa dagat, bapor—bapór, sakayán

BODY, n.—katawán—lawas — lawas

BOIL, v.—pakuluín—pagbukal — pabukalón

BOIL, n.—pigsá—hubag — hubág, uyapós

BOLD, adj. — matapang, waláng gulat—maisug—maisug, wala'y hadlok

BOLO, n.—iták, gulok—sundang—binangon

BOLT, v.—trangkahán—trangkahan, paglayat—pintalán, pitalâ

BOMB, n.—bomba—bomba, pagbomba—bomba

BOND, n.—talì, pyansa, kásunduan—pasalig, talikala, baligtos—pyansa

BONDAGE, n.—pagkaalipin—kaulipnan—pagkaulipon

BONE, n.—butó ng karné—bukog—tul-an

BOOK, n.—aklát, libró—basahon, libro—libro, tulun-an

BOOKKEEPER, n. — taga-ingat-kuwenta — tenedor de libro — tenedorya

BOOTBLACK, n.—manlilinis ng sapatos, limpya-bota — taglinis sa sapin—manoglimpya-botas

BORDER, n.—gilid, hangganan—utlanan, mohon—dulonan

BORE, v.—yamutín, abalahín, butasin—paglungag, laayan — samongón, buhoan

BORROW, v.—manghirám, humirám, hiramín—paghulam, pagulos—hulám, humulám, manghulám

BOSOM, n.—dibdíb, sinapupunan, ilalim—dughan, sinati—dughan, balataán

BOSS, n.—punò, tagapamahalà — amo, agalon—agalon, tagdumala

BOTH, pron.—kapwà, siláng, dalawá—ang duroha—silá nga duhá

BOTHER, v.—abalahin, guluhín—samok, pagsamok—samongón

BOTHERSOME, adj.—nakayáyamót, nakagúguló—masamokon—samokan, masamóngon

BOTTLE, n.—bote, botelya—botilya—botelya

BOTTOM, prep.—sa ilalim—sa ilalum—sa idalum

BOUGH, n.—sangá—sanga sa kahoy—sangá

BOULDER, n.—malakíng bató — dakung bato—dalagkong bató

17

BOUNDARY, n.—hangganan—ut-lanan, mohon—dulonan

BOUNTY, n.—biyayà, kasaganaan—kaluoy, kamahatagon—bugáy, kahamungayaan

BOUGHT, v. — bumilí, binilí — mapilit, napalit—bumakál

BOUQUET, v. — pumpón ng mga bulaklák—pungpong sa bulak—pungpong nga bulak

BOW, n.—panà, arkó ng biyolín—pana, pagyukbo, dulong sa sa-kayan—panâ

BOWER, n.—malilim na páhinga-han—tinai—kasudlan

BOWL, n.— mangkók—panaksan—yahóng

BOX, n.—kahón, lalagyán—kahon—kahón

BOX, v. — suntukín, butahlín—pagsuntok, pagsumbag—sumba-ganay

BOY, n.—batang lalaki, utusáng lalaki—batang lalaki—batà nga lalaki, suluguón nga lalaki

BOYISH, adj.—mukháng batà — mabinataon, lakin-on—payaón

BRACELET, n.—pulseras, galáng—pulseras—pulseras

BRAID, n.—tirintás—sinapid—sa-lapid

BRAIN, n.—utak—utok—utok

BRAKE, n.—preno—pugong, pre-no—preno

BRANCH, n.—sangá—sanga—sa-ngá

BRAN, n.—darák—tahop sa hu-may—lintok

BRAND, n.—taták, guhit, markà—patik, marka, timaan—marka

BRASS, n. — tansô — tumbaga, bronse—sawáy

BRAVE, adj.—matapang, waláng gulat—maisug—maisug

BRAVE, v.—sagasain — sungso-ngon—lamposanay

BREAD, n. — tinapay—pan, tina-pay—tinapay

BREADFRUIT, n.—rimas, langkâ—kamansi, kolo — bunga sang kamansi, koló

BREADLINE, n.—pila sa límusan—laray sa nagpalimus—pila sa pakilimsan

BREADTH, n.—lapad, luwáng — kalapdon—lapad, sangkad

BREAK, v.—sirain, basagin, putu-lin—pagbuak, pagbasag, pagbali—buongon, utdon

BREAKDOWN, n. — paghintô, panghihinà—pagkaguba — inog-pugóng

BREAKFAST, n.—almusál, aga-han—pamahaw—pamahaw

BREAST, n.—dibdíb, suso—dug-han—dughan, suso

BREVITY, n.—kaiklián, iklî— ang kamub-on—kalip-otón

BREATH, n.—hiningá—gininhawa—ginhawa

BREATHLESS, adj.—hindî halos makahingá—wala magginhawa, naghinga-hinga—dî halos maka-ginhawa

BREED, v.—mag-anák—pagpaliwat, pagpasanay — magpanganák. mangliwát

BREEDING, n.—kinagawián, pinag-aralan—kagawian, bangkaagan—buluadán

BREEZE, n.—hihip ng hangin, simoy—hinuyohoy—harupoy

BRETHREN, n.—magkakapatid—igsoon—mag-ulotod

BRICK, v.—laryo, tisà—tisa, bika—tisà

BRIBE, n.—suhol — hiphip, suborno—pabuya

BRIBE, v.—suhulan—paghiphip—pabuyahan

BRIBERY, n.—pagsuhol — panghiphip, panuborno—pasuhot

BRIDE, n. — kasintahang babae, nobya—pangasaw-onon, nobya—nobya

BRIDEGROOM, n.—nobyo, .kasuyong lalaki — pamanhonon, nobyo—nobyo

BRIDESMAID, n.—abay — babayeng abay sa kasal—abay

BRIDGE, n.—tuláy, tulayan, pagitan—tulay, taytayan—taytay

BRIDLE, n.—busál, renda, pangakay—rinda—busál, renda, inogtuytoy

BRIDLE, v.—akayin, putulin, agapayan—agakon—tuytoyán

BRIEF, n.—maiklî, maigsî — mubo—malip-ot

BRIGADE, n.—hukbó—pundok sa sundalo, brigada—gubán

BRIGAND, n. — masamáng loób, magnanakaw—tulisan — tulisán. makawat, manog-atí

BRIGHT, adj.—makináng. makintáb. maliwanag, matalino—mahayag, madan-ag, masinabuton—masanag, maalam

BRIGHTEN, v.—paligayahin. painumín—paghayag, pagpasaya—pahalipayon

BRILLIANT, adj. — maningníng. matalino—masilakon, masiga — masili. masiling, mangin-alamon

BRINK. n.—gilid, pampáng—kilid, daplin—kilid. pangpang

BRING, n.—dalhin—dad-on, dad-a—dalhon

BRISK. adj.—masiglá, mabilís — malagsik, mapiskay—mapagsik, maabtik

BRITTLE, adj.—babasagín, malutóng, madalíng mabalì — tago, gabok—buongón, matapók

BROAD, adj.—malapad, malawak —malapad, lanatad — malapad, masangkad

BROADCAST, v.—ihayag, ipamalità—pagsibya sa kahanginan—ipahayag (sa radyo)

BROIL, v.—iihaw, idaráng—pagsugba, pagdangdang — sinugba, iparilya

BROKE, adj.—waláng-walâ, mahirap — walay nahot—walâ gid, balasubas

BROOD, n.—mga akay — liwat, paglumlom—mga tuytoy

BROOK, n.—batis—sapa-sapa—linaw

BROOM, n.—walís—silhig—silhig

BROTH, n. — sabáw—sabaw—sabáw

BROTHER, n.—kapatíd na lalaki —igsoong lalaki—utod nga lalaki

BROTHER-IN-LAW, n. — bayáw —bayaw—bayáw

BROTHERHOOD, n. — kápatiran —pag-igsuonay—kautoran

BROW, n.—kilay — agtang, bona, kilay—kilay

BROWN, adj.—kayumanggí, kulay-kaki—tabunon — kayumanggì, duág kaki

BRUISE, n.—bugbóg, pasâ, galos —bun-og—pakris

BRUSH, n.—eskoba, sipilyo, damuhán—brutsa, sipilyo, sagbutan—eskoba, kahilamnan

BRUSH, v.—linisin, kuskusín — brutsahan — eskobahan, kuskusón

BRUSQUE, adj.—waláng-galang, waláng pinag-aralan—walay tahud—walay katahuran, walay tinun-an

BUBBLE, n.—bulâ—bula—bukál

BUCKET, n.—timbâ, baldé—timba —timbà, balde

BUD, n.—buko, pasimulâ—putot, piyoos—bukol

BUDDY, n.—kasama, kaibigan—sagabay, abyan — kaupod, abyan

BUDGET, n.—badyet — talaan sa gugolan—badyet

BUGGY, n.—kalesa, karitela—kalesa, tartanilya—kalesa, karitela

BUGLE, n.—tambulì, trumpeta—trumpeta—trumpeta, budyong

BUILD, v.—magtayô, gumawâ—pagtukod—magpasad, maghikut

BUILDING, n. — bahay, gusalì - balay—baláy

BULB, n.—bombilya — bombilya, malingin nga buok—bombilya

BULK, n.—lakí, kapál, dami—kadak-on, kadaghanon—bulto, dakû, damò

BULKY, adj. — makapál, matambók—mabultohon, ugdo—bulto, madamul

BULL, n.—bakang lalaki, toro—tore kun bakang laki—baka nga lalaki, toro

BULLDOZE, v.—takutin, bantaán —paghulga, paghadlok — pahugon, pahadlukón

BULLET, n.—bala, punlô—bala—bala

BULLETIN, n. — búlitín — boletin, pahayag—bulitín

BUMP, n.—untóg, bukol—huboy, hubag—bunggò

BUMP, v. — umpugín, barilín, banggaín—pagbangga, banggaan—bumunggò, bungguón

BUNCH, n. — kumpól, langkáy—sipi, bulig—sipî

BUNDLE, n. — bigkís, balutan—putos, bantal— bugkós

BUNDLE, v.—talian, bihisan, puluputan — pagputos, pagbangan —bugkosón

BUNGLE, n.—pagkakámalî—pagsayop—sariwaol

BURDEN, n. — pásanin, bigát—palas-anon, kabug-at — palasanon

BURDENSOME, adj. — pabigát, pang-abala—makasamok, makabalda—mabug-at, mabaknal

BUREAU, n.—káwanihán, kahón, lalagyán—buhatan, buro—buró

BURGLAR, n.—manloloób, magnanakaw, tekas—kawatan—makawat, tulisán

BURGLARIZE, v.—looban, nakawan—pagkawat, kawatan — kawatán

BURIAL, n. — libíng, pagbabaón —lubong—lubóng

BURN, v.—sunugin — pagsunog, paso—sunugon

BURST, v.—pumutók, sumilakbó —pagbuto, mabuslot—lumupók, bumusaag

BURY, v.—ibaón, ilibíng—paglubong, pagluyong—ilubóng

BUSH, n.—maliít na punungkahoy — kalibonan — magagmay nga punô sang kahoy

BUSINESS, n.—kalakal, gáwain, hanapbuhay — patigayon, buhat —negosyo, palatikangan

BUSY, adj.—okupado, may ginágawâ, abalá — daghag buhat daghag libang — okupado, masakù

BUT, conj. — subali't, nguni't — apan—apang

BUTCHER, n.—magkakarné, mámamatay ng hayop—mangingihaw, matadero—manog-iháw

BUTLER, n.—mayordomo, tagapangasiwà sa táhanan—mayordomo—mayordomo

BUTTER, n.—mantikilya—**manti-kilya**—mantikilya

BUTTERFLY, n.—paruparó—**alibangbang, kaba-kaba** — alibangbang

BUTTON, n.—butones—**butones**—butones

BUTTON, v. — ibutones, isará—**ibutones**—ibutones

BUY, v.—bumilí—**pagpalit**—bumakál

BUYER, n.—mámimili, tagabilí—**pumapalit**—manogbakal

BY, prep.—ni, sa siping, sa tabí ng —**ni, pinaagi sa**—sa, sa luyó, sa higád sang

BY-GONES, n.—lumipas, nakalipas, kahapon—**ang nangagi, ang kagahapon**—nagligad

BY-LAW, n.—tuntuning panloób—**sumbanan**—kinaugalíng nga sulondan

BY-STANDER, n.—nanónoód, nakakákita, nakasásaksî — **ang maghinan-aw**—tumalan-aw

— C —

CAB, n.—kotse, awto—**awto, kotse**—kotse, auto

CABARET, n. — bahay-sáyawan, **kabaret**—kabarét, sautan

CABBAGE, n. — ripelyo—**repolyo** —repolyo

CABIN, n.—dampâ, silíd sa bapór, kamarote — **payag, kamarote**—kamarote

CABINET, n. — mesang sulatán, gabinete—**sulatanan, gabinete**—gabinete

CABLE, n.—kablegrama—**hatudkawat, kablegrama** — kablegrama

CAD, n.—masamáng tao, waláng galang—**banyaga, way ulaw** —huróshurós

CAFETERIA, n.—kapiteryá — **kapihanan, kan-anan**—kapiterya

CAKE, n. — kakanín, bibingka, keyk—**torta, bibingka** — keik, bibingka

CALAMITY, n. — sakunâ, masamáng pangyayari—**katalagman, kalisdanan**—distresa, kalamidád

CALDRON, n.—kaldero, lutuán—**kaldero**—kaldero

CALENDAR, n.—kalendaryo, talaarawán — **kalendaryo** — kalendaryo

CALF, n. — bintî, guyà, bakang maliít—**nati sa baka, bitiis**—pusopusoán, tinday (baka)

CALL, n.—tawag—**tawag**—tawág

CALL, v. — magbisita, tumawag, tawagin—**pagtawag, pagduaw**—tawagon

CALM, v.—patahimikin, papanatagin—**malinaw**—palinongón

22

CALUMNY, n.—paninirang-puri—
butang-butang, pakaulaw—bu-
tángbutang

CAMERA, n. — kámerá, kodak,
pangkuha ng larawan — kodak,
kamera—kamerá, kodak

CAMP, n. — kampo, páhingahan,
larangan — kámpo, puy-anang
patag—kampo, patag

CAMPAIGN, n.—kampanya, kilusán — kampanya, singkamut—
kampanya

CAN, n.—lata—lata—lata

CAN, v.—maáarì — makahimo —
mahimo

CANAL, n.—kanál, dáluyan ng tubig—kanál, aglanag tubig—kanál

CANCEL, v.—burahín, kaltasín—
pagpapha, pad-on — panason,
kanselahón

CANDID, adj.—tapát, bukás na
loób — madayganon — bukás,
tampad

CANDIDATE, n.—kandidato — pilionon, kandidato—kandidato

CANDLE, n.—kandilà — kandila,
espirma — kandilà

CANDLELIGHT, n.—liwanag ng
kandilà—silaw sa kandila — sanag sang kandilà

CANDY, n.—kendi — karmelitos,
matam-is—kendi, dulse

CANE, n.—bastón, tungkód—baston, sungkod—baston

CANNER, n.—tagapagsilíd sa lata—maglalata—taglata

CANNIBAL, n.—mángangaing-tao
—balbal, mokaog tawo—mangà-
ngaon-táo

CANNON, n.—kanyón — kanyon,
lantaka—kanyon

CANNOT, v.—dî maáarì—dili mahimo—dî mahimò

CANOE, n.—isáng urì ng bangkà
—matang sa bangka—bangkà

CANTEEN, n.—kantín — kantina
—kapeterya

CANTER, n.—takbóng banayad—
mahinayng paglakaw—tintin

CANVAS, n.—lona — lona—lona,
kanbas

CANVASS, v.—mag-ipon, mangu-
ha—pagpanguha — magtigayon
sing pilì

CAP, n.—gora, takíp—gora, tak-
op—gora

CAPABLE, adj.—may-kaya, maylakás — takus, makahimo—makasaráng

CAPACITY, n.—kaya, lakás, lulan, lamán—ang katakus—may
ikasaráng

CAPE, n.—ungós ng lupà sa dagat, tangos—lawis—siwíl

CAPITAL, n.—puhunan, kabesera
o punungbayan, malakíng titik
—puhonan, kaulohan — kapital,
kabesera

CAPITALIZE, v.—pamuhunanan,
puhunanin — pagpamuhonan —
pahunanan, kapitalán

CAPITULATE, v.—sumukò—pag-lunga, pag-ampo—yumaúb

CAPTIVE, n.—bilanggô, bihag — bihag, dinakpan—binilanggò, bihag

CAPTIVITY, n.—pagkakábilang-gô, pagkakáhuli—ang pagkabi-nihag—pagkabilanggò, pagkadakúp

CAR, n.—karo, sasakyán, awto-karo, awtomobil—karo, auto, salakyan

CARAVAN, n.—samahán sa pag-lalakád — ambahan — gubán (sang mga manglalakaton)

CARBARN, n.—himpilan ng sa-sakyán—karohan, garahe—esta-sionan sang salakyan.

CARD, n.—tarheta, baraha—tar-heta, baraha—baraha, tarheta

CAREER, n.—karera — karera—karera

CAREFUL, adj.—maingat, maala-láy—mabinantayon — mahina-longon

CARELESS, adj.—pabayâ, mapag-pabayà, bulagsák—danghag, la-ngas, tanga—uyayâ

CARELESSNESS, n.—pagpapaba-yà, kawaláng-ingat—ang pagka-danghag, pagkatanga — pagkau-yayâ

CARESS, n. — himas, pagmama-hál—parayeg, karinyo—hagup-hagupon

CARFARE, n.—bayad o tiket sa sasakyán o tren—bayad sa sak-yanan—bayad sa tren ukón sa salakyan

CARGO, n. — lulan ng bapór o kargá, kargamento—luwan—lulan

CARPENTER, n. — anluwagi — panday—panday sa kahoy, kar-pintero

CARPET, n.—alpombra, panakíp sa sahíg — alpombra, banig sa salok—alpombra

CARRIAGE, n.—karwahe, sasak-yán, tikas—karwahe, bayhon — karwahi

CARRIER, n.—tagadalá, tagaha-tíd—tagdala, taghatud—tagda-lá, tagdul-ong

CARRY, v.—dalhín, bunatin, pasa-nín—pagdala, pag-alsa—dalhon, hakwatón, pás-anón

CART, n.—kalesa, karitón—karo-mata—kalesa, karitón

CARTOON, n.—kartón, guhit-la-rawan — tawo-tawo — kartón, karikatura

CARVE, v.—umukit, gumawâ, ba-luktutín — pagkulit, pagsilsil —bumanghay, dibuhista (sa ka-hoy)

CASE, n.—usapín, kahón—kahim-tang, sumbong, sudlanan — ka-hitabô, kaso

CASH, n.—kuwarta, salapî—salapi kuwarta, pilak

CASHIER, n.—kahero, tagapagpa-lít o tagatanggáp ng kuwarta—kahero, tagdumala sa kuwarta—kahero, kuymi

CASSAVA, n.—kamoteng-kahoy—balanghoy, kamoteng kahoy — kamote-kahoy

CAST, v.—ihagis, ihugis—ilabay, itampog — ipilák, ihabóy

CAST, n.—tauhan sa palabás — talay sa magdudula — gumuluà

CASUAL, adj.—pasumalá—panag-sa — kasualidád

CASUALTY, n.—sakunâ, kamáta-yan—naangin sa hitabo, patay —kahitaboán

CATALOG, n.—katálogó, tálaan—talaan, katalogo—katalogó

CATARRH, n.—sipóng mabigát—sip-on—kataro, sip-on

CATCH, v.—hulihin, saluhín, sa-puhín — pagsalo, pagdakop — dakpon, sal-on

CATCH, n.—huli—dinakpan, sini-kop—dakúp

CATERPILLAR, n. — malaking uód — dakung ulod — atataro

CATHEDRAL, n.—katedrái—ka-tedral, simbahang daku — ka-tedral, simbahan

CATTLE, n.—mga baka—mga ba-ka—mga baka

CAUCUS, n.—pulong, miting—sa-but-sabut, kawkus — miting, kawkus

CAUSE, n. — dahilán, sanhî—hi-nungdan, nakaingon—kaso, ka-bangdanan

CAUTIOUS, adj.—maingat, alalay —mabinantayon, mapanagan-on —mainandamon

CAVALCADE, n.—kawan ng mga mángangabayó—panon sa nag-kabayo — manogkabayó

CAVE, n.—kuweba, yungíb — la-ngub — kweba, lungíb

CAVERNOUS, adj.—malakí—da-ku uyamot—dakû kag masang-kad

CEASE, v.—tumigil, humintô, lu-mubáy—paghunong, undang — dumúlog

CEASELESS, adj.—waláng hintô, waláng humpáy—walay hunong, walay undang — walay dulog

CEILING, n.—kísamé—kisami — kisamé

CELEBRATE, v. — magdiwang, magsayá — pagsaulog — labíng mataas

CELEBRATION, n.—pagbubunyi, pagdiriwang—saulog, kasadyaan —magsaulog, magsadya

CELEBRITY, n.—kilalá, tanyág—bantug, inilang tawo — dung-ganon, lutáw

CELERY, n.—kinsáy — kinsay — kinsay

CELL, n.—silíd—bílangguan, kúlungan—atub, bilanggoan, prisohan — suiód-bilanggoan, bukotán

CELLAR, n.—silong, bodega—bodega, silong sa balay — silong, bodega

CEMETERY, n.—líbingan—kalubngan, sam-ang, lubnganan — lulubngan, patyo

CENSORIOUS, adj. — mapagbat:, mapamuná — salawayon — mabinalak-on

CENSUS, n.—bilang, senso—senso —sensus

CENTENNIAL, n.—sandaang taón —ikagatus — gatuson ka tuig

CENTER, n.—gitnâ, sentro — taliwala, kinataliwad-an — tungâ, sentro

CENTERPIECE, n.—panggitnâ— — taliwad-ong butang — katung-anan

CENTIPEDE, n.—alupihan—uhipan - - talimbabaga

CENTRAL, adj. — nasa gitnâ, nágigitnâ — natilawala, kauyokan — sentral, tungâ-tungà

CENTURY, n.—ikasandaáng taón —gatusan—isagatuson ka tuig

CEREAL, n.—bungang butil ng halaman—bungang linugas (mais, humay) — lamigas nga kalan-on

CEREMONIOUS, adj. — mapagabalá, mabusisi — makuti-kutihon, mabusi-sion — masinadyahon

CEREMONY, n.—seremonya, pagdiriwang — saulog, seremonya—seremonya

CERTAIN, adj. — tiyák, walángmalî—tino, piho — pat-ud, syerto, walay sayúṇ

CERTAINLY, adv.—tunay, totoó, oo—dayag nga piho — tunay, kamatuoran, huo

CERTIFICATE, n. — katibayan, sertipiko—kalig-onan, sertipiko —sertipiko

CERTIFY, v. — patunayan—pagmatuod — pamatuod

CHAGRIN, n.—kayamutan, kabiguán—paungot—kaugót

CHAIN, n.—tanikalâ, kabít, kadena—talikala, kadena — ikadena, italikalâ

CHAIR, n.—silya, úpuan—lingkoranan—siya

CHAIRMAN, n.—pangulo, pµnò—pangulo, daku-daku — tsirman

CHALK, n.—atisa, yeso—tisas — yeso, iso

CHALLENGE, n.—hamon, paghamon—paghagit, hagit — hangkat

CHAMELEON, n. — hunyangó — mananap tigbalhig panit—tambalihán

CHAMBER, n. — silíd, kámará—lawak — kamará

CHAMPION, n. — kampeon — kampiyon — kampeón

CHANCE, n.—pagkakáfaón—kahigayonan — kahigayonan

CHANGE, v.—palitán, halinhán, baguhin—pagpabaylo, pagbag-o — baylohán, islan

CHANGE, n.—suklî, pagbabago-suklì, kabalhinan — sag-ulì

CHANNEL, n.—kanál, daanan ng tubig—agianan sa tubig kun dagat — kanál

CHANT, n.—awit, pag-awit, dasál —awit, laylay kanta - amba (sa simbahan)

CHAPEL, n.—kapilya, simbahang maliít—kapilya, simbahang gamay — kapilya

CHAPERON, n.—taga-alagà, kasama — tigbantay, kauban — ibid-ibid

CHAPTER, n. — kapítuló, pangkát, kabanatà—anib, kapítulo—kapituló, bahin

CHARACTER, n.—káraktér, urì o ugalì, katángian, pagkatao, ka-ugalián—titik, batasan, kinaiya sa tawo -- karakter

CHARGE, n.—bayad, lagak—pagpabayad, pagsumbong — bayad, bilí

CHARGE, v.—pagbayarin, pagbintangán, singilín — pabayaron pagpasangil — pabayaran, pabilhan, sukton

CHARGABLE, adj. — maaaring pabayaran, maáaring ipagbintáng — mahimong pasanginlan, mahimong pabayaron — papabayaran

CHARIOT, n.—karo, sasakyán — karo, salakyan—karo, karwahi

CHARITY, n.—kawanggawâ, kabutihang-loób—kaluoy — karidád, buhat sa kaluoy

CHARM, n. — halina, gayuma, pang-akit — kapiskay, kaanyag, lumay—lumáy

CHARM, v.—akitin, hulihin, bighaniin—pagdani, paglumay—lumayón

CHARTER, n.—pahintulot ng pámahalaán, kasulatan·ng pagkakátatag—pagtugot sa kagamhanan, kalig-onan sa pamunoan—paghinakay sa isá ka bapór

CHASE, n.—paghabol, habulán—gukdanay, lutosay--lagás, lagsanáy

CHASE, v.—habulin—paggukod—lagson

CHASTITY, n.—kalinisang-ugali o puri — kagawiang malinis — kaulay

CHAUFFEUR, n.—tsupér, nagpápalakad ng awto—tsoper, sapyor —tsopér, sapyur

CHEAP, adj. — mura, mababang halagá—kubos ang bili, barato —barato, manubô ang bilí

CHEAT, v.—dayain, lokohin—paglimbong — dayaon

CHECK, v.—suriin, pigilin — pagusisa, pagpugong — usisaon, sayasaton

CHECK, n.—tseke, marká—tseke —tséke, marka

CHECKER, n.—tagabantáy—tigusisa, tigbantay—tag-usisà

CHEEK, n.—pisngi—aping — pisngi, guyá

CHEER, n.—a'íw, sayá, tuwâ — kamaya, kalipay, kasayn—sadya, hugyaw

CHEERFUL, adj.—masayá, maligaya—maya, malipayon — ma sadya, malipayon

CHEERLESS, adj. — malungkót waláng sayá—magul-anon, way kalipay—mamingaw

CHEESE, n.—keso—keso—keso

CHEMISE, n.—kamisón—kamison —kamisón

CHEMIST, n.—kímikó—kemiko—kemikó

CHEMISTRY, n.—kímiká—kemika—kemiká

CHEST, n.—dibdíb, kabán — dughan, baul—dughan, kabán.

CHEW, v.—nguyaín — pag-usap, pagmama—usangon

CHICKEN, n.—manók—manok —manúk.

CHICKEN FLEA, n.—hanip—pulgas sa manok—dapaw

CHICKEN-HEARTED, adj.—mahinang-loób, duwág — talawan, mahadlokon—matalaw

CHIEF, n.—punò, pangulo, líder—pangulo, líder — punò, pangulo, hepe

CHIEF CLERK, n. — punong-kawaní — labawang manunulat — punong-takigrapista

CHILD, n.—batà—bata—batà

CHILDBIRTH, v. — panganganák —panganak—pagpanganák

CHILDHOOD, n.—kabataan—ang pagkabata—pagkabatà

CHILDLESS, adj.—waláng anák —walay anak — walay anák, baw-as

CHILDREN, n.—mga batà—mga bata—mga batà ukón kabataan

CHILL, n.—ngiki, gináw—tugnaw panugnaw—ginakalambre

CHIMNEY, n.—tsimeneá, páusukan—bagting sa lingganay—tsimenea, alasonan

28

CHIN, n.—babà—suwang — sag-
ang

CHISEL, n.—paít—tigib — sinsel
tigíb

CHOICE, n. — pilì, hirang—pini
lian, pinili—pilì

CHOIR, n.—koro, mga mang-aawi
—mga mag-aawit sa simbahar
—koro, mangangamba

CHOKE, v. — sakalín, pahintuín
pasakan — pagtuck, pagluok —
kug-on, sungsongán, pasakan

CHOOSE, v. — pilìin, hirangin —
pagpilì—pilíion

CHOOSY, adj.—salawahan, mapa
milì—humilì—salamwanan, ma
pislì

CHOP, v.—putul-putulin, tadtarín
—pag-ad-ad, paghiwa, pagtad
tad—hatukhatukón, tadtarón

CHRIST, n.—Kristo — Kristo —
Kristo

CHRISTIAN, n. — Kristiano —
Kristohanon—Kristohanon

CHRISTMAS, n.—Paskó ng Panganganák—Pasko sa Pagkatawo—Paskua sa Pagkatáo

CHURCH, n.—simbahan—simba
han—simbahan

CIRCLE, n.—bilog, lipon, samahar
—lingin, kapunongan — bilóg
manipu'on, tinlingoban

CIRCULAR, n. — palibot-sulat —
sulat-palibot—palibot-sulát

CIRCUMSTANCE, n.—pangyayari, pagkakátaón—kahitaboan —
kahitabuán, kahigayonan

CITIZEN, n.—mámamayán—lung-
soranon—banwahanon

CITIZENSHIP, n. — pagkamáma-
mayán — dakbayan, siyudad —
pagkabanwahanon

CITY, n.—siyudád, lunsód — lung-
sodnon—siudád, dakbanwa

CIVIC, adj.—pambayan—bahin sa
lungsod, sibil—tungód sa banwa

CIVILIZE, v.—bihasahin—pagsibi-
lisar—maabiabihon, sibíl

CLAIM, n. — pag-angkín — angkon—angkon

CLAIM, v.—angkinín — pag-ang
kon—angkonón

CLAM, n.—kabibi, halaán—kabibi,
tuway—tuwáy, litog

CLAMMY, adj.—malagkít, mala
míg—mahagkot, mabugnaw
makaput, mapilít

CLAP, n.—palakpák, tunóg--pak-
pak—palakpak

CLAP, v.—pumalakpák, isará —
pagpakpak, pagtakop—pumalak-
pak, itiklop

CLASP, v.—pisilín — pagpig-it —
pislon, kamustahón

CLASP, n.—pangkabít, kalawit-
kaw-it—tabiron

CLASS, n.—urì, klase — matang,
saring—sarí, klase

29

CLASSIC, adj.—pambihirà, tanyág —talagsaon, klasika—klasikó

CLASSIFICATION, n.—pagbubu-kúd-bukód, pag-uuri-urì—pagla-in-lain—pagsarî

CLATTER, n.—ingay — kabanha, aringkil-kasikas—gahud

CLAUSE, n.—sugnáy — sukip — tumbok

CLAW, n.—kukó—kuko sa mana-nap—kamumuo ukon kukó (sa hayup)

CLEAN, v.—maglinis—paglinis — maninlò

CLEAN, adj.—malinis—malinis — matinlò

CLEANER, n.—tagapaglinis—tig-linis, maglilinis—manogtinlò

CLEAR, adj.—maliwanag—maha-yag, matin-aw—maathag

CLEARANCE, n. — paghuhusay, pagtuós, paglilinis—katin-awan, kalinisan—paghusayáy

CLEMENCY, n. — pagpapatawad, pagkaawà—pasaylo — pagpata-wad, pagkaluoy

CLERK, n.—kawaní, tagasulat — manunulat—takigrapó

CLEVER, adj.—matalino, maligsi —maliksi, maabtik—batíd

CLICK, n.—tunóg na matalím—inggit nga tingog, imik—tagring (sang talúm)

CLIFF, n.—batóng matarík, bun-dók na matarík — pangpang, bung-aw — tukarón nga pang-pang ukón bukid

CLIMATE, n.—klima, singáw ng lupà, panahón — panahon, klima —klima, panahón

CLIMAX, n.—kasukdulán—kulba-hinam nga yugto—putokputokán

CLIMB, v.—umakyát — pagsaka, pagkatkat — sumakà

CLINCH, n.—paraán ng pagtatalì ng malakíng lubid—panaggakus —pagbalû sang dakû nga lubid

CLING, v.—tumangang mahigpít, kumapit — paggunit, paghawid, pagkumbabit—baluón, hugton

CLINIC, n.—págamutan, klíniká—tambalanan, klinika—klinika

CLOAK, n.—balabal, panakíp—ku-po—kunóp

CLOCK, n.—orasán, relós—takna-an—orasán, taknaan

CLOG, v.—harangan, barahán — pagbalda, pagpuot—suponán, ba-rahón

CLOSE, v.—sarhán, takpán, isará ipinid—pagtak-op, pagsira—sir-han, takpan, isirá, itakúp

CLOSET, n.—muntíng silíd, pána-bihan—pansayan, sibay—diótay nga kwarto (suludlan sing yang-kutyangkut)

CLOSE-UP, n.—málapitan — sa-duol—malapít kaayo

CLOTH, n.—damít, kayo — saput besti—ulós, sapút, tela

CLOTHE, v.—bihisan, damitán — pagsaput — islan, ílisan (sa panapton)

CLOTHESLINE, n.—sampayan—hayhayan—halayán

CLOTHING, n.—damít, kasuutan —mga saput, panapton — bayù, panapton

CLOUD, n.—ulap—panganud, gabon—panganod

CLOUDY, adj.—maulap, malabò - gabonon, halap—magal-um

CLOWN, n.—tagapagpatawa, bobo—bokon, komiko — komikero, tarso

CLUB, n. — batutà, kapisanan — batota, puspos, kapunongan—batota, talapoanan, klùb

CLUE, n.—himatón—timailhan — sandigan

CLUSTER, n.—kumpól, pilíng, buwíg—bulig, pongpong—bulig

CLUTCH, v.—hawakan, pigilan — gunitanan, paggunit—kalaptan, pulonggan

COACH, n.—tagaturò, tagasanay, kotse, karwahe—kotse, tigtudlo, tigbansay—tagtudlò, tagahanas, kotse, karwahi

COACH, v. — turuan, sanayin — pagtudlo, pagbansay—pagtudló, hanason

COACHMAN, n.—kutsero, kotsero, mamilino—kutsero

COALITION, n.—pag-iisá, pagpipisan—paghiusa, panag-abin — pag-isaháy

COARSE, adj.—magaspáng, malaswâ—bagal, dili pino, halhag, sagalsalon—mabahúl

COARSENESS, n.—kagaspangán, kabastusán, kasagwaán — ang kabagal, kasalbahisan—kabaholán, kabastosán

COAST, n.—pampáng, baybayin—baybayon, kabaybayonan—pangpang, baybayon

COAT, n.—ameríkana, barò—ameríkana—amerikana, bayù

COCK, n.—tandáng — manok, sonoy—mungâ

COCKEYED, adj.—dulíng, sulimpát—sulimaw, libat, manokon—libát

COCKPIT, n.—sabungán — bulangan, sabongan—bulangán

COCKROACH, n. — ipis—uk-ok—tanga

COD, n.—bakaláw—bakalaw—bakaláw

COERCION, n.—pamimilit — pamugos, panglugos—pamílit

COIN, n.—salapî, kuwarta, barya —salapi, manintabos—salapi, pilak, sensilyo

31

COINAGE, n.—gáwaan ng kuwarta—pamuhat sa salapi — buhatán-kuarta

COLD, adj.—malamíg — mabugnaw, sip-on—mabugnaw

COLLAPSE, v. — mápalugmók, mátumbá—pagkatumba, pagkapukan—mauy-oy, mapukan

COLLAR, n.—kwelyo — liog, kuwelyo—kwelyo

COLLECT, v. — maningíl, magipon — pagpaningíl, pag-ipon, pagtigum—sukót, supton

COLLECTION, n.—nápaningilán, kalipunan—tinigum, kinubrahan —napanuktan

COLLECTOR, n. — tagasingíl —maniningíl—manunukot

COLLEGE, n.—kolehiyo—tunghaan, kolehiyo—kolehiyo

COLLISION, n. — banggaan — bangga, banggaay—banggaay

COLOR, n.—kulay—bulok, kolor—duág

COLUMN, n.—hanay; haligi—haligi, lindog—kolumna, kubay

COMB, n.—sukláy—sudlay—husáy

COMB, v.—suklayín, halughugín —pagsudlay—husayon

COMBAT, n.—away, babág, labanán—away, gubat—away

COMBAT, v.—sugpuín, labanan—paggubat, pagsumpo—awayáy

COMBINATION, n. — kombinasyón, pagkakáunawaan—panagipon, kombinasyon — kombinasyon

COMBINE, v.—magsama, pag-isahín—pagtipon, pag-uban — tingób, tingbon

COMBUSTIBLE, adj.—madalíng magliyáb o magdingas — madaling masunog—malakután

COMFORT, n.—alíw, ginhawa — kaharuhay, katagbawan—kasulhay

COMFORT, v.—aliwín—paglingaw —libangón

COMFORTABLE, adj.—maginhawa, ginbawa—haruhay — masulhay, komportable

COMFORTER, n.—tagaalíw, tagaalagà—tiglingaw—taglibáng

COMIC, n.-adj.—kómiká, mapagpatawá—komika, kataw-anan—komiká, kaladlawan

COMICAL, adj. — nakakátawá—kataw-anan, makapatawa—ma kahalam-ut

COMMAND, v.—mag-utos, atasan —pagsugo—magsugò, mando

COMMANDER, n.—punò, tagapagutos — labawng magsusugo, komandante—punong . manogsugô ukón manogmando

COMMEMORATION, n.—paggu-
nitâ sa alaala, pag-aalaala—han-
dumnanan—pahanumdum, kome-
morasyon

COMMENCE, v.—pasimulán, um-
pisahán—pagsugod—sugoran

COMMENCEMENT, n.—pagtata-
pós, pasimulâ — katapusan, si-
nugdanan—belada (sa eskwelahan)

COMMEND, v.—purihin—pagda
yeg, pagdayo—dayawon

COMMENT, n.—pansín, puná—pahayag, hunahuna—pagalupangod

COMMERCE, n.—kalakal, komersiyo—patigayon, komersiyo—ko-
mersyo

COMMERCIAL, adj.—komersiyá
—patigayonon—komersyal

COMMISSION, n.—lupon, pors
yento—komisyon, porsiyento —
komisyon

COMMISSIONER, n.—kinatawán
representante—komisyonado, tinugyanan—komisyonado

COMMIT, v.—gumawâ, mangakè
— paghimog, butang—magbuhat
magpangakò

COMMITTEE, n.—lupon, komité
—komite—komité

COMMON, adj.—karaniwan, pam-
bálaná — kasagaran — ordinaryo, kumón

COMMUNICATION, n.—pahatíd,
pakikipag-usap, talâ—hatud-ka-
wat, komunikasyon — komunikasyon

COMMUNITY, n.—bayan, nayon,
baryo—lungsod — banwa, puók,
baryo

COMPANION, n.—kasama, kaak-
báy—kauban, kakuyog—kaupod

COMPANIONSHIP, n.—pagsasa-
ina—panag-uban, panagkuyog —
pag-inuporáy

COMPANY, n. — samahan, kom-
panyá—katiponan, kompaniya—
kompaniya, kumbuyahan

COMPARE, v.—iparis, ihalintulad,
ipareho—pagtandi, pagtanding—
ipaanggid, ipatulad

COMPARISON, n. — pagpaparis,
pagtutulad, paghahambíng—pa-
nagtandi, panaghuwad—pagpaanggid, pagpatulad

COMPARTMENT, n.—pitak — lawak, sulod—partisyon

COMPASSION, n.—awà, habág—
kaluoy—awà, kaluoy

COMPATRIOT, n.—kababayan—
katagilungsod—kasimanwa

COMPEL, v.—pilitin—pagpugos—
piliton

COMPENSATION, n.—kaupahán,
bayad—bayad, suhol — kompen-
sasyon

COMPETE, v. — makipaglaban, makipag-unahán — pagpakigtagus, pagsalmot — makigtatok, makig-unaháy

COMPILATION, n. — pagsasamasama, kalípunán — pagtampo, mga tinampo—pag-ulolupod

COMPLAIN, v.—tumutol, magsumbóng, dumaíng — pagtutol, pagsumbong—mamalabag, magsumbong, magyamo

COMPLETE, adj.—ganáp, buô, tapós — hingpit, tibuok — bugos, kompleto

COMPLETE, v. — tapusin, buuín, ganapín — paghuman, pagtapus —tapuson, bug-osón

COMPLEXION, n.—kulay ng balát, laló na ng mukhâ—pamanit, bulok sa panit—kutis, kompleksyon

COMPOSE, v.—magbuô, kumathâ —pagtagik, paghimo—humanón, pasaron

COMPOSER, n. — mangangathâ ng tugtugin—tagsulat sonata, maghohoni — manghuhumán (sa musiká)

COMPOSITION, n.—kathâ, kayarián—tinagik, sinulat—pagkahumán, pagkapasad,. komposisyon

COMPREHEND, v.—maunawaan maintindihán, maliwanagan pagsabut—mahangpan, masanagán

COMPREHENSION, n.—pagkakáunawà, pagkakáintindí—sinabtanan—pagkahangúp, pagkaathag

COMRADE, n.—kasama, kaibigan, kaisá, kapanalig — kauban, kaanib—kaupod, kahirup

CONCEAL, v.—ikublí, itagò, iiihim—pagtago. paglimud — itagò ilikún

CONCEDE, v.— tanggapín, umayon—pagtugyan, pagseguro —batonon, magpaayón

CONCEIT, n. — paghahambóg sa sarili—pagarbo sa kaugalingon —pagpahambog sa kaugalingon

CONCEIVE, v.—maglihí, akalain —pagsabak, pagpangisip—magpanamkon, magmabdus

CONCERN, n.—samahan, pakialám, pag-aalaala—kapunongan, may labut, kabalisa — updan. buylogán, pahanumdumón

CONCENTRATE, v.—buuín, tipunin—pagtingub, paghiusa—bugosón, tingbon (sa isip)

CONCENTRATION, n. — kulungán, ipunán—tiguman, tampohan—bulukotán, tilingban

CONCERNING, adj.—tungkól sa, ukol sa—mahitungod sa, bahin sa—tungód sa, bangód sa

CONCERT, n.—konsiyerto, tugma-an—konsiyerto sa honi, kahusay —konsyerto

CONCEPTION, n.—pagkakáintin dí, akalà, paglilihí—pagpanamkon, pinasabutan — pagkahangúp, pagpanamkon

CONCLUDE, v. — tapusin, wakasán, magtapós—pagtapus, paghukom—tapuson

CONCLUSION, n.—resulta, katapusán, hatol—hukom, katapusan —katapusan, pamatbat, resulta

CONDEMN, v.—hatulan, parusahan, sumpaín—pagsilot, pagsaway—pamatbatán, silutan, kondenahón

CONDEMNATION, n.—hatol, parusa, sumpâ—silot, matamayong, hukom—silut, hukman

CONDITION, n.—kalágayan, ayos, kahingian — kahimtang, pagkabutang—kahimtangan

CONDITIONAL, adj.—may pasubalì—may kasabutan—kondisional

CONDUCT, n. — kilos, pag-uugalì —gawi—gawî, pagkinaugalì

CONDUCT, v.—samahan, magdaos, ihatíd—pag-uban, paghatud —updan, hiwatan, dul-ongón

CONFECTION, n.—matamís, kendi—matam-is, karmelitos—dulse

CONFEDERATION, n.—samahan. kalipunán—katiguman, kapunongan—konpederasyon, katilingbanan

CONFER, v.—makipagharáp, makipagpulong — pakigsabut-sabut, pakigsulti—makigsapul

CONFERENCE, n. — panayám, pagpupulong — sabut-sabut, tigum—konperensya, pagsilinapul

CONFESS, v.—mangumpisál, ipagtapát—pagkompisal — pangumpisár, panuaron

CONFESSION, n.—kumpisál, pagtatapát, pagsasabi — kompisal, kompisyon — kumpisár, kompesyon

CONFIDENCE, n.—tiwalà—pagsalig—salíg

CONFIDENTIAL, adj.—lihim, waláng nakaáalám, kapalágayangloób—tinago, ato-ato — masaligan

CONFINE, v.—hanggahan, tumigil—pagpahimutang sa dapit — dulonan

CONFIRM, v.—patotohanan, patunayan, sagutín — pagsanong, pagmatuod—pamatud-an, kilalahon

CONFIRMATION, n. — patotoó, sagót, kumpíl — sanong, kumpil —kompirma

CONFLICT, n.—labanán, guló — kasamok, kasumpakian — awayáy, gamó

CONFISCATE, v.—ilitin, samsamín—pagsakmit—konpiskahón

CONFUSION, n.—kaguluhan, kagitlahanan — kaguliyang — kagamohán

CONGESTION, n. — pagbabará, pagkakaguló—kadasok, gubot — pagkasupón, pagkinagamo

CONGRESS, n.—konggreso, kapulungáng mambabatás—balaoranan, kongreso — kongreso

CONGRESSMAN, n.—konggresista, isáng kaanib ng konggreso—magbabalaod, kongresista—kongresista

CONJECTURE, n.—palagáy—hunahuna, pangagpas — pagkabig, paghaum

CONJUGAL, adj.—pangmag-asawa—sa asawag-bana—pag-asawaháy

CONNECT, v.—ikabít, idugtóng—pagdugtong, pagsumpay — isugpon, iangút

CONNIVANCE, n. — sabuwatan, pagkadugtong, paglambigit — sugpon, angút

CONNIANCE, n. — sabuwatan, pakikipag-ayos — pakigkombuya, pakigsabut—hinimbonán

CONNIVE, v.—makipag-alám, makipagsabuwatan — pagpakigkombuya—makighimbon

CONQUER, v.—supilin, sakupin, talunin—pagbuntog, pagparot—dag-on, sakupon

CONQUEROR, n. — tagasakop manlulupig—magbubuntog, mananaog—tagsakup

CONQUEST, n. — pagsakop, pagkalupig—kadaugan — pagsakup, pagkalupig

CONSCIENCE, n. — budhî, konsvensya, damdamin — tanlag — konsyensya, balatyagon

CONSCIENTIOUS, adj.—matiyagâ—mabunahunaon — mahimulaton

CONSCIOUNESS, n. —. damdamin, pakiramdám, malay—balatian, paghimatngon—pamatyag

CONSCRIPT, n.—pálistahang-sá-pilitán—pasalista — pilitáy nga listahay (sa armi ukón nebi)

CONSENT, n. — pagsang-ayon-ang pagtugot, katugotan—pagsugót

CONSENSUS, n.—pagkakáísá — hinlusang hunahuna—paghiliusa

CONSEQUENCE, n.—bunga, kinálabasán—sangputanan — bunga, hinimulatan

CONSIDER, v.—ayunan, tanggapín — paghunahuna —.kabigon, patugsilingon

36

CONSIDERABLE, adj.—malaki, masiyado, mahalagá — dakuan, takus hunahunaon—takús kabibon

CONSIDERATION, n.—pakundangan, pagtingín, pagbibigáy — hatag, hunahuna — konsiderasyon, patugsiling

CONSIST, v.—binúbuô, kinalálamnán—sinakpan—ginatapoan

CONSOLATION, n.—kagaanan ng loôb, kaaliwán—konsuylo—konsolasyon, kinabubut-on

CONSTANT, adv.—lagî, pálagián, waláng pagbabago, tapát — makanunayon—pirmo, unáy

CONSTITUTION, n.—pátakarán, pangangalawán, saligáng-batás —panglawas, batakan-balaod — palatukorán

CONSTRUCT, v.—itayô, gawín — pagtukod—pasaron

CONSTRUCTION, n.—pagtatayô —katukoran — palasarón

CONSULT. v.—ipagtanóng, humingî ng payo, magpatingín—pagpakisayud—ipamangkut, ipangutana

CONSULTATION, n.—pagpapatingín, pagtatanóng, pakikipagusap —pakisayud—ipausisà

CONTAGIOUS, adj. — nakáhahawa — mananakud — makalalaton

CONTAMINATE, v.—ihawa, hawahan—pagtakod, pagdahig — ipalatón

CONTAIN, v.—maglamán — pagsulod, pagsakop—kaundan

CONTEMPT, n.—pag-iríng, paghamak—pagtamay, pagdant — tamay, pasipala

CONTEND, v.—ipagtalo, ilaban, panindigán — paglalis — ipangapin, pangapinan

CONTENTED, adj.—nasísiyahán —natagbaw—naayawan

CONTENTS, n.—lamán—ang sulod—kaundan

CONTEST. n.—páligsahan, timpalák, labanán, pakikipag-sukatán—bangga, indigay, tiglay — paindis-indis

CONTEST, v.—tutulan, labanan, usigin—pagtutol, pagsupil — pamatukan, pamalabagan

CONTINUOUS, adj.—palagî, sigtsigi, waláng pa'id—nagpadayon, kanunay — padayon

CONTINUE, v.—magpatuloy, dugtungán—pagpadayon — magpadayon

CONTOUR, n.—ayos, guhit—huima kahimtangan—kinuritan

CONTRACT, n.—kásunduan, pakikipagyarî, kontrato—kasabutan, kontrato—kontrato, kasugtanan

CONTRACTOR, n.— ang nakíkipagyarî, kontratista — tigsabut, kontratista — kontratista

CONTRADICTION, n.—pagkakásalungatan — panagsumpaki — pagsupok, supokan

CONTRARY, adj.—laban, kasalungát, di-ayon, balintunà—nahasupak, nahasupil — kaaway

CONTRAST, n.—kaibahán—kalainan—kasihayan

CONTRASTING, adj.—magkaibá, dî-magkabagay — malainon, masukwahion — magkatuhay

CONTROL, n.—pagpipigil, kapangyarihan — pagpugong — kohtrol, pamugóng

CONTRIVE, v.—umisip, gumawâ, umayos — pagpakigsangga — umisip, maghimud-os

CONTROLLER, n.—tagapigil, pinunò ng pámahalaán—tigpugong, punoan sa kagamhanan — tagpugóng, opisyal sa gobierno.

CONTROVERSY, n. — gusót, dipagkakásundô, away — panagsumpaki, panag-away — dîmaghangpanay, dî-maghisugot

CONVELESCENT, n.—nagpápagalíng, taong galing sa sakít—nagpahiuling masakiton — nagapaayo-ayo (gikan sa balatian)

CONVENIENT, adj.—nakasísiyá, nakagágaán — hamugaway — makapaayaw

CONVENTION, n.—pagpupulong, panayám—panagtigum — konbensyon, pagsilinapul

CONVERSATION, n.—pakikipagusap, úsapan—sulti-sulti, kolokabildo — sabtanay

CONVERSANT, adj. — masalitâ, maalam—makisultihon, mahibalo — palahambal

CONVERT, v.—hikayatin, pilitin —pagdani, pag-awhag — haylohón

CONVEY, v.—ilipat, ihatíd—paghatud—ipaalinton

CONVEYANCE, n. — paghahatíd, sasakyáng tagapaghatíd — ang paghatud, salakyanan — isaylo (sa panublion)

CONVICT, n.—bilanggô, náhatulan ng húkuman—sinilotan, makasasala — binilanggò, napamatbatán sang hukmanan

CONVICTION, n.—pananalig, paniniwalà—pagtuo, silot — pagsalig, pagtuo

CONVINCE, v. — pasang-ayunin, papaniwalain—pagpatuo, pagpauyon — papatihon, konbinsido

CONVIVIAL, adj.—masayá, masa-yahin—malipayon — masadya, masadyahon

COOK, n.—tagapaglutò -- manlu-luto, kosinero — kusinero kusi-nera, manoglutô

COOL, adj.—malamíg, mahangin —bugnaw, hayahay — mabug-naw, mahangin

COOPERATION, n. — pagtutulu-ngán — pagbinuligay — paghi-nangpanay

COOPERATE, v.—tumulong, ma-kiisá, makisama — pagbulig — pagbinuligáy, pag-inuporáy

COP, n.—pulís—polis — polís

COPY, v.—isalin, sipiin, huwarán — paghulad, pagsundog — huád, kopya

COPYRIGHT, n.—tunay na pag-aarì ng isáng gumawâ—katu-ngod-pagpanag-iyag sinulat — tunay nga pagkatag-iya sang taghikut

CORD, n.—pisì, malíít na lubid, tal̀'—pisi, higot — pisì, diótay nga lubid, kordon

CORDIAL, adj. — tapát na loób, ayon sa pusò—kinagsingkasing bunayag sing kabubut-on

CORDIALITY, n.—katápatan, ka-butihan — kaaghop, kamaayog buot — pagkabunayag

CORK, n. — tapón—sungsong — duol

CORN, n.—maís, kalyo — mais, kalyo — maís, kibul (sa t̄jil)

CORNER, n.—sulok—suok, sibay —pamusorón

CORNY, adj.—waláng kuwenta, hindî tunay—walay hinungdan, taphaw — wala'y pulós, di-tu-nay

CORPORATION, n. — samahan, korporasyón — katiponan, kor-porasyon — korporasyon

CORPSE, n.—bangkáy—minatay bangkay

CORPULENCE, n.—tabâ, kataba-an—katambok — tambok, mu-wà

CORRECT, adj.—tamà, maayos—husto, tukma — tamà, husto, sibù

CORRECT, v.—baguhin, isaayos, iwastô—pagtul-id, pagtarung — tadlongón

CORRESPOND, v.—makipagsula-tán—pagpakigsulatay — magsu-latay

CORRESPONDENCE, n.—sulat, kalatas—mga sulat — sulátay

CORRIDOR, n.—pasilyo, daanang makitid—agianang piut, pasilyo —pasilyo

CORRUPT, adj.—di-malinis, ma-rumíng-budhî—mahugaw, ma-laksot — mahigkò

CORRUPTION, n. — kabulukán, kahalayan, pagsusuhulán — kahugawan, kalaksotan — kaga garukán

CORSET, n.—kursc, korpino—hapin sa lawas, korpinyo — korsc, korpinyo

COST, n.—halagá, kabayarán — bili, bayranan — bili, bayad

COSTLY, adv.—mahalagá, mahál —mahal — mahál

COTTON, n.—bulak—doldol, gapas — bulak

COTTON TREE, n.—punò ng bulak — kahoyang doldol — bulak sang bulak

COUCH, n.—supá, hiligán, higaan higdaan, sopa — sopá, idagan

COUCH, n.—supá, hiligán, hígaan pag-ubo, ubo — umubó

COUNCIL, n.—kapulungán — katiguman, hunta — pulolungan, konsehos

COUNSEL, n.—payo, tagapayo — tambag, sambag — lugpay, mananabang

COUNT, n.—bilang—lhap — isip

COUNTENANCE, n.—mukhâ — panagway — nawóng, dagway

COUNTERACT, v.— hadlangán, talunin—pagsumballk — balabagan

COUNTERFEIT, adj. — kaparis, huwád—huwad, mini — huád

COUNTRY, n.—bansá, bukid o labás ng bayan—nasud, bukiran— pungsod

COUNTRY-PEOPLE, n.—taga-bukid, taga-parang—bukidnon, taga-banika — bukidnon

COUNTY, n—lalawigan, isáng bahagi ng estado—lalawigan, purok — isá ka bahin sang estado

COUPLE, n.—dalawá, ang magasawa—duroha, magtiayon—duhá, mag-aṣawá

COURAGE, n. — katapangan, lakás ng loób—kaisug—kaisug

COURSE, n.—daán, lutô kung bagá sa pagkain, takbó—dalan, linutoan sa sud-an—kurso, alagyan, lutò (sa pagkaon), dalagan

COURSE, v.—paraanín, patakbuhín — pagpaagi, pagpadagan — paagyon, padalaganon

COURT, n. — húkuman, kortehukmanan, hawan—korte, hukmanan

COURT, v.—ligawan, hingín, lumigaw—pag-ulitawo — kaluyagáy, daluáy

COURTEOUS, adj. — magalang, mapitagan—matinahuron — matinahuron

COURTESY, n.—paggalang, pitagan sa pamamagitan — katahuran—kortesiya

COUSIN, n.—pinsan—ig-agaw — pakaisá

CRIB, n.—sabsaban, hígaan ng batang maliít—pasongan, katre sa bata—katre sang lapsag

CRICKET, n.—kuliglíg, isáng larô ng mga Inglés—kulilig, dulang Ingles — siriritan, isá ka hampang sang mga Inglés

CRIME, n.—kasalanan o sala — kasal-anan, krimen, salaod—kasal-anan ukon salâ

CRIMINAL, n.—kriminál, salarín —makasasala, kriminal—kriminal, tagpatáy

CRIPPLE, n. — piláy, di-makalakad—bakol—lupóg, di-makalakát

CRIPPLE, v.—pilayan, pahigaín pabagsakín — pagbakol, pagpiang—piáng, tambalà

CRIMSON, adj.—mapulá—mapula —mapulá

CRITICISM, n. — pansín, puná, bati--panaway—pamasul, panawáy

CRITICIZE, v.—pansinín, punahín —pagsaway, pagtamay — sayawón, basaulon, patalupangdon

CROP, n.—ani—ani, abut sa yuta —alanyon

CROSS, v.—tumawíd, bumagtás— pagtabok, pagtapon — tumabók, lumaktud

CROWN, n.—putong, korona—purong-purong, korona, — korona, puróng

CROWNED, v.—pinutungan, kinoronahan — pagkorona, pagpurong-purong — kinoronahan, pinurongán

CRUEL, adj.—malupít, mabagsík, tampalasan—mabangis, tampalasan—mapintas, tampalasan

CRUELTY, n.—kalupitán, kabagsikán—kabangisan, kapintasan —kapintas, katampalasan

CRUMB, n.—mumo, piraso—momho—mumho, dinukdok

CRUMBLING, v. — bumábagsák, naáagnás—pagkapukan, pagkahulog—bumulidbulíd, nadunot

CRUMPLED, adj.—gusót, lamukót —gubut, kalkag—yukót

CRUSH, v.—durugin — pagpígsat, pagkumot—dunoton

CRY, n.—sigáw, iyák, tawag—hilak, singgit, tawag—hibi, singgit, tawág

CRYSTAL, n.—kristál, bubog — bildo, kristal—kristal

CUCUMBER, n.—pipino, katimon —pipino—pipino

CUFF, n. — punyós — punyos — punyos, palakoan

CULPABILITY, n.—kasalanan — kasal-anan—kasal-anan

CULTIVATE, v.—mag-alagà, maglinang, magtaním, patubuin — pag-ugmad, pag-alima, paggalam—talaumahón

COVER, n.—takíp, isáng tanghalian o isáng hapunan—taklob, tabon, kubiyertos — takúp, hapín, isá ka panyagahón ukón panyaponón

COVET, v. — pagnasaan, pag-isipan—pagpaninguha, pagpangandoy—interesán

COWARD, adj. — duwág, mahinang-loób—talawan, hadlokan—taslawán

CRAB, n. — alimango, alimasag, maramot — kasag, alimango, agukoy—alimango, kalampay

CRACK, v.—sirain, patunugín, biyakín—pagbuak, pagtipak—gision, patunogón, buk-on

CRACK, n.—basag, biták, punit—liki, basag—buóng, litík, gisî

CRACKER, n.—galyetas—galyeta —galyetas

CRADLE, n.—duyan, hígaan ng sanggól—duyan — duyan, abóyabóy

CRANKY, adj. — sirá-sirâ, ulól, sumpungin — saputon, kuwanggol—gisigisión, hanginón, alabuton

CRASH, n.—lagitík, banggaan, lusob—bangga, dam-agay — sunggoay, santikan, dalasaón

CRASH, v.—pasukin, banggaín—pagyuhot, pagsulod — sudlon, sunggoán

CRAVE, v—nasain, naisin, hangarín — pagpangandoy — handumón, tinguhaón

CRAVING, n.—nais, hangád, gustó — pangandoy, gusto — handum, pagtiñguhâ

CRAWL, v.—gumapang — pagkamang—kumamang

CREAM, n.—gatâ ng gatas, ang pinakamabuti, krema — gatas, krema, labing maayo—gatâ, krema

CREATE, v.—lumaláng, gumawâ — pagmugna, pagbuhat—laláng tukíb

CREATION, n. — nilaláng, paglaláng, likhâ, santinakpán — minugna, binuhat—ginlalang, tinukíb

CREATURE, n. — kinapál, hayop, nilalâng—ginama, binuhat, linalang—linaláng, hayup

CREDIT, n.—kapurihán, pautang —utang, dungog—kreditó

CREEK, n.—batis—sapa—sapâ

CREVICE, n. — guwáng, butas, awáng—lungag, buho, gawang—buhò, inutlan

CREW, n.—ang mga tauhan sa sasakyán, pangkát—grumete, olagad sa sakyanan—grumete

CRIED, v.—umiyák, tumangis — mikiilak, mitiyabaw—humibi, tumangis

CULTURE, n. — pinag-aralan, pag-aalagà—hibangkaagan, pagalima—tinun-an

CUNNING, adj.—tuso, magdarayà—abtik, malimbongon — toso, madayà

CUP, n.—tasa, sartín—tasa - tasa, sartin

CUPBOARD, n.—paminggalan, taguán ng pagkain—aparador sa sud-an — pingganan, talagoán sing pagkaon

CURE, v.—gamutín, pagalingín—pagtambal, pagbulong—bulngon paayohon

CURE, n.—kagálingan, gamót — pagkaayo, tambal — kaayohan, bulóng

CURIOUS, adj.—usyoso, mausisà, mapakialám—masusihon, makisayud—osyoso, mahilabton

CURRENCY, n.—pananalapî—sa lapi, panalapi—pamilak

CURRENT, n.—koryente, kasalukuyan, agos—kuryente, sulog—koryente, kinarón, ilig

CURRICULUM, n.—kurikulúm — kurikulum—kurikulum (pagtulun-an)

CURSE, n.—tungayaw, sumpâ — panghimaraut, balikas — pamuyayaw

CURSE, v.—isumpâ, tungayawin, murahin—pagbalikas, paghimaraut—buyayawon

CURSORY, adj.—madalî, maikli mabilís—dinalian, pasiplat, matulin—madalî, madasig

CURTAIN, n.—kurtina, tabing — tabil, kortina—kortina

CURVE, n. — baluktót, tambok, umbók, likô — baliko, likoag — kurba, tikû, bawod

CUSHION, n.—kutsón, almuhadon —kultson, unlan—kutson, almohadón

CUSTOM, n.—ugalì, gawî, kinamulatan—batasan, gawi—batasan, kinabatasan

CUSTOMER, n.—sukì—suki—suki

CUT, n.—putol, hatì, hiwà — samad, putol—utdon, tung-on, hiwaon

CUTLERY, n. — mga kasangkapang panghiwà — kagamitang mahait—kasangkapan sa paghiwà

CYCLE, n.—ikot, bilog, pagbalík—panaglibut, lingin—libot, pabalík

CYCLONE, n.—ipuipo — hanging kusog, bagyo—alimpulos

CYMBAL, n.—pómpiyáng — piyang-piyang—pompiyang

CYNICAL, adj. — waláng tiwalà, suspitsoso, mapag-akalà—matahapon, walay pagtuo—walay salíg

CYNOSURE, n.—tampulán, minámataán — tinumong sa mata, atraksiyon — buluyokán

43

— D —

DAILY, adj.—araw-araw—adlaw-adlaw, matag-adlaw—adlaw-ad-law

DAINTY, adj.—maliít, malinis, ka-ayaaya—diyuting, malinis—ma-hinhín, mahinlò

DAIRY, n.—gatasán — gatasan-gatasán

DAIRYMAID, n.—maggagatás na babae — maggagatas babaye—manoggatás nga babáe

DAIRYMAN, n.—maggagatás na lalaki—maggagatas lalaki—ma-noggatás nga lalaki

DAM, n.—patubigan—paambakan sa tubig—dam, palatubigan

DAM, v.—hadlangán—pagbalda — dam, punongan

DAMAGE, n.—kapinsalaan, sirà—kadauí, kagusbatan—kapierde-ban

DAMAGE, v. — dumhán, sirain, pinsala'n—pagguba, pagdaut — pierdehón

DAME, n.—dalaga, babae—babaye, dalaga—dalaga, babáe

DAMNATION, n.—sumpâ, galit — tunglo—debosyon

DAMP, adj.—basa-basâ, pawisán—humod, may pagkabasa — basâ-basà, mahuramul

DAMP, v.—palamigán, basaín — pag-umog, pagbasa—palabugna-wan, bas-on

DANCE, n.—sayáw, sáyawan — sayaw, sadsad—saut

DANCER, n.—mánanayaw—mag-sasayaw—manogsaút

DANGER, v.—panganib—katalag-man—makatalagam

DANGEROUS, adj.—mapanganib, nakatátakot—makuyaw, maka-palisang — talagam-an, haladlo-kan

DAPPER, adj. — pusturyoso, ma-ayos—sitsiriko, luho — postor-yoso, gwapo

DARE, v.—pangahasán, hamunin —pagpangahas, paghagit — pa-ngahsán, hilabtan

DARE, n.—hamon—pangahas, ha-git—hangkat

DARK, adj.—madilím — mangit-ngit, madulum—madulóm

DARKEN, v.—padilimín — pag-ngitngit, pagkisdum—padulmon

DARKNESS, n.—kadilimán—ka-ngitngit, kadulum—kadulumón

DARLING, n.—mahál, irog, giliw —hinigugma, minahal — mahál, hinigugma, pinalanggà

DARN, v.—tahiín, sulsihán—pag-sulsi pagpilot—tahión, surihón

DART, n.—palasóng maigsî, kisláp—gapasan, tuling lupad — panínga malip-ot

DASH, v.—tumakbóng mabilís — pagdagan nga kusog — dumalagan sing madasig

DATE, n.—takdâ, takdaan, típanan, petsa—pitsa—talanâ, petsa

DAUGHTER, n.—anák na babae—anak babaye—anák nga babae

DAUGHTER-IN-LAW, n.—manugang na babae—umagad nga babaye—bayáw nga babáe

DAWN, n. — madalíng-araw, bukáng-liwaywáy—kaadlawon, kabuntagon—pamanagbanag

DAWDLE, v.—magpalipas, magatubili—pagpalabay sa takna — paligaron, awatón ang tinión

DAY, n.—araw—adlaw — adlaw

DAYDREAM, n. — panaginip, hangarin, naʼs—mga damgo, handurawan—handurawan

DAZE, n.—tulíg — panglipong — bunglan, natinglan

DEAD, n.—patáy—patay—patáy

DEAF, adj.—hingí—bungol — bungol

DEAL, v. — makisama, makipagpaiitan, makipag-usap—pagpaidgaabut, pagpahirit—makigbahin, makighisugtanay

DEALER, n.—mángangalakál, tagapagbilí — magpapatigayon — manogpanagtag, manogbaligya

DEAR, adj.—mahál—mahal, hinigugma, pinangga—mahál

DEATH, n. — kamátayan—kamatayon—kamatayon

DEATHLESS, adj. — waláng kamátayan — walay kamatayon—walay kamatayon

DEBATE, n.—pagtatalo, pagpapálitan ng kurò—lantugi, sangka sa katarungan—debate, baisáy

DEBT, n.—utang—utang—utang

DEBUT, n.—pagpapakilala sa lipunan—unang pagpaila sa katilingban—pagkalutáw

DECAY, n.—pagkabulók, sirâ—ka·gabok, katun-as—pagkagabók

DECEIT, n.—pagdarayà, kataksilán—limbong — pangdayà, pamudhì, panglimbong

DECEIVE, v.—manlinláng, magdayà, magtaksíl — paglimbong, paglipot—limbongán, budhián

DECEMBER, n.—Disyembre—Disiyembre—Disiembre

DECIDE, v.—magpasiyá, hatulan—paghukom, paghinayak — pakamaayo, pamatbatán

DECISION, n.—kapasiyahán, pasiyá, hatol—hukom—pamatbat, ginpakamaayo

DECK, v.—hapág ng sasakyáng dagat—salog sa sakayan—salúg sang sakayán

DECK, v.—gayakán, palamutihan —tungtonganan—punihán

DECLARATION, n.—pagpapahayag, salitâ — asoy, pahayag — asoy, pinahayag

DECLARE, v.—magpahayag, magsalitâ—pag-asoy, pagpahayag — magpahayag, magpangasoy

DECLINE, v.—tanggihán. manghinà—pagdumili, pagkunhod — pamatukan, sikwayón

DECORATE, v. — magpalamuti, maggayák, pagandahin. palamutihan—pagdayan, pagtahum —magpuní, punihán

DECOY, n.—pain, panghalina — paon—paón, buyukon

DECREASE, v.—paliitin, bawasan —pagdiyutay, pagkunhod — buhinan, padiótayon

DECREE, n.—utos, pahayag—sugo, mando, baod—sugò, pahayag

DECREPIT, adj.—matandà, mahinà—tigulang, mahinay, luyahon — maluya (sa katigulangón), inutil

DECRY, v.—sisihin—pagbasul — basulon

DEDICATION, n.—handóg, paghahandóg, alay—halad, pahanungod—dulot, halad

DEDUCTION, n. — bawas, pagaakalà, pag-iisip — pagkunhod, kunhod—buhinan

DEED, n.—gawâ, katibayan—buhat, kalig-onan—buhat, binuhatan, kalig-onán

DEEM, v,—ipalagáy — pagsabut, paghunahuna—kabigon, tulotimbangon

DEEP, adj.—malalim—halawom— madalum

DEEPNESS, n.—kalaliman—kala. wom—kadalumón

DEER, n.—usá—usa—usá

DEFACE. v.—dungisan, sirain — pagpanas, pagpapas — dagtaán, musingan

DEFAMATION, n.—dungis, sira, batík sa karángalan—pakaulaw, pagbuong sa dungog—pakahuyan, musing sa kadungganan

DEFEAT, n.—pagkatalo—pagpildi. pagbuntog—pagkalutos

DEFECT, n. — kasiraan, kakulangán—apan, depekto — kakulangán, depekto

DEFEND, v.—ipagtanggól, ipaglaban—paglaban—pangapinan

DEFENSE, n.—pagtatanggól, pakikipaglaban—panalipod — pagpangapin

DEFERENCE, n. — pagbibigáy pagsunód — paghiuyon, pagsunod—pakig-ugyon

DEFY, v.—hamunin labanan — paghagit, pagsukol—hangkatón, pamatukan

DEFORMITY, n. — masamáng ayos, kasakunaan — lawasnong kadaut—masaw-a nga hulag

DEFRAUD, v.—salbahihin, dayain, lukuhin — pagtikas, paglimbong—dayaon, lokohon

DEGREE, n.—grado, antás, pinagaralan, titulo—grado, silid—grado, halintang

DEJECTION, n.—pagkabigô, kahirapan — kapakyasan, kalisdanan—pagkapasó, pagkamingaw

DELAY, n.—pagpapaliban, págkaantala, abala—kalangan — awatón, atrasohon

DELEGATE, n.—kinatawán, sugò, representante — tinugyanan, delegado—delegado, tiglawás, representante

DELETE, v.—alisín, awasín, tanggalín—pagpapas; pagpala — kuhaon, buhinon, paksíón

DELICATE, adj.—maselang, mahinà — bantayanan, delikado—halalongán, matapók

DELICIOUS, adj.—masaráp, may mabuting lasa—lamian, tam-is—malalimon, mananám, marimis

DELIGHT, n.—kaligayahan, ligaya, lugód—kalipay, kangaya — kalipay

DELIGHTFUL, adj.—puspós ng ligaya, puspós ng alíw—makalilipay—lugom sa kalipay

DELINQUENT, adj.—pabayâ, hulí sa pagbabayad—ulahing mobayad—delingkwente, atrasado sa pagbayad

DELIRIOUS, adj.—nahíhibáng — nagdiliryo—nagasalimuáng

DELIVER, v. — dalhín, ibigay, mag-anak, iligtás — paghatag, pagtunol—dalhon, idul-ong, ipanganák

DELIVERY, n.—paghahatíd, kaligtasan, panganganák—pagpahatud, pagpanganak, kaluwasan —pagdul-ong, pagdalá, pagkapanganák

DEMAND, n. — pangangailangan, hingî, hilíng—pangayo — kinahanglanon, pangayò

DEMARCATION, n. — hanggahan —mohon, pangutlanan—dulonan

DEMOCRACY, n. — demokrasya pagkakápantáy-pantáy — demokrasya, angay-angay — demokrasya, pag-alalangay

DEMONSTRATE, v.—ipaliwanag, ipakita, ipaglabar — pagpakita, pagpasundayag — ipakità, ipaathag

DENIAL, n.—di-pag-amin, pagpapahindî, pagtangg í— paglimod —himutigón, paninghiwaláón

DENOUNCE, v.—isumbóng, isuplóng—pagsumbong, pagsaway — isumbong, idenunsya

DENSE, adj.—masinsín, matindí, makapál—dasok, libon, baga — maikit, madamul

DENUDE, v. — hubarán, alisán, tanggalán—paghukas, pagtangtang — ubahan, hublasán

DENY, v.—tanggihán, ipagkailâ—pagdumili, pagbalibad — panghimutigón, panghiwalaón

DEPART, v. — umalîs, lumisan — pagbiya, paggikan, paglakaw — lumakát. naghimulág

DEPARTMENT, n.—kágawarán, departamento—tipik sa buhatan, departamento — departamento, bahin

DEPEND, v.—umasa, manangan— —pagsalig—magsalig

DEPENDENT, n. — alagà, páka-inín, empleado, tangkilik—nag-salig, pinakaon—sinagurán, pa-lakan-on

DEPICT, v. — ipakita, ilarawan, ipahiwatig—paghulagway, pag-larawan—ipakitâ, ilarawan

DEPLORE, v.—ikalungkót, ipang-hinayang—paghinugon, paghisu-bo—igasubô, kanugonan

DEPORT, v.—itapon sa ibáng lu-paín—paghingilin sa laing yuta —itapuk sa ibán nga kadutaan

DEPOSE, v, — alisín, ibagsák sa tungkulin — pagpalagput sa ka-tungdanan — pahalinón sa ka-tungdanan

DEPOSIT, n. — lagak, diposito — tinipigan, deposito — deposito, tipig

DEPOSITION, n. — ang paglala-gak, ang pag-aalís sa katungku-lan,kasulatan, sinumpaán — si-numpaang pahayag sa saksi — pagkatipig, pagkadepositó, pag-kasesante sa trabaho, kasulatan nga sinumpaán

DEPOT, n. — lagakán, himpilan, arsenal—tapokanan sa mga bu-tang, depo—halantalan, arsenal

DEPRAVED, adj. — masamâ, bu-lók, malaswâ—dautan, maluod—pagpangagaw

DEPRIVE, v. — alisán, baw'an — pag-agaw, pagkuha — kuhaan, bawian

DEPRIVATIONS, n. — kahirapan, kawalán—kalisdanan, kawad-on pagkawalâ

DEPTH, n.—lalim, kalaliman — giladmon—dalum, kadalumón

DEPRESSED, adj. — malungkót, waláng-siglâ — masulob-on, minghoy — masubô, walay ka-pagsik

DERIDE, v. — tuyaín, uyamín — paglibak, pagdaut-daut — liba-kón, batakon

DERIVE, v.—kunin, hanguin — pagkuha — patakason, batakon

DERELICT, n.—kawawà, hampas-lupà, kulang-palad—dagsa, tima-wa, anud sa dagat—makaluluoy, wala'y palad

DESCEND, v.—pumanaog, bumabâ — pagkanaug, pagpaubos — pumanaog, lumusad

DESCENDANT, n.— pinagmulan, pinanggalingan—kagikan, kaliwatan—kaliwatan

DESCRIBE, v.—ilarawan, isalaysáy, iuiat—pagsaysay, pagbatbat --ilarawan, isaysay

DESCRIPTION, n. — paglalarawan — saysay, batbat, asoy — paglarawan

DESERT, v.—lisanin, iwan, pabayaan—pagbiya, pagtalikod—talikdan, halinán

DESERT, n.—iláng, lupang tigáng —desiyerto, yutang-bonbon—desierto, banlas

DESERVE, v.—maging dapat, nanararapat—pagkatakus, pagkaangay—mangindapat

DESIGN, n. — bangháy, dibuho, budlís, balangkás, tangkâ—dibuho, pagbuiit—dibuho, banhay

DESIGN, v.—tangkain, balangkasín, idibuho — pagdibuho—desinyo

DESIGNATE, v. — ilagáy, piliin, iturò — pagtudlo, pagbutang — ibutáng, idesignar

DESIGNER, n. — magbabangháy, dibuhista, tagaguhit—magbubulit, dibuhista—manogdesinyo, dibuhista, tagbanhay

DESIRABLE, adj. — kanais-nais, mainam — tinguha-on, kagustohan—halandumon

DESIRE, n.—nasà, hángarin—tinguha—bandum; tiling ahaór

DESIROUS, adj.—punô ng hángarin—matinguhaon — punô sing handum

DESOLATE, adj. — mapangláw, malungkót — mamingaw, mamingawon--wala'y paglaum, masinulub-on

DESPAIR, n.—kawaláng pag-asa, kasukdulán ng hirap—kawaỉay paglaum—wala'y paglaum, masiyado ka imol

DESPERATE, adj.—waláng pagasa—maputong, nawad-ag paglaum—nawalaán sing paglaum

DESPISE, v. — hamakin, libakín, alipustaín—pagyubit, pagtamay —tamayon, libakón, buyayawon

DESPOIL, v.—nakawan, alisán—pagtungina—kawatan, nadulaan

DESTINATION, n. — hanggahan, patútunguhan, kapalaran — tumong, dangpanan — kaladtoan, kapalaran

DESTINED, adj.—itinalagá, inilaán—nadestino—destino

Destroy

DESTITUTE, adj. — dukhâ, waláng-walâ, marálitâ — timawa,
rabanit, makaluluoy—kinulabus

DESTROY, v.—sirain, wasakin, gi-
baín — pagguba, pagdugmok —
wasakón, gubaón

DESTRUCTION, n. — pagkasirà,
pagkawalâ, kamátayan — ang
pagkaguba, kagusbatan—pagkawasák, pagkamatáy

DETAIL, n.—bagay-bagay, maliít
na bahagi o sangkáp — digyu-
tayng bahin—diótay nga butáng
ukón magagmay nga butáng

DETACH, v.—ilayô, tanggalín, alisín—paglaksi, pagbulag—paksi-
ón, ukabón, hukson

DETAIN, v.—pigilin, abalahin —
pagpugong, paglangan—punggan

DETECT, v.—subukan — pag-ila,
paghimatngon — tukibón

DETECTIVE, n.—tiktík, detebtib
— tiktik, detiktib — detiktib,
lampitáw, sekreta

DETENTION, n. — pagkakápigil,
pagkakákulóng — ang pagkabi-
langgo, pagkapugong — pagka-
hunong, pagkapugóng

DETERMINATION, n. — masidhíng paghahangád, kapasyahán
—ang tinguhang hugot — hugót
mga pagtiguhâ

DETERMINED, adj.—náhahandâ,
nátatalagá — malugoton, mapaninguhaon—kapat-urán

DETONATION, n.—putók — buto
nga masipa—lupók

DETOUR, n.—likô, baling—likoan
—likô, likáw

DEVELOP, v.—pabutihin, pasulu-
ngin, painamin—pag-ugmad —
pasaron, kaayohon

DEVELOPMENT, n.—pagsulong.
pagtubò, paglináng — kaugma-
ran—pag-uswag

DEVIATE, v.—umibá, bumago, lu-
mihís—paglihay, paglain sa tumong — bumag-o, tumuhay, lu-
mikday

DEVICE, n. —paraán, kasangkapan, kagamitán—paagi, kasangkapan — kasangkapan, kagamitán

DEVIL, n.—demonyo, diablo, hayop—yawa, demonyo—panuláy.
yawà

DEVISE, v. — gumawâ, umisip.
umimbento—pagbuhat, pagmugna—magtukíb, magbuhat, mag-
imbento

DEVOID, adj.—kulang, walâ—kulang—kulang

DEVOTE, v. — tumalagá, iukol.
ibigáy — paghalad, pagpalabi-
ihalad

DEVOTION, n. — pagmamahál,
pagtingín, kabanalan — pagmahal, debosyon—paghalad. paghigugma, pagkabalaan

DEVOUR, v.—ubusin, lamunin, siraín — pagsubad, paglamon — uboson, lamunon, papason

DEVOUT adj. — maka-Diyos, deboto, taus-pusò—maki-Dios, santolon—deboto, Diosnon

DEW, n.—hamóg—yamog—tun-og

DEXTERITY, n.—kahusayan, kasanayan, katalinuhan—kabatid, kahanas, kaliksi — kahimpitán, kinaadman

DIABOLIC, adj.—masama, makahayop, nakatátakot—makahadlok, yawan-on — makahadlok, kinaadman

DIAGNOSIS, n.—pagkilala kung bagá sa sakít—usisa sa sakit—pagsayasat (kon sa balatian)

DICTIONARY, n. — diksiyonario, talátinigan—kapulongnan, diksiyonaryo — diksyonaryo, kapulongan

DIALECT, n.—wikà, wikain, sálitaan—sinultihan, pinulongan — hambal

DIARY, n.—taláarawán, tálaan — inadlawng talaan — lista-adlawan

DIAPER, n.—lampín, sapín—lampín, hampin—lampin, hapín

DICE, n.—dais—dais—dais

DICTATE, v. — diktahán, idiktá, utusan, pag-utusan — pagsugo, pagdiktar—diktahán, idiktá, suguon

DICTATION, n.—utos, sinabi — pinasulat, diktasyon — dinikta, hinambal

DICTION, n. — pananalitâ—panglitok —panghambal

DIFFERENCE, n. — pagkakaibá-kakulangán — kalainan sa kakulangan—pagkatuhay, kakulangán

DIFFERENT, adj.—ibá—lain, lahi —ibán, tuhay

DIFFICULT, adj. — mahirap, malalim—malisud, makuli — mabudlay, maiwat

DIFFICULTY, n.—kahirapan, kalaliman—kalisdanan, kakulian—kabudlay, kaiwaton

DIFFIDENT, adj. — mahihiyain, waláng-kibò — maulawon, hilumon—mahuluy-on, rumóy

DIFFUSE, v. — ikalat, isabog — pagsabwag, pagkaylap—isab-og, ipalapta

DIG, v. — humukáy, kumutkút, maghukáy — pagkutkot, pagkubkob, pagkalot — kumutkot

DIGEST, v. — tunawin, iklián — pagtunaw, paghilis — tunawon, lip-otán

DIGEST, n.—mga lathalang pinaiklî—minugbong sinulat — pinalip-otán

DIGNIFIED, adj.—marangál, kapitá-pítagan—maligdong — talahuron

DIGNITY, n.— kamahalan, karángalan — kaligdong — kamahalan, kadungganan

DILIGENT, adj. — masipag, mapag-arál, masikap — matulonanon, kugihan — mapisan, palatuon, mahimulaton

DILEMMA, n.—pagkakásubò—kalibog—pagkatiplang

DILUTE, adj. — haluan, bantuan, tubigan—sagolan, saktan, lasawon — samoan, tubigan, palasawon

DIM, adj.—malabò, madilím—mangi:ngit, hanap — masagir-um, madulóm

DIME, adj.—sampúng séntimós — napulo ka sintabos—napulò ka sentimós

DIMENSION, n.—kasukatan, sukat—sukod—takús

DIMNESS, n.— kalabuan, kadilimán—kaingitngit, kahanap—kasagir-um, kadulumón

DIMPLES, n.—biloy, butas ng pisngí—kandiis — yupók (sa pisngi)

DIN, n.—ingay, guló—kasaba, kabanha—kagahud, kagamó

DINE, v.—kumain—pagkaon—kumaon

DINGY, adj. — marumí, maitín marungis — mahugaw, nginb, naglago—mahigkò

DINNER, n.—pagkaing pangunahín, pinakamasaganang pagkain sa maghapon—panihapon—panyapon

DIP, v. — isawsáw, magsawsáw, isalok — pagtuslob — isawsaw, ikandos

DIRECT, v.—pangasiwaan, patnugutan, turuan, isama—pagdumala, pagtudlo, pagtultol—direkto, dumalahan, ubayán

DIRECTION, n.—bandá, utos, direksiyón, pangangasiwà, panuto —ang pagpangulo, pagpanudlo— kaladtoan

DIRECTOR, n. — patnugot, tagaturò, tagapangasiwà—magdumala, pangulo, direktor—direktor, manogdumala

DIRECTORY, n. — listahan, sulatan, talaan—listahan, direktoryo —direktoryo

DIRGE, n.—agunyás, awit sa patáy—agoniyas — agoniyas, punebre

DIRT, n.—dumí—hugar, buling— higkò

DITRY, adj. — marumí, malaswâ —mahugaw, bulingon — mahigkò

DISABILITY, n.—kasakunaan, kawaláng-lakás, kasawián—lawas nong kakulian-kabilinggan — pagkainutil

DISADVANTAGE, n.—kasahulan,
kagípitan—ang kapig-utan, des-
bintahu—disbontaha, pagkawala'y ikasaráng

DISAGREE, v. - - tumutol, di-su-
mang-ayon — pagsupak — dî
nagpasugót

DISAPPEAR, v. — mawalâ, magtagò, maglahò - - pagkahanaw,
pagkawaglang—pagkadulà

DISAPPOINT, v.—biguín—paghí-
gàwad—nalus-awán

DISAPPOINTMENT, n. — pagkabigô, pagkasawî — kahígawad,
kahlubos sa buot — pagkapalso,
nalugaw-an

DISAPPROVE, v.—ipakilala, ipaglaban, huwág sang-ayunan —
pagsalikway, dili pagdawat —
dí-pagpasugtan

DISARM, v.—alisan .ng panlaban
—tangtangan sa armas—kuhaan
sing inog-away

DISASTER, n.—kapahamakán, sakunâ, guló—tnakuyawng hitabo,
katalagman — kapabamakan,
desgrasya

DISBURSE, v.—gastahín, gugulin
—paggugol — gastohón, hingu-
yangon

DISCHARGE, n. — pagpapaalís.
pagpapatakbó, paputók — ang
pagkahawa, ang pagkabuto —
pagpahalín, pagpalupók

DISCHARGE. v.—paalisín, paputukín—pagpahawa, pagpabuto—
paha inón, palukpon

DISCIPLINE, n.—disiplina, pagtuturò, kaayusán, kautusán —
displina, kalagdaan — disiplina,
pagtadlong sa kinamatarung

DISCLOSURE, n. — paghahayag,
pagkakahayag—usa ka pagpadayag — pagpahayag

DISCOURAGE, adj.—huminâ ang
loób, manlupaypáy, bigô — ka-
wad-ag kasibut — pagkalus-aw,
pagkatalaw sang buót

DISCORD, n. — pagkakásirâ, di-
pagkakasundô — kasumpakian,
di-pag-uyon — pagkadisgusto

DISCOVER, v.—tuklasín, hanapin
—pagkaplag — tukibón, pangitaon, dihoncn

DISCOVERY, n.—pagkakátuklás,
pagkakakita, pagkaalám — ka-
kaplagan, kamugnaan — pagka-
tukíb, pagkadihon

DISCREET., adj. — maingat, mapagkákatiwalaan — mabinantayon, kasaligan — mahinalongon,
macaligan

DISCRIMINATE, v. — magtangi-
tangì—pagpihig-pihig — magpa-
sulabí

DISCUSS, v. — magta'o, pag-usa-
pan—paglalis, paglantugi, pag-
hisgutay — magbaisáy, maghi-
sayranay

DISCUSSION, n.—pagtatalo, pag-uusap—lantugi, lalis, hisgut-hisgut — pagbaisáy, paghisayranay

DISDAIN, v. — hamākin, tuyaín, abahín—pagdaut, paglibak—hikayan, libakón

DISEASE, n.—sakít—sakít — balatian

DISEMBARK, v.—lumunsád, umahon, lumakad — pagtakas, pagkawas — lumusad, tumakas, lumakát

DISGRACE, n. — kasiraáng puri, batík—kaulawan, kabuongan sa dungog — desgrasya (sa babáe), namusingan

DISGRACEFUL, adj. — nakahíhiyâ, nakasísirang puri—makauulaw, makadaut sa dungog — makahuluya, desgrasyada

DISGUISE, n. — pagbabalát-kayô, pagtatagò—pagtakuban — paghinagô, pagpakunókuno

DISGUST, n.—pagkayamót, pagkasuyà — kapikal, kalugut, disgusto — pagkadisgusto, pagkataká

DISGUSTED, adj.—nayamót, nasuyà, nabigô — pagkapikal, disgustado — nadisgusto, natak-an

DISGRUNTLED, adj. — masamâ ang ulo, yamót, bugnót—nanuve, magbagutbot, nagngulob — maakigón, dingút

DISH, n.—pinggán, ulam — pinggan, sud-an — pinggan, tulanhan, pagkaon

DISHONEST, adj. — magdarayà, manluluko — malimbongon, dili ligdong — dayaon, manogbuáng

DISLIKE, v.—kayamután, kainisán—paghinaway, pagkaluod — antipatikó, makatalaka

DISLOYAL, adj. — di-tapát—mabudhion, di-manunongon — dîtampad, dî-bunayag

DISMAL, adj.—malungkót, madilím, nakapangíngilabot—masulob-on, subo — mamingaw, makangilidlis

DISMISS, v.—pauwiín, huwág itaním sa isip—pagpahawa, pagsalikway — papaulion, dî-pag-isulód sa isip

DISMISSAL, n. — pagpapaalís — ang pagkapahawa, ang pagkalagpot — pagpahalín

DISMOUNT, v.—bumabâ, ibabâ—pagkawas, pagkanaug — kumubós, hukson, dismontar

DISOBEDIENCE, n. — tigás ng ulo dî-pagsunod, pagsuwáy—kamasupilon, kagahig-ulo — malalison, palasuay

DISORDER, n.—guló, gusót—kasamok, kagubut, kaguliyang — gamó

DISORDERLY, adv.—maguló, waláng ayos—samok, gubut—magamó, wala'y kahim-ongán

DISOWN, v. — alisán, bawian,
itakwíl—pag-iway, pagsalikway
—tabugon, dî-pagkilalahon

DISPERSE, v.—pakalatin, paghi-
wáhiwalayin — pagpakaylap,
pagbulag-bulag — palapnagkón,
tapatón

DISPLAY, n.—ladlád, pakita, pagtatanghál — pasundayag, pagpakita, ladlad — pasundayag

DISPLAY, v.—magpakita, iladlád,
itánghál — pagladlad, pagpasundayag — ipasundayag

DISPLEASED, adj.—nagalit, nayamót, nabuwisit — pagkapikal,
nanuyo, gitak-an — matak-an

DISPOSAL, n.—nais, kapangyarihan, kagustuhan—pagbuot, kagahum — pagbuót, kinabubut-
on

DISPOSE, v. — ayusin, ipamigay
ipagbilí — paghusay, pagbaligya
—husayon, ipanghatag, ibaligyà

DISPUTE, n.—pagtatalo, paglala-
ban, pagkakagalít—lantugi, ka-
suk-anay, way — pagbinaisáy,
pag-ilinaway

DISRUPT, v. — sirain, lansagín,
pahintuín—pagbungkag, pagbalda, paghunong — gub-on, wasakón, pauntatán

DISSATISFACTION, n.—pagkabigô, di-kagustuhan, di-wastô —
walay-katagbaw, walay kagustohan — dî-nagakaigò, dî-naayawan

DISSENT, v.—tumutol, di-umayon
—pagsupak, pagtutol, pagsukwa-
wahi — namatuk, dî-nagpaayón

DISSOLVE, v.—tunawin, lansa-
gin—pagtunaw, pagbungkag —
tunawon, kanawon, bungkagón

DISSUADE, v. — pigilin — pagpugong — punggan

DISTANCE, n.—layò, kalayuan—
gilay-on — layô, kalayuón

DISTANT, adj.—malayò—malayo,
halayo — malayô

DISTASTEFUL, adj. — di-ayos,
malaswâ—maluod, way-lami —
dî-igò, wala'y lalim

DISTINCT, adj.—ibá, maliwanag,
tangì, ibáng-ibá—lahi, lain, malinaw — ibán, tuhay, maafhag,
pinasahî, tuhay kaayo

DISTINGUISHED, adj. — tangì,
bukodtangì, náiibá—inila, tinamud, halangdon — katuhayan,
kapinasahî, kinatuhay

DISTRACT, v.—abalahin, guluhín
—pagsamok, pagkabig — awatón, gamohón

DISTRESS, n.—hirap, sakit, ka-
pighatian—kalisud, kasakit, ka-
subo — kasubô, kamingaw, kalisúd

DISTRIBUTE, v.—ipamigáy, ipamahagi, paghatiin—pagpanghatag, pagpanabwag — ipanghatag, ikataka:a

DISTRUST, n.—kawaláng-tiwalà, di-pagtitiwalà — kawalay pagsalig — wala'y pagsalig, dî-musa'igan

DISTURB, v.—abalahin, gambalain, guluhín — pagsamok, paggubut — tublagón, gamohón

DISUNITE, v.—paghiwalayín, lansagín, pagkagalitín — pagbulag, pagbungkag — bulublagon, panghukson

DITCH, n. — kanál, pácaluyan—kanal — kanál, iligán

DIVE, v.—sumisid, lumundág — pagtiurok, pagbinawo — sumulíp, lumumpat

DIVERGE, v. — umibá, lumayô—paglain, paghilayo — umibán, nag'ayô

DIVERSE, adj.—bukód, nálibá — lahi, lain-lain — tuhay, pinasahí

DIVERT, v.—aliwín, ilikô, baguhin — paglingaw, pagliko, paglibag-o — lingawón, ilikô, balhinón

DIVEST, v. — alisán, tanggalán—paghukas, pagtangtang — kuhaan, huksan

DIVIDE, v. — hatiin — pagpikas pagtunga — tung-on

DIVINE, adj. — banál, marikít—balaanon, langitnon — balaan, mahinhin, Diosnon

DIVISIBILITY, n.—pagkakáhatì-hatì—pagkabahin-bahin — pag tulungà

DIVISION, n. — paghahati-hatì pagkakáhatì — kabahinan — pagtungâ

DIVORCE, n. — diborsyo, paghihiwaláy — kabulagan, diborsiyo — diborsyo, paghimulagay (sa mag-asawá)

DIVULGE, v.—isiwalat, ipahayag, ipagtapát—pagpadayag, pagtugan — ituad, ipahayag, itampad

DIZZINESS, n.—hi'o, pagkahilo—lipong, pagkalipong — lingin, atipuycng

DO, v.—gawín, isagawâ — pagbuhat, buhata — buhaton, tumanon

DOCILE, adj.—maamô, sunúd-súnuran—anad, masunoren — mahagúp, masinulundon

DOCKYARD, n.—págawaan o pákumpunihan ng mga bapór — bansalan sa barko, baradero — ulobrahan sang sakayán ukon bapór

DOCTOR, n. — manggagamot — mananambal — doktór, manogbulong

DOCTRINE, n.—doktrina, panini-
walá — doktrina, tinuhoan —
doktrina, pagtuo

DOCUMENT, n. — kasalutan, du-
kumento—kalig-onan, dokumento — dokumento, kasulatan

DODGE, v.—iwasan, layuán, ilagan—paglikay, paglihay — likawán, palayoán, lihayán

DOG, n.—aso—iro—idô

DOLL, n.—manikà—dulaan, mon-
yeka — manyika

DOLEFUL, adj.—ma ungkót, madilím — mamingawon, masulob-
on — masubô, masagir-um

DOMAIN, n. — lupaín, nasásaku-
pan, kaharián — gingharian —
kadutaan, kaharian

DOMESTICATED, adj.—pinaamò
—gianad, minanso — ginpaha-
hagúp

DOME, n.—bubungáng bilóg, s'm-
boryo—malinging atop — bubongán nga bilóg, simboryo

DOMESTIC, adj.—maainô, pantá-
hanan — maanad, panimalaynon
—balaynon, maki-baláy

DOMICILE, n.—tírahan, táhanan
bahay — pinuy-anan, panimalay
—puluy-an, baláy

DOMINION, n.—pamamahalà, pá
mahalaán — yutang-sakop, do-
minyo — ginsakpan

DOMINANT, adj.—makaharì, makapangyarihan, matigás—maha-
rion, mamandoon — harianon,
makagalahum

DON, v.— isuót—pagsul-ob — isuk-
sók

DONOR, n.—ang maybigáy, may-
regalo, may-alay — taghatag,
tag-amot — duloť, regalo

DOOM, n.—parusa, kapalaran, kamátayan — sangputanan, kawa-
laan, katapusan — silut, kapalaran, kamatayon

DOOR, n.—pintô, búkasan—ganghaan. puitahan — pwertahan,
ganhaan

DOORKNOB, n. — tangnán ng
pintô — gunitanan sa ganghaan
—kalaptan sang pwertahan

DOORLATCH, n.—sárahan, susi—
yawihanan — yabihán

DOPE, v.—lukuhin. hiluhin—pag-
tonto, paghilo — buangon

DOSE. n —dosis, takal ng gamót
—sukod sa tambal — dosis, talaksan sa bulóng

DOT, n.—tuldók, oras, panahón—
tulbok, takna — pintok, oras,
panahón

DOUBLE, n.—dalawá, doble—du-
rcha, doble — duhá, kapid, doble

DOUBLE-CROSS, v.—saltahihin,
lokohin, linlangín — limbongan,
luiban — buangon, limbongán

DOUBT, v.—mag-álinlangan, mag-
duda—pagduhaduha, pagduda—
magpangduhaduha

DOUBTFUL, adj.—nakapag-aalin-
langan, waláng mintís, waláng
duda — waya duhaduha — wala'y duhaduha, wala'y lisá

DOVE, n.—kalapati, batubató —
salapati, salampati — pating,
salampati

DOVETAIL, v.—pagtamain—pag-
kasibo, pagtukma — sibuon

DOWNCAST, adj. — lúlugó-logó,
napatungó—masulob-on — paidalum, masinulub-on

DOWNSTAIRS, adv.—sa ibabâ ng
bahay o hagdanan — sa silong
sa balay — idalum sang baláy
ukón hagdanan

DOWNRIGHT, adj.—biglâ, tuwíd
—kalit, tarung — tadlong

DOWNWARDS, adv. — pababâ—
paubos — paubóş, paidalum

DOZEN, n.—dosena, labindalawa
—dosena, napulog-duha — dosena, napulo'g duhá

DRAFT, n.—dibuho, tseke, pulutóng ng mga kawal, hihip ng
hangin—krokis, tseke, huyop sa
hangin — dibuho, tseke, gubán
sang hangawáy, huyóp sang hangin

DRAFTSMAN, n. — mandidibuho,
tagagawâ ng plano—magdidibu-
ho, tagbuhat plano — manogdi-
buho, tagubhat sang plano

DRAG, v.—hilahin, kaladkarín —
pagguyod, pagguroy — butongon, sagnoyón

DRAGNET, n.—panghuli parrilò-
sapyaw, pangsikop — panikup

DRAGONFLY, n.—tutubi—sili-sili
--tumbak-tumbak

DRAIN, v.—alisán ng tubig—pag-
hubas — pamalihan, sag-ahán

DRAINAGE, n.—kanál, takbuhan
ng tubig—kanal, lutsanan sa tubig — kanál, iligán sang tubig

DRAMA, n.—dulà—dula, drama—
drama, palaguaon, pulawan

DRAMATIZE, v. — isadulà, dulain
—pagdula, dulaon -- idrama

DRAPES, n.—kurtina, takíp—kurtina, tabil — kortina, takúp

DRAW, v.—gumuhit, hilahin, bunutin — pagkudlit, pagbutad —
magkurit, butongon, gabuton

DRAWER, n. — tagaguhit, kahón
ng mesa — tagkudlit, hunos —
tagkurit, kahón (sa lamisa)

DRAWL, n. — ungol — ungal —
ungal, ugayong

DREAD, n.—pangambá, takot —
kahadlok, kalisang — kugmat,
hadlok

DREADFUL, adj. — nakapangá-ngambá, nakatatakot — maka-hádlok, makakulba — makaku-lugmat, makahaladlok

DREAM, n.—panaginip, hángarin —damgo — damgohanon

DREAMY, adj.—marikít, nanána-bík—madamgohon — makada-lamgo

DRESS, n.—bihisán, damít, suót—bestida, saput, sinina — bayù

DRESS, v.—suutan, bihisan, lini-sin, ayusin — pagsaput, pagsul-ob — bayoan, islan, tinloán, hi-piron

DRESSMAKER, n. — kusturera, mánanahi — mananahi, modista —kosturera, mananahi

DRESS SHOP, n.—pátahian, tin-dahan ng damít—tahianan, tin-dahan sa sinina — talahian, tin-dahan sang bayúon

DRESSY, adj.—pustura, maayos, marikít—pustorawo, himiste — postura, mahipid, magayón

DRIFT, v. — umanod, padalá sa agos—pag-anud, pataban sa su-log — inanod, nagpadaldal sa ilig

DRIFTING, v.—umáanod, nagpá-patangáy, nagpápadalá—nagpa-anud, nagpataban — inanod. di-naldal sang ilig

DRILL, v. — butasan, magsanay, sanayin, paputukán — lungagan, pagbuho, pagpabuto — buhoan, barinahan, hanashanason

DRINK, v. — inumín, uminóm—pag-inum, inum — ilimnon, umi-nóm

DRIP, n. — paták, tulò — pagtulo, pagpatak — tulò

DRIVER, n.—ang nagtátabóy, ang nagpápalakad ng sasakyán, tsu-pér, kutsero — ang paggiya sa sakyanan — magtabog, ang na-gapalakát sang salakyan, tso-per, kotsero

DRIZZLE, n.—ambón—alindahaw, talithi — talithi

DROOP, v.—manlupaypáy, yumu-kô — pagyuko, pagloyloy—pag-dukô, loyloy

DROOPING, adj. — nalálantá — nagkatagak, nagkalaglag — na-gakalayóng

DROP, v.—ihulog, ilaglág—paghu-log, pagtagak — ihulog, ituntor.

DROWN, v.—malunod, lunurin—paglumos — nalumós, lumson

DROWSY, adj.—nag-áantók, ma-bigát ang katawán—madukaon, katulgon — ginatuyó, maluya ang lawas

DRUG, n.—gamót, pampatulog—tambal, pagpatulog — bulóng, inogpatulog

DRUGSTORE, n.—botika—botika, tindahag tambal — botika

DRUM, n.—tamból, bombo—tambol, bombo — tambor, bombo

DRUM, v. — ulit-ulitin, tumuktók —pagsubli, pagtambol — bombohón

DRUNK, adj.—lasíng, langó—hubog — malá

DRUNKARD, n.—lasenggo, mánginginom — palahubog, palainum — palahubog

DRY, adj.—tuyô, tuyót—uga, mala —hubóg

DUAL, adj.—dálawahan — tagurhaay — tigduhá

DUBIOUS, adj.—álinlangan, di-tiyák—alang-alang, way-seguro—maduhaduhaon, dî-pat-ud

DUCK, n.—pato, bibi, itik—pato, itik—pato, bibi

DUCTILE, adj.—maunat—mainat —maunat

DUE, prep.—ukol sa, hinggíl sa, nátatakdâ—gumikan sa, bayranan—tungód sa, bangód sa

DUEL, n.—labanán ng dalawá — estokada sa duha — sambuwaáy sang duhá

DUET, n.—dálawahang tinig—duweto, awit-tagurhaay—duhá ka tingog

DULL, adj. — mapuról, dî makináng, pulpól, waláng siglá—habolan, maluya, way-kinabuhi — mahabol, malubóg, maluya

DUMB, adj.—pipi, di-marunong—amang—apâ, buhóng

DUMMY, n.—pantalya—pantalya, pahoy—pantalya

DUMP, v.—ibagsák, ibabâ, ihagis —pagyabo, pag-ítsa — itugdang, ihabóy

DUPLICATE, n.—ikalawá, kapareho, katulad—hulad, huwad — duplikado, ikaduhá

DUPLICATE, v.—tularan, parisan, ipareho—paghuwad, pagpariho—tularan, parehoan

DURING, adv.—sa panahón ng, sa loób ng—sa sulod sa, sa panahon sa — sa sulód sang, sa panahón sang

DURATION, n.—tagál, hinaba-habà—gidugayon—kadugayón

DURABLE, adj.—matibay, pang-matagalan — malungtaron, matunhayon—mahunit

DUSKY, adj.—madilím, maitím—dagtum, maitum — madulóm, libon-dulóm

DUST, n.—alikabók, alabók—abug —yak-ok

DUST, v. — palisán, paspasán—

DUTY, n.—tungkulin, buwís, pagbabantáy—katungdanan, buhis, sa adwana—katungdanan

DWARF n.—unano, maliít na tao —inano, tawong gamitoy—inano, putót nga taó

DWARFISH, adj.—bulilit, pandák, maliít—dwendihon, inanohon — dwende, itór

DWELL, v.—manirahan, tumirá, isipin— pagpuyo—magpuyô

DWELLING, n.—tírahan, bahay—puloy-anan, balay — puluy-an, baláy

DYE, n.—tinà, kulay—tina, bulok —lugóm

DYING, v.—namámatáy, nangángapús, naghíhingalô — pagkamatay, pagpinai—tagumatayon, nagahimumugtò

DYNAMIC, adj.—makapangyarihan, magilas, mapusók—maabtikon, makagagahum—makagalahum, makangilidlis

DYSPEPSIA, n. — di-pagkatunaw dili-matunawan, dili-mahilisan—dî-matunawan

— E —

EACH, pron—bawa't isá—tagsa, tagsa-tagsa—tagsatagsa

EAGER, adj.—sabík, nasásabík — matinguhaon—matinguhaon

EAR, n.—tainga—dalunggan—dulunggan

EARLY, adv.—maaga — sayo — temprano

EARMARK, v.—tatakán, markahán — pagmarka, pagtimaan—timbrehán, markahán

EARNEST, adj. — maalab, masikap, taimtím — mahinangpon, maikagon—mahimulaton

EARNING, n. — kita, pinagkakitaan—kinitaan, pinangitaan — kinitaan

EARING, n. — hikaw—mga aritis--aritos

EARTH, n.—lupà, daigdíg—yuta, kalibutan—dutà, kalibutan

EARTHLY, adj.—makalupà, makamundó — yutan-on, kalibutanon—dutan-on

EARTHQUAKE, n.—lindól—linog —linog

EARTHWORM, n.—bulati — wati—lagó

EARWAX, n.—tutulí—atuli—atutulí

EASE, n.—katiwasayán, kasaganaan—kasayon—kasulhayan, kahim-ongán

EASIER, adv.—lalong madali o lalong magaán—labing masayon—mahapós

EASILY, adv.—may kadalián—sa kasayon—kahaposán

EAST, n.—silangan — sidlakan — sidlangán

EASTER, n.—Paskó ng Pagkabuhay—Pasko sa Pagkabanhaw—Paskua sang Pagkabanhaw

EASTERN, adj.—silanganan, taga-silangan — sidlakanon, taga-sidlakan—sidlanganon

EASY, adj.—madalî, magaán — masayon—madalî, mahapós, tayuyon

EAT, v.—kumain—pagkaon — kumaon

EAVESDROP, v. — makiníg, maniktík—pagpaniktik — manilag, mamatîbatì

EBONY, adj.—maitím, itím—maitum, itum — maitúm, itúm

ECCENTRIC, adj. — biglá-biglâ, sumpungin—saputon, tandugon —patarasak, alabuton

ECHO, n.—alingawngáw—lanog—lanóg (sang tingog)

ECLIPSE, n.—eklipse, pagsasalubong ng buwán at araw—eklipse—eklipse

ECONOMY, n.—pagtitipíd, pagaayos ng mga súliranin ng táhanan—ang pagdaginot, kainot — makinuton

ECSTASY, n.—kasarapán, kaligayahan, kasiyahan — kalaliman, kahimayaan—kalipayan, kaayawan

EDDY, n.—ipuipo, alimpuyó—buhawi, alimpuos—alimpulos, buhawi

EDGE, n.—dulo, talím, sukdulan, gilid—tumoy, suwab, ngilit — punta, talúm, kilid

EDGY, adj.—di-mapalagáy, maynerbiyos—nerbiyoso, kuyawanon —nerbioso

EDIBLE, adj.—makakain—makaon—kalan-on

EDICT, n.—pahayag, batás, alituntunin—mando, kasugoan — patalastás, kasugoán, pagsulundan

EDIFICE, n.—gusalì—balay sinimento—baláy

EDITOR, n.—patnugot ng páhayagán—editor, pangulo—editór, manogdumala

EDUCATE, v.—pag-aralin, túruan—tagtudlo, magtutudlo — patun-on, tudloán

EDUCATOR, n.—tagapagturò — tagtudlo, magtutudlo — manunudlò

EDUCATION, n.—pagtuturò, pinag-aralan — bangkaagan, edukasyon — pagtulun-an

EEL, n.—igat, palós—kasili—sili

EERIE, adj.—nakatátakot, nakapanghíhilakbót — makahahadlok, makalilisang—makahaladlok, makasiligni

EFFECT, n.—bisà, bunga—sangputanan—bunga, kinaayo

EFFECTIVE, adj.—mabisa, magalíng, mabuti—masangputon, maayo—maayo, epektibo

EFFEMINATE, adj.—parang babae, binabae—bayot, babayen-on —para sa babáe

EFFICIENCY, n.—kahusayan, kabutihan—kamaayo, katakus—kinaayo

EFFORT, n.—pagsisikap, pagpupunyagî — paningkamut — paghimud-os, paghimulat

EFFRONTERY, n. — kabastusán, pagkawaláng galang, katapangan—kahambugan, kawalay tahud — kabastosán, pagkawala'y katahurán

EFFULGENCE, n.—kariktán, kagandahan—kaanindot, kahayag, sidlak—kaambong, kaanyag, kagayón

EGG, n.—itlóg—itlog—itlog

EGGPLANT, n.—talóng—talong—talóng

EIGHT, n.—waló—walo—waló

EIGHTEEN, n.—labingwaló—ikanapulog-walo—napulo'g waló

EIGHTEENTH, n.—ikalabingwaló —ikanagulog-walo — ika-napulo'g waló

EIGHTH, n.—ikawaló—ikawalo — ikawaló

EITHER, pron.—alinmán, kahit alín sa—bisan hain—bisán diín, bisán anó

EJACULATE, v.—mápasigáw, mabiglâ—paghidalian, paghisinggit sa—makasinggit, mahinlaián

EJECT, v.—paalisín, palayasin — pagpahawa, pagpalayas—pahalinón, tabugon

ELAPSE, v.—lumagpás sa taning —paglapas sa tagal—nakaligad sa pinat-ud

ELASTIC, adj.—malambót, hanáhatak—inat-inat, mabira-bira—mahumok, maunat

ELATED, adj.—nataás, nagúguluhán, nasiyahán—nalipay, nahimuot — pukatód, kagamohán, naawayan

ELBOW, n.—siko—siko—siko

ELDER, adj.—matandâ, nakatátandâ—magulang—maguláng

ELECT, v.—ihalál, piliin—pagpili, pilion—pilion

ELECTION, n.—hálalan, pilian — piliay—piniliay

ELECTOR, n. — manghahalál, mamboboto, botante—pumipili, elektor—pumilili, botante

ELECTRICITY, n. — electrisidád, dagitab—dagitab, elektrisidad — elektrisidád, sugáng-kilás

ELECTRIFY, v.—pasubuhín ang damdamin—pagpadílaab sa pagbati—pahaganhaganon (ang balatyagon)

ELECTROCUTE, v.—koryentihín, bitayín sa koryente — pagsunog sa dagitab — koryentehón, patyon sa koryente

ELEGANT, adj.—makinis, kaayaaya, makisig, postura — ambongan, pustorawo—mahinlò, manayanaya, mabukdo, postura

ELEMENT, n.—elemento, símulain, bahagi—elemento, bahin — elemento, sulugoran

ELEMENTARY, adj. — pasimulâ, pang-una, panimulâ — paninugdan—elementarya, ginsugoran

ELIGIBLE, adj.—maáarì, nárarapat—takus, madawat—mahimò, dapat

ELIMINATE, v.—alisín, talunin—pagsalikway, pagpildi — kuhaon, lutoson

ELEVATE, v.—itaás, purihin — pagpataas, pagbayaw—dayawon, itib-ong

ELEVATION, n.—kataasan, taás—kahitas-an—pukatód, banglid

ELEVATOR, n.—mákináng pantaás, elebetor—makinang paubospataas—makiná nga inogbatak, elebetor

ELEVEN, n.—labing-isá — napulog-usa—napulo'g isá

ELEVENTH, adj. — ikalabing-isá — ikanapulog-usa—ikó-napulo'g isá

ELITE, n.—tampók, krema, tangì —ang uyok, krema — tampok, krema, pinasahî

ELONGATION, n.—kahabaán — ang kataas—kalabaón

ELOPE, v.—magtanan, tumakas—pagtaban—magtabanáy

ELOQUENCE, n.—kahusayan sa pagbigkás o pananalitâ—kabatid manulti — kahimpitan magmitlang sang tinagâ

ELSE, adj.—kung hindî, o kayâ—kondíli, kun kaha—kondì

ELSEWHERE, adv.—sa ibáng poók—sa laing dapit—sa ibán nga duóg ukón duóg

ELUSIVE, adj.—madulás, mabilís, mailáp, mapagkawalâ—madanglog, lisud-hisakpan — madanlog, madasig, mailá

EMACIATED, adj.—payát — niwang, daut, namiyaok — maniwang, kulyapís

EMANCIPATION, n.—kalayaan—kaluwasan—katibawasan, kaluasan

EMBALM, v.—embalsamuhín, gamutín — pagtabal, pagembalsamar—embalsamahón

EMBARRASSED, adj.—nápahiyâ—naulawan, nanlipaghong—nápahuyâ, nahinalian, nakatabinás

EMBARRASSMENT, n.—kahihi-
yán, kabiglaanan—kaulawan —
kahuluy-an, kahinalián

EMBEZZLE, v.—lustayín—pagtikas, pagdispalko—lamukuson

EMBLEM, n.—sagisag — timaan,
timailhan—emblema, patimaan

EMBRACE, n.—yakap, yapós—ga-
kus—hakson

EMERGE, v.—lumabás, lumitáw,
humusót — paggula, paglutaw,
pagguho- lumutáw, lumusót

EMERGENCY, n. — panahón ng
mahigpít na pangangailangan —
panahon sa kapit-os, emerhen-
siya—emerhensya

EMIGRANT, n.—nangingibáng bayan, dayuhan—lumalangyaw, la-
lin—dumalagsà, manluluntad

EMIGRATE, v. — mangibáng bayan, dumayo—paglalin, paglang-
yaw—mangluntad

EMINENCE, n.—kadakilaan, kabantugán, katanyagán — kama-
dungganon, kahalangdon — ka-
banfogán, pagkalutáw

EMINENT, adj.—tanyág, kilalá,
bantóg—halangdon, dungganon,
bantugan—kilala, lutáw, bantog

EMPEROR, n.—emperadór — em-
perador—emperadór

EMOTION, n.—damdamin—balatian, pagbati—balatyagon

EMPIRE, n.—imperyo, kaharián—
imperyo, ginghárian — imperyo,
ginharian

EMPLOY, v. — pagawín, ipasok,
paglingkurín pagtrabahuhin —
paggamit, pagpatrabaho—pabu-
haton, pamugonon, patrabahuon

EMPLOYEE, n.—kawaní, empleado, ang naglílingkód — kawani,
empliyado—empleado, alagád

EMPLOYER, n.—ang may patra-
baho, amo, punò—agalon, amo
—amoy, tag-iya

EMPLOYMENT, n.—hanapbuhay,
gáwain, káwanihan, trabaho, pi-
napasukan.—buhat, trabaho, em-
pliyo palamugnan, palangitan-
an, trabahoán

EMPORIUM, n.—tindahan—tindahan, baligyaan—tindahan

EMPTY, adj. — waláng lamán —
walay-sulod, haguka — wala'y
unód

EMULATE, v.—parisan, hagayan
—pagsundog, pag-awat — tularan, bagayan sing gahúm

ENABLE, v.—magbigáy-kaya, bigyán ng kaya o lakás—paghatag.
katakus, paghatag higayon—pa-
ninguhaán

ENACT, v.—gawíng batás, ipag-utos, ilabás, mulíng gawín—**paghimog baod, pagbalaod** — buhaton nga kasugoán

ENCIRCLE, v.—kulungín, paligiran, pakisamahan—**paglibot, libutan**—kulongón, palibotan

ENCLOSE, v. — isilíd, paligiran, ipaloób, palibutan — **pagsulod, pagsukip**—isulód

ENCLOSURE, n.—kalakip, looban —**linabat, kinoralan**—libonon

ENCORE, n.—pag-ulit — **pasubli, pausab** — liwatón, suliton

ENCOUNTER, v.—magtagpô, mákasalubong, mátagpuán—**pagsugat, pagtagbo**—magkitaáy, magsugataay

ENCOURAGE, v.—pasiglahín, palakasín—**pagdasig, pag-abiba** — paisugon

ENCOURAGEMENT, n.—palakásloób, pagpapasiglá — **kadasigan, abiba**—magpakaisug

ENCROACH, v. — samantalahín, pasukin—**pangahas nga pagsulod** —hingalitán sudlon

ENCUMBRANCE, n.—pabigát, talí, sagabal — **pamug-at, sabal, balda**—pamató

END, n.—katapusán, wakás, dulo, kaduluhan—**katapusan, tumoy**—katapusan

ENDANGER, v.—isubò sa masamâ, mapasamâ, manganib—**pagbutang sa kuyaw** — ibutáng sa katalagman

ENDEAVOR, n.—hángarin, pagsumigasig, pagsisikap—**paninguha, tingusbawan** — handum, tilinguhaán

ENDEAVOR, v. — pagsikapan, magsumigasig, hángarin, magsumakit — **pagpaninguha** — himud-osán, tinguhaán, maghimulat

ENDLESS, adj.—waláng katapusán, patuluyan—**walay-katapusan**—wala'y katapusan

ENDURANCE, n.—pagtitiís, tagái tatág, lawig—**agwanta, lanat** — pagbatás, pag-antus

ENDURE, v.—pagtiisán, palawigín, matagalán—**pag-antus, pagagwanta**—batasón, padugayon

ENEMA, n.—labatiba — **labatiba, kalibang**—labatiba

ENEMY, n.—kaaway, kalaban, kaalít—**kaaway, kaatbang** — kaaway, kasumpong

ENERGETIC, v.—malakás, masigasig—**mabaskug, maabtik, malagsik**—makusog, mapagsik, makagalahum

ENERGY, n.—lakás, sipag, kaka-yahán—**kusog** — kusog, kapisan

ENFORCE, v.—pagtibayin, isakatuparan, ipatupád—**pagpatuman**

ENFORCEMENT, n. — pagpapatupád, pagpapatibay — **katumanan**—pagpabakud, pagpatuman

ENGAGE, v.—kasunduín, upahan—**pagsabut, pag-abang** — kasugtanan, hisugtan

ENGAGEMENT, n. — kasunduan, tipanan—**kasabutan, panagtrato** —paghisugot

ENGAGING, adj.—magiliw, mainam, mapamihag — **mahigalaon, makabigon**—mangaluyág

ENGINE, n.—mákiná—**makina** — makiná

ENGINEER, v. — iturò, pangasiwaan — **pagtudlo, pagdumala** — itudlò, dumalahan

ENGINEER, n.—inhinyero, makinista—**batid sa makina, enhinyero**—enhenyero, makinista

ENGULF, v. — sakupin, lamunin, lulunín, takpán—**pagsakop, paglamon**—sakupon, tunlon, takpan

ENHANCE, v.—palakihín, painamin, pabutihin—**pagpaayo, pagpausbaw**—padakuón, patahumón

ENIGMA, n. — paláisipán, hiwagà —**tanghaga** — palaisipán, makatilingala

ENJOY, v. — ikagalák, ikaligaya, magsayá — **paglingaw, paglipay, pagpahimulos**—hiaguman

ENLARGE, v. — palakihín, luwangán, pahabain—**pagdaku** — pasangkarón, padakuón

ENLARGEMENT, n.—pagpapalakí, pagpapahabà — **pinadaku** — pagpasangkad, pagpalapad

ENLIVEN, v.—pasayahín, pasiglahín—**pagpadasig, pagpasadya** — pasadyahón

ENORMOUS, adj.—malakíng-malakí, labis—**daku uyamot, labihan kadaku** — tuman kadakú, kapin

ENOUGH, adj.—sapát na, tamà na—**igo, igo na**—nagakaigò, tamà na

ENRAGE, v. — pagalitin, papagalabin — **pagkasuko, pagpalagot** —paakigon, painitón

ENROLL, v.—magpalistá, magpasulat, magpatalâ — **pagpalista, pagpatala**—magpalista

ENTER, v. — pumasok, tumulóy, ipasok — **pagsulod, pagdayon** — magsulód, dumayón, sumulód

ENTERTAIN, v.—libangín — **pagabi-abi, paglingaw**—lingawón

ENTERTAINMENT, n. — líbangan, kasáyahan, salubong—**kalingawan** — kalingawan, kasadyahan, tamyawón

ENTHUSIASM, n.—siglá, sigasig —**kadasig, kaikag**—kapagsik

ENTICE, v.—akitin, hibuin, gayu-
mahin—pagkabig, pagbihag—lumayón

ENTIRE, adj.—lahát, buô — tibuok, ang tanan—bug-os, tanán

ENTITLE, v.—karapat-dapat, ná
bibilang, may-karapatán — paghatag katungod—manginbagay

ENTRANCE, n.—pasukán, pintô,
dáanan — agianan, sudlanan —
suludlan, pwertahan, alagyan

ENTREAT, v. — makiusap, himukin, mamanhík—pagpangamuyo,
pagpangiliyupo — makighambal,
makig-alugáy

ENTREATY, n.—pamanhík, pakiusap, himok — pangamuyo, pa-
ngiliyupo—pangabáy, alungáy

ENTRY, n.—pagpasok, ipinasok—
ang pagsulod, ang apli—pagsulód, ginsulód

ENTWINE, v. — ipulupot—pagba-
liktos—ibalû

ENUMERATION, n. — pagbibi-
láng—pag-ihap, ihap, pag-isip—
pag-isip

ENVELOPE, n.—sobre — sobre—
sobre

ENVELOPE, v.—balutin, paligiran
—paglikos, paglibut — putson,
palibotan

ENVIRONMENT, n.—paligid, poók na pinagkálakhán — kahimtangan—palibot, puók nga gin-
pasangkarán

ENVIOUS, adj.—naiinggít, maing-
gitin—masinahon, maibugon
nahikaw, naibug

ENVY, n.—kainggitán, pangingim-
bulo—kaibug, kasina — kaibug,
kahikaw

EPIDEMIC, n.—salot, laganap na
sakít—makaylapong sakit, epi-
demya—sarút, pisti

EPIDERMIS, n.—balát, anit—panit—panit

EPIC, n.—isáng tulâ ng kabayanihan—balak sa kabayanihan —
isá ka binalaybay sa pagkabaganihán

EPISODE, n.—yugtô, kabanatà—
yugto—episodyo, sulugponan

EQUAL, n.—patas, pareho, mag-
katimbáng, tumbás—magsama,
pariho, katumbas—patas, pareho, magkatimbang, tumbas

EQUIVALENT, n.—kapareho, ka-
tumbás, kaparis—tukma, kapari-
ho—katumbas

ERASE, v.—burahín, alisín—pagpapas, pagpala—panason

ERASER, n.—pamburá—papas, ig-
papala—inogpanás

ERASURE, n.—pagkaburá—pina-
laan—pagpanas

ERECT, v.—magtayô, tumuwíd—
pagtukod, pagpatindog—magpasad, tadlong

ERECT, adj.—tuwíd, matigás —
tul-id, tanus—tadlong, matig-a

EROSION, n.—pagkabuwág, pag-kaagnás — ang pagkapudpod — pagkabulag, pagkahagas

ERR, v.—magkamalî—pagkasayop —magsayúp

ERRAND, n.—utos, gáwain—sugo —sugò, buluhatón

ERROR, n.—kamálian, pagkaká-malî—sayop—kasaypanan, pag-kasayúp

ESCAPE, n.—pagtatanan, pagta-kas—paglayas, pag-ikyas, pag-kagiw—pagpalagyo

ESCORT, n.—kasama, bantáy, ta-gapagtanggól — kauban, bantay —kaupod, bantay, tagpangapin

ESSENCE, n. — pabangó, lamán, katás—kahumot, duga—esensya, pahumót, kaundan, pinugaán

ESSENTIAL, adj.—kailangan, pá-ngunahín—kinahanglan, hinung-danon—kinahanglan, tig-una

ESTABLISH, v.—magtatág, mag-tayô — pagtukod, pagbutang—magpasad, magpatuk

ESTATE, n.—pag-aarî, lupaín, ka-lágayan—kabtangan, kayutaan, kahimtang — estado, pagkabu-táng

ESTEEM, n. — paggalang, pagpa-palagáy — gugma, pagmahal—pagtahud, pagpakigbagay

ESTEEM, v. — pakiharapán, iga-lang — paghigugma, pagpangga pagmahal—tahuron

ESTIMATE, n.—tasa, tantiyá, hu-là—kalkulo, tagna — pagtansya, paghaumhaum

ESTIMATE, v.—tasahan, tantiya-hín, pag-aralan—pagkalkulo — pagsulagma—tansyahón, haum-haumon

ETERNAL, adj.—waláng kamáta-yan, waláng katapusán, waláng hanggán—walay-katapusan, wa-lay-kahangturan—wala'y kama-tayon, wala'y katapusan, wala'y dulonan

ETIQUETTE, n.—batayán ng ki-los sa lipunán—lagda sa pama-tasan—etiketa sa katipunan

EVAPORATION, n.—pagkatuyô kasingaw—pagpamalá

EVEN, adj.—patag, pantáy — pa-tag, tupong—patag, hanip

EVEN, adv.—kahit, noón pa man —bisan pa, maskin—bisán pa

EVENING, n.—gabí—gabli—gab-i

EVENT, n. — pangyayari, nangya-ri, nakaraán—hitabo, nangagi—hitabô, kaligaran

EVER, adv.—lagì, kailán man, ka-hit, gaano—sa kanunay, sa gi-hapon—pirme, tubtob kon san-o, kutob kon san-o

EVERLASTING, adj.—waláng ka-tapusán, waláng kamátayan — tunhay, way-katapusan — wala'y katapusan, wala'y kamatayon

EVERY, adj.—bawa't isá—matag usa—tagsatagsa

EVERYBODY, pron.—bawa't isá, bawa't tao—tagsa-tagsa, matag tawo—tagsa, tanán

EVERYONE, pron.—bawa't isá, lahát—matag tawo—tagsa ka butáng, tanán

EVERYTHING, n.—bawa't bagay, lahát—matag usa, tanan—tagsa, tanán

EVERYWHERE, adv.—sa bawa't dako, sa lahát ng poók—sa tanang dapit, bisan diin—bisán diín, sa tanán nga puók

EVICTION, n.—pagpapaalís, pagpapalayas—ang pagpahawa, ang pagpalayas—pagpahalín, pagtabog

EVIDENCE, n.—patotoó, pinangh, háhawakan, katunayan—kamatuoran, kalig-onan, pruyba—kamatuoran

EVIDENT, adj. — malinaw, maliwanag, halatâ — dayag, matinaw, lutaw—maathag, masanag, masat-umán

EVIL, n. — masamâ, kasamaán, dyablo—dautan, kangil-aran, diyablo—malain, panuláy

EVINCE, v.—ipakilala, ipahalatâ —pagpalta, pagpasabut — ipakilala, ipakitâ

EVOLUTION, n.—pagbabago, pagiibá, pagtubò—kabalhinan, kausaban — pagbalhin, pag-uswág, pagtuhay

EXACT, adj.—waláng kulang, tamà, wastô, tumpák — sibo, tukma—sibù, wala'y kulang

EXACTING, adj.—mapaghanáp — mapangitaon—mapangitaón

EXAGGERATE, v.—palabisan, palakihín — pagpakapin, pagpalabaw—hingapinán, pasangkarón

EXALTATION, n.—pagtaás, pagpupuri — hingaping pagdayeg, pasidungog—pagtib-ong, pagdayaw

EXAMINATION, n. — pagsusulit, pagsusurì, paglilitis—pasulit, eksamin — eksaminasyon, pagsalawsaw

EXAMINE, v.—sulitin, suriin —pagsusi, pag-usisa — sayasaton, salawsawón

EXAMINER, n.—tagasulit, tagasurì — magsususi, tag-usisa—manogsayasat, manogsalawsaw

EXAMPLE, n.—halimbawà, ulirán — sanglitanan, panig-ingnan — halimbawà, huaran

EXASPERATING, adj. — nakákayamót, nakákaabala — makapagil-as, makabalda—makatalaka, makaalawat

EXCEED, v.—higitán, lampasán—paghingapin, paglabaw — labawán, kapinán

EXCEEDINGLY, adv.—masiyado, lubós—hilabihan, labihan—lubos, kakapinán

EXCEL, v. — manaíg, mamayaní, manguna—paglabaw, paghawod —mangibabaw, manguna

EXCELLENT, adj. — kaayaaya, magalíng—maayo kaayo, dataygon—matandos, maayo

EXCEPT, prep.—máliban, liban sa —gawas sa—luás (sa, nga)

EXCEPTION, n. — pagtatangì, pagbubukód, náiibá, nátatangì, pambihirà — ang pagkalahi, katalagsaon—pagkatuhay, labot pa

EXCESS, n.—kalabisán, sobra, kabigatán—kapín, sobra — sobra, kapín

EXCESSIVE, adj. — labis-labis — nagningapin, naghinobra—sobra kaayo

EXCHANGE, v. — pagpapalít — pagbaylo, pag-ilis—pagbaylo

EXCITE, v.—gulatiń, guluhín — pag-agda, pagpakugang — kibután, gamohón

EXCITEMENT, n. — gulat, guló, tuwâ—kasibut, kahikurat, kahiulpot—kibút, gamó, hinugyaw

EXCLAIM, v.—bumulalás, sumigáw—pagtuaw, pagsinggit — tumuáw

EXCLUSIVE, adj.—tangì—kaugalingon, walay lain—pasahî

EXECUTE, v.—isakatuparan, bitayin—pagtuman, pagbitay—tumanon, bitayon

EXECUTIVE, n.—tagaganáp—pangulo, magdumala—dumalahán

EXERCISES, n.—pagsasanay, programa, palátuntunan — pagbansay, belada — paghanashanas, programa, palatuntunan

EXERCISE, v.—gamitin, magpalakás—paggamit, pagpaugnat — maghanashanas, gamiton

EXCUSE, n. — pagpapaumansín, dahilán—pasangil, hinungdan — magpermiso, magpasaylo

EXCUSE, v.—dahilán, magdahilán, magpatawad — pagpamalibad, pagpasaylo—kabangdanan, magpamalibad, magpatawad

EXHAUST, v.—uousin, hapuin — paghurot, paglugwa — ubosoń, hapuon

EXHIBIT, n.—pagtatanghál—pasundayag—pagpahayag

EXIST, n.—mabuhay, lumagî, mamalagì—pagpuyo—nagapuyô

EXISTENCE, n.—kabuhayan, pamamalagì—panimuyo, kinabuhi —kabuhian, kaluntarán

EXIT, n.—labasan, pintuan—guianan—guianan, pwertahan

EXODUS, n.—paglabás, paglipat—pagpanggula, pamahawa — pagguâ, pagsaylo

EXONERATE, v. — pawaláng sala—pagluwas, pag-ilang way-sala—luasón sa salâ

EXPAND, v.—palaparin, lakihán, magpaluwág — **pagpadaku, pagpalapad** — palaparon, padakuón, pasangkarón

EXPATRIATE, v. — paalisín sa isáng bayan — **pagpapabalik sa nasud** — tabugon sa isá ka banwa

EXPECT, v.—asahan, antayín — **pagpaabut, paghulat** — hulatón, saligan

EXPECTATION, n.—pag-asa, bagay na maasahan—**pagpinaabut, butang gilauman**—paglaum, butáng nga masaligan

EXPEDITION, n.—paglalakbáy—**panaw-pangayam** — pagpanakayon, paglagulad

EXPENSE, n.—gugol, gastos—**kagugolan**—gasto, hinguyang

EXPENSIVE, v.—mahál, mahalagá—**mahal, bililhon**—mahál, mabilí

EXPERIENCE, n.—karanasán, pinagdaanan—**kasinatian, kabatid**—pinanilagan

EXPERT, adj.—bihasá, sanáy — **batid, hanás** — sampaton

EXPERIMENT, n.—pagsubok—**sulay-sulay**—pagtiláw, pag-eksperimentar

EXPIRE, v.—mamatáy, matapos, malagót—**pagkamatay, pagkatapus**—mamatáy, matapos, mahunos

EXPIRATION, n. — kamátayan, katapusán, takdâ — **kamatayon, katapusan**—kamatayon, katapusan

EXPLAIN, v.—ipaliwanag — **pagtin-aw, pagpasabut**—ipaathag

EXPLODE, v.—paputukín, magalit—**pagbutó, pagkasuko**—palukpon, maakig

EXPLOIT, v.—pagsamantalahán, pakinabangan — **pagpahimulos, pahimudsan**—hingalitán, himuslan

EXPLORE, v.—tarukín, tuklasín—**paghibalag, pag-usisa** — laguladon, tukibón

EXPORT, v.—mangalakal o **magbilí** sa ibáng lupaín, maglabás ng kalakal upáng ipagbilí sa ibáng lupaín — **pagpadalag produkto sa laing nasud**—eksporte, paalintonay

EXPOSE, v.—ihayag, ipahayag — **pagpadayag, pagtukas** — ipahayag

EXPRESS, n.—isáng matuling biyahe, túluyang takbó—**matuling panaw, matuling sakyanan** — tadlong nga panakayon

EXPRESSIVE, adj. — makahulugán—**mahuloganon**—may kahulogán

EXTEND, v.—pahabain, palugitan —pagpataas, pag-uswag—pala- baon, tugotan

EXTENT, n.—lakí, abot, nasása- kop — ang abuton, gidak-on — ipaabót, ipaalinton

EXTINGUISH, v.—patayín, hipan —pagpalong—palongon, huypon

EXTORT, v.—kuwartahan — pag- hinapi—pabuyahan

EXTRA, n.—dagdág—dugang, so- bra—hinugang, ekstra

EXTRACT, v.—alisín, hingán — pagpuga—pugaon

EXTRAORDINARY, adj.—tangì, di-karaniwan, pambihirà—talag- saon, kahibudnganan — pasahî, tumalagsahon

EXTRAVAGANT, adj. — mapag- gastá, bulagsák, lábis — usikan, gastador—burarâ, gastadora

EXTREME, n.—dulo, hulí, sukdu- lan—kinatumyan, kinaupsan — punta, ukbong

EXTRICATE, v.—lusután — pag haw-as—lulutsan

EYE, n.—matá—mata—matá

EYE-BALL, n.—bilog o bola ng matá—kalimutaw—kalimutáw

EYE-BROW, n.—kilay—kilay—ki- lay

EYELASH, n.—pilík-matá—pilok —amimilók

EYELID, n.—talukap ng matá — tabon-tabon—ulaklob

EYEWITNESS, n.—saksí, nakaki- ta—saksi—saksi, nakakità

— F —

FABLE, n. — salaysáy, pábulá, nagtúturò ng isáng aral, kuwen- to—kinaraang sugilanon, leyen- da—panugiron, sinadto'ng sugi- lanon

FABRIC, n.—habi, tela, damít — panapton—ulós, bayuón

FABRICATION, n.—katakata, ga- wá-gawâ—binuhat-buhat — pa- tôpatò

FACADE, n.—harapán, pangha- ráp — nawong, atubang—atu- bangon, umatubang, nawóng

FACE, v.—harapín, humaráp — pag-atubang—atubangan

FACILITY, n.—kadalián — kasa- yonan, kasangkapan — kahapo- sán

FACSIMILE, n. — kopya, repro- duksiyón — hulad, reproduksi· yon — kopya, huád, reproduk- syon

FACT, n.—katotohanan—katinuo- ran—kamatuoran

FACTORY, n.—págawaan, pábri-
ká—kam-anan, pabrika—pabri-
ǩa, dawdawan

FACULTY, n.—mga gurò, isipan,
kakayahán—kaisipan, panon sa
magtutudlo—sampaton nga ma-
nunudló, may-ikasaráng

FADE, v.—mangupas, mawalâ —
paglubad, pagkahanaw—duma-
ay, lumus-aw, nanglayà

FAIL, v. — mahulog, di-magawâ,
malaglág—pagpakyas — mahulog, dî-matuman

FAVOR, n.—tangkilik, paglingap,
pagbibigáy—utang-buot, palihug
—utang nga buót

FAVORABLE, adj. — sang-ayon,
mabentaha, mainam—may bintaha, mauyonon—ugyon, maayo

FAVORITE, n.—minámahál, paborito, itinátangì—kinaham, pinalabi—pinalanggà, paborito

FEAR, v.—katakutan, ilagan —
pagkahadlok, paglikay — kala-
hadlokán, lilikawán

FEARFUL, adj.—natátakot, naka-
pangángambá—kahadlokan, ma-
ǩalilisang — makahaladlok, makatalagam

FEASIBILITY, n.—ikapangyáyarì
—kasayonan—mahitabô

FEAST, n. — pistá, handaan, káinan—pangilin — pista, handaan,
ba ló

FEAT, n.—kabutihán, katángian-
buhat sa katakus—kinaayo

FEATHER, n.—balahibo, pakpák
—balhibo—balahibo, pakpak

FEATHERY, adj. — mabalahibo,
malambót, makinis—balhiboon,
mahumok — mabalahibo, mahumok, mahinlò

FEATURE, n. — itsura, pagmu-
mukhâ, katángian, ayos—panagway, kagawian—dagway, kahimtangan

FEBRUARY, n.—Pebrero—Pebrero—Pebrero

FEE, n.—bayad, upa — bayranan,
plitihan—bayad, hinakay

FEEBLE, adj.—mahinà—mahinay,
maluya—maluya

FEED, v.—pakanin, busugín—pagpakaon, pagbahog — pakan-on,
busgon

FEED, n.—pagkain — pagkaon —
pagkaon

FEEL, v. — danasin, maranasan,
damdamín—pagbati, paghikap—
batyagón

FEELING, n.—damdamin — balatian, pagbati—balatyagon

FEET, n.—mga paá—mga tiil —
mga tiíl

FEIGN, v.—magdahilán, mag-ayos
magkunwarî—pagpasangil, paglansis—mamalibad, magpakunô-
kuno

FELICITATE, v.—batiin, handu-
gán—pagpahalipay — pangibulahanan

FELT, v.—náramdamán—nabati-
an, hibatian—nabatyagán

FELONIOUS, adj.—masamâ, ma-
kamámatáy, makasalanan—dautan, masal-anon — makagud,
makassalà, makamalatay

FEMALE, n.—babae, kababaihan
—babaye—babáe, kababáen-an

FENCE, n.—bakod, bakuran, ha-
lang—labat, koral—kudál

FEND, v.—iwasan, hadlangán —
pagbabag, pagbalda—balabagan

FERN, n.—pakô—pako — kunya,
pasák

FEROCIOUS, adj.—mabangís, ga-
nid—mabangís, mapintas — mabangís

FERRET, v.—hanapin—pagpangita, pagsiksik—litaón

FERRY, n.—sasakyán sa pagta-
wíd sa tubig, balsá, tawiran —
balsa—balsa

FERTILE, adj.—matabâ, malusóg
—tabunok, mabungahon — matambok, mabungahon

FERTILIZE, v. — patabaín, palu-
sugín—pagpatambok — patam-
bokón

FERVENT, adj. — mainit, napu-
sok, masigasig—mainiton, madi-
laabon—mainitón, masupok.

FESTIVITY, n.—pistá, kasayahan
— pangilin — kahamungayaan,
kadagayaan

FETCH, v. — kaunín, sunduín —
pagkuha, pagsundo—sugaton

FETE, v.—ipagdiwang, ipaghandâ
—pagsaulog—handaán, hiwatan

FETID, adj.—masansáng, mabahò
— baklagon, mabaho — mahar-
ang, mabahò, maantud

FETISH, n.—galíng, anting-antíng
—anting-anting, birtud—anting-
anting

FEVER, n. — lagnát—hilanat—hilanat

FEVERISH, adj. — mainit, may-
lagnát—gihilantan, mainit—ma-
alangaang

FEW, adj.—kauntî, ilán — pipila,
diyutay—pilá, diótay

FICKLE, adj.— sálawahan, kabila-
hakán

FICTION, n. — waláng katotohanan, gawa-gawâ, di-likás — su-
gilanong taphaw o bakak—wala'y kamatuoran, pinatuk sa isip
nga wala'y sandigan

FIDDLE, n.—gitara, biyolín — biyolin—byolín

FIDELITY, n.—pagtatapát, katapatan — kamadayganon, kaligdong—kabunayag

FIDGETY, adj. — nerbiyoso, di-
mápakalí, malikót — nerbioso,
hulagán

75

FIELD, n.—bukid, kabukiran — uma, basakan, patag—ulumhan, patag

FIENDISH, adj.—makahalimaw—yawan-on, demonyohon—hayup-hayupon, sapatsapaton

FIERCE, adj. — mabangís, mabalasik, mabagsík — mabangís — mabangís

FIERY, adj.—maapóy, mainit—kalayohon, mainiton—mahingalayohon, mainitón

FIFTEENTH, adj. — ikalabinlimá, panlabinlimá — ikanapulog-lima —iká-napulo'g limá

FIFTH, adj.—ikalimá, panlimá — ikalima—ikálima

FIFTH-COLUMN, n. — tiktík, ispiyá, taksíl—tiktik, espiya—kinta-kolumna, ispiya, maninilág

FIFTY, n.—limampû—kalim-an — kalim-an

FIG, n.—igos—igos—igos

FIGHT, n.—away, suntukan, labanán—away, bugno, sumbagay — away, sumbaganay, tusay

FIGURATIVE, adj.—di-likás, makahulugán, matalinghagà — panagwayon, dili-tinuod—dî-tunay, makatalanhagà

FIGURE, n.—larawan, numero o bilang, ayos, anyô — panagway, numero — laragway, numeró ukón isip, dagway

FIGUREHEAD, n.—ulong-kahoy tautauhan—kahoy, tawo-tawo — ulo nga kahoy, táotáo

FILE, n.—kikil, salansán—limbas —bal-ag, tinumpokan

FILE, v.—isalansán, kikilin—paglimbas, pagpasaka — hantalón, bal-agán

FILL, n. — kahustuhan, kasiyahang loób—katagbawan, kaigoan—kaigoan, kaayawan

FILL, v.—punuín, lagyán—pagpuno—pun-on, butaon

FILM, n.—pelikulá—lilas, pelikula —pelikulá

FILIBUSTER, n.—pilibustero, laban sa bayan—pilibustero, kaaway sa lungsod — pilibustero, batok sa banwa

FILTH, n.—dumí, bahò—hugaw—higkò, garúk

FILTRATE, v.—salain—pagsala—salaon, patalasón

FINALLY, adv.—sa katapusán, sa wakás—katapusan—katapusan

FINANCE, n.—pananalapî, salapî —panalapi—manggad

FINANCIER, n.—kapitalista, tagagugol—sapianon, kapitalista—kapitalista

FIND, v.—hanapín—pagpangita—pangitaon

FINE, adj.—pino, magandá, multá pino, takum, silpi—pino, multa, tabís, mahining

FINE, v.—multaḥán, parusahan—pagsilpi, pagmulta — multahán, tabisán, silutan

FINGER, n.—dalirì—tudlo—tudlò

FINGERPRINTS, n.—taták, marká ng mga dalirì — timaan sa tudlo—marka sang mga tudlò

FINGER WAVE, n.—kulót sa kamáy—kulong sa tudlo — bawod sang mga tudlò

FINISH, v.—tapusin, wakasán —pagtapus, paghuman—tapuson

FINISH, n. — katapusán, wakás, pagkakáyarì — katapusan, sangputanan — katapusan, pagkahumán

FIRE, n.—apóy, init—sunog, kalayo—kalayo

FIREBRAND, n.—dupong, taga-pagsulsól—magsusugyot — manunugyot, agipó

FIREMAN, n.—bombero, tagapatáy ng sunóg—bombero, tigpatay sa sunog—bombero

FIREWOOD, n.—panggatong, kahoy—sugnod — inoggatóng, kahoy

FIREWORKS, n.—paputók, kuwitis—kuwitis — kwites, puegos artipisyales

FIRM, adj —matatág, matigás — magahi—makabud, matig-a

FIRM, n.—bahay-kalakal, kompaniya, samahan—balay sa patigayon—baláy-palatikangan, kompaniya,. kumbuyahan

FIRMNESS, n.—katigasan, katatagán—kagahi, katigson — katig-ahán, kabakurán

FIRST, adj.—una, pang-una—unanahauna—una, tig-uná

FISH, v.—mangisdâ, hulihin—pangisda, pagsikop—mangisdà, manikup

FISHERMAN, n.—mángingisdâ—mangingisda, mananagat — mangingisdà

FISHERY, n.—paláisdaan—isdaan—plaisdaan

FISHY, adj.—maisdâ—isdaanon—maisdà

FIST, n.—suntók, kamáy — kumo —sumbag, inumol

FISTIC, adj.—mapanuntók—pinaagi sa kumo—manunumbag

FIT, adj.—nárarapat, lapat, bagay, angkóp—angay, sibo, takus —sigo, bagay

FIT, v.—iangkóp, isukat, ibagay—isigo, ibagay—itakús

FITTING, n.—pagsasaayos, pagsusukat, sukat — kasiboan, kasukdanan, pagsibo — pagkasibù, pagkabagay

FIVE, n.—limá—lima—limá

FIX, v.—ayusin, kumpunihín, patibayin — **pag-ayo, pagpahimutang**—kaayohon, pabakuron

FIXTURE, n.—kasangkapan, kabit—**kasangkapan, kahimanan**——kasangkapán

FIZZLE, v.—sumagitsít na magningas at bigláng mamatáy — **pagsirit**—sumurò

FLABBY, adj.—mahinà, yayát, tuyót—**luyahon**—maluming

FLAG, n. — watawat, bandilà—**bandila**—bandera, hayahay

FLAP, n.—hampás, tunóg — **dagpas, tunog**—pakpak, tunóg

FLARE, n.—liwanag, kisláp—**siga, hayag**—igpat, masilì

FLASH, n.—kisláp, bilís — **kidlap**—igpat, hagurót

FLASHY, adj. — pasikat, mabilís, makisláp—**makidlapon, mahambogon**—hambog, maabtik, makilán

FLAT, adj.—patag, waláng katás, malapad—**patag**—matapan

FLATTER, v.—puri-purihin—**pagulo-ulo**—dayáw-dayawon

FLATTERY, n.—papuri, pagtuyâ, pag-uyám—**ulo-ulo, ulog-ulog** — ulointuon

FLAVOR, n.—lasa, timplá—**lami, timpla**—lalim

FLAW, n.—sirà, depekto—**sipyat, depekto, apán**—litík, dcpekto

FLEA, n.—pulgás—**pulgas**—bitik·

FLEE, v.—magtanan, lumipád — pagkagyo, **paglayas**—magpalagyo, lumupád

FLEECE, v.—hubarán, nakawan—pagpanapi, **panapian pinsagi sa** limbong—panitan, upakan

FLEET, adj.—maliksí, mabilís — lagsik, **tulin**—makisáy, madasig, buke de gera

FLEETING, adj.—panandálian — hinanali, **madalion**—padali

FLESH, n.—lamán, karné—**unod**—kaundan, karne

FLICKERING, adj. — áandáp-andáp, namamatáy, malamlám — **himalatyon, nagpirát-pirat—nagaigpat**-igpat, nagakipaw-kipaw

FLIGHT, n.—paglipád, pagtakas—**lupad**—paglupád, pagpalagyo

FLIGHTY, adj. — palit-palit, kapritsosa, nakahíhilo — **mabalhinon, laagon**—mabaylohon, mailá, kapritsosa

FLIMSY, adj.—marupók, mahinà —gabok, **mahinay, mahuyang**—matapók, mahuyang

FLING, v.—itapon, ipukól—**pagsalibay, paglabay**—ibunal, ipasalipadpad

FLIPPANT, adj.—magasó, malandî—**kiat, kundatan**—hulagán

FLOAT, v.—lumutang, maanod — **paglutaw, pagpaanud**—lumutáw, karosa

FLOAT, n.—karosa, balsá—**karosa**—karosa, balsa

FLOCK, n.—kawan—tapok, panon
—kahayupan

FLOCK, v.—magpunpón, magtagpô, magsama-sama — pagtapok,
pagpanon—magtililipon, magti-
naboay

FLOOD, n.—bahâ—lunop, bahá—
bahâ

FLOOD, v. — bumahâ, dumami,
nabasâ—gilunopan, gibahaan —
bumahâ

FLOOR, n.—sahíg, lapág—salog
—salúg

FLORA, n.—mga taním ng poók
—mga tanum sa lasang—Dios
sang mga bulak sang Romano

FLORID, adj.—mabulaklák, makintáb, magayák—mabulakon—
mabulakon

FLORIST, n.—magbubulaklák —
magbubulak—manogbuhat bulak

FLOUR, n.—harina—harina—ari-
na

FLOURISH, v.—sumaganà, dumami—pagtubo, pagdagsang — du-
magayà, dumagsà

FLOW, n.—agos, takbó, anod —
inagas, agos—ilig, tubód

FLOW, v.—umagos, bumuhos, ibuhos, patuluin — pag-agas, pag-
agos—umilig, tumubód

FLOWER, n.—bulaklák—bulak —
bulak

FLOWERING, adj.—namúmulak-
lák—bumubuklad, namiyoos —
gapamulak

FLUCTUATE, v.—pagalawín, itaás o ibabâ, mag-atubili—pagpalihok, pagpaulpot-ulpot — suma-
lipadpad, pumapaladpad

FLUENT, adj.—mabuting magsalitâ, malinaw—larino, matin-aw
manulti — tayuyon maghambal,
maathag, alagisod

FLUID, n.—anó mang tumútulò
gaya ng tubig, langís, ibp.—tubigon—pluido, matubigon

FLUTTER, v. — ipagpág, ibukás,
igaláw — pagkapa-kapa, pagbukas—magkapákapá, magkuyam-
pad

FLY, n.—langaw—langaw — langaw, lupád

FLY-LEAF, n.—pagitan, pamasak
—blangkong panid sa libro —
sumal-ut

FOAM, n.—bulâ—bula, buwa—bukál

FOAM, v.—bumulâ—pagbula pag-
buwa—bumukál

FOE, adj.—kaaway, kalaban—kaaway, kaatbang — keaway, kasumpong

FOG, n.—ulap na hamóg — alisngaw sa tun-og—gamhon

FOGGY, adj. —maulap, di-maliwa-
nag—hanap, yamogon—magam-
hon

FOLD, n.—sakop, kapangyarihan
—sakop, ginsakpan — sinakupan, kalibutanon

FOLD, v.—tiklupín, ilupî—pagpi-
lo, pagtiklop—piluón, piuron

FOIL, v.—biguín—pagpakyas—pahugon

FOLIAGE, n.—mga dahon—kada-
honan—mga dahon

FOLK, n.—tao, lipi o lahì, mga
kamag-anak—katawhan, banay
—táo, kaliwatan

FOLLOW, v.—sumunód, sundán—
pagsunod—sumunód

FOLLOWER, n.—tagasunód, alagád—sumusunod, alagad—sumu-
lunod, alagád

FOLLOWING, adj.—ang sumúsu-
nód—ang mosunod—masunód

FOLLY, n.—kaululán, kapilyuhán,
kamálian—kabuang, kapulpol—
kabuangán

FOND, adj.—nagígiliw, mawilihín,
maibigín—mahigugmaon — ma-
wilihon

FONDNESS, n.—pagkawili, pag-
kagiliw — kamahigugmaon —
pagkawili

FONDLE, v.—hipu-hípuin, híma-
sin — paghapohap — hulohapu-
lason

FOOD, n.—pagkain — kalan-on,
pagkaon—pagkaon

FOOL, n.—haling, ulól, loko—buang, kwanggol, tonto—buangit,
buáng-buáng

FOOLISH, adj.—ulól, hangál-ha-
ngal-hangal, buang-buang—buang

FOOT, n.—paá, paanán, ibabâ—ti-
til—tiíl, tiilán, talapakán

FOOTLIGHTS, n.—tanghalan, entablado, eksena—entablado, be-
ladahan—entablado, esena

FOOT-LOOSE, adj.—malayà, wa-
láng-talì—luwas, wala-gapusa—
mahilwayon, wala'y higót

FOOTSTEPS, n.—mga bakás ng
yapák—lakra sa tiil—tinapakán

FOR, prep.—pará, ukol sa, pará
sa, sa—alang, sa, tungod sa —
para sa, tungód sa

FORBEARANCE, n.—pagtitiyagâ,
pagbibigáy—pailub — pagpailub

FORBID, v.—ipagbawal, ipag-utos
—pagdili, did-an—djlian

FORBIDDEN, adj.—bawal—gina-
dili, ginadid-an—ginadilian

FORCE, n.—lakás, pilit—kusog—
kusóg, pilit

FORCE, v.—pilitin, pangyarihin—
paglugos, pagpugos—piliton, pa-
kusgan

FORE, n.—unahán—unahan—unahán

FOREARM, v.—sandatahan, laka-
sán, ihandâ — pag-andam batok
sa ataki—manginlaman

FOREHEAD, n.—noó—agtang, bu-
ná—agtang

FOREBODING, n. — guniguní—
—tagna sa dautang umaabut—
handurawan

FOREIGN, adj.—tagaibáng lupaín, náiibá, nababago, dayuhan—langyaw—taga-luás

FOREIGNER, n. —tagaibáng-bayan, estranhero, dayuhan — lumalangyaw—dumuluong, estranhero

FOREGO, v.—bitiwan, pabayaan, ipaubayà—pagbuhl, pasagdan — buy-an, pabayaan

FOREGONE, adj.—nakatítiyák-nasiguro, hitag-anan—makapalat-ud

FOREMAN, n.—kapatás, katiwalà —kapatas—kapatás

FOREMOST, adj.—káuná-unahan, nangúnguna — labing una — labing una

FORENOON, n.—bago tumanghalì—kaudtohon—hingudtohon

FOREST, n.—kakahuyan, gubat—kakahoyan, kalasangan—kagulangan

FOREVER, adv. — magpakailanmán—sa kahangturan, hangtud anus-a—katubtohan

FORFEIT, v.—likumin, ilitin — pagluwat, paghatag—butongon

FORGE, v.—huwarán, pandayín—paghuwad, pagpanday — ilogón, pandayón

FORGET, v.—limutin — pagkalimot—limutan

FORGETFUL, adj.—makalimutín —malimuton—malimuton

FORGER, n. — manghuhuwád — maghuhuwad—mangingilóg

FORGIVE, v.—magpatawad, patawarin—pagpasaylo — patawaron

FORGIVENESS, n.—kapatawarán —pasaylo—kapatawaran

FORGOTTEN, adj.—nakalimutan, nalimot — hinikalimtan — nalimutan

FORK, n.—tinedór, pandurò—tenidor—tenedór

FORLORN, adj.—waláng pag-asa, malungkót, napabayaan—walay-paglaum, biniyáan—wala'y paglaum, masinulub-on, ginpatumbayaan

FORM, n.—hubog, hugìs—dagway, porma—dagway, porma

FORMAL, adj. — pormál, hustó, matimpî—pormal, ligdong—pormal, mahipos

FORMER, adj.—dati, náuunâ — kanhi, sa una—sadto, sinadto

FORMERLY, adv.—noóng una, dati-rati—kanhi—sadto anay

FORSAKE, v.—pabayaan, limutin, iwan—pagbiya, paglimot — patumbayaan, kalimtan, bayaan

FORT, n.—kutà—kuta — kutà

FORTH, adv.—pasulóng, sa malayò—ngadto padulong — sumulong

FORTHCOMING, adj.—dárating—umaiabut—palaabuton

81

FORTNIGHT, n. — dalawáng linggó—duha ka semana—kinsenál

FORTUNATE, adj. — mapalad—palaran, bulahan—bulahan, mapalaron

FORTY, n.—apatnapû — kap-atan —kap-atán

FORWARD, v.—ipadalá—sa unahan—sumulong, nakig-uná

FOUL, adj.—mabahò, marumí, ditapát, nakapópoót—mabaho, mahugaw, hiwî—mabahò, mahigkò, garúk

FOUNDATION, n.—batayán, pasimulâ, baligi—sukaranan, katarokan — salandigan, sulogoran, haliginhan

FOUNTAIN, n.—batis, pinagmúmulán, bukól—busay — busáy, ponda

FOUNDER, n.—nagtatág, nagsimulâ, nanguna—magtutukod — nagpatuk, tagtukod

FOUR, n.—apat—upat—apat

FOURSOME, n.—apatan—tagupatay—apatán

FOURTEEN, n.—labíng-apat—nabulog-upat—napulo'g apat

FOURTEENTH, adj. — ikalabingapat — ikanapulog-upat — ikánapulo'g apat

FOURTH, adj.—ikaapat—ika-upat —ikap-at

FOUR-O'CLOCK, n.—alas kuwatro, ikaapat—ika-upat ang takna—ikap-at, alas kwatro

FOWL, n.—ibon, manók — langgam, manok—pispis, manúk

FOX, n.—hayop na sora, alamíd—milo, mananap samag iro—sora

FOXY, adj.—magdarayà, manlilinláng—abtik, ilmbóngan—madayà, maluíb

FRACTION, n.—kalahatì, kapilas, kaputol—katipik, kaputol—katungâ, kabahin, kautód

FRAGILE, adj.—babasagín, marupók—daling-mabuak, huyáng—buongón, matapók

FRAGRANT, adj.—mabangó, mabusilak, maamóy — mahumot, maamyon—mahumót, maamyon

FRAIL, adj.—marupók, mahinà—mahuyang, daút—matapók, mahunâ

FRAME, n.—kuwardo, balangkás —kuwadro, paglaraw—kwadro, pagbalayon

FRANK, adj.—bukás, hayág, tuwíd—madaygaṅon—tampad

FRANKNESS, n. — pagkahayág, háyagan, pagkabukás — kamadayganon—katampad

FRATERNITY, n.—kápatiran, samahan—**kapunongan, pundok** — pag-ulolutod

FRAUD, n.—pagdarayà, panlilinláng—**limbong, kawihian**—pagdayà

FRAUGHT, adj.—punúng-punô — **puno nga labihan**—kunsarán

FREE, adj.—malayà, waláng-sagabal — **luwás, libre, gawás** — hilway, wala'y salabton

FREEDOM, n.—kalayaan—**kaluwasan, kagawasan**—kahilwayan

FREEZE, v. — lumamíg, magíng yelo, mamuô—**pagpagahi sa yelo** —tumugnaw, nangínyelo

FREIGHT, n.—lulan, bayad sa lulan—**luwan, karga**—lulan, bayad sa lulan

FRENZY, n.—guló, pagkaulól — **kasamok, kaguliyang**—buangít

FREQUENT, adj.—madalás, malimit—**kanunay**—masunson, pirme, lagi

FRESH, adj.—sariwâ, bago—**lab-as**—lab-as

FRET, v.—magulumihanan—**pagkasuko, pagkagipod**—mahunusbo

FRIDAY, n.—Biyernes—**Biyernes** —Biernes

FROG, n.—palakâ—**baki**—pakâ

FROLIC, n.—paglalarô, pagsasayá **—kasayaan, kalipayan** — paghinampang, pagsinadya

FROLICSOME, adj.—magasó, ma-

paglarô—**masaya, malipayon** — masadyahon

FROM, prep.—galing sa, buhat sa, sa—**gikan sa**—gikan sa, halín sa

FRONT, n.—haráp, unahán, pambungad — **atubangan** — atubangan, unahán, tig-una

FROST, n.—busilak, lamíg—**tibugok nga tubig, yelo**—pagkabugnaw

FROTH, n.—bulâ, paimbaháw na karunungan — **bulá** — umindakál, nangibabaw sa kinaalam

FROWN, v.—mangunót ang noó, sumibangot — **pagkunot sa agtang**—kumurisong

FROZEN, v.—nalamigán, namu nanigás—**gipanugnaw, pagpanibuok**—nabugnawán, namilógbilóg

FRUGALITY, n.—katipirán—**kainot, daginot**—kamakinuton

FRUIT, n.—bunga, bungangkahoy **—bungahoy**—bunga'ngkahoy

FRUITFUL, adj.—saganà, mabunga—**mabungahon** — mabungahon

FRUSTRATE, v. — biguín, hadlangán—**pagpakyas** — pas-awón, balabagan

FRY, v.—ipirito—**pagprito, paggisal**—iprito

FUEL, n.— panggatong, kahoy — **sugnod**—gatóng

FULFILL, v. — isaganáp, totohanin, isagawâ, ganapín — **pagtuman**—tumanon

FULFILLMENT, n. — kaganapán
—katumanan—pagkatuman

.FULL, adj.—punô, lipós, busóg—
puno, busog—punô, busóg

FULLY, adv.—ganáp, punúng-punô—sa kapuno—bug-os, napunô

FUN, n.—siste, birò, kasayahan—
tiaw, kasayahan—lahúg, kasadyahan

FUND, n.—pondo, panggugol, pre-
su-puwesto — panggugol, presu-
pwesto — pondo,-pre-supwesto,
hilinguyangon

FUNERAL, n.—libíng, paglilibíng
—lubong—lubóng

FUNGUS, n.—amag—uhong — bu-
lak-bulak

FUNNEL, n.—embudo—embudo—
embudo, tayonán

FUNNY, adj.—nakákatuwâ, nakatátawá — kataw-anan, makapatawa—makahalam-ot

FUR, n.—balahibo ng hayop—mahumok balhibo sa mananap—balahibo sang hayup

FURIOUS, adj. — napópoót, nagngángalit—napikal, naimpito sa
kasuko—masingkì

FURLOUGH, n.—bakasiyón—bakasyon, pahuway—bakasyon (sa
armi)

FURL, v. — iladlád — pagladlad,
pagkayab—ihumlad

FURNACE, n.—hurno, ápuyan —
hudno, kayohan—hurno, dalabu-
kán

FURNISH, v.—magkaloób, sangkapán, bigyán, pagkalooban —
pagsangkap, paghiman — hatagan, sangkapán

FURNISHING, n. — kasangkapan, kagamitán — kasangkapan,
kagamitan — kasangkapán, kagamitán

FURNITURE, n. — kasangkapan
sa bahay—kasangkapan sa balay
—kasangkapan

FURTHER, adj.—higít ang kalayuan, lalong malayò, at sakâ pa
—lapas nga gilay-on, ug labut
pa—tuman kalayô, labíng malayô, kag

FURTHERANCE, n.—pagpapatu-
loy—pagpadayon—kasugponán

FURTIVE, adj. — malihim, marahan — mabinantayon, hinay-hinay—malikumon

FURY, n.—dikít, sulsól, pusible—
naghinagaping kasuko—masing-
kion

FUSION, n.—pag-iisá, pagsasama
—paghiusa, pagtipon — isahón,
tingbon

FUSSILADE, n.—bárilan, pútukan
—linuthangay, pinusilay—lutha-
ngay

FUTILE, n.—waláng maáasahan, waláng saysáy — walay-dapat, mapakyason—wala'y masaligan, wala'y pulós

FUTURE, n. — kinábukasan, ang dáratíng — kaugmaon, umaabut —palaabuton, buan-damlag

— G —

GAIN, n.—tubò, pakinabang, kahigtán—tubo, ganansiya, kapin —ganansya, saplid, daúg.

GAIN, v.—magtubò, makinabang, lampasán—pagtubo, paggananslya — magganansya, magsaplid, magdaúg

GALE, n.—malakás na hangin— kusog nga hangin—buhawi

GALL, n.—apdó—apdo—apdo

GALLANT, adj. — matapang, galante—maisug—isganán, galante

GALLERY, n.—galerya o úpuang nasa itaás, tanghalan—galeriya —galerya

GALLON, n.—takaláng may lamáng 4.2 litro, galón—galon— galón, sulukban nga may unod sing 4.2 ka litro

GALLOP, n.—galáw na may paluksó, tumakbóng may paluksó —dagan-sagol-ulpot—galope, liktinan

GAME, n.—larô, mga ibon—dula, pangayam ug langgam — hamnang

GANDER, n.—gansâ — gangsa— gansà

GANGPLANK, n.—tuláy, andamyo—latayan, andamyo—andamyo, latayán

GANGRENE, n.— kangrena, pamamagâ—kanggrena, kamayo—. kangrena, kalamayó

GAPE, v.—ngumangá, tumulalà— pagnganga—nahayanghag

GARAGE, n.—garahe, silungan ng sasakyán — garahe, pasilongag awto—garahe

GARB, n.—suót, damít—saput, sinina—bayuón, panapton

GARBAGE, n.—dumí, sukal--basura—basurahán

GARDEN, n.—hálamanán, hardín, tániman—tanaman—hardin

GARDENER, n.—maghahalaman, hardinero, tagapagtaním ng halaman — bantay sa tanaman— hardinero

GARDENIA, n.—rosál — rosál — rosál

GARGLE, n.—mumog, pangmumog—limogmog—mangalimóg

GARLAND, n.—putong na bulaklák, kuwintás—pungpong bulak —pungpong nga mga bulak nga palangolintason

GARLIC, n.—bawang — **ahos, bawang**—ahos

GARMENT, n.—kasúutan, damít —**saput, besti**—panaptoń

GARTER, n.—ligas—**ligas**—ligas

GAS, n.—petrolyo, gaás—**gas, petrolyo**—petrolyo, gas

GASH, n.—hiwà, kalmót—**samad** —nagulót

GASP, v.—humingal — **paghangal** —nagahapûhapô

GASPING, adj.—humíhingal—**nagahangal**—ginahapò

GATE, n.—pintô, daanan — **ganghaan**—pwertahun

GATHER, v. — ipunin, magtipon, mag-umpukan—**pag-ipon, pagtigum**—tiponon, tumpukón

GATHERING, n. — lipón, umpukan; kasáyahan — **katiguman,** panagtipon—tinipon, maḷipayon

GAY, adj.—masayá, kaayaaya — **ngaya, malipayon** — masadya, malipayon

GAUDY, adj.—bulgár, masagwâ—**mangil-ad, talamayon** — bulgar, masaw-a

GAUNT, adj.—yayat, payát—**daút, naghigos**—hayát

GAZE, v.—tumingín — **pagtutok, pagtan-aw**—tumingâ

GAZING, v.—tumitig, tumingín—**nagatutok, nagatan-aw**—tumulok

GEN, n.—hiyas, mahalagáng batő, pilì—**pahiyas, batong-mahal** —hiyás

GERMINATE, v.—tumubò — **pagtubo**—sumingil

GENERAL, n.—henerál, karaniwan, panlahát—**kadaghanan, tanan-tanan, heneral**—henerál, tanán-tanán

GENERATE, v.—mag-anák, tumubò, labasán—**pagpakuryente, pagpanganak**—magpatubás, manganák

GENERATION, n.—salin ng lahì, isáng panahón—**kaliwatan, kapanahonan** — kaliwatan

GENEROUS, adj.—mapagkaloób, mabuting-loób, maawaín, mahabagín—**manggiluy-on, mabination**—maalwan, maluluy-on, mahinatagon

GENIAL, adj. — masayá, mabuting makiharáp—**buotan, mahigalaon — malipayon, bunayag** makig-atubang

GENIUS, n. — henyo, marunong, dalubhasà — **makinaadmanon, henyo**—henyo, mangin-alamon

GENTLE, adj.—maamò, mahinahon, mabinì—**maaghop, ligdong** —mahagúp, mabuot

GENTLEMAN, n.—maginoó—**tawong-hamili**—talahuron

GENTLY, adv.—dahan-dahan—sa mahinay—hinay-hinay

GENUINE, adj.—tunay, lantáy, likás—tinuod, tunay—tunay

GEOGRAPHY, n.—karunungan sa mga lupaín, heograpiya—heograpiya—heograpiya

GERM, n.—mikrobyo — kagaw—mikrobyo, kagaw

GERMICIDE, n.—pamatáy ng mikrobiyo—pamatay sa kagaw — inogpatay sang mikrobyo

GET, v.—kunin—pagkuha, pagdangat—kuhaon

GHASTLY, adj.—maputlâ, nakasísindák—ngilngig, makuyaw — malapsì makatalagam

GHOST, n.—multó—kalag, ungo, multo—kalág

GIANT, n. — higante, malalakíng tao—higanti—higante

GIBBERISH, adj.—waláng-liwanag, nagbúbubulóng—mangulobon, di-masabtan — pitlà, nagapurotikol maghambal

GIFT, n.—kaloób, regalo, handóg, alay—gasa, regalo hinatag—regalo, dulot

GIGGLE, n.—ngisi, tawang nakilitî—tingsi, ngisi—barangisí

GILL, n.—hasang—hasang—asang

GINGER, n.—luya—luy-a—luy-a

GIRDLE, n.—bigkîs, talì sa baywang—bakus sa hawak — bugkos, higút sa balikawáng

GIRL, n.—batang babae, nobya, katipán—batang babaye, nobya —batang babáe, nobya, katipan

GIST, n.—ubod, kabuuán — ubod, kinatibuk-an—ubod

GIVE, v.—magbigáy, ibigáy, magkaloób—paghatag — maghatag, magdulot

GLAD, adj.—masayá, natútuwâ—masayá, malipayon—masadya

GLADNESS, n.—katuwaan, kasáyahan—kasayá, kalipayan — kasadyahan

GLANCE, n.—sulyáp · — pasiplat, pasiklap—siplat

GLANCE, v.—sumulyáp, sulyapán —pagsiplat, pagsiklap—pasiplatán

GLARE, n.—liwanag na nakasísilaw—kasulaw, lamdag — sanag nga makasisilaw

GLARING, adj.—maliwanag, malakí, nakasísilaw—masnlaw, mahayag kaayo—masilì, makasisilaw

GLASS, n —salamín, baso—bildo, baso—baso, kristal

GLAMOUR, n. — panghalina, gayuma—malumayong kaanyag — makalulumay, makabuluyok

GLEAM, n.—sinag, banaag — silaw, dang-ag—banaag

GLEAN, v.—mamulot, pulutin — pagpunit, pamudyot — maninigput

GLEE, adj.—katuwaan, galák—kalipay, kangaya—kalipayan

GLIB, adj.—masalitâ, madaldál—babá-on, tabian, matabi—bâbaan

GLIDE, v.—magpadulas, magpatangáy sa hangin, lumipád—pagpadaílos, paglutaw sa hangin—magdalus-os, magpadain-as, magpahuyóp sa hangin

GLIMPSE, n.—sulyáp, tingín, tanáw—pasiplat, tutok—siplat, tulok

GLITTER, n.—kináng, kisláp — kidlap—igpat

GLOOM, n.—lungkót, lamlám, dilím—kasubó, kadulóm—masubô, mangitngit

GLOOMY, adj.—madilím, malungkót, malamlám—subó, madulóm —masagir-um, mamingaw

GLORIOUS, adj.—maluwalhatî — mahimayaon—mahimayaon

GLORY, n.—lualhatì, kaluwalhatian—himaya, kahimayaan — himayà

GLUE, n.—kola, pandikít —, kola, papilit—kolá, glue

GLUTTON, n.—matakaw, masibì —dawó, hakúg, dakug-habhab—maasab, dalúk

GLOW, n.—baga, liyáb, sinag — siga, hayag—siga, baga

GLOWING, adj.—nagbábaga, nagliliyáb—nagasiga, nagadilaab — nagadabadaba

GO, v.—yumao, umalís, lumakad—paglakaw, pag-adto—lumakát

GOAT, n.—kambíng—kanding — kanding

GOD, n.—Bathalà, Diyós—Bathala, Dios—Diós, Makaako

GODLY, adj.—maka-diyós — maki-Bathala, maki-Dios—diosnon

GODDESS, n.—diyosa—diyosa — diosa

GODMOTHER, n.—ninang, iníiná —maninay—maninay

GOLD, n.—gintô—bulawan—bulawan

GOLDEN, adj. — mala-gintô, parang gintô, ginintuán—bulawanon, daw bulawan—bulawanon

GOLDSMITH, n.—latero, pandáy pilak—platero, magbubulawan—platero

GOOD, adj.—mabuti, magalíng — maayo—maayo

GOODWILL, n.—pakikisama, pag-kakakilala—pakigdait — pagka-bunayag

GOOD-BYE, v.—paalam na, adi-yós, diyán na káyó—adyos, ari-na-ako—paalam, adiós, dirâ ka ná

GOODNESS, n. — kabutihan—ka-ayohan, kamaayo—kaayohan

GOOSE, n.—gansâ—gangsa, pato —gansà

GORE, v.—suwagín — pagsungay, pagsungag—sungayon

GORGEOUS, adj. — magandáng luhhâ, marikít, marilág—mata-hum, maanyag, mabihagon—ma-anyag, maambong, magayón

GORMAND, n.—matakaw, mabu-ting kumain — hingaon, dakug-kaon—maasab

GOSPEL, n.—ebangehlyo—ebang-helyo, santos nga sulat—ebang-helyo

GOSSIP, n.—tsismis, satsatan —tabi, honghongihong—katâ-katà

GOVERN, v. — mamahalà, sakla-wín, pangasiwaan—pagmando—but-an, gamhan

GOVERNMENT, n. — gobyerno, pámahalaán — kagamhanan — gobierno, pangulohán

GOVERNOR, n.—gobernadór, pu-nong lalawigan—gobernador, pa-muno-lalawigan — gobernadór, pangulopuód

GOWN, n.—damít na panlabás, to-ga, kasúutang panghigâ—sinina sa balay—panapton, toga, bata

GRAB, v.—dakutín, agawin, sak-lutín — pagsakmit, pag-ilog — hugakumon

GRAB, n.—dakót, agaw, saklót — inagaw, agawán, ilogáy — huga-kum, agawon

GRACE, n.—kabutihan, kaganda-han, biyayà, dasál sa pagkain—grasya, kaambong — kaalwan, bugáy, grasva

GRACEFUL, adj.—magandá, kaa-ya-aya, mabikas — maambong, grasyosa—maalwan, mabugayon

GRACIOUS, adj. — mapagbiyayà, magiliw — maparaygon — ma-pagbugáy

GRADE n. — grado, antás, bai-táng—grado, matang — grado, halintang

GRADE, v. — graduhin, antasán, markahán — pagmatang, pag-marka—gradohan, halintangán

GRADUAL, adj. — dahan-dahan, untí-untî, atáy-atay — anam-anam, hinay-hinay, tagidyut — amát-amát, diótay-diótay

GRADUATE, n. — tapós, nakata-pos, graduadó — nakatapus, gradwado—gradwado

GRADUATE, v.—magtapós—pag-tapus, paggradwar — maggra-dwar

GRAIN, n.—butil—lugas, humay— lamigas

GRAMMAR, n.—gramátiká, bala- rilà—gramatika, pulonglaan — gramatika, lantipulong

GRAND, adj.—malakí, dakilà — daku, hamili—dakû, dungganon

GRANDEUR, n.—kalakhán, kada- kilaan, katanyagán — kadaku, kahamili—kadakuón, kadungga- non, kalutáw

GRANDFATHER, n.—nunò, ing- kóng, lolo—apohang lalaki—lolo

GRANDMOTHER, n.—nunò, impó, nunong babae, lola — apohang babae—lola

GRANDSON, n.—apó—apo nga la- laki—apó

GRANT, n.—ang ipinagkákaloób— hatag, katugotan — ginhatag, ginpahanugot

GRANT, v.—ipagkaloób, ibigáy — paghatag, pagtugot—ihatag, ipa- hanugot

GRAPE, n.—ubas—ubas—ubás

GRASP, v.—tumangan, tanganan, hawakan — paggunit sa puan, paghakgom — kaptan, hugaku- mon

GRASS, n.—damó — sagbut, balili —hilamón

GRASSY, adj. — madamó—sagbu- ton, balilihon—mahilamón

GRASSHOPPER, n. — luktón, ba- lang—alasiwsiw—tibakla

GRATEFUL, adj.—tumítingín na nagpápasalamat — mapasalama- ton — matinalamdon, mapasala- ton

GRATER, n. — kudkuran—kudko- ran—kudkoran

GRATIFY, v.—pagbigyán—pagha- lus—paghatagan

GRATIS, n.—waláng bayad, gra- tis, libre—walay bayad, gratis— gratis, wala'y bayad

GRATITUDE, n.—utang na loób, pasasalamat — utang-kabubot- on, pasalamat—utang nga buót, pasalamat

GRAVE, adj.—malubhâ, maselan —malisud, grabe — grabe, ma- lubhà

GRAVE, n.—hukay, libingan—lu- bong, gilubngan—kutkot, lulub- ngan

GRAVITY, n.—bigát, kalubhaán— kabug-at, kagrabe—bug-at, ka- lubhaán

GRAY, adj.—abuhín, kulay-abó — abuhon—abohón

GRAZE, v.—manginain ng damó —pagsibsib—manghaláb

GREASE, n.—grasa, sebo — sebo, grasa—grasa, sebo

GREASY, adj.—madulás, mináb, makintáb—mantikaon, madang- log—madanlug, mahining

INDEPENDENT, adj. — may ka-
saṙinlán o pagsasarilí, malayà—
makinaugalingon—hilway

INDESCRIBABLE, adj.—di-maki-
lala, di-masabi, di-mailarawan —
dili-ikaasoy, dili-ikasugid — dî-
makilala, dî-mabungát, dî-mala-
rawan

INDICATE, v.—ipakita, iturò —
pagpasabut, pagtudlo — ipakità,
itudlò

INDICATION, n.—tandâ, tagaturò—timaan, marka—tandà, ubáy

INDIFFERENCE, n. — waláng
saysáy, pagwawaláng bahalà —
ka-walay pagtagad—wala'y kaangtanan

INDIGENT, adj. — nangángailangan, mahirap — nauyamot, timawa—nagakinahanglan, kinulabos

INDIGNATION, n.—poót, galit—
kasuko, kapikál—dumót, akíg

INDIRECT, adj. — paliguy-ligoy,
di-túwiran—paliko-liko, balikog
—dî-tadlong, palikûlikù

INDIVIDUAL, n.—tao, bukód, sarili, kanyá-kanyá—ang tawo, kaugalingon, iya-iya—kinugalíng,
kinaiya

INDISPENSABLE, adj.—lubháng
kailangan, kailangang-kailangan
—kinahanglan kanunay — kina-
nanglan gid

INDISPOSED, adj. — may diná-
ramdám, may kauntíng sakít—

masakiton, may gibati — may
paghinakít

INDIVISIBLE, adj.—hindî mahá-
hatì—dili mabahin — indî matu-
ngâ

INDOLENT, adj.—tamád, waláng
ginágawâ — taslakán, tapulán,
patay-patay—tamád, wala'y na-
isgan

INDUCE, v.—mang-udyók, upatán
—pagdani, pagpugós—sugyotón

INDUCEMENT, n.—upát, udyók—
butang makadani—sugyot

INDULGE, v.—mamalagì, magpa-
kagumon—pag-apil-apil, pagba-
tig kaluoy—magkaluoy, magta-
mod, maglingíg

INDUSTRIOUS, adj.—masipag —
kugihán, makugihon—mapisan

INDUSTRY, n.—pagkabuhay, hanapbuhay, kasipagan—industriya, kakugi—industriya, kabuhian

INEFFICIENT, adj. — di-sanáy,
di-marunong, waláng-kaya—dili
mahibalo, dili takús—dî-anád, dî-
makaisrut, wala'y ikasaráng

INEVITABLE, adj. — di-maíwa-
san—dili kapugngan, dili kalika-
yán—dî-malikawán

INFALLIBLE, adj.—di-magkáka-
malî—dili-masayóp — dî-magsa-
yúp

INFANT, n.—sanggól, batà—bata
nga masuso — lapsag, batà nga
diótay

INFECTION, n. — pagkakáhawa, pamamagà, pagkakaroón ng nanà—ang pagmaná, impeksiyon—makalalatón, nagabanóg, inpeksyon

INFERENCE, n.—hakahaká, akalà, intindí—ang pagpasabut, ang pagpatuo nga mao — palakamaayohón

INFERIOR, adj.—mababà sa urì, marupók—ubós sa matáng, baratohón—magpakaubós

INFIDELITY, n.—di-pagtatapát—ang kawalay tinuhoan, kalimbóngan sa panumpa—dî-tampad

INFINITE, adj.—waláng hanggá—walay-kahangturaa — wala'y dulonan

INFIRM, adj. — mahinà, úugód-ugód—maluya, tukbilon, sakitanon—maluya, nagaigod

INFLUENCE, n.—lakás o kapangyarihan sa ibá, inpluensiya—diwanhong gahum, impluwensiya — inplwensya, kaangtanan sa ibán

INFORM, v. — magbigáy alám, magbalità—pagpahibalo, pagtahó—magpasayud, magbalità

INHABIT, v.—tirahán, manirahan—pagpuyó—puy-an

INHABITANT, n. — naninirahan, nakatirá—pumopuyo, molupyó—pumuluyò

INHALE, v.—langhapín, suminghót, singhutín—pagsuyop ug hangin—hakluón

INHERENT, adj.—natural, likás, katutubò — kinaiya, natural — kinaugalì, kinamat-an

INHERENT, adj.—naturál, likás, na—pagsunod sa kabilin—magpanublì

INHOSPITABLE, adj. — masamáng ugálì di-makupkop — dili makiangayon, dili maabiabihon —malain sing batasan, dî-mainakupón

INHUMAN, adj.—waláng damdamin, di-makatao—dili tawhanon — wala'y balatyagon, dî-táohanon

INITIAL, n.—unang titik ng pangalan, pasimulâ — unang titik sa ngalan — unang letra sang ngalan

INJECT, v.—duruin, ipasok—pagtusok, pagtupok, dagum—tuslukón, itublok

INJURE, v. — masaktán, manakít — pagsamad, pagdagmal—sakitón

INJURY, n.—kapinsalaan, sakit—samad, lawasnong kadaut—kalaglagan, kasakitán

INJUSTICE, n.—kaapihán, pagkawaláng katwiran — panglupíg,
inhustisya—wala'y katarungan

INK, n.—tinta—tinta—tintà

INKLING, n.—pagkakáalám, hi-
nuhà—pasambingay — pagkahi-
sayud, pagkahaumhaum

INMATE, n.—kasambaháy, preso,
bilanggô—bilanggo, priso — kaupod, binilanggò

INN, n.—bahay-túluyan — balay-
abtanan—baláy-dalayonán

INNER, adj.—loób, sa kalooban—
sa sulód—kasudlan

INNERMOST, adj.—káloób-looban
—sa kalládman, labing sulód —
sa sulod pa

INNOCENCE, n. — pagkawalang-
malay, kalinisan—kawaláy salá,
katarung—wala'y hinalung-ong,
matarung

INNOCENT, adj. — waláng malay, waláng kasalanan — walay
salá—wala'y hinalung-ong, wala'y kasal-anan

INNOVATE, v.—baguhin, magbago—pagbag-o, pag-usab — bag-
ohón

INQUIRE, v. — magtanóng, mag-
usisà—pagsukót, pagsusi — ma-
kigasyud, mag-usisà

INQUISITIVE, adj.—mausisà, mapakialám—masukoton, mausisa-
hon—mausisaón, mahilabtanon

INSANE, adj.—ulól, sirâ ang ulo,
oalíw—buáng, kuwanggol — buang

INSANITARY, n.—marumí—ma-
hugaw, mahimi—kahigkoán

INSECT, n.—hayop na maliít na
waláng gulugód, kulisap na gaya ng langaw, bubuyog—diyutay nga mananap, buyóg, pak-
an—hayup nga magagmay

INSECURE, adj. — mapanganib,
mabuwáy—makuyaw, dili seguro—di-hilway, makatalagam

INSERT, v.—isingit — pagsal-ut,
pagsukip—isal-ut

INSIDE, n.—loób—sulód—sulód

INSIDE, adv.—sa loób, nasa-loób
—sa sulód—sa sulód

INSIST, v.—ipilit, igíít — pagpa-
mugós—piliton

INSISTENT, adj.—mámimilit, mapilit—malugoson, mapugsanon—
pagpamilit

INSPECT, v.—suriin, magsiyasat
—pag-usisa, pagsusi, paghiling—
usisaon, sayasaton

INSPECTION, n.—pagsusurì, pag-
bibisita—ang pakisusi — pagpa-
ngusisà, pagsayasat

INSPECTOR, n.—tagasurì, tagasiyasat — magsususi, tig-usisa—
inspektor, manog-usisâ

INSPIRATION, n.—inspirasyón — lamdaman—lalaumán

INSPIRE, v. — magbigáy-diwà — pagdasig—maglaum

INSTANCE, n. — halimbawà—pananglitan—halimbawà

INSTANT, n.—isáng sandalî—tipik sa panahón—isá ka tinión, gilayón

INSTEAD OF, prep.—sa halíp ng —inay, imbis sa—tigaylo sang, tingali

INSTINCT, n.—katutubong kilos o gawì—kinaiyang gawi—kinabubut-on

INSTITUTE, n.—instituto, pámulaan—tunghaan—instituto

INSTITUTE, v.—magtatág—pagtukod, pagtarok — magpatuk, magpasad

INSTITUTION, n.—kaugalián, paraán, pasanayán—kabatasanan, paagi, tulunghaan—kinabatasan, paagi, halanasán

INSTRUCT, v.—magturò — pagtudlo, pagsugo—magtudlò

INSTRUCTION, n.—pagturò—panudlo—pagtudlò

INSTRUMENT, n.—kasangkapan — galamiton, kasangkapan, tulonggon—kasangkapan

INSULT, v.—hamakin, insultuhín —pag-insulto, pagpakaulaw—insultohón, pakahuy-an

INSULT, n. — insulto, paghamak, pag-alipusta—pakaulaw, tamay, insulto—insulto, pahuy-an

INSURANCE, n.—seguro, katibayan—seguro sa kinabuhi kun butang—seguro sa kabuhi ukón butáng

INSURE, v. — iseguro, isakatibayan—pagseguro—ipaseguro

INTACT, adj.—buô, hindî nagágaláw—tibuok, wala kulangi—bugos, bilóg, walâ matandog

INTELLIGENCE, n. — katalinuhan, kaalam—salabutan, kaalam —kinaalam, kinaadman

INTELLIGENT, adj. — matalino, maalam—masinabuton, maalam, utokán — maalam, mahinangpanon

INTEND, v.—magbantâ, umakalà, mag-akalà—paghunahuna, pagtinguha — magbukò, magproponér

INTENSIFY, v.—pasidhiín, palubhaín—pagpainit, pagdasig — palutawón

INTENT, n.—hángarin, balak—tuyo, gikinahanglan—handum, tuyò

INTENTION, n.—iníisip, nais, intensiyón—tuyo, hunahuna — ginahunâhunà, ginahandum, intensiyón

INTER, v.—ilibíng, ibaón—paglubong—ilubóng

INTERCEPT, v.—harangin, hadlangán — pagtagbo, pag-atang—
lambatán, sugataón

INTEREST, n.—tubò, patubò, pag-
káwili, kawilihán — tubo, tung-
long, interes—interés, kawilihan

INTERESTED, adj. — interesado,
nagkákagustó—may-hilig, interesado—interesado, nakagusto

INTERLUDE, n.— pagitan—kapu-
lihay, tipik nga panahon—gin-
utlan

INTERIOR, n.—loób, looban—ang
sulod—sulód, kasudlan

INTERPRET, v.—isalin, ipaliwanag — paghubâd, pagbadbad —
lubarón

INTERPRETER, n. — taga-salin,
taga-paliwanag — taghubad,
maghuhubad—taglubád

INTERROGATE, v.—magtanóng,
itanóng—pagsukot, pagpangutana — magpamangkut, ipamangkut

INTERRUPT, v.—gumambalà, su-
mabad, gambalain—pagsakgaw,
pagsamok—sumamóng, umawát

INTERVAL, n.—pagitañ—kapuli-
hay, interbalo—gin-utlan

INTERVENE, v.—mamagitan, makialám—pagbabag, pagsalmot—
namalabag, nagpahilabót

INTO, prep.—sa, sa loób—sa sulod
—sa, sa sulód

INTOXICATION, n.—pagkalasíng,
kalasingan—kahubog — pagka-
hubóg, kahulugbon

INTREPID, adj. — waláng gulat,
matapang—maisug, mapintas —
wala'y ginahadlokán, maisug

INTRICATE, adj.—maguló, salí-
salimuót—gubut, makuti — magamó

INTRODUCE v. — magpakilala,
ipakilala—pagpaila — magpakilala, ipakilala

INTRODUCTION, n.—pagpapakilala—paila-ila—pagpakilala

INVADE, v. — lumusob, sumalakay, lusubin — pagsulong, pagdasdas—sumalakay

INVASION, n. — salakay, lusob,
paglusob—dasdas, sulong—salakay

INVENT, v.—umimbento, lumik-
hâ—pagmaugna — umimbento,
nagtukíb

INVENTION, n. — imbento, likhâ
—minugna—imbento, tukíb

INVENTOR, n.—imbentor, ang lu-
mikhâ—mamumugna — imben-
nagtukíb

INVEST, v.—maglagáy ng puhunan, maggugol—pagbutang puhonan—magbutáng sing puhunan

INVESTIGATE, v.—magsiyasat—pagsusi, pag-usisa—magsayasat

INVISIBLE, adj.—di-makita, nakatagò—dili makita — dî-makittan

INVITATION, v.—anyaya, paanyaya—pagdapit, agda—pangagda, pangdapit

INVITE, v.—mag-anyaya, anyayahan—pagdapit, pag-agda—magpangagda, magpangdapit

INVOLUNTARY, adj. — di-kusà, di-sadyâ—dili tinuyo—dî-hungód

INVOLVE, v.—magsangkót, isangkót, ihalò—paghiapil, paghisalmot—nahilabtan, nalamitá

INWARD, adv. — náloób, sa dakong loób—sa suIod, pailalum—nasulód, nasuók

IODINE, n.—yodo—tintura de yodo—yodo

IRE, n.—galit—kalagot, kasuko—akíg

IRON, n.—bakal, plantsa — puthaw, plansa—salsalon, plantsa

IRON, v.—mamalantsa — pagpamalansa—mamalantsa

IRREGULAR, v.—di-panáy — dili pong

IRRIGATE, v.—patubigan — pagpatubig—patubigan

IRRIGATION, n.—patubig—patubig sa uma—irigasyon

IS, v.—ay—mao ang—amó

ISLAND, n.—pulô, isla—pulo isla—pulû, isla

ISLE, n.—maliít na pulô — diyutayng pulo—diótay nga pulû

ISOLATE, v.—ibukód, pag-isahín—paglain, pagbulag — ituhay, isahón, lainón

ISOLATION, n.—pagkakábukód, pag-iisá—ang pagkalain, pagkabulag—pagkatuhay, paglaín

ISSUE, n.—usapín, labás ng páhayagán—tema sa lantugi, gula sa mantalaan — salabton, guâ sang pamantalaan

ISSUANCE, n. — pagpapalabás, pagbibigáy—pagpagula — pagpaguâ, pagdespatsar

ISTHMUS, n.—makitid na lupang nagkakabít sa dalawáng malawak na lupaín—pirasong yuta kasiwil sa lain—makitíd nga dutà nga nagaangót sa duhá ka malapad nga kadutaan

IT, n.—yaón, iyán, siyá—siyá, kaniya—inâ, ató, siá

ITCH, n.—katí, pagkatí, galís — katol, gilok—katúl

ITCHY, adj.—makatí—makatol — makatúl

ITEM, n.—isáng bagay sa tálaan—butang, ihap, usa ka bahin—isá ka butáng

ITS, pron.—kanyá—ang iyang — íya

ITSELF, pron.—yaón sa sarili o siyá sa sarili — iyang kaugali. ngon—siá sa kaugalingon

112

— J —

JAB, v.—dunggulín — **pagsuntok,** pagtudyok—huyapán

JACKFRUIT, n.—langkâ—**nangka** —langkà

JAIL, n.—bilangguan, piitan—**bi-langgoan, atub**—bilanggoan

JAIL, v.—ipiit, ikulóng, ibilanggo —**pagbilanggo**—ibilanggò

JAM, n.—matamís, miting, pulu-tóng—**matam-is,** duot sa kataw-han—dinulse nga prutas, kagu-tók sa trapikó

JAM, v.—barahán, pag-ipunan — **pagpiut, pagdutdotay** — kinagu-tok, binalabag

JANITOR, n.—tagapaglinis at ta-gaingat ng isáng bulwagan, di-yánitór—**maglilinis sa lawak-bu-hatan** — dyanitór, manogtinlò-opisina

JANUARY, n.—Enero, unang bu-wán ng taón—**Enero** — Enero, una nga bulan sang tuig

JAR, n.—gusì, bangâ—**tadyaw, ba-nga, tibud**—bangâ-bangà

JAR, v.—yanigín—pag-uyog, **pag-yogyog**—uygon

JARGON, n.—ingay, guló—**banha, sulting yagaw** — binansulì nga hambal, dì-tadlong nga hambal

JAW, n.—pangá — **apapangig** — sag-ang

JEALOUS, adj. — mapanibughuin, mapanaghiliín — **masinahon, abubhoan**—maimon

JEALOUSY, n.—panibughô, selos —**pangabubho** — kaimon

JEER, n.—pagtuyâ, pag-uyam — **yam-id, sulinga**—libák, tumboy, hikayan, buyayawon

JEER, v.—tuyain, tuksuhin—**pag-yam-id, pagsulinga** — paglibák, pagtumboy, paghikay

JELLY, n.—haleya—**haliya, gula-man**—haliya

JERK, n.—baltakín—**paglagnot** —itib-ong

JEST, n.—pagpapatawá—**pagtiaw, pagpatawa**—pagpakadlaw

JEST, v.—patawanin, biruin—**pag-lawón,** lahugón

JESTINGLY, adv.—pabirô — **sa pagpatawa**—palalahug

JEW, n.—Hudyó—**Hudiyo** — Hudi-yo

JEWEL, n.—hiyás, alahas — pahi-yas **ingon sa mutya, bulawan**—hiyás, alahas

JEWELER, n.—maghihiyás, mag-aalahás—**magbabaligya** mga pa-**hiyas**—manog-alahás

JILT, v.—itakwil, iyán—**pagsalik-way, pagbiya**—isikway

JINGLE, n. — kalansíng — **gag-mayng ingganay**—linagating

— K —

KERCHIEF, n.—panyô, takíp — panyo—panyò

KEROSENE, n.—petrolyo, gaás— gas, petrolyo—petrolyo, gas

KETTLE, n.—pákuluan ng tubig —kaldero—kaldero

KEY, n.— susì—yawi—yabi

KEYNOTE, n.—pambungad, tampók— panguna—panguna

KICK, n.—tadyák, sipà—sipa, tindak, patid—tindak, sipà

KICK, v.—sipain, paalisín—pagsipa, pagpatid—sipaon, tindakán, pahalinón

KIDNAP, v.—dukutin, itagò—pagdagit—kidnap, tabanon, kuoton

KID, n.— batang kambíng, batà— bata, kanding nati—tinday sang kanding, batà

KID, v.—biruin, lokohin—pagbinata, pagtiaw—lahugón, lokohon, intuón

KIDDING, n.—birò, panloloko — tiaw, pangomidya—lahúg, uloinintón

KILL, v.—pumatáy, patayín—pagpatay, pagluba — pumatáy, patyon

KILLING, n.—pátayan, pagpatáy —ang pagpatay—patyanay

KIN, n.—kamag-anak — kabanay, kadugo—kaparientehan

KIND, adj.—urì o klase, mabait, maawaín—matang, maluloy-on —sarî, klase, maluluy-on

KINDERGARTEN, n.—páaralán ng mga batang waláng pitóng taón—tunghaan sa kabataan — buluthoan sang kabataan nga kubós sa pitó ka tuig

KINDLE, v.—magsindí, magpaningas, susuhan—pagdagkot, pagpasiga — magsindi, magdabuk, gatongan

KINDLING, n. —pagpapaningas, ningas, sindí—dagkot, siga daub —pagpadabdab, dabadaba

KINDLY, aj.—maawaín, ayon sa kabáitan—pinaagi sa kaluoy — maawaon, mainunongon

KING, n.—harì—hari—harì

KINGDOM, n.—kaharián—gingharian—ginharian

KISS, v.—halikán—paghalok—halukán

KISS, n.—halík—halok—halúk

KITCHEN, n.—kusinà, lugál na pinaglúlutuan — kosina, luotan, abuhan—kusina, digamohán

KITE, n.—boladór, saringgola — banog-banog, tabanog—boladór, saranggola

KITTEN, n. — kutíng, maliít na pusà—gamitoy nga iring—kutî, diótay nga kuríng

KNAVE, v.—magdarayà — limbongan—madayà

KNEE, n.—tuhod—tuhod—tuhod

KNEEL, v.—lumuhód, luhód—pagluhod—lumuhód, luhód

KNELL, n.—tugtóg ng kampanà—tugtog sâ agoniyas—basál sang lingganay

KNIFE, n.—kortapluma, lanseta, kutsilyo—korta, lansita, kutsilyo—kortapluma, lansitas, kutsilyo

KNIFE, v.—kutsilyuhin, saksakin—pagdunggab, pagkautsilyo — lansitason, bun-on

KNIGHT, n. — kabalyero, taong mahál—kabalyero—kabalyero

KNIT, v.—maggansilyo — paggansilyo—magpangansilyo

KNOB, n. — tanganán ng pintô, umbók—gunitanan sa ganghaan

—uluyatán-pwertahan

KNOCK, n.—tuktók, katók—tuktok—-tuktok

KNOCK, v.—tumuktók, patumbahín — pagtuktok — tumuktok, tumbahón

KNOT, n.—buhól, bukó—baliktos, balighot—balû, bukó

KNOW, v.—unawain, alamín — paghibalo, paghisayud—hibal-an, hisayran

KNOWING, adj.—marunong, nakákaintindí—mahibalo, nasayud—nahibal-an, nahangpan

KNOWLEDGE, n.—kaalamán, karunungan—kahibalo, kaalam — kaalam, kinaadman

KNOWN, adj.—kilalá, tanyág — nailhan, inila — kilala, lutáw, dungganon

KNUCKLE adj. — sugpungan ng dalirì at kamó — kumo—kamumuo

— L —

LABEL, n.—tandâ, marká, taták—papel-timaan—etiketa, tandà, marka

LABEL, v.—tandaán, markahán—pagtimaan, pagmarka — etiketahan, tandaán, markahán

LABOR, n.— paggawâ, trabaho — buhat, trabaho — pagtrabaho, pagpamugon

LABOR, v. — magtrabaho, gumawâ — pagbuhat, paggama — magtrabaho, magpamugon

LABORER, n.—manggagawà, trabahadór — mamumuhat, mamumuo—mamumugón, trabahadór

LACE, n.—laso, panalì, puntás — laso, tagkos—laso, engkahi

115

LACE, v.—itali, ilaso — paglaso,
pagtagkos—ilaso, engkahian

LACK, v. — magkulang, walâ—
pagkulang—kulang, kulabos

LACK, n.—kawalán, kakulangán—
ang kakulang—kakulangán

LAD, n.—binatà, batang lalaki —
bata nga lalaki—ulitóo, batang
lalaki

LADDER, n.—hagdán, hagdanan,
panhikan—hagdan, hagdanan —
hagdanan

LADLE, n.—sandók, tikbô—luwag
—luwág

LADY, n.—babaing may dangál,
babaing marangál — babayeng
hamtong—babáeng mahipid, babáeng dungganon

LAG, v.—magpaiwan, magpahulí
— pagkabiya, pagka-iwit—magpabilin, magpaulihí

LAGOON, n.—maliít na loók o lawà—lo-ok, laguna—diótay nga
linaw, sapâsapà

LAID, v.—ilapag, ilagáy—pagbutang, paghilona—ibutáng

LAKE, n. — dagat-dagatan, loók;
lawà—lanaw, lin-aw—sapâsapâ,
linaw

LAMB, n.—kordero, tupang maliliít—karnerong nati — kordero,
karnero nga diótay

LAME, adj. — piláy, maiklî ang
isáng paá—piang, pungkol—piáng, malip-ot ang isá ka tiíl

LAMENT, v.—managhóy, manangis—pag-agulo, pagguol—manganduhoy

LAMENTATION, n.—panaghóy,
panangis—mga agulo, kaguol —
pagpanganduhoy

LAMP, n.—ilawán, lamparâ—suga, lamparahan—kingki, lampa-
rá

LAND, n.—lupà—yuta—dutà

LAND, v.—lumunsád, bumabâ sa
lupà — pagtakas, paglandig —
humugpà, dumungkà

LANDLORD, n. — kasero, ang
may-arí ng páupaháng bahay —
kasera, tag-iyag balay — kasero, tag-iya sang baláy-hinaka-
yán

LANDSCAPE, n. — tánawin —
talan-awon—talan-awon, danyag

LANE, n.—isáng makipot na daanan—dalan nga hagip-ut—banas

LANGUAGE, n.—salitâ, lenguahe,
wikà—pinulongan, sinultihan —
hambal, lenguahe

LANKY, adj.—mahabà, payatin—
gangkaw, mataas — malabà,
mayagpis

LANTERN, n.—paról—parol, suga
—paról

LAP, n.—kandungan, isáng pag-
ikit o inog—sabakan, pagtila —
sabak

LARCENY, n. — pagnanakaw, panguumít—pangawat, pangiriw —pagpangawat, panglapyà

LARD, n.—mantikà—mantika — mantikà

LARGE, adj.—malakí, malawak—daku, maluag — dakû, masangkad

LARGELY, adv.—kalakihán — sa kimadak-an—kadakuón, kasangkarón

LARK, n.—pamamasyál — pamasiyo—hulátlakát

LASH, n. — pamalò, palò, hiwà, hampás—bunal, ptuti, palo — putik, hampak, hiwà, lapdos

LASH, v.—hagupitín — pagbunal, pagpalo—pitkon, lapdosán

LAST, n.—hulí, katapusán—katapúsan, kaulahian—katapusan

LASTING ad.—pangmatagalan—malungtaron, matunhayon—kadugayón

LASSITUDE, n.—kapáguran—kakapoy, kalapoy—kapóy

LATE, adj.—hulí, ang. yumao — awahi, anhing — anhing. nakalumbos

LATELY, adv. — di-kátagalan, kailán lamang—dili pa dugay—sining karón lamang

LATER, adv.—lalong hulí, sa bandáng hulí—unya na, sa ulahi — ulihi kaayo

LATHER, n.—bulâ—buwa—bukól

LAUD, v.—purihin — pagdayeg, pagdayo—dayawon

LAUGH, n.—tawa—katawa—kadlaw

LAUGH, v.—tumawa—pagkatawa —kumadlaw

LAUGHTER, n.—halakhák—katawa, talidhay—harakhak

LAUNCH, v.—magsimulâ, pumasok—paglansad—magpapili

LAUNDRESS, n.—labandera, babaing tagapaglabá — babayeng manlalaba—labandera, babáeng manoglabá

LAUNDRY, n.—palabahan, paglalalabá—labhanan—palalabhan

LAVISH, adj.—masiyado, bukángpalad—mausikon — buhahâ

LAVATORY, n. — hugasán, labatoryo—hugananan, hilam-osan—hugasán, hilam-osán

LAW, n.—batás—balaod—kasugoán, layí

LAWFUL, adj.—makabatás, ayon sa batás — subay sa balaod—manglalayí. sunô sa layí

LAWLESS, adj.—waláng kiníkilalang batas—masupilon sa balaod—wala'y ginakilala nga kasugoán

LAWN, n.—damuhan—hawan, balilinhan—hilámnan

LAWNMOWER, n.—pamutol ng
damó—igtutupi sa balili—makiná sa panghilamón

LAWSUIT, n.—usapín, asunto —
asunto, buruka—asunto, kasabà

LAWYER, n. — abugado, mánananggól — manlalaban, abogado—abogado, mananabang

LAX, adj.—pabayâ, maluwág —
pinasagdan, huyang—uyayâ

LAY, v.—ilapág, ihigâ — pagbutang, paghiluna—ibutáng, pahig-
daón

LAZY, adj.—tamád, batugan—tas-
pukan, tapulan—matamad

LEAD, v. — manguna, nangúnguna, akayin—pag-una—manguna,
magpanguna, mag-ubáy

LEADER, n. — tagapaguna, punò,
lider—punoan, lider—lider, ma-
ngunguna, punòpunò

LEAF; n.—dahon—dahon—dahon

LEAFY, adj.—madahon—madahon
—madahonon

LEAGUE, n.—liga, samahan, kapisanan—liga, katiponan — liga,
kahut-ongán sang humalampang

LEAK, n.—tulò, butas—tulo—tulò,
lubót

LEAN, v.—sumandál, humilig —
pagkahilig, pagsandig — suman-
diay, sumandig

LEAN, adj.—payát, waláng lámán
—daut, niwang, yagpis— maniwang, hayát, kulakíg

LEAP, v.—lumundág, lumuksó —
paglukso—lumumpat, lumukso

LEARN, v.—mátutuhan, pag-aralan—pagtuon, pagkat-on — tun-
an

LEASE, v.—upahan sa malaong
panahón, paupahan—pag-abang
—hinakayan sa malawig nga pa-
nhón, hinakayán

LEASH, n.—talì, panalì—pisi, lu-
bìd—higút

LEAST, adj.—pinakamaliít — labing diyutay—labíng diótay

LEATHER, n.—balát—panit—panit

LEAVE, v. — mag-iwan, yumao,
umalís — paggikan, pagbiya —
ibilin, lumakát, naghalín

LEAVE, n.—pag-alís, pagyao —
hamubong bakasyon — paghalín,
paglakát

LECHEROUS, adj. — mapanipsíp,
magulang—masupsopon, alima-
tokon—manunugyot, toso

LECTURE, n.—panayám, pangaral — matulon-anong pamumu-
long—laygay, paathag, lektura

LECTURE, v.—mangaral, iturò —
pagpamulong, pagpañudlo —
manglaygay, magtudlò

LEER, v.—pitsarahan, irapan —
pagsiplat, pasiklap—papirután,
pahuloyán

LEFT, n.—kaliwâ—wala—walá

LEFT, v.—iniwan, naiwan—**pagbi-ya, lubiyaan**—binilin, nabilin

LEFT-HANDED, adj.—kaliwete—**walhon**—walís

LEG, n.—hità, bintî — paa—paa, hità

LEGACY, n.—mana, pamana—**kabilin**—sublì, panublion

LEGAL, adj.—ayon sa batás—**subay sa balaod**—sunô sa layí

LEGEND, n.—alamát — **leyenda,** kasugiran—gintunaan

LEGIBLE, adj.—mababasa — **mabasa**—mabasâ

LEGISLATE, v.—gumawâ ng batás—**paghimog balaod**—magpatuk sing layì

LEGISLATIVE, adj. — ayon o tungkól sa paggawâ ng batás, pambatás — **mahatungod sa pamalaod** — palatukán layí, balidharan

LEGISLATURE, n. — legislátura, kapulungang mambabatás—**dalam, balaoranan**—lehislatura

LEGITIMACY, n. — kapanganakang ayon sa batás—**pagkaanak nga tinuod**—kapanganakán

LEISURE, n.—mga sandalíng malayà—**panahong lingaw**—tinión nga wala'y obra

LEMON, n.—limón, dayap, kalamansí—**suwa, lemon**—limón, dalayap, kalamansí

LEND, v.—magpahiram, magpautang—**pagpahulam, pagpaulos** —magpahulám, magpautang

LENDING, n. — pagpapahirám, pagpapautang — **nagpahulam, nagpaulos**—pagpahulám, pagpautang

LENGTH, n.—habà—**gitas-on**—labà

LENT, n.—Mahál na Araw—**Kuwaresma, Mahal nga Adlaw**—Balaan nga Adlaw

LESS, adj.—kulang, lalong maliít —**kulang, labing diyutay** — kulang, kubós

LESSON, n.—aral, pag-aaralan — **pagtulon-an**—tulun-an, leksyon

LEST, conj.—baká sakaling — **tingali pa man**—basì pa lang, kubós na gid

LET, v.—pabayaan, pahintulutan —**pagtugot, pagpaabang**—pahanugotan

LETHAL, adj.—mapanganib—**makuyaw**—makatalagam

LETTER, adj.—liham, sulat, titik —**sulat, titik**—sulá:, letra

LETTUCE, n.—litsugas — **litsugas** —litsugas

LEVEL, n.—patag, pantáy—**patag,** tupong—patag, hanip, matapan

LEVEL, v.—patagin, pantayin — **pagpatag, pagtupong**—tapanon, patagon

LIBEL, n. — kasiraan, paninírang puri sa pamamagitan ng isáng lathalà—libelo, salang pakaulaw —libelo, binutig nga pagbantalà

LIBERAL, adj.—mapagbigay, liberal—manggihatagon — mahinatagon, liberál

LIBERATE, v.—palayain — pagluwas—hilwayón

LIBERTY, n.—kalayaan—kaluwasan, kagawasan—kahilwayan

LIBRARIAN, n. — tagapamahalà ng librerya o aklatan — tagdumala sa basahonan—librero tagtatap-tulun-an

LIBRARY, n.—basahán at páhiraman ng mga aklat, aklatan—basahonan—balasahán, libreriya

LICENSE, n. — pahintulot, lisensiya — pagtugot, lisensiya—lisensya, pahanugot

LICENSED, v.—pinahintulutan — tinugotan, lisensiyado—ginpahanugotan, lisensyado

LICK, v.—paghimod — pagtilap, pagparot—kusipad

LICK, n.—takíp, tungtóng — panilap—takúp, taklub

LIE, n.—kasinungalingan — bakak —kabutigán

LIE, v.—magsinungaling, mahigâ —pagbakak — magbinutig, maghigdà

LIEUTENANT, n. — tenyente — tenyente—tenyente

LIFE, n.—buhay—kinabuhi — kabuhì

LIFE-GUARD, n. — tagapagligtás —bantay sa kinabuhi—tagluáskabuhì

LIFT, v.—buhatin, mataás, itaás— pag-aisa, pagsakwat, pagbuswat —hakwatón, batakon

LIGHT, n.—ilaw, liwanag—kahayag, ilaw, iwag—sugâ, kasanag

LIGHT, adj.—magaan, marahan— magaan, hinay—mamag-an

LIGHT, v.—sindihán—pagdagkot, pag-iwag—sindihán

LIGHTEN, v.—gaanan, ilawan — pagpagaan—pamag-anán, sug-an

LIGHTNING, n.—lintík, kidlát — kilat, liti—kilát

LIKE, adj. — katulad, kapareho, kamukhâ, gaya—sama, maingoningon — katulad, pareho, kanawóng

LIKE, v.—nasain, magkaroón ng lugód — paghiangay, pagkagusto —handumón, luyag

LIKEN, v.—ipareho, itulad—paghisama, pagpareho — ipareho, itulad

LIKELY, adv.—marahil, maaring mangyari—hayan, tingali — nagakaanggid

LIKEWISE, adv. — gayón din, sakâ pa rin—ingon man usab—amó man, isá pa

LILT, n.—kiliti—gilok, magilokon—itik

LIMB, n.—sangá, hita, bintî, paá, kamáy—sanga, bahin sa lawas—sangá, hitâ, batíis, tiíl, kamút

LIME, n.—apog, bunga ng dayap, kabuyao—apog—apog

LIMELIGHT, n.—lente, liwanag—kahayag—lente

LIMITATION, n.—hanggahan, ta-takdaán—utlanan, hangturan — dulonan, talaksan

LIMIT, n.—hanggá—kinutoban — tubtob sa

LIMIT, v. hanggahán—pagsukod, pagisda—utlan

LIMITLESS, adj.—waláng hang-gán—walay utlanan, way sukod—wala'y dulonan

LIMPING, adj.—papilay-piláy — nagtakiang, piangon—pagpiangkul

LINE, n. — guhit, sapin sa loób, tandâ—badlit—kurit, hapín sa sulód, tandâ

LINEAGE, n.—labî, pinagmulán—kaliwatan—kaliwat, gingikanan

LINEN, n.—lino, de ilo—de ilo—lino, de ilo

LINGER, v. — magtagál, magpa-ikut-ikot — paglangay-langay—maghukmong, maglisngadlisngad

LINGERING, adj.—matagál, pa-ulit-ulit — malangay-langayon, laygay—manglisngad

LINGUIST, n.—dalubhasà sa wi-kà—batid sa mga pinulongan—sampaton sa hambal

LINK, n.—dugtóng, tuláy — lang-gikit, dugtong—sugpon, talabid

LINK, v.—pagdugtungín, tulayín, pag-abutin—paglanggikit, pag-dugtong—sugponón, talabiron

LION, n.—león, mabangís na ha-yop—liyon—león

LIONIZE, v.—pagkalipunpunán—pagpasídungog — pagsalosalohan

LIP, n.—labì, ngusò—ngabil, wait—bibíg

LIQUID, n.—anomang malambót at tumutulo, likidó, lusáw—tu-big, likido—likidó

LIQUIDATION, n. — pagsasará, pagbibilí — pamaligyang hutda-nay—paglikidár, pagbayaráy

LIQUOR, n.—alak, inuming maka-lalasíng—alak, bino—alak, ilim-non nga makapahubóg

LIST, n.—talaan, sulatan—talaan, listhan—listahan

LIST, v.—italâ, isulat, ilistá — pagtala, paglista—isulát, ilista

LISTEN, v.—makiníg, pakinggán —pagpamati, pagpatalinghog — mamatì, pamatian

LITERACY, n. — karunungan sa pagbasa at pagsulat — kahibalo sa pagsulat-basa—kinaadman sa pagsulát kag pagbasa

LITERATE, adj.—marunong bumasa at sumulat—mahibalo sa pagsulat-basa — mahibaló magsulát kag magbasa

LITERATURE, n. — literatura o mga gawang isinulat, pánitikán —katitikan, literatura — literatura, panulát

LITTLE, adj.—maliít — diyutay, gamay—diótay

LIVE, v.—mabuhay, mamuhay, tumirá — pagpúyo, pagkabuhi — mabuhì, mangabuhì

LIVELY, adj.—buháy, maliksi — sadya, abtik, lagsik — kabuhì mapagsik

LIVELIHOOD, n.—kabuhayan — panginabuhi—kabuhian

LIVER, n.—atáy—atay—atáy

LIVESTOCK, n. —alagang mga hayop—hayopan—hinuptan nga mga hayup

LOAD, v.—ikargá, ipasán, ilulan, dala — pagluwan, pagkarga — ikarga, ipapas-an, ilulan

LOAF, n.—tinapay na malakí, parang unan, pan Amerikano — pirasong pan—tinapay nga dakû, daw ulonan, pan amérikano

LOAN, n.—pautang, pahirám — utang- hulam—pahulaman

LOAN, v.—magpautang, magpahirám — pag-utang, paghulam— magpahulám

LOATHE, v. — mayamót, isumpâ, pandirihan—pagdumot, pagkasilag—magkataká, maghilayô

LOATHESOME, adj.—nakapandidiri, kasumpá-sumpá — masilagón, madumtanon—talak-an, hililayoán

LOBBY, n.—hintayan, patayuan— tindoganan, hulatanan—hulatan

LOCAL, adj.—ukol sa poók o bayan na kinaroroonán, pampoók —mahatungod sa kaugalingong dapit—lokál, natungód sa puók ukón banwa

LOCATE, v.—hanapin, maglagáy —pagpangita, pagbulong — pangitaon

LOCATION, n.—kinároroonán, ki nálalagyán—nahimutangan, dapit—kinahamtangán

LOCK, n.—tranká, kandado, susí —yawihanan, trangka—trangka, kandado, pitalâ, yabihán

LOCK, v.—isusí, itranká—pagyawì, pagtrangka — ikandado, itrangka, ipitalâ

GREAT, adj.—dakilà, malakí, kahanga-hangà—daku, bantugan—ungganon, dalayawon

GREATNESS, n. — kalakhán, kadakilaan—kadaku, kabantug — kadungganon, kadalayawon

GREEDY, adj. — masakím, matakaw, timawà—hakog, daló—dalúk, hakabán

GREEN, adj. — berde, luntian — lunhaw, berde—berde, lunhaw

GREET, v.—batiin, salubungin — pagtimbayá—pangibulahanan

GREETING, n.—pagbatì, pagsalubong—timbayá — pagpangibulahan

GRIEF, n.—kalungkutàn, dalamhatì—kasakitan, kasub-anan — kasulub-on

GRIEVANCE, n. — sumbóng, dalamhatì—sumbong, reklamo — pagbatás, pagkalisúd

GRIEVE, v.—magdalamhatì, malungkót—pagsubò — magbatás, magkalisúd

GRILL, v.—iihaw, tanungín nang másinsinan—pag-usisa, pagsusisusi—usisaon, pisápisahon

GRIN, n.—ngitî, ngisi—ngisi, tingsi, yuhom — yuhóm, ngisi, barangisí

GRINNING, v. — nakangisi — nagpahiyum, nagtingsi — nakangisi, nagabarangisí

GRIND, v. — gilingin, dikdikín — paggaling—galingón, dukdukón

GRINDER, n. — tagagiling, gilingán, dikdikan—galingan—galingán, dulukdokan

GRIP, n.—pisíl, hawak—pig-it — pisíl, kaptan

GROAN, n.—daíng, ungol, hinagpis—agulo, muló, pangagho — ugayong, ingus

GROGGY, adj.—lasíng, hiló — lipóng, hubóg, nagsapinday — hubóg, naling-an

GROSS, adj.—magaspáng, matindí —halhag, napulogduha ka dosena—mabahúl

GROUND, n.—lupà—yuta, pasikaran—dutà

GROUP, n. — lupón, pulutóng — pundok, panagtapok—hubón, gubán

GROVE, n.—kakahuyán—kakahoyan—kakahoyan

GROW v.—tumubò, sumupling — ang tubo, ang tinuboan—tumubò, sumingíl

GROWTH, n.—pagtubò, tubò—ang tubo, ang tinuboan — pagtubò, tubò

GUARANTEE, v.—garantiya, garantisahan, sagután — pasalig, garantiya—garantiya, pasalig

GUARD, n.—bantáy, talibà—bantay, magbalantay—bantay

GUESS, n.—tantiyá, hulà—banabana, tagna—pakút

GUEST, n.—bisita, panauhin—dinapít, pinasidunggan — dumuluaw, bisita

GUIDE, n. — patnubay, tagaakay, tagaturò—giya, magtutultol — ubáy, tuytoy

GUIDE, v.—akayin, turuan, patnubayan—pagtultol — ubayán, tuytoyán

GUILD, n. — sámahan, kapisanan —katiponan, kapunongan—katilingban, talapoanan

GUILE, n.—pang-akit, panloloko, panghibò—lansis, lumáy—panglumáy, pasalíg-salig

GUILT, n.—kasalanan — kasalanan—kasal-anan

GUILTY, adj.—maykasalanan, salarín—ang tagsala, makasasala —makasasalà

GUILTY, adj. — maykasalanan, makasalanan—may sala, sad-an —may kasal-anan

GUISE, n.—balatkayô—takuban— kunókuno

GUITAR, n. — gitara, kudyapî — sista, gitara—gitara

GULLIBLE, adj. — tangá, madaling lokohin, mapaniwaiaín—matuhotuhoon—ilintuon

GUN, n.—baríl, sandata — pusil, luthang—luthang, rebolber

GURGLE, v. — magmumog, magbanláw ng bibíg—paglimogmog —pangalimóg

GUSH, n.—butas, tulò—pugsit sa tubig—lubót, tulò

GUST, n.—halip, bugsô, (ng hangin)—huyop sa hangin, hoyuhoy—dalimuos

GUTTER, n.—kanál, alulúd—kanál—kanál, sagbotan

— H —

HABIT, n.—ugali, gawî, kasúutan —batasan, gawi—ugalì, kinabatasan

HABITABLE, adj.—maáaring tirahán—kapuy-an—mahimò puyan

HABITUAL, adj.—karaniwan, palagian—nabatasan, naandan — kanaandan, hulukmongan

HAD, v.—nagkaroón — pagkaduna —nakahupót

HAG, n.—matanda, mangkukulam —barángan nga tigulang, usikán —tigulang, manoghiwít

HAGGARD, adj.—payát, malalim ang matá—lapóy, hagó, laglum ug matá—layát, madalum ang matá

HAIL, n. — batî, pagsalubong — pagtawag, pagtimbayá — pangibulahan

HAIR, n.—buhók—buhok, balhibo —buhók

HAIRDRESSER, n. — tagapagayos 'ng buhók—tag-atiman sa buhok—taghipid sang buhók

HAIRPIN, n.—ipit sa buhók—kimpit sa buhok—kimpit sa buhók

HALE, adj.—malusóg, mabuti ang katawán — baskug, maayog lawas—mabukod, matibunog

HALF-BRED, n.—mistiso—mestiso, kulibog—mestiso, kalibugán

HALF-HEARTED, adj.—malamíg, malambót—bugnaw, way-kaikag —mapainumuron, mapaulubson

HALF-PAST, n.—kalahatî, medya —labay sa katungá—tungâ ang nakapasár

HALF-WIT, n. — luku-lukó, sirásirâ, utu-utô — angól-angól, hangál-hangál—buangít, ilintuon

HALL, n.—pulungán, sala, bulwagan, pasilyo—hawanan, sala sa balay—sala, kadak-an, salapulán

HALT, v.—pahintuín, pigilin—paghunong, pag-undang—padulogon

HALT, n.—hintô, pigil — hunong, undang—dulog

HAM, n.—hamón—hamón—hamón

HAMMER, v.—pukpukín, martilyuhín — pagdukdok, pagpakáng —martilyohón

HAMMER, n.—martilyo, pamukpók—martilyo, pakáng—martilyo

HAMMOCK, n.—duyang yantók—duyan—duyan

HAND, v. — ibigáy, iabót — pagabut, pagtunol — ihatag, iduhol, itunghol

HAND, n.—kamáy—kamut — kamút

HANDKERCHIEF, n. — panyô, panyolito—panyo, pahíd—panyò

HANDFUL, adj.—isáng dakót, kauntî, sandakót—usa ka pudyot —isá ka hakúp

HANDLE, n. — tanganan, hawakán, pakialamán—puan, kaptanan, pagkupot — kalaptan, pakaw, hilabtan

HANDMADE, adj.—gawâ sa kamáy—binuhat sa kamut—buhat sa kamút

HANDSOME, adj.—magandá, matikas—ambongan, barugan—mabuot

HANDY, adj.—madalíng gamitin kung ibig—daling gamiton—mahapós gamiton

HANDWRITING, n. — porma ng pagsulat, sulat-kamáy — agi sa kamut, sinulatan — porma sa pagsulát, agi sa kamút

HANG, v.—ibitin, magbitin, isampáy—pagbitay—isablay, ihaláy

93

HANGER, n.—sabitan — sab-itan, sablayan—salab-itan, sablayan

HANGING, n.—sampáy, bitin — mga binitay, sinablay — sablay, kabit

HAPLESS, adj. — sinásamâ, kulang-palad—kinabsan sa palad— wala'y palad, kinulabos

HAPPENING, n. — pangyayari— hitabó—kahitaboan

HAPPILY, adv. — kabutihang palad, buóng kasáyahan—kamalipayon—kamalipayon

HAPPY, adj. — maligaya, masayá —masayá, malipayon — malipayon, masadya

HARBOR, n. — punduhan ng sasakyán, takbuhan, silungán — pundohanan sa barko—dungkaan

HARBOR, v. — pumundó, tumabí, sumilong, waláng diñáramdám o samâ ng loób—paglungót-lungót, paghambin—dumungkà

HARD, adj.—matigás, mahirap — magahi, malisud—matig-a

HARDEN, v. — patigasín — pagpagahi—pinatig-a

HARDSHIP, n. — kahirapan, paghihirap—kalisdanan, paglisud-lisud—kahul-anan

HARD-UP, adj.—waláng-walâ, nagígipít—naglisud, pit-os — kulabos, nawad-an

HARDLY, adv. — may kahirapan, bahagyâ nang—lugos, may-kalisud—halóshalusón

HARDWARE, n.—mga kasangkapang bakal—kasangkapang puthaw—mga kasangkapan nga salsalon

HARDY, adj. — malusóg, malakás —kusgan, gahi-on, lig-on — makusog, matibunol

HARK, v.—makiníg, pakinggán— pagpamati, pagpaminaw — magpamatî, pamatian

HARM, n.—kapinsalaan, masamâ, kasamaán—kadaut, kadautan — kalaglagan, kalainan

HARMONY, n. — pagkakasundô, pagkakatugmâ — panagduyog, panagbagay — paghangpanay, paghilirup

HARMONIOUS, adj. — pagkakásunduan, tahimik — mabagayon, maduyogon — paghinangpanay, paghinirupáy

HARNESS, n.—singkáw, riyenda —gwarnasyon, rinda—ryenda

HARSH, adj.—bastós, tampalasan, mabagsík — harás-harás, parásparás—bastos, harásharás

HARVEST, n. — ani — ting-ani, tingpupó—ani

HARVEST, v.—umani, mag-ani—
pag-ani—mag-ani, mangani
HAS, v.—mayroón, may — aduna,
may—may arà, may
HAS-BEEN, n.—dati-rati—lawós,
miagi na—sadto anay, sadto'ng
pilá lang
HASTE, n.—pagmamadalî, kabig-
laán—ang pagdali-dali, apura —
pagdalî-dalì, hakûhakù
HASTEN, v.—magmadalî, dalí-da-
liin, biglaín—pagdali. pag-apura
—dalián, aporahón
HASTY, adj. — nagmámadalî, pa-
biglá-bìglâ — madali-dalion —
pagsakû-sakû
HAT, n.—sumbrero, sambalilo —
kalo—kalù
HATCH, v.—pisaín—pagpisó—luo-
ban agád mapusâ (sa mga itlog)
HATE, v.—magalit, mapoót—pagdumot, kasilag, kawalay-gusto
—magpangakig
HATEFUL, adj.—nakaíinís, nakapópoót—madumtanon, kadumta-
nan—makaalakig
HATRED, n.—poót, galit, pagka-
inís — dumtanay, kasilagay —
dumót, pagkataká
HAUGHTY, adj.—hambóg, mapagmataás—hambug, mapahitas-on
—hambog, bugalón
HAUL, v.—hila, hilahin, batakin—
pagbitad, pagguyod — bitaron,
butongon, guyoron

HAVE, v.—magkaroón, mayroón,
may—pagkaduna, adunay—mag-
hupót
HAWK, n.—lawin—banug, uwak—
dapáy
HAY, n.—ginikan, dayami—daga-
ming layá—dagami
HAZARD, n.—kagipitan, hadláng
—balda, babág, kalisdanan—makatalagam
HAZY, adj. — malabò, maulap —
mahalap, gabonón — malubog,
masagil-um
HE, pron.—siyá (lalaki)—siya (lalaki)—siá (lalaki)
HEAD, n.—ulo, pangulo, pángu-
luhán—ulo, pangulo, punoan —
ulo, pangulo, punò
HEADACHE, n.—sakít ng ulo —
labad sa ulo—sakít sang ulo
HEADED, v.—patuloy, patungo—
paingon, padulong, pinangulohan
—padayon, padulong
HEADING, n.—ulo, panguna, mu-
la, pamuhatan—ulohan—tig-uló,
tituló
HEAL, v.—gamutín, pagalingín—
pagbulong, pagtambal—bulngon,
paayohon
HEALTH, n.—katáyuan o kalágayan ng katawán, kalusugán —
panglawas—ikaayong-lawas

95

HEALTHY, adj. — waláng sakít, malusóg — maayog-lawas, baskug — wala'y balatian, matambok

HEAP, n.—tambák, buntón — tipun-og, lagundok, tambak—hantal, tinumpokan

HEAR, v.—makiníg, pakinggán — pagpatalinghug, pagpamatí — mamatí, pamatian

HEARD, v.—ibalità, ipahayag — nadungog, gindungog — ibalità, ipahayag

HEARING, n. — paglilitis, pakikiníg—husay, pagusisa — pagkità, pagpamatí

HEARSAY, n.—balità, katá-katâ, tsismís — tahó, asoy-asoy, sulting-hatúd—binalità, katâkatà

HEART, n.—pusò, gitnâ—kasingkasing, kinataliwad-an—kasingkasing, tagipusuon, ubod

HEARTY, adj.—nasa pusò, masayá—kinasingkasing — makinasingkasingon, masadyahon

HEAT, n.—init, kainitan—init, kainit—init, kainit

HEATHEN, n.—pagano, dî kumíkilala sa tunay na Diyós—irihis, walay-Dios—pagano, dî nagakilala sa tunay nga Diós

HEAVE, v.—itaás, iangát—pag-alsa, pagbaswat, pagsakwat — pataason, paangkatón

HEAVEN, n. — langit, kalangitán —langit—langit, kalangitan

HEAVENLY, adj. — makalangit, napakainam — langitnon — langitnon

HEAVY, adj. — mabigát, matimbáng—mabug-at—mabug-at

HECKLE, v. — tuyaín, lokohin, kantiyawán — pagsuliyaw, pagsugsog—libakón, buangon, lahugón

HEDGE, n.—bakod na halaman—pagsuliyaw, pagsugsog, — palpal sang tanúm

HEED, v.—mag-ingat, makiníg — pagpamatí, pagtagad — maghalong, mamatí

HEEDLESS, adj.—waláng ingat—walay-pagtagad, danghag — buhahâ, dî-mainandamon

HEIGHT, n.—taás, kataasan—gitas-on—taas, kataasan

HEIR; n. — tagapagmana—manunurod sa kabilin (lalaki)—manunublì

HELL, n.—impiyerno, párusahán ng mga makasalanan—ispidno—impierno

HELL-CAT, n. — mapaghigantí, mangguguló — babayeng dumianon, barangán—manghimalús

HELLO, inter.—kumustá, hoy — komosta, hoy—kamusta ka, ma-ano-ano ka man, hálo

HELP, n.—tulong, pagdamay, abuloy—hinabang, panabang — bulig, unongan, amutan

HELPFUL, adj. — matulungín, maalalay—matinabangon, mabuligon — mabinuligon, mainunongon

HELPLESS, adj.—waláng magawâ, waláng katulong, mahinà—pinasagdan, way-mahimo — wala'y mahimò, wala'y igkasangkul

HEN, n.—inahín (sa manók)—himungaan—mungâ

HENCHMAN, n. — tauhan, katulong—sakop, katabang —·tináo, kabulig

HEN-PECK, adj. — talú-talunan, kayang-kaya—manandis, daug—ilisgan

HENCE, adv.—buhat ngayón, dahil dito—busa, tungod niini—sugod karón, tungód siní

HER, pron.—siyá (babae) — siya (babaye)—iya (babáe)

HERD, n.—kawan, pulutóng—panon sa hayop—kahayupan

HERD, v.—itabóy, kulungín—pagpundok, pagtapok—tabugon, bukuton

HERE, adv.—dito—dinhi, diri — dirí

HEREAFTER, adv. — buhat ngayón—sukad karon, sa umaabut —sugod karón

HEREBY, adv. — sa pamamagitan nitó—uban niini, ania lakip — sa kalalangan siní

HERETOFORE, adv.—dati — sukad niadto—sadto

HERITAGE, n.—mana, pamana—kabilin, masunód—panublion

HERMAPHRODITE, n.—binabaé —bayot, babayen-on — binabáe, agî

HERNIA, n.—luslós—tuyob, supot —kagisón, torion

HERO, n.—bayani—bayani — baganihán

HEROIC, adj.—bayani, magitíng—bayanihon—pagkabaganihán

HERPES, n.—buni, katí — bun-i, sakit sa panit—empiene

HERSELF, n.—so kanyáng sarili (babae) — iyang kaugalingon (babaye) sa iyá kaugalingon (babáe)

HESITATE, v.—mag-atubili, mag-alala — pag-ukon-ukon, pagpanagana—mangduhaduha

HESITATION, n. — pag-aalala, pag-aatúbili — ukon-ukon, panagana—pagpangduhaduha

HEW, v.—ukitin, putulín—pagsiak, pagbugha—lukiton, sib-akón, wasayon

HIBERNATE, v. — magpalipas, magparaán—pagpalabay sa panahon—magpaligad

HIDE, n.—balát, kuwero—pagtago, panit sa mananap — panit,
kuwero

HIDEOUS, adj.—nakatátakot, na-
kagúgulat — makapalimbawot,
mangilngig—makahaladlok, ma-
kakululbà

HIGH, adj.—mataás, matayog —
mataas, mahabog—mataas

HIGHBROW, adj. — marunong,
mataás — mahibalo, maalam —
mangin-alamon, mataas sing agtang

HIGHWAY, n.—lansangan ng bayan, kalsada, daán—nasudnong
dalan, karetera—nakawaán nga
dalan

HIKE, v.—maglakád, lumakad —
pagbaklay, tiniil nga lakaw —
maglakát, maglupâ

HILARIOUS, adj.—mapagpatawá,
masayá — masaya-on, kataw-
anan—masadya, makahalam-ot

HILL, n.—buról, muntíng bundók
—bungtod, puntod — pukadtód,
banglid

HILLOCK, n.—punsó — gamayng
bungtod, laundok—bakolód

HILLSIDE, n.—sa tabí ng buról—
kiliran sa bungtod—sa kilid sang
bungsod

HILT, n.—tatangnán, hawakán —
pu-an sa espada—uluyatán, pakaw

HIM, pron.—siyá, sa kanyá (la-
lake)—siya, kaniya (lalakí) —
siá, sa iya (lalaki)

HIMSELF, pron.—sa sarili niyá—
iyang kaugalingon (lalaki) — sa
iya kaugalingon (lalaki)

HIND, n.—hulihán, sa likód, usáng
babae—sa likoran, sa luyo — sa
likúd nayon, usá nga babáe

HINDER, v. — abala, abalahin,
hadlangán—pag-ulang, pagbalda
—awatón, punggan

HINDMOST, n. — káhulí-hulihan,
kulalat — sa kaulahian, labing
iwit—kaulihian, kulihót

HINT, n.—paalaala, senyas — pasambingay — pahanumdum, sinyas.

HINTERLAND, n. — kalagitnaan,
ilaya—kalasangan, kailayahan—
katung-anan, ilayá

HIP, n.—pigî—hawak, bat-ang —
balikawáng

HIRE, v.—upahan — pag-abang,
abangan—suholan

HIS, pron.—kanyá—kaniya (lalaki)—iya, sa iya

HISS, v.—sumutsót — pagsusot,
paghuthot — sumutsot, sumitsit,
nanagutsot

HISTORICAL, adj. — makasaysa-
yan, boses—salaysayon, kaaginhon—maragtason

HISTORY, n.—kasaysayan — kasaysayan—kasaysayan

HOBBY, n.—paglilibáng, katuwaan, líbangan—kalingawan, libángan—kalingawan

HOG, n.—baboy—babuy—baboy

HOLD, n.—hawak, pigil — gunit, kupót, kaptan, huptan — kapút, pugóng

HOLD, v. — pigilin, hawakan — pagpugong, paggunit — kaptan, punggan

HOLDER, n. — tagatangan, sisidlán—maghuhupot—tagkapút, suludlan

HOLE, n.—butas — lungag, buhó, bangág—buhò-

HOLIDAY, n.—pistà, araw na pangilin—pangilin, kapistahan — pista, adlaw sang pagpahuway

HOLLOW, n. — hungkág, waláng lamán—haguka, walay-sulod — bangkak, wala'y unód, gweko

HOLY, adj.—banál, madásalin — balaan, santos — balaan, matinuohon

HOLY THURSDAY, n.—Huwebes Santo—Huwebes Santo—Huebes Santo

HOME, n.—táhanan, sariling bayan—balay, pinuy-anan—baláy, kaugalingon nga banwa

HOMELY, adj. — pangit, karaniwan, hindî mapagpanaóg — malaksot, panimalaynon—balaynon

HOMEWORK, n. — gáwaing-bahay, leksiyón—buluhaton sa balay, leksiyon—buluhatón sa baláy, leksion

HONEST, adj.—tapát, di-sinungaling—ligdong, dili bakakon, dili limbongán — tampad, matamparon

HONEY, n.—pulut-pukyutan—dugos—dugós

HONOR, n.—dangál, puri, karángalan—dungog, kadungganan—kadungganan, dungóg

HONOR, v.—parangalán, igalang — pagpasidungog, pagtahud — padunggan, tahuron

HONORABLE, adj. — marangál, dakilà — halangdon, madungganon—talahuron, halangdon

HOOD, n.—takíp ng ulo, takíp—pandong sa ulo—takúp sa ulo

HOOF, n.—kukó ng hayop—kuko sa mananap—kukó sang hayup

HOOK, n.—kalawit, pangalawit — tagá, kaw-it—bunít, ganso

HOP, n.—luksó, kandirít—lukso—tintin, lukso, tumbò

HOP, v.—lumuksó, kumandirít — paglukso — lumukso, tumintin, tumumbò

HOPE, v.—umasa, asahan—paglaum, laum—paglaum

HOPELESS, adj. — waláng pagasa, waláng ináasahan—walaypaglaum—wala'y paglaum

HORDE, n.—kawan, lipon—**panón** —kagubanán

HORIZON, n.—lugál na parang tagpuan ng langit at lupà—**ka-punaw-punawan** — sulobangan, bulutlakan

HORN, v. — sungay, pansuwág — **sungay, budyong**—sungay, budyong

HORRIBLE, adj. — nakapangingi-labot, nakatátakot o nakasísindák—**makalilisang, makahahadlok**—makangilidlis, makakulugmat

HORROR, n.—sindák, kilabot — **kalisang, kuyaw** — makahaladlok, makasiligni

HORSE, n.—kabayo—**kabayo**—kabayo

HORSEBACK, n.—likód ng kabayo—**likod sa kabayo**—likúd sang kabayo

HOSE, n.—medyas, gomang pandilíg—**midyas, bomba sa tubig**—medyas, goma nga inogbunyag

HOSPITAL, n. — ospitál; bahay-págamutan—**tambalanan, ospital**;—ospitál, bululngan

HOST, n.—óstiyá, ang may panauhin, pulutóng—**ostiyas, tag-alagad sa bisita**—ostiyá, tagbaláy

HOSTILE, adj. — galít, mapanlabán—**mabatukon, masupilon** — akíg, masuayon

HOT, adj.—mainit, maapóy, mapusók—**mainit, init**—mainit, nagahingalayó, masupog

HOTBED, n.—pinamúmugaran — **yutang iabunog mga tanum** — salab-ogan

HOTEL, n.—otél, bahay-túluyan—**otel, balay-abangan**—otél

HOUR, n.—oras—**takna** — oras, teknà

HOUSE, n.—bahay, tirahan—**balay, puy-anan**—baláy, puluy-an

HOUSEHOLD, n. — sambahayan, bahay — **panimalay, sulod-balay** —panimaláy

HOUSE OF REPRESENTATIVES, n.—Kapulungan ng mga Kinatawán o Mambabatás—**Balay sa mga Tinugyanan, dalam**—Kamara de Representantes

HOVEL, n.—kubo, barung-barong —**bayong-bayong, payag** — payág

HOW, adv.—paano, gaano—**unsaon, unsa na**—paano, anó

HOWEVER, adv.—gayón man, kahit ganoón—**bisan pa niana, bisan unsaon**—sa amó man, bisán subóng

HOWL, n.—ungal, hagulgól, sigáw —**ulang sa iro, ta-ól** — taghol, uwang

100

HUGE, adj.—malakí—daku kaayo —dakú

HUE, n.—kulay—bulok—lugóm

HUG, v.—yapusín, yakapín—paggakus, paghakop—hakson

HUM, v.—humuni, umawit nang marahan — paglaylay, paghagonghong—mag-ugóy-ugoy

HUMAN, n.—tao, maka-tao—tawo, tawhanon—táo, táohanon

HUMBLE, adj.—mapagpakumbabâ—mapaubsanon — mapainubuson

HUMID, adj. — basá-basâ, namámasâ—humód, basa-basa — basâ-basâ

HUMOR, n.—kondisyón, pagsisistì, katatawanán — kataw-anan, makapatawa — kahalam-otan, kaladlawan

HUMOROUS, adj.—masayá, palatawá, mapagpatawá — katawanan, makapatawa — makahalam-ot, makapakadlaw

HUMPED, adj.—hukót — makahadlok—makalilisang

HUNCHBACK, n.—kubà — buktot —buktot

HUNDRED, n.—isáng daán o sandaán—usa ka gatus—gatús, ginatús

HUNDREDTH, adj.—ika-isangdadaán, daán o ikasandaán—gatusan, ika-gatus—gatusón

HUNGRY, adj. — gutóm, nagúgutom, nanánabík — gutúm, gigutom—gutóm, magulutmon

HUNK, n.—malakíng piraso, bahagi—dakung-buok — dakú nga kihád ukón hiwâ

HUNT, v. — mangaso, mamaríl, maghanap—pagpangayam, pagpangita — mangayám, mangluthang

HUNTER, n. — mángangasó, mámamaríl — mangangayam — mangngayám, mangluluthang

HURL, v.—ihagis, ipukól—pag-itsa, pagsalibay—ihabyog, ipukol

HURRAH, inter.—mabuhay, sigáw ng tagumpáy — singgit sa kalipay, mabuhi—mabuhì, kabáy pa

HURRY, v.—magmadalî, bilisán—pagdali, dalia—dalián

HURRY, n.—pagmamadalî — ang pagdali—pagdalî

HURRY AND SCURRY, n.—kaguluhan—kaguliyang sa pagdinali —dalî-dali

HURT, v. — saktán, pasakitan — pagsamad, pagdaut — sakitón, samadon

HURTLE, v.—mamahagis, manilapon—pagbuagya sa pagkabangga, paglagpot — masihón, síkulón

HUSBAND, n.—asawa (lalaki) — bana—bana

HUSH, v.—tumahimik, magpatahimik—paghilum—paghipos

HUSH, n.—katahimikan, dî pag-galáw — **kahilum, kamingaw** — kahiposan, wala'y tingog

HUSK, n.—bunót, balát ng niyóg —**bunot sa lubi**—bunót

HUT, n.—kubo, dampâ—**payag** — payág

HYBRID, n.—mistiso — **kulibog,**

mestiso — mestiso, kalibugán

HYMN, n.—awit, kantá—**alawiton, kalantahon** — imno, kalantahon, pungsodnon

HYPOCRITE, n.—mapagkunwarî, mapagbalatkayô — **tigpagawal, inapihigon** — manogpakunóku-no, mahinaguón

— I —

ICE, n.—yelo—**yelo**—yelo

ICE CREAM, n.—sorbete—**sorbe-te, pabugnaw**—sorbete

ICY, adj.—malamíg, parang may yelo—**bugnaw, daw may yelo** — inabugnaw, daw may yelo

IDEA, n. — kuru-kurò, palagáy inisip—**mitna, idiya**—hunâhunà, kaisipán

IDEAL, adj.— mithî, minímithî uli-rán—**mithi, tinguha, sulundon** — sulundan, huaran

IDENTICAL, adj. — magkatulad, magkapareho—**managsama,** pa-riho— magkatulad, magkaanggid

IDENTIFY, v. — kilalanin, suriin, sinuhin—**pag-ila, pagtino**—kila-lahon, sayasaton, pasin-ohón

IDIOM, n.—kawikaan, kasabihán — sulultihon, pinulongan — ka-tinagaán hurubaton

IDIOTIC, adj.—hangál, malukulu-kó **hangal-hangal, pulpol** — bu-angit, hanginón

IDLE, adj.—batugan, tamád, bu-lakból — **taslakan, bulakbol** — tamád

IDLENESS, n.—katámaran, pag-bubulakból—**katapol, kataslak**—katamarán

IDOL, n.—idolo, diyús-diyusan —**idolo, diyos-diyos** — idolo, díos-dios, dulódiwata

IDYLLIC, adj.—marikit sa pani-ngín, ukol sa buhay-bukid—**bu-kidnon, lansangnon** — mahandu-rawon, umanhon

IF, conj.—kung—**kon**—kon

IGNITE, v.—pagdingasin, sindihán —**pagdagkot, pagpakayo**—paka-rábkarabon

IGNOMINY, n.—kahihiyán, kasi-raán — **kaulawan, kapildihan sa dungog** — kahuluy-an, pakahuy-an

IGNORANCE, n. — kamangma-ngá —**kaburóng**—kamagoán

IGNORANT, adj. — mangmáng, mulalà—burón, hubó sa kaalam —mangô

IGNORE, v.—dî-pansinín, abaín — pag-iway, pagsikway, di-tagdon —dî-pagsapakon

ILL, adj.—may sakít, malubhà — masakíton, balatianon—masakitón

ILL-BRED, adj.—di-nag-aral, waláng-galang — musimos, walay-bangkaagan, way-tahud—wala'y tinun-an

ILL-CONCEIVED, adj. — masamángparaán—mangil-ad pagkaisip—malain nga padugì

ILL-DISPOSED, adj.—masamáng ugalì, may-kasamaan — hilig sa demonyo, dautag batasan—malain sing pamatasan

ILLEGAL, adj.—labág sa batás, malî—supak sa balaod — batok sa kasugoán

ILLEGITIMATE, adj. — labág sa batás, di-ipinahíhintulot — sukwahi sa balaod, anak sa gawas —batok sa kasugoán, anák sa luás

ILL-GOTTEN, adj.—ninakaw, masamáng pinagmulán — kinawat, tinikas—kinawatan

ILLITERATE, adj.—dî marunong sumulat at bumasa, di-nag-aral —dili makasulat ni makabasa—dî-makahibaló magsulát

ILL-MANNERED, adj. — masamáng ugalì—dautag-gawi—malain sing batasan

ILLUSTRATE, v.—ipaliwanag sa pamamagitan ng larawan o halimbawà—paghulagway — ipahayag sa kalalangan sang laragway ukón halimbawà

ILLUSTRATION, n. — larawan, halimbawà—hulagway, larawan, dibuho—laragway, pananglitan

ILL-NATURED, adj.—bugnót, talipangan—putong, pikon—pikón

ILLUMINATE, v. — ilawan, liwanagin—paghayag, sug-an—sugay, 'pasanagan

ILLUSION, n.—maling akalà, panaginip—handuraw, damgo—sayúp nga pagtuo, damgohanon

IMAGE, n.—larawang-diwà, larawan—larawan—larawan

IMAGINATION, n.—gunitâ, guniguní —. handurawan, palandong —hunâhunà, handuraw

IMAGINE, v.—gunitaín, ipalagáy —paghanduraw, pagpalandong— hunáhunaon, handurawon

103

IMBECILE, adj. — mapuról, sirá-sirâ—buangón, pulpol—mahabul

IMITATE, v.—gayahan, parisan—pagsundog, pag-awat—ilogon

IMITATION, n. — huwád, pággagaya — hinulad, minaomao — huád, inilog

IMMACULATE, adj.—malinis, dalisay—malinis, mahinlo—matinlô, dalisay

IMMATURE, adj.—batà pa, murà—bayong, linghod pa — lamhagaya — hinulad, minaomao — huád, inilog

IMMEDIATE, adj.—kagyát, agád—diha-diha, karon-dayon—gilayón

IMMEDIATELY, adv. — kaagád, kapagdaka—sa labing madali — sa gilayón

IMMENSE, adj.—malapad, malakí, waláng hanggán — halapad, dakuan uyamot — malapad, wala'y dulonan

IMMERSE, v.—ilubóg, ilublób — paglubóg, pagtuslob — itugdang

IMMIGRANT, n.—imigrante, dayuhan, pumasok sa ibáng bayan upáng manirahan — lumaiangyaw — mangluluntad, manglulugayaw

IMMINENT, adj.—dárating, nálalapít — umalabut, nagkaduol—ginapaabót-abót

IMMODEST , adj. — masagwâ, bastós—bastos — masaw-a, bastos

IMMORAL, adj.—waláng-hiyâ — walay-ulaw-law-ayan — wala'y huyâ, mahigkò ang kaisipán

IMMORTAL, adj.—waláng kamátayan—matunhayon, way-kamatayon—wala'y kamatayon

IMMOVABLE, adj. — di-magaláw, —waláng-damdám — dili-malihok—dî-matióng, dî-mahulag

IMMUNITY, n.—ligtás sa, katángian, kaligtasan — ang kadilitakdan—hilway sa, kahilwayan

IMP, n.—pilyo, salbáhe—salbahis nga bata—banihót, retobado

IMPART, v.—magbigáy, ipahayag, iturò — pagtudlo,. paghatag — maghatag, magbahin, ipahayag, itudlò

IMPAIR, v.—pahinain — pagdaut, pagluya—pahináy-hinayon

IMPASSABLE, adj. — di-maráraanan—dili-kaagian — dî-maagyan, wala'y alagyan

IMPASSIVE, adj.—makaharì, matigás, waláng-damdám. — makiharion, walay-pagbati — harianon, matigdas, wala'y halatyagon

IMPATIENT, adj.—yamót, waláng pagtitiis, di-matiyagâ — walaypailub — kataká, wala'y pagbatás, matinalak-on

IMPEDIMENT, n.—hadláng, sagabal—balabag, balda — balabag, awát

IMPENDING, adj.—dumáratíng—umaabut—manog-abót

IMPERSONATE, v.—katawanin—pagpanundog sa tawo — hikayan, libakón

IMPERTINENT, adj.—waláng galang, waláng halagá—walay-dapat, way-tahud—wala'y katahurán. wala'y bilí

IMPORT, n.—kalakal na galing sa labás ng bansá o ibáng bansá—kabtangan gikan sa laing nasud —importe, balaligyaon gikan sa luás

IMPORT, v. — bumilí ng kalakal ng ibáng bansá — pagpasulod produkto gikan sa gawas—magbakál gikan sa luás

IMPORTANCE, n. — kabuluhán, kahalagahán — kahinungdanon —kinahanglan

IMPORTANT, adj. — mahalagá, makabuluhán—hinungdanon, bilílhon — kinahanglanon, kamapuslanon

IMPOSE, v.—mag-atang, igíít — pagpahamtang sa lugos — duholan

IMPOSSIBLE, adj.—di-maáari, di-magágawâ—di-mahimo, di-mabuhat—dî-mahimò, dî-mabuhat

IMPOVERISH, v.—papaghirapin—paghimog, timawa, pagkabus — paantusón

IMPRESSION, n.—impresiyón, taták, kuru-kurò, kakintalán—patik sa hunahuna — pakút-pakut, impresyon

IMPRESS, v.—itakdâ, pilitin, ikintál—pagmarka, pagpatik — tímbrehán, bag-ohón, husayon

IMPROVE, v.—pabutihin, ayusin, baguhin—pag-usbaw, pag-uswag —paayohon, bag-ohón, husayon

IMPROVEMENT, n. — pagiging mabuti, gasulong, pagbabago — kausbawan, kauswagan—pag-uswag, pagbalhin

IMPURE, adj.—marumí, di-malinis, di-wagás — mahugaw, dili lunsay—mahigkò, dî-dalisay

IMPUTATION, n.—binténg, akalà — pagpasangil, ang pasangil, butang-butang — butáng-butáng, han-an

IN, prep.—sa loób, sa—sa, sulod sa—sa sulód, sa

INBORN, adj.—likás, kinágisnán —kinaiyanhon—kinabun-agán

INCENSE, n.—insiyenso—insenso, kamanyang — insenso, kamangyan

INCH, n.—pulgada (2.54 centimetro)—tudlo, pulgada — pulgada, dalî

INCIDENT, n.—pangyayari—hita-bo—pagkahitabô

INCIDENTALLY, adj. — di-sinásadyâ—sa wala tuyoa — dî-hungód

INCITE, v.—sulsulán, pag-initin—pagsugyot, pag-init — sugyotón, paakigon

INCLINATION, n.—hilig, gustó—hilig—duyóg

INCLINE, v.—yumukô o iyukô — pagyukó, paghirig — pagkatakilid, pagkaduyóg

INCLUDE, v.—isama, ilakip—paglakip—ilakíp, ibuylog

INCOGNITO, v. — di-kilalá—wala magpaila, di-paila — kamalamalahán, dî-nakilala

INCOHERENT, adj. — waláng liwanag, malabô — nagkayungit, nagkayabag—dî-nagaalalangot

INCOME, n.—kiníkita, sahod—pinangitaan, kinitaan — kinitaan, suhol

INCOMPARABLE, adj. — waláng kapareho, waláng katulad o kaparis—talagsaon, way-kaparis—wala'y katulad

INCOMPETENT, adj. — di-marunóng, waláng-kaya—dili-takus—dî-makahibaló, wala'y ikasaráng

INCOMPLETE, adj.—di-hustó, kulang—kulang—dî-husto, kulang

INCREASE, n.—pagdami, paglaki, dagdág—dugáng. punó — padamuon, dugangan

INCREASE, v.—damihan, dagdagán—pagdugang, pagpunó — dugangan

INCREDIBLE, adj. — di-mapaniwalaan, di-totoó—dili-katuhoan, bakak—dî-mapatihan, dî-matuod

INCURABLE, adj.—waláng paggalíng—walay pagkaayo — wala'y kaayohan

INDECENT, adj. — mahalay—malaw-ay—masaw-a

INDEED, adv. — tunay ngâ, siyá ngâ—tinuod, bitaw, diay — amó inâ

INDEFATIGABLE, adj. — masipag, waláng pagod—mapanlimbasugon, way pagkaluya—mapisan, wala'y pagkataká

INDEFINITE, adj.—malabô, waláng katíyakan—walay piho, hanap—wala'y kapat-urán

INDENTION, n. — urong, pasok, palugit sa, marhen sa kaliwâ—marhin, blangko sa walang tampi sa papel—isul, ipasulódsulód, antad sa walá

INDEPENDENCE, n. — kasarinlán, paglayá, kalayaan — kaugalingnan—kaluásan

INDEPENDENCE DAY, n.—Araw ng Pagsasarilí—Adlaw sa Kaugalingnan — Adlaw sang Kaluásan

106

LOCKJAW, n.—paninigás o pagsasará ng pangá—**panggahì sa apapángig** — sag-angón

LOCOMOTIVE, n. — mákiná ng tren—**makina sa tren** — makiná sang tren

LOCKUP, n. — pansamantaláng kúlungan—atub—kitaypuni nga bukotán

LODGE, n.—kapisanan, táhanán, tuluyan — **balay-abutanan** — lingkuran sa sine

LODGE, v.—tumirá, tumulóy — **pagpuyo, pagloklok** — magpuyô, magdayón

LOFTY, adj.—mataás, marangál —**hataas, malayog, dunggganan**—mataas, bugalón, kataasón

LOG, n.—kahoy na malakíng pinutol, troso—**kahoy, troso**—troso

LOGIC, n. — pangangatwiran — **pangatarungan** — lohiká, sandigan sang pagpangatarungan

LONE, adj.—nag-íisá—**nag-inusara**—isahanon

LONELY, adj.—nag-íisá, malungkót—**nag-usara, nagsubo** — isá isa, mamingawon

LONESOME, adj. — malungkót, di-makalí—**mamingawon** — mamingaw, masinulub-on

LONG, adj.—mahabà, nasaing mataimtím, matagál—**taas, mataas** —malabà, kadugayón

LONGSHOREMAN, n.—kargadór o mambubuhat ng mga kargá ng bapór—**kargador, maghahakot**—kargadór ukón manoghakwat sang karga sang bapór

LOOK, n.—itsura, **ayos—tan-aw**, panagway—itsura, dagway

LOOM, n.—habihán—**hablanan** — hablon

LOOP, n.—salabíd, silò—**laang, higot sa laang**—siúd, pinil-an, salabayán

LOOSE, adj. — magkalág, maluwág, di-nakatalì — **maluag, nakabuhì**—hubaron, nakabuhî, nalugakán

LOOSEN, v.—luwagán, pakawalán —**pagluag**—hugakán, buy-an

LOOT, n.—nakaw, pinagnakawan —**kinawat**—kawat, kawatan

LORD, n.—Panginoóng Diyós—**Ginoo, Makagagahum** — Ginuong Diós, Makaakò

LOSE, v. — mawalâ, magwalâ — **pagkawala, pagkapildi**—pagkapierde, pagkaparút

LOSS, n.—pangulugi, pagkawala —**kawad-on, kapildihon** — pagkapierde

LOT, n.—pitak ng lupà, kapalaran —**pirasong yuta, palad**—lote nga dutà

123

LOUD, adj. — maingay, matunóg, malakás—matunog, maşaba — magahud, magansal

LOVE, n.—pag-ibig, pagmaınahál —gugma—paghigugma, pagpalanggà

LOVELY, adj. — kaibig-ibig, magandá — matahum, maanyag — mahigugmaon, magayón, maambong

LOVER, n.—mangingibig, kásintahan, kaligawán — hinigugma — manoghigugma, hinigugma

LOW, adj.—mababà, dukhâ—hamubo, ubos—manubô, kubós

LOYAL, adj.—tapát na loób—maunongoh—tampad ang buót

LOYALTY, n.—pagtatapát, katapatan—ang kamaunongon—pagkatampad, kabunayag

LUCK, n.—kapalaran, suwerte — kapalaran, swerte — kapalaran, swerte

LUCKY, adj. — mapalad, masuwerte — palaran — mapalaron, may swerte, palaran

LUDICROUS, adj.—katawá-tawa —kataw-anan—makahalam-ot

LUMBER, n. — tablá, kahoy na malakíng naputol — tabla, kahoy ng ginabas—tapì, siniadsiád nga tapì

LUMP, n.—bukol, katipunan, umbók—bugon—bukól, lanóg

LUNATIC, n.—ulól, sirâ ang isip —buangon, hangal — buangít, rendido ang ulo

LUNCH, n.—tanghalian—paniudto —panyaga

LUNG, n.—bagà—baga—bagâ

LURE, v.—akitin, dayaiŋ—pagbihag, pagdani—buyukon, budhián

LURE, n.—pang-akit, patibong — pamihag, panglumay — pangbuyok, pangpaón

LURK, v.—manubok, magbantay —pagpanuop, pagbantay—manilag, maningadsingád

LUSH, adj.—makatás, matabâ — supang, daghag duga—madugà, malubod

LUST, n.—kahibuan, kayamuan, luho—kaibug, gana—hingabót

LUSTER, n.—kináng, kabantugán kumináng — kasilaw, kidlap — masilì, sililawán

LUXURIANT, adj.—marami, makakapál—malabong — madamò, dagayà

LUXURIOUS, adj.—maluho, mabisyo—maluho, mahal — mabisyoso, luhoso

LUXURY, n.—bisyo, luho—kaluho —bisyo, luho

LYE, n.—lihya—lihiya—lihiyá

— M —

MACHINE, n.—mákiná—makina —makiná

MACHINERY, n. — makinarya. kasangkapan — mahitungod sa makina—makinaryas

MACHINIST, n.—makinista—makinista—makinista

MAD adj. — napópoót, nalóloko. nagágalit — nabuang, napungót —buángbuáng

MADAM, n.—ale, ginang—ginang —tyâ, ginang

MADDEN, v.—napoót, nagalit.— pagkabuang, pagkasukó — nagsalimuáng

MAGAZINE, n.—mágasín o bodega ng baril at pulburá—magasin, luklókan sa bala—magasín. bodega sang rebolber ukón polborá

MAGIC, n.—engkanto, salamangká — salamangka — madyik, mahikó, salamangka

MAGICAL, adj.—engkantado, kaakit-akit — ingkantohanan — engkantado, enkantohanon

MAGICIAN, n.—salamangkero — salamangkiro — salamangkero, madyikero

MAGISTRATE, n. — mahistrado, hukóm—mahistrado, maghuhukom—mahistrado, hukóm

MAGNATE, n.—mayaman, mataás na tao—sapian, tawong halangdon — manggaran, dungganon nga táo

MAGNET, n.—batobalani—batóbalani—bato-balani

MAGNETIZE, v.—akitin — paglipong, paglimot—balanion

MAGNIFICENT, adj. — napakagandá, dakilà — matahum uyamot — tuman katahúm, tuman kadungganon

MAID, n.—dalagita, babae utusán—dalaga — dalagita. babaé, suluguón

MAIDENLY, adj.—mahíyain mabini — maulawon — mabuyaon, matahapon

MAIL, n.—koreo, mga liham—koriyo, sulat—koreo, mga sulat

MAIL ORDER, n.—bílihan sa koreo—panugon pinaagi sa koriyo —koreo, palanagtagan-sulát

MAIN. adj. — pangulo, panguna, gitnâ ng dagat — nag-una, mangulo—tig-uná, kalalawran.

MAINSTAY, n.—taga-kandilí, lakás—sinaligan—tagsakdag

MAINTAIN, v. — umalalay, kumandilí, kumupkóp — pagbaton, paghupot — magsakdag. maginakúp

MAINTENANCE, n. — sustento, abuloy, pagkandilí — sustento, alíma—sustento, ginasagúd

MAJESTIC, adj. — dakilà, marangál, mataás—halangdon, harianon, — dungganon, lutáw

MAJESTY, n.—karángalan, kataasán — kaharianon, kataasan — kadungganan, kalutawán

MAJOR, adj., n.—higít ang kalakihán, tungkuling mataás sa kapitán—labawg bahín, opisyal sa kasundalohan—kapín ang dinakoan, komandante

MAJORITY, n.—nakarárami, karamihan—kadaghanan, kinabagan—kadamoan

MAKE, v.—gumawâ, yariin—pagbuhat, paghimo—magbuhat, humanón

MAKE, n.—urì, pagkakagawâ, yarì—matang, pagkabuhat — sarî, pagkabuhat

MAKER, n.—tagagawâ — tagbuhat, taghimo—tagbuhat

MAKESHIFT, adj.—pansamantalá—minantinil—tigtalal-us

MAKE-UP, n. — ayos pagbabago, pampagandá—paanyág sa dagway — maninguhâ, make-up, magpaanyag

MALE n.—lalaki—lalaki—lalaki

MALEFACTOR, n.—salarín, kriminál, aliktiyá — makasasala—dalakpon, kriminál

MALCONTENT, adj.—di-nasísiyahán—dili-tagbaw—dî-naayawan

MALEDICTION, n.—sumpâ, denunsiya—maldisyon, pagtunglo—sulumpaon, sulubulón

MAN, n.—tao, lalaki—tawo, lalaki—táo, lalaki

MAN, v.—pangasiwaan, táuhan—pagmaniho — dumalahan

MANAGE, v.—mangasiwà, pangasiwaan — pagdumala — pagadumalahan, tatapon

MANAGER, n.—tagapangasiwà — magdudumala — manogtatáp

MANDATE, n.—utos, pahayag — sugo, baód — sugò, mando

MANGROVE, n —bákawan — katunggan—bakhawan

MANGLE, v.—durugin, hiwain — pagdugmok, pagwatás-watás — lapâlapaón

MANHOOD, n.—kabinataan, pagkalalaki—pagkalalaki — pagkahamtong (lalaki)

MANICURIST, n. — manikurista, tagapag-ayos ng kukó—manikurista — manikurista, tagtatapkukó

MANIFEST, n.—pahayag, pakita—pahayag, katin-awan — pabutyag, manipesto

MANIFOLD, adj. — marami, ibá-ibá—daghan, ubay-ubay — madamò, sarîsarì

MANIPULATE, v.—hawakan, huwarín, huwarán — pagmaniho, pagpaagi—maniobra, hinikutan sa kamút

MANKIND, n.—sangkatauhan — katawhan—pagkatáohanon

MANNER, n.—pinag-aralan, mabuting ugali, kabutihang ugalì—pamatasan — tinun-an, pinanilagan

MANSION. n.—malakíng bahay—dakung balay—puly-anan

MANSLAUGHTER, n.—di-sinásadyáng pagpatáy—pagpatay ug tawo—dî-hungód nga pagpatáy

MANTLE, n.—sapín sa dulang o sa mesa—hapin sa lamisa—mantil

MANUAL, adj.—gáwaing-kamáy—kinamut nga buhat — hilikutón sa kamút

MANUFACTURE, n.—gawâ, produktọ, yarì—ginama, binuhat — dawdaw, produkto

MANUFACTURE, v.—gawín, yariin—paggama, pagbuhat—magdawdaw, magprodukto

MANUFACTURER, n. — tagagawâ, tagayarì — manggagama — tagdawdaw, tagprodukto

MANY, adj.—marami—daghan — madamò

MAP, n.—mapa—mapa — mapa

MARBLE, n.—marmól — marmol —marmol

MARCH, n.—Marso — Marso — Marso

MARCH, v.—magmartsa, lumakad ng kademiya—pagmatsa — martsa

MARE, n.—kabayong babae—kabayong bayé — kabayo nga babáe

MARGIN, n.—gilid, tabi—daplin, tubo—kilid, higád

MARITAL, adj.—tungkól sa pag-asawahan—mahitungod sa pag-asawa—natungód sa pag-asawaháy

MARK, n.—tandâ, marká, taták—marka, patik — marka, tandà, timbre

MARKET, n.—pámilihan, palengke, tiyangge—tiyanggihan—tindahan, merkado

MARKET, v. — ipagbilí, itindá—pagtinda, pagpaniyanggi — ibaligyà, itinda

MARRIAGE, n.—kasál, pag-aasawa—kasal, kaminyoon — kasál, pag-asawaháy

MARRIAGEABLE, adj.—panahón ng pag-asawa—mahimong mangasawa—panahón sang pagpangasawa

MARRY, v.—mag-asawa, magpakasál—pagpangasawa, pagkasái
mag-asawa ukón magpamana,
magpakasál

MARTYR, n. — martir—sinakit,
martir—martir

MARVELOUS, adj.—kahanga-hangà, kataka-taká—kahibudngan
—katingalahán

MASCULINE, adj. — panlalaki—
bahin sa lalaki—panglalaki

MASK, n.—máskará, panakíp ng
mukhà—taptap, maskara—mas-
kará

MASON, n.—kantero, kasapi sa
masónerya—masón, panday sa
tisa — kantero, manogkalapati-
semento

MASONIC, adj.—tungkól sa mga
masón—mahatungod sa Masón
—natungód sa mga Masón

MASQUERADE, n. — balatkayô
dispras—lispras—disprás, sapút
sa saut nga dî-makilal-an

MASS, n.—misa, tumpók—Misa—
misa

MASSACRE, n.—patayan—pamatay ug daghan—patyon

MASTER, n. — panginoón, ulo,
pag-aralan—agalon, amo — agalon, ulo, tun-an

MASTER, v.—málamang ganáp na
ganáp—agalon, amo — agalon,
ulo

MASTHEAD, n.—palo ng sasakyán, bahagi na nagsásaád ng
halagá ng páhayagán buwán-bu-
wán o taún-taón, ang pangalan ng páhayagán at ang nagmámay-arì—palo sa sakayán, ulo-
hán sa mantalaan — palo sang
bapór, tig-ulong dinalán sang
pamantalaan

MAT, n.—baníg, latag—banig—
baníg, pahirán

MATCH, n. — pósporó — posporo,
indigay, sangka—posporó

MATCH, v. — pagbagayin, ilapat,
iagpáng — pagbagay, pagparis,
pagparang—ibagay, isibù

MATE, n.—kasama, opisyál sa sasakyáng dagat, asawa—kauban,
katipon—kaupod, opisyal sa bapór, asawa

MATERIAL, n. — kasangkapan,
sangkáp—igdadapat, kasangkapan—kasangkapan

MATERIALISTIC, adj. — malabis
na mapaghangád sa salapî —
makisapi, mahilig sa kwarta—
kapín ang paghandum sa pilak

MATERIALIZE, v. — maganáp, magkatotoó — pagkatuman — matabô, mamatud-an

MATTER, n.—bagay, kadahilanan —butang—butáng, pamalibad

MATTER, n.—lamán, usapín, bagay—unod, butang, sultihanan —unód, kasabà, butáng

MATTRESS, n.—kutsón—kultson —kutson

MATURE, adj.—magulang, sapát sa gulang, mahihinóg na—gulang, hamtong, hinog — gulang, sibù sa gulang, bangkalawagón

MATURITY, n.—kapanahunán — kagulang, kahamtong — kapanahonán, tigpanahón

MAUL, v. — bayuhín, durugin — pagbukbok, pagmakmak — bayhon, dukdukón

MAY, n —Mayo —Mayo—Mayo

MAYBE, adj.—bakâ sakalì, marahil—tingali, kaha—ayhan, basì pa lang

MAYFLOWER, n. — Bulaklák ng Mayo—mga Bulak sa Mayo — Bulak sa Mayo

MAYOR, n.—alkalde, punò — alkalde, pamuno-lungod — alkalde

MAXIM, n.—kawikaan, kasabihán —panultihon, suloltihon — hurubaton

MAZE, n.—salí-salimuót — agtanang likoliko, .labirinto — katingalahán

ME, pron.—akó, sa akin—ako, kanako—akó, sa akon

MEADOW, n. — damuhán, lupang patag—balilinhan, patag—patag, halalban

MEADOWY, adj.—madamó, patag —puno sa balili, patagon—patag, madamong hilamón

MEAL, n.—pagkain—pagkaon — pagkaon

MEAN, adj. — mababà, bastós— bastos, dautan—malwan, bastos

MEANDERING, adj.—palikú-likô —naglikoliko—palikûlikù

MEANING, n.—kahulugán — kahulogan—kahulogán

MEANTIME, adv. — sa pagitang panahón, samantala—samtang— samtang nga

MEANWHILE, adv.—samantala, habang—camtang—samtang sa

MEASLES, n.—tigdás — dapdap, pamuto, lisay—tipdas

MEASLY, adj.—nakákahiyâ—akakaulaw—makahuluyà

MEASURE, n.—sukat, panukat, takalán—sukod — takús, talaksan

MEASURE, v.—sukatin, takalin— pagsukod—takson, sukbon

MEAT, n.—lamán, karné — unod, karne—karne

129

MECHANIC, n.—mekánikó, ukol sa mákiná—mekaniko—mekanikó, natungód sa makiná

MEDAL, adj.—medalya—medalya —medalya

MEDDLE, v. — makialám, makisangkót—pag-apil-apil — pagpahilabót

MEDDLING, n. — pakikialám — apil-apil, samok-samok — pahilabtan

MEDICINE, n.—gamót, lunas — tambal, bulong—bulóng

MEDITATION, n. — pagwawarì, pagninilay—pagpalandong, paghinuktok — pagpasibûsibù

MEDIUM, n.—paraán, kainaman —paagi, kasarangan—paagi, kasarangan

MEEK, adj. — maamò, mababang loób—maaghop—mahagúp, mabuot

MEET, v.—magtagpô, magkita — pagsugat, pagtagbo, paghibalag —magkitaáy, magtaboay

MEETING, n.—pulong, pagtatagpô, miting—tigum, miting—miting, pulongpulong

MELANCHOLIC, adj.—malumbayin, malungkutin → masulob-on masub-anon—masinulub-on

MELODY, n.—melodiya, himig— paningog, tono, awit—melodiya

MELT, v.—magtunaw, matunaw— pagtunaw, paghilis—tunawon

MELTING, adj. —. tunawan, poók ng paghahalu-halò — nagkatunaw, nagkahilis—tunawán

MEMBER, n.—kaanib, kagawad, kasapì—sakop, kaanib—katapo

MEMBERSHIP, n. → pag-anib, pagkakasapi — ang pagkasakop, pagkakaanib—pagtapò

MEMBRANE, n.—lamad—manipis nga panit—lanyatlanyat

MEMORIAL, n.—alaala, handóg— handumanan, bungdo — handumanan

MEMORIZE, v.—isaulo, tandaán, kabisahín—pagsab-ulo — isaulo,

MEMORY, n.—alaala — handurawan—handumanan

MENACE, n.—panganib—hulga — katalagman

MEND, v. — magkumpuní, magtagpî, pabutihin—pagtapak, pagayo—kaayohon

MENDICANT, n.—pulubi, nagpapalimós—maglilimos, palimos — pobre, nagapakilimós

MENDACIOUS, adj.—mapagkailá —bakakon—malikumon

MENTION, n.—pagbanggít—hisgut, paghisgut—hinambitán

MERCENARY, adj. — mukháng kuwarta—makisapi—makipilak

MERCHANDISE, n.—panindá, kalakal—tinda, baligya — inogtin-
da, balaligyà

MERCHANT, n.—mángangalakál
—magpapatigayon — mamaligyà, negosiante·

MERCIFUL, adj.—mahabagín, habág—maluloy-on, manggiluy-on
maluluy-on, maawaon

MERCILESS, adj.—waláng awà—
walay puangod, mabangis—wala'y kaawà

MERCY, n.—awà, kaawaan, habág—kaluoy, puangod—awà, kaluoy

MERE, adj.—lamang, panáy—lamang—lamang, pulós

MERGER, n. — pagsasama, pag-
iisá — pag-ipon,. panag-ipon -
pagtilingub

MERIT, n.—halagá, karapatán —
bili, merito—bilí, kamahalon

MERITORIOUS, adj.—mahalagá,
karapat-dapat — bilihon, dalaygon — malahalon, bagay gid

MERRY, n.—masayá—sadya, malipayon—masadya

MESSAGE, n.—pabalità, pasabi,
kalatas, mensahe — sulat, mensahe, pahayag—mensahe, paha-
túd

MESSENGER, n.—utusán, sugo—
sinugo—mensahero, taghatúd

METAPHOR, n.—pagpaparis, pagtutulad—kahularan — pagpapa-
reho, pagpaanggid

METEORIC, adj.—biglâ, mabilís
—kalit, kilatnon—hinalì, maabtik

METER, n.—metro, panukat —
metro, sukod—metro, barahán

METHOD, n. — paraán, kapara-
anan—paagi — paagi, padugì

MICROSCOPIC, adj.—nápakaliít,
di-mákilala—labihan kadiyutay
—tuman kadiótay, dî-mákilala

MIDDLE, n.—gitnâ, kalagitnaan
taliwala—tungâ, katung-anan

MIDNIGHT, n.—hatinggabí — tu-
ngang-bagli—tunga'ng gab-i

MIDST, n.—kalagitnaan, gitnâ —
kinatung-an, tunga-tunga—katung-anan, tungâ

MIDWIFE, n.—hilot, komadrona
— mananabang — manoghilút,
paltera, komadrona

MIGHT, n.—kapangyarihan, lakás
Kusog, gahum — kagamhanan,
ikasaráng

MIGHTY, adj.—malakás, makapangyarihan — kusgan, gamha-
nan — makagalahum, makasaráng

MIGRATORY, adj.—palipád-lipád,
lipat-lipat—balhin-balhin — pa-
sulosaylo, pabalhin-balhin

MILD, adj.—mahinay, malamíg—
mahinay, malumo—suabe, mabugnaw

MILDEW, n.—tagulamín — agup-
op—tagiptip

MILE, n.—milya, 1760 talampakan
—milay—milya, 1760 ka tapak

MILEAGE, n.—dami ng milya —
milyahan—milyahe

MILITANT, adj.—laging handâ—
kanunay andam—pirmeng handà

MILITARY, adj.—tungkól sa hukbó sa lupà—sinundalo, militar-
hangawáy

MILITATE, v.—labanan, lumaban
—pagbatok — nagabatô, naga-
away

MILK, n.—gatas—gatas—gatas

MILK, v.—gatasan—gatasan—gatasan

MILKFISH, n.—bangós — bangos
—bangus

MILL, n.—gilingán—galingan—ga-
—lingan

MILLER, n.—manggigiling, tagagiling—maggagaling — manog-
galing, taggagalíng

MILLING, v.—gumigiling—paggaling—nagagalíng

MILLION, n.—angaw—milyon —
milyon, ramak

MILLIONAIRE, adj.—milyonaryo
—milyonaryo—milyonaryo

MILLIONTH, adj.—ikaisáng mil-
yón—ikamilyon—ikaisá ka milyon

MIMIC, n.—manggagaya—manu-
nundog—mang-ilog

MIND, n.—isip—kaisipan—isip

MIND, v.—pansinín — pag-isip,
paghunahuna—sapakón

MINE, pron.—akin—ako, akoa —
akon

MINE, n.—lugál na pinanggalingan ng gintô o ibáng metál—
minahan—mina, dulangán

MINER, n.—magmimina, tagakuha ng gintô o ibáng metál—minero—minero, mangdudulang

MINGLE, v.—makihalò, makisama
— pagsagol, pagpakigtipon —
magpasilabót, makighimbon

MINIATURE, adj.—maliliít — diyutay, gamay—diótay kaayo

MINISTER, n.—ministro, pangulo,
ng isáng káwanihán—ministro,
pari—ministro

MINISTER, v.—maglingkód, asikasuhin—pagsilbi, pag-alagad —
pag-alagád

MINOR, n.—walâ pa sa gulang,
batà pa—bata pa, ubos—linghod,
batà pa

MINT, n.—págawaan ng salapî—
am-anan sa salapi—buluhatán-
pilak

MINUTE, n.—minuto, talâ ng pulong, maliít—gutlo, minuto, diyutay—minuto, tinión

MIRACLE, n.—milagro, himalâ — tugahala, milagro—milagro, katanhagaan

MIRE, n.—balahò—lapok, yanang —lay-on

MIRROR, n.—salamín—salamin—salamíng, kristal

MIRROR, v.—salaminín—pagsalamin, pagpanamin—espeho, larawanán

MIRTH, n.—katuwaan — kalipay, kasayá—kasadyahan

MIRTHFUL, adj. — matuwain—imalipayon, saya — malipayon

MISCELLANEOUS, adj.—samatsamot, ibá-ibá—kalandrakas, lain-lain—yangkutyangkut

MISCHIEF, n.—kaguluhan, kalikután—kasamok, kaguliyang — katontohan, kasutilán

MISCHIEVOUS, adj. — magulo, salbahe — kapilyo, kasalbahis—kalokohan

MISERABLE, adj.—abâ, sawi, nakaháhambál—makaluluoy, alaut —makaluluoy

MISERY, n.—dálitâ, hirap — katimawa, kakabus—kaimolón

MISFORTUNE, n.—sakunâ, paghihirap — kaantusan, kaalautan —pagkaimol

MISS, n.—Binibini, Bb. — Gining, Dalaga—Gining, Gn.

MISTRESS, n.—panginoóng babae, babae, nobya—babayeng agalon, kirida—agalon nga babáe, babáe, nobya

MISTAKE, n.—malî, kamálian — sayop—sayup

MISTAKE, v.—ipagkámali—pagkasayop—nakasayúp

MISTY, adj.—malabô, maulap mahalap, malubog — malubóg. magal-um

MIX, v.—haluin, pagsamahin — pagsagul—samuon, mesklahón

MIXTURE, n.—bantô, halò, lahók —panagsagul, saksak—simbog

MOAN, v.—managhóy—pag-agulo --manganduhoy

MOAN, n. — panaghóy — agulo— panganduhoy

MOB, n.—manggugulo—magubutong panon—manggamó -

MOBILE, adj.—palakad-lakad — malihok—palakát-lakat

MOCK, v.—uyamín, tuyaín—pagyubit, pagtamay—libakón

MOCKERY, n. — pagtuyâ, paguyám—yubit, tamay—paghikay paglibák

MODE, n.—ugali, paraán — gawi, paagi — pamatasan, hulag, moda

MODEL, n.—ulirán, modelo—panig-ingnan, modelo — sulundan, modelo

MODERATE, adj.—katamtaman, kainaman—kasarangan — kasarangan

MODERN, adj.—bago, kasalukuyan—bag-o, binag-o — binag-o, kinarón

MODERNISTIC, adj.—makabago —bag-ohanon—makibag-o

MODEST, adj.—mahinhín, matim pî—mapaubsanon — mahinhin, mahipos

MODIFICATION, n.—pagbabago —pagka-bag-o, kausaban—pagbag-o

MOIST, adj.—pawisín, namámasámasâ—yamog, nag-umog—hunog, hulas

MOISTURE, n.—pagkabasâ, basâ —umog, kabasa—pagkahun-og, pagkahulmas

MOLE, n.—nunál—ila—alum

MOLEST, v.—abalahin, molestiyahín—pagsamok — molestiahón, pangabayón

MOMENT, n.—sandalî — katipikpanahon — tinión

MOMENTOUS, adj.—mahalagá — kaaginhon—malahalon

MONARCH, n.—harì, monarka— hari, monarka—harì, monarka

MONARCHY, n.—kaharián—gingharian, monarkiya—ginharian

MONDAY, n.—Lunes — Lunes— Lunes

MONEY, n. — salapî, kuwarta— salapi—kuarta

MONEY-BAG, n.—kalupî — puyo sa sapi—kuarta-pagkitan, pitaka

MONEYED, adj.—masalapî, mayaman—sapian, adunahan—makuarta, manggaranon

MONKEY, n.—matsíng, unggóy— amo, unggoy—ibóy, amû

MONKEY, v.—paglaruán—pagdula-dula, pag-inamo—hampangán

MONSIEUR, n.—ginoó — ginoo (Pranses)—halangdon

MONSTER, n.—hayop na malakí at nakatátakot — aliwas, higanting mananap — hayup nga dakû kag makahaladlok

MONSTROUS, adj.—nakatátakot labihan kadaku, makalilisang — makahaladlok

MONTH, n.—buwán—bulan — bulan

MONTHLY, adj.—buwanan—binulan—bulanán

MONUMENT, n.—bantayog, monumento—bungdo, bantayog — monumento, batong-daán

MONUMENTAL, adj. — malakí, dakilà—mabungdoon, alasoyon —kadungganon

MOOD, n.—himig, kondisyón, panagano—gawi, buot — kondisyon, kinaugali

MOODY, adj.—walâ sa kondisyón, waláng kibô—hilumon, mahinuktokon, luyahon — walâ sa kondisyon, dî-mahamtang

MOON, n.—buwán—bulan—bulan

MOONLIGHT, n.—liwanag ng buwán—bulanon—sanag sang bulan

MOONSTRUCK, adj. — sirá-sirâ, ulól—buang, kwanggol, tonto— —linakbayán-bulan, linakaranbulan

MORAL, n. — kaugaliáng wagás, banál — pagtnlon-an — kinabubut-on nga balaan

MORBID, adj.—masakitin, mahinà, masasakitín — maluyahon, masakiton—masakitón

MORE, adv.—higít, lalò—dugang pa, labi pa, labaw pa—kapín, labí

MOREOVER, adv.—higít sa rito - labaw pa niini, gawas niini — kapín siní

MORNING, n.—umaga—buntag—aga

MOROSE, adj.—mapagmaktól, yamót — tanga, magul-anon, masuk-anon — mamamakdol, masingkì

MORSEL, n.—kapiraso, kauntî — diyut, momho—momho

MORTAL, n.—tao, nilikhâ—ang tawo, may kamatayan—mortál, tao, tinuga

MORTALITY, adj.—dami ng kamátayan — gidaghanon sa mangamatay—kadamuón sang kamatayon

MORTALLY, adv.—malalim, malubhâ—naglisud, grabe — mada lum, malubhà

MOSQUITO, n.—lamók—lamok—lamúk

MOSS, n.—lumot—lumot—lumot

MOST, adv.—karamihan, higít sa —ang kadaghanan, ang nagalabi —kadamoan

MOTH, n.—gamugamó — anunugba—lamlok, baláy-atataro

MOTHER, n. — iná, nanay, ináy, imâ—inahan, nanáy — ilóy, nanáy, nay

MOTHERED, v.—kupkupín, alagaan—pag-alaga, pagmatutó — sakdagón, inakupón

MOTHERHOOD, n. — pagiginginá—ang pagka inahan—pagkailóy

MOTION, n. — galáw, paggaláw, mungkahì—lihok—hulag, pakamaayohón

MOTIVATION, n. — adhikaín, pangganyák—pagpalihok — palakamaayohón

135

MOTIVE, n.—pakay, adhikâ—tuyo, katarungan—halambalan

MOTLEY, ad.—ilan-ilán, iba-ibá — lain-lain, kalandrakas—sarîsari ang duág

MOTOR, n. — motór, makiná— motor, makina—motór, makiná

MOTORCYCLE, n.—motorsiklo — motorsiklo—motórsiklo

MOTORIZED, adj.—mga may motór—motorisado—de motór

MOTORMAN, n.—motorman, ang nagpápalakad ng motór—tigpalihok sa motor—motórman, ang nagapalakát sing motór

MOTTO, n.—sáwikaín, kasabihán —lagdaanong pulong—hurubaton

MOULD, n.—molde, hubugin, hulmahan—hulmahan—molde, húr-mahan

MOULD, v.—hulmahín, hubugin— paghulma—hurmahón, moldehón

MOULDER, n.—taga-molde, tagahubog—maghuhulma, taghulma —taghurma, tagmolde

MOUNT, v.—umakyát, sumakáy— pagsakay, pagkabayo—sumakáy, sumakà

MOUNTAIN, n.—bundók—bukid —bukid

MOUNTAINOUS, adj.—mabundók—pulok-bukid, tungason — bukíd-bukíd

MOURN, v.—magluksâ, ipagluksâ —pagminatay pagloto—magloto, lotohan

MOUSE n.—dagâ—ilaga, ambaw bagtok—ilagâ

MOUTH, n.—bibíg—baba—bâbà

MOUTHFUL, adj.—labis, marami, sansubò—usa ka hungit—isá ka dapal

MOUTHPIECE, n.—tagapagsalitâ, bibíg o bungangà—bokilya, galamiton sa baba—taghambal

MOVE, v.—lumipat, bumagó — pagbalhin, paglihok—humulag

MOVABLE, adj.—alsáhin, gálawin —mahimong lihokon—hulagon

MOVEMENT, n.—kilusán, paggaláw—lihok, kalihokan—pagsaylohay

MOVING PICTURE, n.—sine—sine, lilas, pelikula—sine

MOW, v.—putulin o putlín—pagputol—putlon, kútlon, utdon

MUCH, adj.—marami—daghan — madamò

MUCUS, n.—uhog—sip-on—kulamug

MUDDLE, n.—gusót, guló—kagubut, kasamok—gumón

MUD-FISH, n.—dalág—haiwan — haloán, puyó

MUD-SKIPPER, n. — talimusák tambasakan—alimusan

MULLET, n.—banak—kalan-on sa isda—balanák

MULTIPLY, v.—paramihin, mag-parami — pagpadaghan, pagsa-nay — padamuon, multiplika-hón

MULTITUDE, n. — karamihàn — kadaghanan, katilingban — ka-damoan

MUNDANE, adj.—maka-mundó—kalibutanon—kalibùtanon

MUNICIPAL, adj.—ukol sa bayan o munisipyo — mahatungod sa lungsod — munisipyo, natungód sa banwa

MURDER, v.—pumatáy ng tao—pagpatay, pagbunó — pumatáy sing táo

MURDER, n.—pagpatáy ng tao — salang pagpatay—pagpatáy sing táo

MURMUR, n.—bulóng—bagulbol, bagulbot—kibut, himulongon

MURMUR, v.—bumulóng—pagbagulbol, pagbagutbot—magkibut-kibut, magdaragilon

MUSCLE, n.—bisig, lamán—braso, unod—kusóg, kaundan

MUSE, n.—diyosa ng arte—bathala sa arte—diwatà sang tali-ambong

MUSE, v.—dilidilihín — paghandum, paghanduraw — pasibusi-buon sa kaugalingon

MUSEUM, n.—museo—musiyo — museo

MUSHY, adj.—pambabae, maloho—alang sa babaye—pangbabáe, salabayon

MUSIC, n.—músiká, tugtóg, tug-tugan—honi, musika — musika, lantonon

MUSICAL, adj.—ukol sa musika, may hilig sa musika—mahitu-ngod sa honi — musikál, natu-ngód sa musiká

MUSICIAN, n.—musikero, mánu-nugtóg—maghohoni, musikero - musikero, manglalanton

MUST, v.—nárarapat, dapat, ka-ilangan—angay, kinahanglan — mangindapat, palasakupan

MUSTACHE, n.—bigote—bigote—bigote, bungot, burangos

MUTE, adj. — tahimik, pipi — amáng—apâ, malinóng

MUTILATE, v.—tadtarín — pag-tadtad, pagtagúd-tagúd—tadta-rón

MUTINY, n.—pag-aalsá, paglaban—aklas sa dagat—pag-alsamen-to, pagpakiggiùs

MUTUAL, adj.—magkakabít, gan-ti-gantí—angay-angay, inató — alalangay

MY, pron.—akin, sa akin — ako, akong—akon, sa akon

MYSELF, pron.—sarili, aking sarili—ako mismo — kaugalingon,
akon kaugalingon

MYSTERIOUS, adj.—katakataká,
kahimáhimalâ—kahibulongan —
katingalahán, katanhagaan

MYSTERY, n.—hiwagâ, katakata-

ká—tugahala, kahibudnganan—
tanhagà, makatalanhagà

MYSTIC, adj.—mapaghimalâ, na-
kapagtátaká—tagolilong — makatilingala

MYOPIA, n.—kalabuan ng matá
—kahalap sa mata—palangdu-
lóm sang matá

— N —

NAIL, n.—pakò, kukó—lansang —
lansang, kukó

NAIL, v.—ipakò — paglansang —
ilansang

NAKED, adj.—hubót-hubad—hubó, hukás—hublas

NAME, n.—ngalan, pangalan —
ngalan—ngalan

NAME, v.—ngalanan—pagngalan
—hingalanan

NAMELESS, adj.—waláng pangalan—walay ngalan—wala'y ngalan

NAP, n.—idlíp—katulog sa palis—
—magpiyong, matulog sa udto

NAPKIN, n.—serbilyeta, pamahi-
ran—pamahid sa ngabil—serbilyeta

NARRATE, v.—isalaysáy, ikuwen-
to—pagsaysay, pagsugid — isaysay sa sugilanon

NARRATION, n.—kuwento, salaysáy—sugid, saysay — pagsaysay
sa sugilanon

NARROW, adj.—makitid, makipot
hiktin, sigpit—makitíd

NARROWLY, adv.—kamuntík na
—diriyut na — nadiótayan lamang

NASAL, adj.—humál—pinaagi sa
ilóng—pungá

NATION, n.—bansá, lahì—nasud
—pungsod

NATIONALISTIC, adj.—makabayan, pambansá — makinasud —
pungsodnon, makig-pungsod

NATIONALITY, n.—lahì — kaliwat — kaliwatan

NATIVE, n.—tubò, anák — lumad
—tumandok

NATIVITY, n.—kapanganakan --
ang pagpanganak — kapanganakán

NATTY, adj.—pustura, maayos—
ambongan, pustorawo—postura,
mahipid

NATURAL, adj.—likás—kinaiya—
kinaiya, naturál

NATURALIZE, n.—tanggapín na
isáng mámamayán — pagsagop
nga lumad-molupyo — kabigon
nga banwahanon

NATURALLY, adv.—siyáng totoó,
nárarapat — dayág na lang —
amo'ng matuod

NATURE, n.—katalagahan, gawî
—kinaiyahan—kinaiya, kinaugalì

NAUGHT, n.—walâ, pagkawalâ—
walá, pagkawalá—walâ, wala'y
kapuslanan

NAUGHTY, adj.--masamâ, malikót—matiawon, siaw — malain,
sutíl

NAUSEA, n. — alibadbád, hilo—
panglimot, panglipong—dalaga-
tón, lingin

NAVIGABLE, adj. —· mapama-
mangkaán—mahimong lawigan
—mapamangkaán, mabalsahán

NAVY, n.—mga sasakyáng dagat
na pandigmâ—mga sakayan ig-
gugubat—nebi

NEAR, adv. or prep. — malapit,
malapit sa—haduol, duol sa —
malapít lang, malapít sa

NEARLY, adv.—halos — diriyut,
hapit—halos

NECESSARY, adj. — kinákaila-
ngan — kinahanglan — kiña-
hanglan

NECESSITY, n. — pangangaila-

ngan—kinahanglanon — kinahanglanon

NECK, n.—liíg—liog—liug

NECKLACE, n.—kuwintás — ku-
wentas — kolintas

NECKTIE, n.—kurbata—korbata
—kurbata

NEED, n.—pangangailangan — gikinahanglan—pagkinahanglan

NEEDLE, n.—karayom, pantahî—
dagum—dagum

NEEDY, adj. — nangángailangan,
naghíhirap, pabayaan — timawa,
nagkinahanglan — nagakinahanglan

NEFARIOUS, adj.—masamâ—mangil-ad, dantan—malain

NEGLECT, v.—magpabayà—pag-
pasagad, di-pagtagad — patumbayà

NEGLECT, n. — pagpapabayà—
ang pagkapinasagdan — pagpa-
tumbayà

NEGLECTFUL, adj. — mapagpa-
bayà—mapinasagdanon — mag-
patumbayà

NEGOTIATE, v.—makipag-ayos,
makipag-alám — pagpakigsabut,
paghíkay—makighangup

NEGOTIATIONS, n. — pakikipag-
ayos, sálitaan—sabut-sabut, ka-
híkayan—pagpakighangup

NEGROS, adj.—isáng taong itím,
maitim—agta, itum—negro, isá
ka maitúm nga táo

139

NEIGHBOR, n.—kapitbahay—silingan—kasilingan

NEIGHBORHOOD, n. — kalapit-lugár, buóng paligid-ligid—kasilinganan — pagkakasilingan

NEIGHBORLY, adj.—malapit — makisilingan—paghilapitay

NEOPHYTE, n.—baguhan—nobato, ihalas—bag-ohanon

NEITHER, adv.—ni, hindî, kahit sino—mi, ni, wala sa duha—ní bisán sin-o

NEPHEW, n.—pamangkíng lalaki—pag-umangkon lalaki—hinablus nga lalakí

NERVE, n.—litid, lakás-loób — kusog, kaisug—nerbios

NERVOUS, n.—matakutín, nerbiyoso—mahadlokon, nerbiyoso — nerbioso

NEST, n.—pugad—salag — pugad

NESTLE, v.—mamugad, humilig—pagkupkop — manilong, makighigdà

NET, n. — lambát, tubò, pakinabang—baling, tubo—lambát, punà, saplid

NET INCOME, n.—linis na kita—pinangitaan—bug-os nga kinitaan

NEUTRAL, adj.—waláng kiníkilingan—walay gidapigan—wala'y ginaapinan

NEVER, adv. —`hindî kailánman —dili bangtud anus-a—indî gid

NEVERTHELESS, adv. — kahit na, maskí na—bisan pa—bisán pa, maskin na

NEW, adj.—bago—bag-o—bag-o

NEWS, n.—balità, mga balità — balita, tahó—balità, mga balità

NEWSPAPER, n.—páhayagán — pamantalaan—pamantalaan

NEW YEAR'S DAY, n.—Baguntaón—Adlaw sa Bag-ong- Tuig—Bag-ong Tuig

NEXT, n.—ang kasunód—ang sunod—masdasón

NIBBLE, v.—manginain—pag-ingkib, pagpaak—manginaon

NICE, adj.—mainam, wastô—maanindot—matahúm, nagakaigó

NICHE, n.—nitso, líbingan—lubnganan, nitso—nitso, lulubngan

NICKEL, n.—nikel, buóng limáng sentimos—nikil, lima ka dakn—nikel, limá ka sentimós

NICKELIZED, adj. — makintáb, pinakintáb—nikilado, pinasinaw —pabadlakón

NICKNAME, n.—palayaw—angga, dagmay—hayû

NIECE, n.—pamangkíng babae — pag-umangkon babaye—hinablus nga babáe

NIGGARD, adj.—maramot, masamáng ugalì—kuripot, balasubas —dalúk, malain sing batasan

NIGHT, n.—gabí—gabii—gab-i

NIGHTMARE, n. — bangungot — daman—damán, hupáy, sala

NIMBLE, adj.—maliksí, mabilís—maliks', abtik — maabtik, mapagsik.

NINE ,n.—siyám—siyam—siám

NINETEEN, n.—labinsiyám—napulog-siyam—napulo'g siám

NINETY, n.—siyamnapû — kasiyaman—kasiamán

NINTH, adj.—ikasiyám—ikasiyam—ikasiám

NIP, v.—putulin—pagsanta, pagputól—utdon

NIPPLE, n.—suso, susuhán—suso, toytoy—ulotngan sang soso

NO, adv.—hindî, walâ—dili, wala indì, walâ

NOBLE, adj. — mahál, mabunyi, marangál—mahal, halangdon — dungganon, lutáw

NOBODY, pron. — walâ ni sino man—walay bisan kinsa—walâ bisán sin-o

NOCTURNAL, adj. — panggabí, paglalamay—gabhianon — hangab-i

NOD, n.—tangô, patangô—lingo, yangó—tangô, tangô-tangò

NOD, n.—tumangô — paglingo, pagyango—tumangô

NODE, n.—bukó, hatì—butang gurutanan—bukó

NOISE, n.—ingay, guló—kabanha, kasaba—gahud, gamó

NOISY, adj.—maingay, maguguló—banha, masaba — magahud, magamó

NOMINAL, adj.—sa pangalan lamang—sa ngalan lamang — sa ngalan lamang

NOMINATE, v.—magharáp, magpasok — pagtuhoy, pagtugpo — magpilì, maglawag

NOMINATION, n. — paghaharáp ng kandidato — ang katugpoan sa pilionon — paghingalan sang palapilián

NOMINEE, n.—kandidato — tinuboy, pilionon—pililión

NONCHALANT, adj. — malamíg, walâ sa loób—bugnaw, wala sa buot—malas-ay, mabugnaw ang buót

NONE, adv.—walâ—wala—walâ

NOR, adv.—ni, hindî—mi, ni, dili bisan—ní, indí, bisán pa

NONSENSE, n.—waláng katuturán—binuang — wala'y kapuslanan

NONSTOP, n.—waláng hintô — walay-undang—wala'y dulog

NOON, n.—tenghaling tapát — udto—udto, hingudtohon

NORMAL, adj.—regulár, karaniwan—ingon sa kanaiya—normal, kinaugalì, kinaandan

NORTH, n.—norte, hilagà — amihanan—aminhan

NORTHERN, adj. — gawíng hilagà—tamping amihanan — na-aminhan

NOSE, n.—ilóng—ilóng—ilóng

NOSEDIVE, v.—magpatihulóg — pagtiurok, pagbinawó—magpaninghulóg

NOT, adv.—hindî, walâ—dili, wala—indì, walâ

NOTABLE, adj.—tanyág, kilalá—inila, halangdon—lutáw, kilala

NOTE, n.—tandâ, sulat, nota ng tugtugin—timaan, mubong suat, nota sa musika—tandà, sulát, nota sang musiká

NOTEWORTHY, adj.—walâ—makadadani—wala'y pulós

NOTICE, n.—paunawà—pahibalo—pahibaló, pasayud

NOTICE, v.—pansinín—pagtamud, paghimatngon—himutaran, talupangdan

NOTICEABLE, adj. — kapuna-puná — kahimatngonan — makabuluyok

NOTIFY, v.—pagsabihan, ipaalám — pagpahibalo, pagpasidaan — pahibal-on,. pasayuron

NOTION, n.—hakà, warì—hunahuna, panahum — pagsigahúm, lalaumán

NOTORIOUS, adj.—kilaláng-kilalá—inila sa pagkadautan—kilala kaayo

NOUN, n.—pangngalan—pangalan —pangalan

NOURISHMENT, n. — pagkaing pampalusóg — pagkaong pagpabaskog—inogpatambok

NOVEL, n.—kathambuhay, nobela—bag-o, nobela—nobela

NOVELTY, n.—bagong bagay o moda—binag-ong butang — kabag-ohán sa bisán anó

NOVEMBER, n. — Nobyembre — Nobiyembre—Nobiembre

NOVICE, n.—baguhan, nagsísimulá—nobato, bag-o—bag-ohanon, nagasugod

NOW, adv.—ngayón—karon—karón

NUDE, adj.—hubô, waláng damít —hubo, hukas—hublas, wala'y bayù

NUDGE, v.—sikuhín, bungguín—pagsiko, pagsikdo—sikohon, masihón

NULL, adj.—waláng halagá—walay bili—wala'y bilí

NUMB, adj.—namámanhíd —namanhud—palamaul

NUMBER, n.—bilang, numero — isip, numero—numero, isip

NUMEROUS, adj.—marami, makapál — daghan, dili-maihap —
madamò, kadamoan
NUN, n.—mongha — mongha —
mongha
NUPTIAL, n.—kasál, kásalan —
kasal—kasál, kasalay
NURSE, n.—narses, tagapag-alagà—nars, bantary sa masakiton
—nars, manogtatáp-masakít
NURSE, v.—alagaan, bantayán—
pag-alima—tatapon, inakupón
NURSERY, n.—páalagaan—lawak
sa mga bata—alaypan, ilinaku-
pán

NURTURE, v. — umisip—pag-isip
—umisip
NUTRITION, n. — kalusugán,
pampalusóg—lawasnong kabas-
kog — katambukón, katibsulón
NUTRITIOUS, adj. — mayaman,
malusóg—puno sa sustansiya —
mabukod, matibunog, matibsol
NUTTY, adj. — malukúlukó, sirá-
sirá—hungóg-hungóg — buáng-
buáng, intù-intù
NYMPH, n.—nimpa, diwatà — di-
wata—katáw, nimpa

— O —

OAK, isáng urì ng punung-
kahoy sa Amériká, akasya—matang sa kahoy—isá ka sarî sang
kahoy sa Amérika
OAR, n.—good—bugsay—bugsay
OATH, n.—sumpâ, panunumpâ —
panumpa, sumpa—manumpà
OBDURATE, adj. — matigás ang
loób, waláng-pusò — gahig kabubut-on, matig-ag kasingkasing
—matigdas sing buót, wala'y patugsiling
OBEDIENCE, n.—pagsunód—ang
pagsugot—masunuron
OBEDIENT, adj. — masúnurin—
masinugtanon—masinulundon

OBESE, adj.—matabâ — tambok,
supang—matambok
OBEY, v. — sumunód, makiníg—
pagsugot—magsunód
OBJECT, v.—tumutol, tumanggí—
pagtutol, pagsupak—mamatuk,
mamalabag
OBJECTION, n.—tutol, pagtanggí
—tutol, supil—batuk, pamatuk
OBJECTIVE, n. — hantungan, lá-
yunin—katuyoan, tuyo—tuluyuón
OBLIGATION, n. — obligasiyón,
tungkulin—katungdanan — ob-
ligasyon, katungdanán

OBLIGATORY, adj.—sápilitán — sa lugsanay, pugsanay—pilitáy

OBLIGE, v — mapilitan, pilitin, pagbigyán—paglugos, pagpugos —piliton, pasundon

OBLITERATE, v.—pawiin, palisín —pagpapha, pagpapas—panason ng wala'y agi

OBLITERATION, n. — pagpalís, paghawì—kapaphaan, pagkahanaw—pagpanas

OBLIVION, n.—limot—kalimot — pagkalimut

OBSCENE, adj.—mahalay — malaw-ay—masaw-a, malaw-ay

OBSCURE, adj.—malabò—mahanap—masagir-um

OBSERVANT, adj.—mapagmasíd -mapaniilron—mahimutaron

OBSERVE, v.—magmasíd—pagpaniid, pagpaminaw—maghimutad, magtan-aw

OBSERVATION, n. — pagmamasíd, tingín—paniid, paminaw — paghimutad, pagtan-aw

OBSOLETE, adj.—lipás na—kinaraan—nag'ligad na, naligaran na

OBSTACLE, n.—sagabal — balabag, ali—samóng

OBSTINATE, adj.—matigás—gahian—matigdas, batúl

OBSTRUCT, v.—hadlangán—pagbalda, pagbahag—balabagan

OBSTRUCTION, n. — nakahalang —ali, balda—nagbalabag

OBTAIN, v.—kumuha, kunin — pagkuha—kumuhà, kuhaon

OBTAINABLE, adj. — mákukuha, maáaring mákuha — mahimong makuha — saráng makuhà, saráng maangkon

OCCASION, n. — panahón, pangyayari pagkakátaón—higayon—panahón, kahigayonan

OCCASIONAL, adj. — paminsan-minsan, pana-panahón—usahay lamang—kon kaisá, sa-panahón, ka-panahonán

OCCIDENT, n.—timog—kasadpanon—katundan

OCCULT, adj. — di-karaniwan—tinagoan, diwaanon — dî-ordinaryo, dî-makit-an

OCCUPATION, n. — hanapbuhay, gáwain, pagsakop — buhat, panginabuhi—palangitan-an, palamugnan

OCCUPY, v. — gumamit, okupahán, sakupin—paghupot, pagsakop—okupahán, sakupon

OCCUR, v.—mangyari, máalaala —pagkahitabo—natabô

OCCURRENCE, n. — pangyayari, pagdatíng—hitabo—kahitaboán

OCEAN, n.—oseano, dagat na malakí gaya ng Pasípikó—dakung dagat—dagat

O'CLOCK, n.—ang oras, ang tak-dâ—sa taknaan—ang oras. ang taknà

OCTOBER, n.—Oktubre — Oktubre — Oktubre

ODD, adj.—gansál, kaibá sa karaniwan—katingad-an, nones — tuhay sa ibán

ODDITY, n.—kalokohan, kaibhán —katingalahan — katuhayan

ODOR, n.—amóy—baho—bahù

OF, prep.—ng, sa, ni, kay—sa, ni, kang—sang, ní, kay

OFF, adv.—malayò— sa layo, halayo—malayô

OFFEND, v.—mamasláng, saktán ang damdamin, pagalitin—pag-daut, pagpakaulaw—manghalit, mamilas sing balatyagon

OFFENSE, n.—pag-alipustâ. sakít ng damdamin—sala, panukol — pagpanghalit, pagpamilas sing balatyagon

OFFENSIVE, adj. — nakaíinís, nanlúlusob—masukolon, madasdason—makatalaka, manalakay

OFFER, n.—alók, dulot—tanyag. halad—dulat, tanyag

OFFER, v.—maghandóg, dulutan —pagtanyag, paghalad—magdulot, magtanyag

OFFICE, n.—tanggapan, tungkulin, opisina—buhatan, katungdanan—opisina, talatapán

OFFICIAL, n.—punô, may kinalaman sa pámahalaán — punoan, opisyal—opisyal, punô-punô

OFFICIATE, v.—manungkól, mangasiwà—pagdumala — mangopisina

OFFSPRING, n.—anák—anak — anák

OFTEN, adv.—madalás, malimit—kanunay—masunson, lagi

OFTENTIMES, adv.—malimit — sa kaninay—masunson, matióntión.

OIL, n.—langís—lana, asayte — langís, lana

OILY, adj.—malangís — lanahon, asaytihon—malangís, malanay

OLD, adj.—matandâ, dati, malaon —tigulang, maas—tigulang. sadto, madugay

OLDTIMER, n.—datihan, matagál —karaang tumitindok—dumaan

OMINOUS, adj. — mapanganib, nagbábalà—may dautan tilimadon — makatalagam, makaalandam

OMIT, v.—alisín, kaltasín, kakalaktáw—paglaktaw — kuhaon, kakasón

ON, prep.—sa ibabaw, sa—sa ibabaw, sa—sa ibabaw, sa

ONCE, adv.—minsan — sa makausa—kon kaisa

ONE, n.—isá—usa—isá

ONE-SIDED, adj.—hindî pareho,
kampî sa isá—**madapigon sa usa**
—**dî-tupong**, apin sa isá

ONION, n.—sibuyas — **sibuyas** —
—siboyas

ONLY, adv.—lamang — **lamang,
usa ra, bugtong**—lamang

ONSLAUGHT, n. — paninibasib,
paglusob—**pagsulong, pagdasdas**
—makangilidlis nga atake

ONWARD, adv.—pasulong—**padayon, sa unahan**—padayon

OOZE, v. — tumulò, pumaták —
pagtulo, pag-agay — humulas,
tumulò

OPALESCENT, adj. — ibá-ibáng
kulay—**lain-laing bulok** —sarîsarì ang duág

OPAQUE, adj.—hindî lusután —
dagtum, hanáp—dî-masinág

OPEN, adj.—bukás, hayág — **bi-
nuksan, inukban**—bukás hayág

OPEN, v.—buksán — **pagbukas,
pag-abli**—buksan

OPENING, n.—butas, pagbubukás
—**lungag**—buhò, bulóksan

OPERATE, v.—operahán, magpa-
lakad—**pagmanlho, pagdisdis** —
operahán, palakton, busbosán

OPERATION, n.—operasyón, pagpapalakad—**palakaw, disdis, yas-
yas**—operasyon, pagpalakát

OPERATOR, n.—ang nagpápalakad, tagapagpalakad—ang **nag-
manlho** — operadór, tagpalakát,
tagpadalagan

OPINION, n.—akalà, kurò—**panahum, hunahuna** — kabubut-on,
panghunâhunà

OPPONENT, n.—kalaban — **kaatbang, kaparang**—kasumpong

OPPORTUNE, adj.—napápanahón
tukma sa higayon—higayon

OPPORTUNITY, n.—pagkakátaón—**kahigayonan**—kahigayonan

OPPORTUNISTIC, adj.—mapag-
samantalá—**maagapon sa higayon**—maghimulós,

OPPOSE, v.—labanan, salungatín
—**pagsupak, pagbatok**—sumpo-
ngón

OPPOSITE, adj.—kasalungát, ka-
tapát—**kaatbang, manag-atbang**
—kabatuk, katimbang.

OPPOSITION, n.—kalaban, ka-
tunggalî — **ang panupak, kaatbang** — kaaway, katusay

OPPRESSED, adj.—apí, nálulupig
—**dinaugdaug, linupigan**—mulî-
mulí, lupigón

OPPRESSION, n.—pagkaapí, pagkalupig — **panaugdaug, panglupig**—pagkalupig, pagmulímulí

OPTICAL, adj.—tungkól sa matá
—**mahatungod sa mata** — natungód sa matá

OPTICIAN, adj. — manggagamot ng salà ng paningín — optiko, doktor sa mata — manogbulong sang panulok

OR, conj.—o, o kayâ—o, kun — ukón

ORACLE, n.—manghuhulà — mananagna, orakulo—orakuló, manoghimalád

ORAL, adj.—pagbigkás o pabigkás—binabá—orál, mitlang

ORALLY, adv.—pabigkás—sa binabaay—pagmitlang

ORANGE, n.—dalandán, dalanghita, kulay—kahil, bulok salmon—kabugaw, duág kabugaw

ORATION, n.—mahalagáng talumpatì—pakigpulong, diskurso — orasyon, malahalon nga pamulongpulong

ORCHARD, n.—hálamanán — tanaman, lagwerta — talamnan, lagwerta

ORCHID, n.—dapò, halaman—waling-waling, bulak nga putì — sarî sang bulak nga matahúm kaayo

ORDAIN, v. — ordenahan, itatág, itakdâ — pagbuot, pagmando — ordenán, isugò, ipabuót

ORDEAL, n.—pahirap — kalisdainan, kapaitan—paantus

ORDER, v.—ipag-utos, magpadalá—pagsugo, pagbaód — isugò, imando

ORDER, n.—utos, ayos—sugo, baód—sugò, mando

ORDERLY, adj.—maayos—mahusay, hapsay—mahipid

ORDINANCE, n.—ordenansa, kautusán — ordinansa, lungsodnong balaod — ordinansa, kasugoán-banwa

ORDINARY, adj.—karaniwan, katamtaman — kasagaran — ordinaryo, kinaugalì, pasagì

ORGAN, n.—organo, kasangkapang natútugtóg na katulad ng piyano—organo, tulonggon—organó

ORGANIST, n.—organista, mánunugtóg ng organo—manunugtog sa organo—organista

ORGANIZATION, n.—kapisanan, pagbubuô — kapunongan, pundok—katilingban, organisasyon

ORGANIZE, v.—magtayô, magbuô —pagtukod—magtukod, magtilingúb

ORGY, n.—paglalasíng, pananampalataya — buhat nga mangilngig— pagpahubóg, pagtuo

ORIENT, n.—silangan — silangan sidlangán

ORIGINAL, n.—pasimulâ, ang pinagsalinan, orihinál—lintunganay, orihinal — orihinál, kinaugalingón

ORPHAN, n.—ulila, waláng magulang—ilo, tuwapós — ilo, wala'y ginikanan

ORPHANAGE, n. — bahay-ampunan—balay sa mga ilo—baláyalaypan

OSCULATE, v.—manghalík—paghalok—manghalúk

OTHER, adj.—ang ibá—ang lain, ang usa—ibán pa

OTHERWISE, prep.—kung dilì, o kayâ—kon dilî—kondì

OUGHT, v.—dapat, nárarapat, kailangan—angay, kinahanglan — dapat, kinahanglan

OUNCE, n.—onsa, Ikalabing-anim na bahagi ng isáng libra—onsa—onsa, ikanapulo'g anum ka bahin sang isá ka librá

OUR, pron.—atin, amin—amo, ato —aton, amon

OURS, pron.—sa amin, sa atin — sa amo, sa ato, kanato — sa amon, sa aton

OURSELVES, pron.—ating sarili, aming sarili—kita—sa aton kaugalingon

OUST, v.—alisín, tanggalín—pagpagula, pagpalagpot—pahalinón

OUSTED, adj.—pinaalís, naalís — pinagula, gipalagpot—pinahalín

OUT, adj.—nasa labás—sa gawas —sa luás, sagwà

OUTBURST, n.—bulalás—bugwak sa pagbati—tumiyabaw

OUTCOME, n.—kinalabasán, kinahinatnán — sangputanan, dadangatan—kinaguaán sinâ

OUTGROWTH, n.—kalagpasán — ang tinuboan—inunahan sa pagtubò

OUTLAW, n.—salarín—makasasala—dalakpon

OUTLINE, n.—balangkás—borador—pagbalayon

OUTSIDE, n.—nasa labás, labás, taga labás—sa gula, sa gawas—sagwà, sa luás, tagaluás

OUTWARD, adj.—patungo sa labás—paingon sa gawas—pakadto sagwà

OVEN, n.—hurnó, pugón—hudnohan—hurno, pugón

OVER, prep.—sa ibabaw, tapós na, higít sa, tungkól—sa ibabaw, natapus na—sa ibabaw, tapos na, kapín sa, tungód

OVER-BEARING, adj.— mapagmataás, suplado—mapahitas-on —bugalón, soplado

OVERCOAT, n.—kapote, balabal —kapote, amerkanang-sapaw — kapote, kunóp

OVERCOME, v.—talunin, daigín—pagpildi, pagbuntog — dag-on, lampasán.

OVERHAUL, v.—linisin, baguhin —paghabwa, paglinis — tinloán, halungkatón

OVERFLOW, v.—umapaw, apawan — pagbaha, paglapaw, pagawas — sumagahay, lumapaw

OVERFLOWING, adj. — saganà umáapaw—nagaawas, nagabaha —dagayà, sagahay

OVERPOWER, v.—talunin, sugpuín—pagbutog—dag-on, lutuson

OVERTAKE, v.—abutan—pag-agpas, pag-apas, paghiapas — abután

OVERTHROW, n.—pagsirà, pagiibá—pagkataub, kapukan—pagpakigbatuk, pagpakigbalhin, pagpakigkulób

OVERTHROW, v.—gumuló, sumirà, itaób — pagtaub, pag-agaw,

pagpukan — nakigbatuk, nakigbalhin, pakulbon

OWE, v. — magkautang, mangutang—pagutang — mangutang, mautangán

OWL, n.—kuwago, isáng uri ng ibon—ngiwngiw, mingok — bukaw

OWN, v.—ariin, sarilinin—pagbaton, pagpanag-iya—iyahon, panagiyahan

OWNER, n.—nagmámay-arì, mayarì—tag-iya — tag-iya

OX, n.—toro, bakang lalaking kinapón—baka nga laki — toro

OXYTONE, adj.—mariín—magahing paglitok—matagsing

OYSTER, n.—talabá—litob, kinhason, takubo—pakinhason

— P —

PACE, n.—hakbáng — lakang — lak-ang

PACIFIC, adj.—tahimik—malinawon — malinóng

PACIFICATION, n.—pagpapaamò, pagpapatahimik—pagpalinaw — pagpalinóng, paghusay

PACK, n.—balutan, bigkís — bangan, putos—pinutsan, binugkosan

PACK, v.—magbigkís, magbalót —pagbangan, pagputos—bugkusón, putson

PACKAGE, n.—balutan, paketeputos—pakite, pinutós

PACKER, n.—tagabalot, mambabalot—tagputos, mamumutos — tagputós, tagbugkos

PADDLE, n.—sagwán—bugsay — bugsay

PADLOCK, n.—susì, kandado — **kandado, panak-op**—yabi, kandado

PAGAN, **n.**—pagano — **pagano** — pagano

PAGE, n.—páhiná, mukhâ, dahon, alagád ng harì—**dahon, panid**—pamihák, pahina

PAGE, v.—pahinahìn—**paghan-ay** —pamihakón, pahinahon

PAGEANT, n.—palabás — **matahum pasundayag**—palaguaon

PAGEANTRY, n.—maluhong palabás—**talan-awong pinasundayag** —lohoso nga palaguaon

PAGING, n. — pagkakapahinà — **paghikay sa panid**—pagpamihák, pagpahina

PAIL, n.—timbâ, baldé — **timba, balde**—timbà, balde

PAIN, n.—kirót, hapdî — **sakit, ul-ol, kahapdus**—sakít, hapdî

PAINFUL, adj.—masakít. makìrót, mahapdî—**masakit, mahapdus**—masakít, nagabusóg

PAINLESS, adj.—waláng sakít— **walay sakit**—wala'y sakít

PAINT, n.—pintá, pintura — **pintal, bulit** — pintura, pinta

PAINT, v.—magpintá, pintahán— **pagpintal, pagbulit** — magpinta, pintahán

PAINTER, n.—pintór, tagapintá— **pintor, mamumulit**—pintor, tagpinta

PAIR, n.—pares, dalawá na **magkabagay—parisan**—paris, magkaupod

PAL, n.—kasama, kaibigan — **abyan, higala**—kaupod, abyan

PALACE, n.—palasyo, bahay-harì **—palasyo, balay sa hari, panting**—palasyo, kastilyo

PALATIAL, adj.—malakíng bahay **—dakung balay, palasyohon** — palasyohon

PALE, adj.—maputlâ, namúmutlâ—**luspad**—malapsì, maluspad

PALISADE, n.—bakod na matutulis—**salipdanan, koral** — kudál nga mataliwis

PALLID, adj.—namúmutlâ — **lusparon**—nagapalanglapsì

PALM, n.—palma, palad—**palad**—palma, paklang, palad

PALTRY, adj.—waláng kabuluhán **—kulang-kulang, diyutay da** — wala'y kabilinggan

PAN, n.—kawali, kasirola—**kaha** —kalahà, kasirola

PANACEA, n.—panlunas sa lahát ng sakít—**tambal sa tanang sakit**—tambal sa tanán mga balatian

PANE, n.—salabín ng bintaná o pintô—**kwadro sa bintana, tamboanon**—salamíng sang bintanà ukón pwertahan

PANEL, n.—dingdíng, sadlakan— hulagway, hut-ong sa mga hu- wes — dingding

PANIC, n.—pagkakagulat, guló— kaguliyang sa kuyaw—pagkaki- bút

PANORAMA, n.—tánawin—talan- awon—talan-awon

PANT, v.—humingal, sumikdó — paghangus — paghapúhapû

PANT, n. — salawál, pantalón — kalsonis—delargo, sarwal

PANTRY, n.—páminggalan—sud- lanan mga pagkaon—talagoán

PAPA, n.—tatay, itáy, tatang — amahan, tatay—tatay, 'tay

PAPER, n.—papíl—papel, manta- laan—papél, bantalaan

PARACHUTE, n.—parakayda — payong-payong, parakayda—pa- rakayda

PARADISE, n.—paraiso—paraiso, tanaman—paraiso

PARAGON, n.—modelo, parisán— sumbanan, modelo — modelo, anggiran

PARAGRAPH, n.—talatà—parapo —parapó

PARALLEL, n. — magkahanay, magkahilera — magkabuyon — magkaubay, pagkulubay

PARALYTIC, adj.—di-makagaláw, baldado—binhuron, paralitiko — paralitokó, baldado

PARASITE, n.—umasa sa ibá — nagsalig sa uban — salíg sa ibán

PARCEL, n.—balutan, bahagi — putos, lona sa yuta—pinutsan, binahin

PARCEL POST, n.—koreo—kor- yo—koreo

PARDON, n.—patawad, kapata- warán—pasaylo—patawad, pag- patawad

PARDONABLE, adj.—mapápata- wad—mapasaylo—mapatawad

PARENT, n.—maglang, amá iná—ginikanan—ginikaana

PARENTAGE, n. — paryentes — kagikan, kagikanan — partidos

PARITY, paré-pareho, magkatu- lad — panag-angay-angay — magkaanggid, magkapareho

PARK, n.—parke, líwasang maha- laman—hawan, parke — parke, plasa sang talamnan

PARK, v. — tumigil, humintô — paghunong — magdulog, mag- parke

PARKING, n.—hintuan — huno- nganan — dulogán, parkehan

PARLIAMENT, n. — kapulungan ng mga mambabatás ng Ingla- terra — parlamento, balay-ba- laoran—parlamento

PARLOR, n.—salas, silíd na tanggapan ng mga panaúhin — lawak-dawatanan, paanyagan — salas, hulót-balatonán

PARSON, n.—kura, parè o pastór—pari, kura, pastor — kura, parì ukón pastor

PARROT, n.—loro—piriko, abukay —periko

PART, n.—bahagi, parte — bahin, pahat—bahin, parte

PARTAKE, v.—makihatì, makisali —pagpakigsalo — makigbahin, makig-ambit

PARTIAL, adj. — hindî pareho, maykiling — kabahin lamang, tipik—dî-pareho, pihakán

PARTICIPATE, v. — makihalò, makisali—pag-apil, pagsalmot— makigsakup, makighimbon

PARTICIPATION, n.—pagsama, pagsali, paglahók — kaapilan, kasalmotan — pagpakidupon

PARTICULAR, adj.—bukód, tangì, maselang — yanong butang — luás, pasahî, pililión

PARTING, n.—paghihiwaláy--panagbulag—pagtulungà

PARTISAN, adj. — magkapartido magdapigon sa pundok—kapartido

PARTITION, n. — paghahati-hatì — pagbahin-bahin — pagbahin-bahin

PARTLY, adv.—isáng bahagi — sa usa ka bahin — isá ka bahin

PARTNER, n.—kasama — sangga, kauban—kaupod

PARTNERSHIP, n.—sámahan sa negosyo, pagsasama — panagsangga — kaupod sa negosyo pag-uporáy

PARTY, n.—lapian, salu-salo — pundok, salo-salo — partido, bunghay

PASS, n.—pases, daán — agianan, pasis — pasis, alagyan

PASS, v.—daanan, dumaán—pag-agi—mag-agi,

PASSABLE, adj. — maráraanan, puwede, maáarì—mahimong kaaian, malabay—maagyan

PASSAGE, n.—pasahe, bayad, bilete, daanan--agianan, plitì — pasahe, hinakay, alagyan

PASSENGER, n.—sakáy o lulan —sumasakay — pasahero, sumalakay

PASSION, n.—masidhíng damdamin — mainítong pagbatì, kasuko—pagpaninghakúl

PASSIONATE, adj.—mainit, mapusók — labihan kamabination —mapaningkakulón

PASSPORT, n.—pahintulot, pasaporte—pasaporte — pahanugot, pasaporte

PASSWORD, n.—hudyát, senyas kontra-sinyas—senyas sa hambal

PAST, adj.—lipás, nakaraán—ang miagi—nagligad

PASTE, n.—pandikít, dikít—papilit, panikit—pasta, inogpilít

PASTIME, n.—líbangan, pamparaán ng panahón—kalingawan—kalingawan

PASTORAL, adj. — mabukirín — banikanhon — palahalban

PASTRY, n.—kalamay — sopas, matam-is, kalamay — kalamay

PASTURE, n.—pastulan—sibsibanan sa baka—halalban

PAT, v.—tapík, tapikín—pagpikpik—pikpik

PATCH, n.—tagpî, tutóp — tapak, pilot — tukáp, hulip

PATCH, v.—tagpián, takpán, husayin—pagtapak, pagpilot — tukapan, hulipan

PATERNAL, adj.—maka-amá, sa panig ng amá—inamahan, amahanon — maki-amáy

PATH, n.—landás, bakás—dalan, subayanan—banas, dalan

PATHETIC, adj. — nakaáawà — makaluluoy, makatandug—makaluluoy

PATHOS, n.—kalungkutan—kasakitan, kahapdusan—kasulub-on

PATIENCE, n.—pagtitiis, pagbabatá—pailub, pag-antus — pagantus, pagpaninghakúl

PATIENT, adj.—mapagtiís — mapailubon, maantuson — mainantuson

PATIENT, n.—maysakít—masakiton—masakitón

PATRIOTIC, adj.—makabayan — bayanihon—maki-banwa

PATRIOTISM, n.—pag-ibig sa bayan, kabayanihan — kabayanihan, patriyotismo—paghigugma sa banwa

PATRIMONY, n.—lupang minana —yutang sinunod — dutang panublion

PATRON, n.—tagakalingà, pintakasi, sukì—suki—sukì, patron

PATRONAGE, n.—kalingà, pagtangkilik—pakigsuki, pagsagop —pagsukì, pagpasulabr

PATTER, n.—takbóng marahan, salitáng mabilís — hinayang dagan, sulting tulin—maliksi, madasig maghambal

PATTERN, n.—parisán, halimbawà—sukdanan, hulmahan — ilogán, sulondan

PAUSE, n. — tigil, hintô — hunong, pahulay — dulog, pahuway

153

PAUSE, v.—tumigil, magpahingá —paghunong, pagpahuway ka-diyut—dumulog, magpahuway

PAVEMENT, n.—latag na bató, dáanan—asiras — alagyan nga baldosa

PAW, n.—kukó o pangalmót ng hayop—kuko sa mananap — ku-kó ukón kamumuo sang hayup

PAW, v.—lamukutin—pagkawras kamasón

PAWN, v.—isanlâ—pagprinda — isangat, iprenda

PAWNBROKER, n.—bahay-sanla-an — balay-prindahan — baláy-sangatán, ahensya

PAY, n.—bayad—bayad, suhol — bayad

PAYEE, n.—ang taong binayaran —tawong gibayaran—balayran

PAYMENT, n.—kabayarán, pag-babayad — bayranan — kaba-yarán

PEA, n.—patanì, gisantes—gisan-te, satsaro—patanì, gisantes

PEACE, n.—kapayapaan, katiwa-sayán — kalinaw, kahusayan — paghidait

PEACEFUL, adj.—payapà, tiwa-sáy—malinawon, makidaiton — mahidaiton

PEACH, n.—magandá, masaráp, melokotón — melokoton, nindot maanyag, manamit, meleko-tón

PEAK, n.—taluktók, tugatog—ki-natumyan—putókputokán

PEANUT, n.—manî—mani—maní

PEAR, n.—peras — peras — peras

PEARL, n.—perlas—mutya—per-las, mutyâ

PEARLY, adj.—makisláp, maning-níng—mutyaanon—masilì

PEASANT, n.—taong bukid, ta-ong-bundók—nrag-uuma, mag-babaul—tagaumá, umanhon, bu-kidnon, mangunguma

PECK, v.—tukaín—pagtuka, pag-tuhik, pagtusik—tuktok

PECULIAR, adj.—kaibá sa kara-niwan — nalahi sa kasagaran—tuhay sa ibán

PEDDLE, n. — ilakò maglakô — pagsuroy-baligya—ilibud

PEDDLER, n. — tagapaglakò sa bahay-bahay — manunuroy ug baligya—manoglibúd sa kabala-yán

PEDESTRIAN, n.—naglálakád—tawong lumalabay—umalagi

PEEL, v.—talupan, balatán—pag-panit—panitan, upakan

PEELING, n.—balát, pinagtalu-pan—panit, gipanitan—pinani-tan, inupakan

PEEP, v.—sumilip, sumungaw — pagsil-ip, paglili—sumid-ing, gu-mawa

PEER, n.—kaurì, kapantáy, daki-
lang tao—katumbas, kasama—
kasarî, lutáw nga táo

PEN, n.—pluma; panulat na may
tinta—dagang, pluma—pluma

PENALIZE, v.—pagmultahín, parusahan, pagbayarín ng multá—
pagsilpi, pagsilot—multhán, lutáw nga táo

PENALTY, n.—multá, parusa—
silot, silpi—multa, tabís, silut

PENETRATION, n. — pagpasok,
pagkakáalám—ang panaglahus,
pamagtuhop—pagpaningsulód

PENCIL, n.—lapis—lapis—lapis

PENITENT, adj.—nagsísisi—ma-
basulon, nagabasul—naghinulsol

PENITENTIARY, v.—bilangguan
—bilanggoan, karsel—bilanggoan

PENKNIFE, n.—kortapluma, lanseta—lansita, korta-pluma—kortapluma, lansitas

PENNILESS, adj.—waláng salapî
walay diyut, way-kangho—wala'y pilak

PENNY, n.—séntimó—sintabo—
séntimós

PENSION, n.—pensiyón, abuloy—
pensiyon—pensyon

PENSIVE, adj.—mapag-isíp—mahinuktokon—palalibug

PEOPLE, n.—mga tao, taong-ba-
yan — mga tawo, katawhan —
mga táo, banwahanon

PEOPLE, v.—tinirahán—pagmu-
lupyo—pinuy-an

PEPPER, n.—pamintá, sili—pami-
yenta, sili—pimienta, gatumbal

PEPPERY, adj. — maangháng —
mahalang—makahang

PER, adv.—bawa't, sa pamamagitan—matagusa—tagsa, sa

PERCEIVE, v.—mamataan, maka-
halatà—pagsabut — panilagan

PER CENT, n.—porsiyento, ba-
hagdán porsiyento—porsiento

PERCH, n.—hapunán o tungtu-
ngan—batuganan—haponán

PERCH, v. — sumampá, tumung-
tóng—pagtungtong—humapon

PERDITION, n.—kawalán ng kinábukasan, pagkapahamak—kawad-on, kapildihon—pagkadulà
sang buás-damlag

PEREGRINATION, n.—paglalakbáy—pagsuroy,   pamagdoy —
pagpanakayon

PERFECT, adj.—sakdál, ganáp,
lubós—hingpit, bug-os—himpit,
lubos

PEREMPTORY, adj. —pahtapós—
matapuson—hingapusán

PERENNIAL, adj. — palagian —
walay katapusan—tuigan

PERFECTION, n. — kasukdulán, kagánapan, kalubusán—kahingpitan, kabug-osan—kahimpitán, kalubosan

PERFORATION, n. — butas—lungag-lungag—buhó, lubótlubót

PERFORM, v.—gumanáp, magsagawâ—paghímo, pagbuhat — maghikut, mag-akù

PERFÓRMANCE, n.—pagkakaganáp, ginawâ—kahimoan, pasundayag—pagkapangakò, pagkatuman

PERFUME, n.—pabangó—pahumot—pahumót

PERHAPS, adv.—marahil, kaypalà tingali—ayhan

PERIL, n.—panganib, pangambá —katalagman, kuyaw—katalagman

PERILOUS, adj. — mapanganib—makuyaw, talagmanon—makatalagam

PERIOD, n.—yugtô ng panahón, tuldók—yugto sa panahon—panahónan, tumbok

PERIODIC, adj. — paná-panahón, tuwî na—nunot sa panahon—tigpanahón

PERISH, v.—mamatáy, pumanaw — pagkamatay, pagkadunot — mamatáy, matapos

PERISHABLE, adj. — madalíng mamatáy o masìrà — madaling mamatay kun madugta—madalî mapatáy ukón madulà

PERJURY, n.—pagsisinungalíng—salang pagpamakak—pagbinutig

PERMANENT, adj.—pampalagian —kanunay, dayon—pirme, unáy

PERMISSION, n.—pahintulot, kapahintukutan—katugotan, pagtugot—pahanugot

PERMIT, v.—pahintulutan—pagtugot—pahanugotan

PERNICIOUS, adj.—mapanirà—makadaut, dautan—mahaliton

PERPETUAL, adj.—patuloy, waláng hintô—sa kanunay—padayon, wala'y dulog

PERSEVERANCE, n.—tiyagâ — pailub—paghimud-os, paninguhâ

PERSEVERING, adj. —matiyàgâ — mapailubon, makanunayon —mahimud-osan, matinguhaon

PERSIST, v.—mamilit—pagpamugos—mamilit

PERSON, n.—tao—tawo—táo

PERSONAL, adj.—ukol sa tao, pansarili—mahitungod sa tawo, kinaugalingon — natungód sa táo, kinaugalingon

PERSPECTIVE, n. — paningín, pagpapalagáy — panan-aw — handurawan

PERSPIRE, v. — pagpawisan — pagdusingot—pabalhas

PERSUADE, v.—akitin, himukin —pagpugos—buyokon

PERSUASION, n.— panghimok, panghikayat—pamugos — pagbuyok

PERSUASIVE, adj. — mainam maghikayat — mapugsanon, makapadani—maayo magbuyok

PERUSE, v. basahin, tingnán — pagbasa—basahon mayo

PEST, n.—peste, salot—pisti, sakit—pesti, sarút

PESTLE, n.—pambayó, halo—alho—hal-o

PET, n.—ang minámahál, ang itinátangì,— pinangga, pinalabi — pinasulabi, pinalanggá

PETITION, n.—kahílingan—tutol-pangayo—petisyon, mangabáy

PETITION, v.—humilíng, hilingán —pagtutol, pagpangayo—pagpangabáy

PETITIONER, n. — ang humíhilíng, ang may kahílingan—ang nangayo, nagatutol—ang nagapangabáy

PETTY, adj.—di-mahalagá—diyutay, dili bililihon—wala'y bilí

PHARMACIST, n.—parmasiyutika — parmasyutika — parmaseutiká

PHILOSOPHER, n.—pilósopó—pilosopo—pilosopó

PHILOSOPHY, n.— pilosopiyá — gumaran, pilosopiya —pilosopiya

PHLEGM, n.—plema, uhog—plema, luwa –plemas, badlù

PHLEGMATIC, adj. — malamíg, walán̄g-siglâ—bugnaw, luyahón —mabundol

PHOTOGRAPHER, n.—retratista, tagakuha ng larawan—maghuhulagway—retratista

PHRASE, n.—pananalitâ, parirala —pasambingay, mugbong pinulongan—-panghambal

PHYSICAL EDUCATION, pangangalagà sa kalusugán—saring sa paugnat sa kusog—hanashanas sa ikaayong lawas

PHYSICIAN, n.—manggagamot, médikó, doktór—mananambal—manogbulong, medikó, doktor

PICK, n. — piko, pilì—piko, pinilian—piko, pilì

PICKLE, n.—atsara, buro, kainán sa labás—atsara—atsara

PICK UP, v.—pulutin—pagpulot, pagpudyot—puluton, pilion

PICTORIAL, adj.—punô ng larawan—himulagway—mga laragway

PICTURE, n.—larawan, retrato—hulagway, larawan—laragway, retrato

PICTURE, v.—ilarawan, iguhit—paghulagway — ilaragway, idrowing

PICTURESQUE, adj. — matanawin, mabista — makalingawng tan-awon—malaragway, mabistahon

PIE, n.—empanada—empanada—panada

PIECE, v.—pagsama-samahin, buuín — pagtibuok — kautód, pinikás, piraso

PIERCE, v.—tumagós, lumagpás, bumutas—paglagpas, paglahus, pagdulot—lumusót, bumuhò

PIERCING, adj.—tumátagós, nakagígimbál—nagalagbas, nagadulot—nagalusót, makatilingil

PIETY, n.—kabánalan—balaanong pagbati—balaanon

PIG, n.—baboy, biík—baboy, baktin—baboy, idík

PIGEON, n.—kalapati—salapati—patíng

PILE, n.—salansán, buntón—tugsok—hinantalan

PILE, v.—magbuntón, salansanín—pagtugsok — maghantal

PILGRIM, n. — ang naglálakbáy, peregrino—manunuaw sa balaanong dapit—peregrino, ang nagadulugok sa mga duóg sang santos

PILL, n.—pilduras—pildoras—pildorás

PILLAGE, v.—nakawan, sirain—pagpanulis, pagpangguba — kawatáy

PILLAR, n.—haligi, tukod—haligi, tukod—haligi, tukód

PILLOW, n.—unan — unlan—ulonan

PIMPLE, n.—tagihawat—bugasbugas—punggod

PIN, n.—ispilé, pandurò—pukpok, alpiril—sibít

PIN, v.—duruin, ipatdá—pagduot—sibton

PINCH, v.—kurót, kumurót, ipitín, hulihin—pagkusi, paglusi, pagkurit—kusî, lusò

PINEAPPLE, n.—pinyá—pinya—pinya

PINE TREE, n.—pino—kahoy nga palo-china—pino

PINCER, n.—ipit, sipit — kimpit kimpit

PINK, adj.—kulay rosas—bulok nga rosas—duág rosál

PINNACLE, n.—kaitaasan—kinatas-an—kahitáasan

PINT, n.—ikawaló ng isáng galón—ikawalong bahin sa galon—ikawaló nga bahin sa isá ka galón

PIOUS, adj.—banál, madasalin—
santolon, diyosnon — balaan,
diósnon

PIPE, n.—pipa, kwako, tubo o
padaluyan—kwako, hunsoy, si-
gopan, tubo—pipa, kwako, tubo
ukón pailigán

PISTOL, n.—baríl, pistola—pistola, luthang—pistola, luthang

PIT, n.—hukay, butas na malalim—lungag, bangag—buhò, kutkot nga madalum

PITCH, n.—alkitrán, tono ng músiká, resin—alkitran, tono — alkitran, tono sang musiká, resina

PITCHER, n. —pitsél, tagahagis
ng bola—pitsil, taglabay sa bola
—pitsel, tagpilák sing bola

PITIFUL, adj.—kaawa-awà, naka-
háhabág—makaluluoy — makaluluoy

PITY, n.—awà, habág, hinayang—
kaluoy—awà, kaluoy

PITY, v.—maawà, kaawaan—pagkaluoy—maluoy, kaluy-an

PLACARD, n. — paskíl—kartil —
paskil

PLACATE, v.—suyuin, pagbigyán
—pagbugnaw — buyokon, hatagan sing dalan

PLACE, n.—dako, lugár—dapit—
lugár, duóg

PLAGUE, n.—salot, peste—sakit,
peste—sarút, penti

PLAGUE, v.—bagabagin, pestihín
pagpakaylap sa sakit—pesti-
hán

PLAIN, adj.—pantáy, patag, maliwanag, malinaw — patag, yano,
tin-aw—patag, matapan, maathag, masilì

PLAINS, n.—kapatagan—kapatagan, kadaruhan—kapatagan

PLAN, n.—plano, bangháy, panukalà—laraw, plano—plano

PLAN, v.—isaayos, iplano—lara-
won, planohon—handumón, planohon

PLANE, n.—katám—sipilya—sa-
piyo

PLANET, n.—planeta, talà—planeta—planeta

PLANT, n.—pananím, halaman —
tanum—tanúm

PLANT, v.—magtaním, magpatu-
bò—pagtanum—ìtanúm

PLANTATION, n. — hasiyenda,
malakíng tatamnán — asyenda,
dakung tanaman—hasyenda

PLASTER, n.—largamasa, pana-
pal—tapal—hampul, plaster

PLASTER, v.—tapalan, dikitán—
pagtapal, pagdikit — hampulán,
plasterán

PLASTIC, adj. — plastiko, bagay
na maáaring hubugin—plastiko
—plastik

PLATE, n.—pinggán, putol na me-
tal—pinggan—pinggan, platò

PLATFORM, n.—pátakarán, entablado—entablado, plataforma—entablado, plataforma

PLATTER, n.—bandehado—bandihado—bandehado

PLAUDIT, n.—papuri, aploso—dalayeg, dayo — aplawso, dayawon

PLAY, n.—larô, palabás sa entablado—dula, drama — hampang, palaguaon

PLAY, v.—tumútugtóg, maglarô—pagtugtog, pagdula—maglanton, maghampang

PLAYFUL, adj.—mapaglarô, makiliti—makidula, madula-dulaon—makighampang, makalamón

PLAYGROUND, n. —pálaruan —hawan-dulaanan—hampangan

PLAYMATE, n. —kalarô— kauban sa dula—kahanpang

PLEAD, v.—makiusap, himukin—paghangyo, pagpangamuyo—makighiugyon

PLEADING, n.—pakiusap, himok—hangyo, pangamuyo — pagpakighiugyon

PLEASANT, adj.—kaayaaya, nakawiwili — makapahimuot, makalipay—makighimbon, makiglipay

PLEASE, v.—umaliw, makalugód—paghimuot—mahimò, balá

PLEASE, v.—maaarì ba, ipaki—

palihug, mahimo ba — palihoga akó

PLEASURE, n.—kaaliwán, katuwaan—kalipay, lingaw-lingaw—kalingawan, kasadyahan

PLEDGE, n.—pangakò, sanlâ—panaad, panumpa — mangakò, manug-an

PLEDGE, v.—mangakò, magsanlâ—pagsaad, pagsumpa — magpangakó, magpanug-an

PLENTY, adj. marami, saganà—daghan, ubay-ubay, naghingapin—dagayà, dagsang

PLOT, n.—banghảy, bantâ—laraw, hunahuna sa pagsukol, pirasong yuta—humon, pagbalayon

PLOT, v.—magbalangkás nang palihím — paglaraw — magbalay sing likúm

PLOW, n.—araro, araruhin—daro, pamugwal—arado, aradohon

PLUCK, v. — bunutin, pitasín — pagkutlo—gabuton, pûpuón

PLUM, n.—siniguelas—bungahoy ingon sa ubas, peras—sirgwelas.

PLUMBER, n.—tubero—plomero—tubero

PLUME, n.—pakpák, plumero — balhibo sa langgam — pakpak, plumero

PLUMMET, v.—mahulog—pagkahulog—pamató

PLUNDER, n.—nakaw, ninakaw—pagkawat, kawat, panghabas—kawatáy

PLURAL, adj.—marami—daghan, labaw sa usa—damò

PLURALITY, n. — nakarárami—pagkalabaw, pagkadaghan—nakapadamò

PLUS, v.—at sakâ—pagkapin — dugangan, isá pa

PLUVIAL, adj.—maulán, basâ — ulanon, basa—maulanon

POET, n.—poeta, mánunulà, makatâ—magbabalak—poeta, mamalaybay

POETICAL, adj. — matulain—balaknon—mabinalaybayon

POETRY, n.—mga tulâ, tulâ — pamalak, pamagay—binalaybay

POINT, n.—dulo, matulis na dulo —tumoy, pagtudlo—punto, mataliwis

POISON, v.—lasunín—paghilo — hiloán

POISON, n.—lason—hilo—hilô

POISONOUS, adj. —nakalálason, —makahilo—makahililô

POKERFACE, adj. —hindî makáhalatâ — butihon — dî-masatumán

POLE, n. — dulo ng mundó, panungkít—tukon — ukbong sang kalibutan, singít, bagát, tukon

POLICE, n.—mga pulís, tanod ng bayan—kapolison, bantay sa kalinaw—polís

POLICE, v.—alagaan, bantayán—pagbantay—bantayan

POLICY, n.—palakad o pamamalakad, katibayan sa seguro—polisa, paagi — polisa, kabakurán sa seguro sa kabuhì

POLISH, v.—pakintabín — pagpasinaw—pabadlakón

POLISHED, adj.—magandáng kilos, makinis—masinaw, mahamis —mahinlô, pinuy-asán

POLITE, adj.—magalar g, mapitagan—matinahuron, maugdang—matinahuron

POLITICAL, adj.—ukol sa polítiká o pámahalaán—lugaynon. politikanhon—natungód sa politiká

POLITICIAN, n.—politikó, marunong sa lakad ng pámahalaán—politiko—politikó

POLITICS, n.—polítiká, pamamaraán—politika, lugaynan—politiká

POLL, n.—tálaan ng mga botante —talaan sa mga pumipili—listahan sang mga botantes

POLL, v.—italâ, magkamít—pagpili, pagdaug—ilista, dag-on

POLYGAMIST, n. — maraming asawa—mansibado, daghag asawa—mandamo'y asawa

POMPOUS, adj. — mapasikat, palalò—mapagawalon, garboso — madayáw, hambog

POND, n.—lawà—linaw, lunangan —tangke sang tubig

PONDEROUS, adj.—malakí— daku, mabug-at—dakû kaayo

POOL, n.—tangke ng tubig, samasama, lawà, bilyár—tangke sa tubig, bilyar — tangkehan sing tubig, pool

POOR, adj.—mahirap, dukhâ, mababà—kabus, timawà—imol, kubós, timawà

POOR HOUSE, n.—bahay-ampunan—balay sa kabus — baláy-alaypan

POPE, n.—papa, pangulo ng simbahang katólikó romano—santo papa—papa

POPEYED, adj. — nanlálakí ang matá—budlatog mata — nagmurahág ang matá

POPULAR, adj.—kilalá, tanyág sa bayan—inila, bantug—kilala, lutáw sa banwa

POPULARITY, n.—katanyagán—kabantug, kainila—kalutawán

POPULATION, n.—mga naninirahan sa isáng bayan—gidaghanon sa pumopuyo—pumuluyò

POPULOUS, adj.—matao—dasok sa tawo—madamong pumuluyò

PORCH, n.—portiko, balkón—balkon, beranda—portiko, balkonahe

PORK, n.—karné o lamán ng baboy—unod sa baboy—unód sang baboy

POROUS, adj.—butas-butas — lungag-lungagon — buhô-buhô, lubótlubót

PORT, n.—puerto, punduhan ng sasakyán—dunggoanan, landiganan—dungkaan

PORTER, n.—bantáy-pintô — bantay sa ganghaan — bantay-ganhaan

PORTING, n.—bahagi, hati, kaputol—katipak, kabahin, katunga—bahin, katungâ, kautód

POSITION, n. — kalágayan, katungkulan — pagkabutang, kahimtang—kahimtangan

POSITIVE, adj.—tiyák — tataw, makapaniguro—maathag, pat-ud

POSSESS, v. — ariin, mayroón, nag-áangkín—pagtag-iya, paghupot—angkunón

POSSESSION, n.—pag-aarì kayamanan — butang napanag-iya, kabtangan—pag-angkon, manggad

POSSESSIVE, adj. — mang-aangkín—maangkonon—mag-angkon

POSSIBILITY, n.—ikapangyáyari —kahimoan—mahitabô

POSSIBLE, adv.—maáarì, mangyáyari—ang mahimo— mahimó,
matabô

POST, n.—koreo, haligi — haligi,
tagdok, koriyo—koreo, haligi

POST, v.—ipastil, ihayag — pagmantala, pagpadayag — ipastil,
idukót

POSTAGE, n.—selyo pará sa lí-
ham—prangkiyo — selyo ukón
prankiyo

POSTAL, adj.—ukol sa koreo —
mahanutgod sa koriyo — natungód sa koreo

POSTERITY, n.—angkán, inapó—
kahangturan, kaliwatan — kaliwatan, inapó

POSTURE, n. anyô, tikas, tayô—
pamarug, postura—dagway, tin-
dog

POT, n.—palayók, bangâ—kulon—
kulon

POTATO, n.—patatas—patatas —
patatas

POTENCY, n.—bisà, lakás — gahum, kusog—gahúm, kusóg

POTENTATE, n.—harì, may kapangyarihan — hari, monarka
—harì, makagalahum

POTENTIAL, n.—natatagong lakás—tinagong kusog — tinagò
nga gahúm

POTTER, n. — magpapalayók —
magkukulon—manogkulón

POTTERY, n.—gáwaan ng palayók—gam-anan sa kulon—dili-
honán-kulon

POUND, n. — librá, kuwartang
Inglés—libra, salaping Ingles—
librá, kuartang Inglés

POUND, v.—pukpukín, bayuhín—
pagdukdok, paglubok — pukpukón, bayhon

POUR, v.—ibuhos—pagbubo, pagyabo, pagtigis—ibûbò

POVERTY, n.—karukhaán, kawalán—kakabus, kawalad-on—kaimolón, kinulabos

POWDER, n.—pulburá, pulbós—
pulbo, abog, binukbok—pulbos,
polborá

POWER, n.—kapangyarihan—gahum, kagahum—gahúm

POWERFUL, adj.—makapangyarihan—makagagahum, gamha-
nan — makagalahum

POWERLESS, adj. — waláng-la-
kás, waláng-kapangyarihan —
mahuyang, way-gahum — wa-
la'y kagamhanan

PRACTICAL, adj. — magágamit,
marunong pumaraan—praktiko,
kinaugalingong pamuhat—prak-
tikál, antigo magpahitò

PRACTICE, n.—pagsasanay—ban-
say-bansay—paghanashanas

PRACTICE, v.—magsanay, sanayin — pagbansay, paghanas
maghanashanas, hanason

PRAISE, n.—papuri—dalayeg, dayo—pagdayaw

PRAISE, v.—purihin — pagdayeg,
pagdayo—dayawon

PRAISEWORTHY, adj. — kahanga-hangà—dalaygon —dalayawon

PRAY, v.—manalangin, magdasál
— pag-ampo, pagpangaliya —
mag-ampò, mangamuyò, manga-
di

PRAYER, n.—dalangin, dasál —
pangadye, panalangin — panga-
muyò, ampò

PRAYERBOOK, n.—dásalan—pa-
ngadyeon—palangadion

PREACH, v.—mangaral, magturò
—pagwali, pagsermon—magwali

PREACHING, n.—pangaral—wali,
nagawali—pagwali

PREAMBLE, n.—páunáng salitâ—
unang pamulong—unang ham-
bal

PRECARIOUS, adj. — waláng tiyák—dili seguro, kaduhaduhaan
—wala'y pat-ud

PRECAUTION, n.—pag-iingat —
pasidaan sa pagbantay — halalongán

PRECEDENCE, n. — nangunang
gáwain o pangyayari — naha-
unang hitabo kun buhat—unang
hilikutón ukón kahitaboán

PRECIOUS adj.—mahalagá mahál—bililhon, mahal — malahalon, bililhon

PREDICATE, n.—panagurì —ma-
tangnon—panagsarî

PREFER, v.—pumilì, humirang—
pagpalabi, pagpihig — pumilì,
magpalabí

PREFERENCE, n. pagpilì—pini-
hig, pinalabi—pagpalabí

PREPARATION, n.—paghahandâ,
handâ—pangandam, panagana—
paghandà; pagpangaman

PRISONER, n.—bilanggô — bini-
langgo—binilanggò

PRIVACY, n.—pagtatagò, paglili-
him—tinagong panimuyo—kinaugalíng

PRIVATE, adj.—lihim, personál—
tinago, kinaugalingon—personál

PRIVATE EDUCATION, n.—pag-
tuturong-pribado — pagpanudlo
nga pribado—eskwela-pribado

PRIVILEGE, n.—tanging karapatán, pribilehiyo—katungod, katugotan—pribelihiyo, katungdanan

PRIZE, n.—premyo, gantimpalà—
ganti—premyo, padyà

PRIZE, v. — itangì, mahalín —
pagganti—ipremyo, dinag-an

PROBABILITY, n.—kalamangáng
mangyari — may kalagmitang
mahitabo, malagmit — mahimò
matabô

PROBABLE, adv.—maáarì, kalpa-
là—hayan, mahimong mahitabo,
malagmit—mahimò

PROBATION, n.—pagsubok—pagsulay—pagtiláw

PROBLEM, n.—súliranin—gumon-
hap, suliran—palaligban, palak-
takon

PROBLEMATICAL, adj.—maguló,
masúliranin—gumonhapon, hu-
losayon—makalilibug

PROCEDURE, n.—paraán, pagpa-
patuloy—paagi, palakaw—paagi,
pagpadayon

PROCEED, v.—magpatuloy, itu-
lóy — pagpadayon — magpadayon, ipadayon

PROCESS, n.—paraán, kasaluku-
yang ginágawâ—paagi — paagi,
pahitò

PROCESSION, n.—prusisyón, pila
—pasunding—prosenyon, katay

PROCLAIM, v. — magpahayag,
magpatalastás — pagsangyaw,
pagpahayag—magpahayag, mag-
patalastas

PROCLAMATION, n. — pahayag,
patalastás—pahayag, kasangya-
wan—pahayag, patalastás

PROCRASTINATION, n. —kata-
maran, pagpapaliban — paglangay-langay, langan-langan —
katamarón, uyayâ

PROCURE, v.—kunin, hanapin —
pagpaninguha, pagsingkamut —
tinguhaón, pangitaon

PROCUREMENT, n. — pagkuha,
paghanap — paningkamut, paninguha—palangitaón

PRODIGAL, adj.—mapagtapón —
mausikon, ligoy—buhahâ

PRODUCE, v.—magbunga, ilabás
—pagpagula, paggama — pabu-
ngahon

PRODUCE, n.—ani, bunga—gina-
man, mga abut—patubson

PRODUCT, n.—bunga, ani, yarì—
ani, bunga—produkto, pinatubás

PRODUCTION, n.—paggawâ, pa-
mumunga—pamuhat, panggama,
pamunga—pinatubsan

PROFANE, adj.—waláng galang
—masipad-anon, way-tahud —
wala'y katahurán

PROFESSION, n. — hanapbuhay,
katungkulan—panginabuhi, kahinguhaan—palangitan-an

PROFIT, v. — magtubò, makinabang—pagpatubo, pagganansiya
—kasaplirán

PROFIT, n.—napalâ, tubò, pakinabang, pakikinabangan—tubo,
ganansiya — nasaplid, naganan-
sya

PROFITABLE, adj.—kapakipaki-
nabang—makapinon, maganan-
siyahon—masaplirán, maganan-
syahán

PROFOUND, adj.—malalim—ha-
lawum, dulot sa bukog—madu-
lúm

PROFUSE, adj.—masaganà— tugob, naghingapin—dagayà

PROGRAM, n. — palátuntunan, programa—tulomanon, programa—programa

PROGRESS, n.—pagsulong— kauswagan—kauswagan

PROGRESS, v. —sumúsulong, lumálagô—paguswag, pag-usbaw —umuswag

PROHIBIT, v.—ipagbawal — pagdili—dumilian

PROHIBITION, n.—pagbabawal —ang pagdili—pagdumilì

PROJECT, n.—balak, panukalà—laraw, bulohaton, proyekto—bulukuón, palasarón

PROLONG, v.—pahabain, patagalín— pagpalugway, pag-inat — palawigon, padugayon

PROMINENT, adj.—kilalá, dakilà —inila kaayo, bantug — lutáw, kinilala

PROMISE, n.—pangakò —pagpausbaw, pagdasig—pangakò

PROMOTE, v.—magtaás, itaguyod —pagpausbaw, pagdasig—padelantohón

PROMOTER, n. — ang nagsúsulong-tagapagtaguyod — tigpausbaw, magdadasig—tagdelanto

PROMPT, v.—napilit,· napilitan—pagdali, pagbaskug—dalián

PROMPT, adj. —maliksí, maagap —madali, mabaskug—madali

PRONOUNCE, v.—bumigkás, bigkasín—paglitok—ilawag, ipahibaló

PROOF, n. — pruweba, patunay, patotoo—kamatuoran — pruweba, pamatuod, patunay

PROPER, adj.—nárarapat, ayos—go, angay— nagakaigò, nagahilituon

PROPERTY, n.— pag-aarì, arì — kabtangan, butang kaugaiingon —pagkabutáng

PROPHET, n.—propeta, manghuhulà—manalagna, propita—propeta, manalagnà

PROPHETIC, adj. — nagsásabi, nagpápahiwatig — matagnaón, matag-anon—nagapanagnà

PROPHESY, v. — hulaan, manghulà—panagna — tagnaán, pakton

PROPORTION, n. — pagkakábagay-bagay — kaigoan, pagkaangay—pag-alalangay

PROPORTIONATE, adj.—nábabagay—naangay, takdong pagkabahin—nagaalangay

PROPOSE, v. — magmungkahì, magpahayag — pagtanyag, pagpahayag — bukò, palakamaayohón

PROPOSITION, n.—panukalà — tanyag, butang pauyonan—bulokuón, pakamaayohón

PROPRIETOR, n.—may-arì—tagiya—tag-iya

PROPRIETY, n.—karapatán, kaayusán—pagka-angayan, pagkabagay, katakus — kahimtangan, kahilabtanan

PROSPECT, n.—tinátanáw, pagasa—palaabuton, paglaum—buás-damlag, palaabuton

PROSPECTIVE, adj. — nálalapít, magiging—umaabut, linauman—manginpalaabutón

PROSPER, v.—managanà, umunlád, yumaman—pag-uswag, pagmadaugon—umuswag

PROSPERITY, n.—paglagô, kayamanan, kasaganaan — kauswagan, kabulahanan—pag-uswag

PROSPEROUS, adj. — mayaman, saganà — mauswagon — mauswagon

PROSTRATE, adj. — manghinà, magpatirapâ—pagkatuy-od, nagbuy-od—naghayanghayang

PROTECT, v.—ipagtanggól, ipagsanggaláng—pagpanalipod, paglaban—pangapinan

PROTECTIVE, adj.—mapagtanggól — mapanalipuron — maapinon

PROTEGE, n. — ampón—inagak, bata-bata—aypon, inakupón

PROTEST, n.—tutol, di-pagsángayon—lalis, tutol — batok, protesta

PROTEST, v. — tumutol, di-umayon—paglalis, pagtutol—makigbatuk, magprotesta

PROUD, adj.—mayabang, hambóg —mapahitas-on, garbuso—bugalón

PROVE, v.—magpatunay, tikman —pagmatuod—pamatud-an

PROVERB, n.—saláwikain — panultihon—hurubaton

PROVIDE, v.—magbigáy ng kailangan, maghandâ — pagsangkap, pagpangandam — maghandà sing kinahanglanon

PROVIDENCE, n. — kalooban ng Diyós, katalagahan—kabubut-on sa Dios—kabubut-on sang Diós

PROVINCE, n.—lalawigan, sakop —lalawigan—kapuorán

PROVISION, n. — baon, pagkain, handâ—balon, kahimanan—balon, pagkaon

PROVISIONAL, adj. —pansamantalá—mantinil—kitaypuni

PROVOCATION, n.—kayamután, pagkakabunsód—hagit, hagad—pagpanugyot

167

PROVOCATIVE, adj. — mapanudyô, mapang-akit — mahagiṭon, mahagarcn — palasugyot, manunugyot

PROVOKE, v.—mag-udyók, pagalitin—pagbagit, pagpainit — painitón

PRUNE, v.—putlán, bawasan — paggunting sa tanum, siriguylas —kapunón, (sa tanúm)

PRUNING, n. — kabawasán, pinagputlán — mga pinutol, mga kinapon—kinaponán (sa tanúm)

PUBLIC, n.—públikó, mámamayán—katawhan, publiko — publikó, banwahanon

PUBLICATION, n.—aklát, páhayagán — pamantalaan — publikasyon, bantalaan

PUBLIC SCHOOL, n.—páaralángbayan—tunghaang lungsod—eskwela—publikó

PUBLISH, v. — ipalimbág, ipahayag — pagmantala — ibantalà, ibalità

PUFF, v.—bumugá, magpapantóg, magpalakí—pagbulhoṭ, pagbuga —burhotán, paburhotán

PUGILIST, n.—boksingero — boksingero, boksiyador—boksingero

PUGNACIOUS, adj. — mapangaway—magubtanon, palaaway— maawayón

PULCHRITUDE, n.—kagandahan —katahuman—katahumán

PULL, n.—batak, hila—butad, guyod—batak, butong

PULL, v.—batakin, hilahin—pagbutad, pagbira—batakon, butongon

PULLEY, n.—kalô—moton—mutón

PULSE, n. pulsó, tibók— pinitik, pulso, kotokoto — pulso, bayóbayo

PULVERIZE, v. pulbusín, durugin—pagpulpog, pagpulbos—pulbosón, dugmukón

PUMP, v.—bombahín, lagyáñ — pagbombag hangin — bombahón

— Q —

QUEEN, n.—reyna, asawa ng harì—rayna, hara—rayna, asawa sang harì, harà

QUEENLY, adj. — parang reyna, marilág — maraynahon — daw sa rayna, haraanon

QUEER, adj.—kakatwâ — katingad-an, bakikaw — kahalamotan

QUENCH, v.—patayín, sugpuín—pagtagbaw, pagpalong — nubwán

QUESTION, n. —tanóng, tutol — **pangutana, sukot, sukna' —** pamangkut, hulusayón

QUESTION, v. — magtanóng — **pagpangutana, pagsukot — mag-pamangkut**

QUESTIONABLE, adj. — kapansin-pansín — **kaduhaduhaan — palamangkuton**

QUESTIONNAIRE, n.—tálaan ng mga tanóng, kuwestiyunanyo— **talaan sa mga pangutana**—listahan sang mga pamangkut

QUICK, adj.—madalî, maliksí — **madalî, lagmit, lagsik**—madalî, maabtik

QUICKEN, v.—buhayin, dallín — **pagpadali**—padalión

QUICKSILVER, n.—asoge—asoge —asogeng buhî

QUIET, adj.—tahimik, waláng kibô—**mahilum, hilumon** — malinóng, wala'y hulohambal

QUIET, v.—patahimikin — **paghilum**—palinongón

QUIETLY, adv.—matahimik — **sa kahilum**—kalinóng

QUININE, n. —kinina, gamót **sa malarya—kinina, tambal sa malarya**—kinina, bulóng sa malarya

QUINTET, n. —límahan, limáng beses—**sinakpag lima** — limahán, limá ka tingog

QUIRK, n.—ngiwî—**kalit nga pagliso**—sambil

QUIT, v.—iwan, umalís, magbitíw —pag-undang, **pagbiya — talik**dan, lumakát, naghalín

QUIVER, v.—manginíg, kumimbót —pagkureg, **pagkuray—mangu**dog, ligbosán

QUIZ, n. — pagsusulit—**pag-usisa, usisa**—pagsalawsaw

QUOTA n.—takdâ, sapát — **kota, kabahinan**—kuota, latid

QUOTATION, n.—sipì, halagá — **bili**—bilí

— R —

RABBIT, n. — koneho—**koniho**—koneho

RABID, adj.—masigasig, mapusók —**mainitong** paglaban — masupog

RABIES, n.—kagát ng asong-ulól, pagkaulól—**sakit gikan sa irong-**buang — kagát sang idû-buang

RACE, n.—lahì, kareta, unahán— **lumba, kaliwat**—kaliwatan, karera, palumbà

RACE TRACK, n.—kárerahán — **lumbaan sa kabayo**—karerahán

RACK, n. — balangkás, sabitán—sab-itanan—salab-itan

RACY, adj.—maliwanag—matulin—madasig

RADIANT, adj. — maliwanag — mahayag, magilakon—mabadla-lakon, masili

RADIO, n.—radyo—radyo—radyo

RADIO, v.—ibalità o ipadalá sa pamamagitan ng radyo—pagsibya sa radyo—ibalità sa radyo

RADISH, n.—labanós—rabanos—rabanós

RAFFLE, n.—ripa—ripa, loteriya—ripa

RAFT, n.—balsá, táwirang kawayan—balsa, gakit—balsa

RAFTER, n.—balangkás ng bubungan—salagunting — pagbalayon (sang baláy)

RAG, n.—basahan, pamunas—nunog pamahid, pahiran—trapo

RAGE, v.—mapoót, mag-init—pagpanuyo, pagkasuko — akíg, dumót

RAGE, n. — galit, poót—panuyo, kasuko, kapikal — mahigkò pahirán

RAGGED, adj. — malabasahan, marumí—nagkagidlay, nagkato—kahig'tuón

RAID, v. — lusubin—pagsulong, paglungkab — maakig, magdumót, manginít

RAIL, n.—riles, barandilya—rilis, barandilya—riles, barandilya

RAILROAD, n. dáanan ng tren—tren—alagyan sang tren

RAIN, n.—ulán—ulan—ulán

RAINBOW, n. — bahaghari—bangaw—balangáw

RAIN TREE, n.—akasya—akasya, akasya

RAINY, adj.—maulán—maulanon—maulán

RAINY SEASON, n.—tag-ulán—ting-ulan—tingulan

RAISE, n. — taás, dagdág—dugang, pataas—pagtaas, pagdugang

RAISE, v.—magtaás, tumindíg—pagpataas, pag-isa, pagbakyaw, pagtanum—pataason, patindogón

RAKE, n.—kalaykáy, pangkalahig—kigi, kahig—kahíg

RAKE, v. kalahigin, kalaykayín—pagkigi, pagkahig—kahigon

RALLY, n.—pagtitipuntipon—tigum, panagdugok — pagtinipontipon

RAMBLE, v. — lumaboy-laboy — paglagoy, pagligoy—maglihúlihû, magtiyógtiyóg

RAMBLING, n. — paglalakád — mga pagligoy-ligoy, laroy-laroy—pagtiyógtiyóg, paglaug

RANCH, n. —rantso, bakahán—rantso, bakahán — rantso, bakanhan

RANGE,, n.—hanay, lagáy, tayô—han-ay, bukiran—irás, kubay

RANK, n.—hanay, urì — ranggo, hut-ong, laray—rango, kubay

RANK, v.—ihanay, humanay—paghan-ay, paglaray — ikubay, iirás

RANKING, adj. — kilalá, mataás — malabaw, hataás — kinilala, mataas

RAP, v.—kumatók — pagtoktok, pagdagpi—nanuktok

RAPID, adj.—matulin, mabilís—matulin, makusog—madasig

RAPTURE, n.—higít na kaligayahan—himaya—kapín nga kalipayan

RAPTUROUS, adj. — nalíligayahang lubós—mahimayaon—lubos nga nahalipay

RARE, adj. — pambihirà—talagsaon—tumalagsahon

RAT, n.—dagâ — ilaga, ambaw bagtok—ilagâ

RATE, n.—halagá, tulin o lakad—bili, kaigoan — bilí, dasig sang lakát

RATHER, adv.—may pagká—labing maayo, masballg—sang sa

RATING, n.—grado, urì—grado, matang—grado, sarì

RATTAN, n. — yantók — uway —uwáy

RATTLE, v.—maingay, kumalampág—pagbanha, kasikas—magahud, magansal

RAVEN, n.—uwák—uwak—uwák

RAVENOUS, adj.—matakaw, gutóm—dawo, hakog, gutúm—hakabán

RAW, adj.—hiláw—hilaw—hiláw, linghod

RAY, n.—sinag—silaw, pasipát—silak

RAZE, v. — masunog, ibagsák —pagsunog, pag-ugdaw—masunog

RAZOR, n.—labaha, pang-ahit — labaha, sipol—nabaha

REACH, v.—abutan, abutín, itaás pag-abut, pagdangat — abtan, dab-utón

READ, v.—bumasa, basahin—pagbasa—magbasa, basahon

READER, n.—tagabasa, aklát, babasahín—magbabasa — buma basa

READILY, adv. — agád, karakaraka—sa kadalian, diha dayon, mouyon—gilayón

READJUST, v.—ayusin—pagpahimutang pag-usab—kaayohon

READY, adj. — handâ—andam — handà

REAL, adj.—tunay, totoó—tunay, tinuod—matuod

REALIZE, v.—gawing tunay, isa-katuparan—pagmatuod, pagpa-kasapi—pagkatuman

REALLY, adv.—tunay, totoó—di-ay, tinuod, sa matuod—tunay

REALM, n.—bandahin, kaharián —gingharian, ginsakpan—gin-harian

REAP, v.—umani, anihin—pangga-lab, pag-ani—anihon

REAR, v.—alagaan, palakihín—pag-alima, pagpadaku—sagurón, sakdagón

REAR, n.—likód, likurán—sa lu-yo, sa likod—sa likód

REASON, n. — katwiran, hunos dili, dahilán—katarungan—ka-tarungan

REASON, v.—maghunosdili, ma-ngatwiran — pagpangataru-ngan—magpangatarungan

REBEL, n.—ang naghíhimagsík,—masukihon, masukulon—maggu-gubot, manriribuk

REBELLIOUS, adj. — mapanghi-magsík—masukolon, magubta-non — manoggubot, manogribúk

REBUKE, v.—pagsabihan—pag-sumbalik-sawáy, pagkasaba —pahanumdumón.

RECALL, v.—maalaala, pabalikin —pagdumdom, pagpatawag —padumdumón

RECEDE, v.—umurong—pagsibug, pagbali, paghunás—kumbós

RECEIPT, n.—katibayan, resibo —resibo, dawat—resibo

RECEIVE, v. — tanggapín, tu-manggáp—pagdawat—batonon

RECEIVABLE, adj.—tátanggapín, papasók—mahimong dawaton—balatonón

RECENT, adj.—karáraán, kailán lamang—bag-o pa lang—siníng karón lamang

RECEPTACLE, n.—lalagyán—bu-tanganan, sudlanan — bulota-ngan

RECEPTION, n.—pagsalubong — madungganong pagdawat, sa-yaw—pagbaton

RECESS, n.—pagpapahingá—ting-pahulay—pagpahuway

RECIPE, n.—paraán ng paglulu-tò—resipe—resipé

RECITATION, n.—pagsasalitâ —lowa, paggaray, panugid—pag-pulongpulong

RECOGNIZE, v.—kilalanin—pag-ila—kilalahon

RECOIL, v.—umurong, umigkás—paglikos, paglabtik—umisul, lu-mikáw

RECOMMEND, v.—itagubilin — pagpaila aron mahiluna — itugyan, patigayonon

RECOMMENDATIONS, n.—mga tagubilin — rekomendasyon — mga pagpatigayon

REMEDIAL, adj.—makalúlunas—makatambal, makaluwas, — makatambal

REMEMBER, v.—alalahanin, tandaán—paghinumdom — dumdumón

REMEMBRANCE, n.—pag-alaala, pagkatandâ, alaala — handumanan—handumanan

REMIND, v.—ipaalala — pagpahinumdom—ipadumdom

REMINDER, n.—paalala—butang makapahinumdom — pahanumdum

REMINISCE, v. — alalahanin — paghanduraw, paghandum — pahanumdum

REMIT, v.—magbayad—pagbayad —magbayad

REMITTANCE, n.—bayad, pagbabayad—bayad—bayad, pagbayad

REMNANT, n.—retaso, labí— salin, tinabas, retaso—retaso, salín

REMODEL, v.—baguhín — pagbag-o—bag-ohón

REMONSTRATE, v.—tumutol — pagtutol—namatuk

REMORSE, n.—pagsisisi, pagtitika — pagbasul, kasub-anan — paghinulsol

REMOTE, adj.—malayò—layo, halayo—malayô

REMOTENESS, n. — kalayuan, pagkakalayò—ang gilay-on, kalayo—kalayoan

REMOVE, v.—lumipat, alisín ilipat—pagbalhin, paglalin — kuhaon, isaylo

REMUNERATE, v. — bayaran — pagbayad, pagsuhol—bayaran

REMUNERATION, n. — kabayarán—bayranan, suhol sa kabudlay—kabayarán

RENDER, v.—magbigáy, magsaulí—paghatag, pag-ulí—maghatag

RENDEZVOUS, n. — tagpuan — abutanan, tagboanan—kilitaán

RENDITION, n.—pagkakáganáp kagánapan—pagkatugtog, pagkáhimo—pagkatuman

RENEW, v.—baguhin — pagbag-o, pagsubli—bagohón

RENEWAL, n.—pagbabago, pagulit—pagbiya, pagluwat — pagbag-o

RENOUNCE, v.—tanggihán, itakwíl — pagluwat, pagsalikway—sikwayón, subulon

RENOVATE, v.—baguhin, ayusin —pagbag-o, pagsungkip — bago, pagkaayo

RENOVATION, n. — pagbabago, pagpapaayos — pang-ayo, panungkip—pagbag-o, pagkaayo

RENOWN, adj.—bantóg kilalá-bantugan — bantog, kinalala

RENT, n.—upa, bayad, enta — abang, bayanan—hinakay, bayad

RENT, v.—ipaupa, ipagpaupa — pag-abang—pahinakayan

REPAIR, n. — pagkukumpuní — ang pag-ayo, pagtul-id—kaayohon

REPAIR, v.—kumpunihín, husayin—pagtul-id, pag-ayo—pagkaayo

REPAST, n.—pagkain—kumbira, salo-salo, pangaon—pagkaon

REPATRIATE, v.—ipabalík, pabalikín — pagpabalik — ipabalík, pabalikón

REPAY, v.—bayaran ulî, magbigáy ng gantimpalà — pagbayad —bavaran liwát, maghatag sing padyà

REPEAL, v.—pawaláng saysáy—pagsubli — himutigón, paninghiwalaón

REPEAT, v.—ulitin — pag-usab, pagbag-o (balaod)—suliton

REPENT, v.—magsisi, magtika — pagbasul — maghinulsol

REPENTANCE, n. — pagsisisi · kabasulan—paghinulsol

REPETITION, n.—pag-uulit-ulit—panubli-subli—pagsulit-sulit

REPLACE, v.—palitán, halinhán —pag-ilis, paghalili, pag-uli — baylohán, islan

REPLACEMENT, n.—kapalít, kahalili — kailis, kahalili — kailis, kabaylo

REPLETE, adj. — punúng-punô — puno kaayo, nag-awás — punô kaayo

REPLY, v.—tumugón, sumagót — pagtubag, pagbalus—sumabát

REPORT, n.—ulat, balità—balita, asoy tahó—report

REPORT, v.—mag-ulat, magbalità —pagtaho, pagbalita — magreport

REPORTER, n.—tagapagbalità — magtataho, magbabalita — reporter, mamalitâ

REPOSE, n. — pahingá — pahuway, pahulay — pagpahuway

REPOSE, v.—magpahingá — pagpahuway—magpahuway

REPRESENT, v. — kumatawán, ilarawan — pagpakita, pag-ilis pagtugyan—magrepresentar

REPRESENTATION, n.—pagtayô, pangangatawán — pakigtugyan —pagpahayag, pag-akù, pagtiglawás

REPRESENTATIVE, n.—kinatawán — tinugyanan — representante

174

REPRESS, v.—pigilin—pagsanta, pagpugong — punggan

REPRESSIVE, adj.—mahigpít — masanta-on, mapugnganon — madumilion

REPRIEVE, v.—suspindihín, ipagpaliban—pag-angan-angan, pagurong—suspendehón

REPRIMAND, n.—balà—kasaba —papamatud-an

REPRIMAND, v. — pagsabihan, pagbalaan, kagalitan — pagkasaba — pamatud-an, hambalán, akigan

REPRISAL, n.—higantí—panimalus—timalús

REPROACH, n.—paninisi—sudya, sikmat, sukmat — pagpamasul, pagpatûtò

REPROACH, v.—halayin, sisihin, bigyáng sala—pagsudya, pagsukmat—basulon, patutoán

REPRODUCE, v.—mag-anák, gumawâ—pagpadaku, paghuwad—magpanganák, magbuhat

REPRODUCTION, n.—pagsusuplíng, pagsasaysáy na mulî—hulad, dinagku—pagpaningíl, pagsaysay liwát

REPROOF, n.—pagbabawal—pagbadlong, pagdili — sayasaton liwát

REPUDIATION, n.—pagtatakwíl, —pagwakli, pagsalikway—pagsikway

REPUTATION, n.—dangál, puri, karángalan — kadungganan — kadungganan, pagkauley

REPUTED, v.—kilalá, balità—naila, nadungog—nakilala, nabalitaan

REQUEST, n.—kahílingan, hilíng, pakiusap — hangyo, palihug — pangabáy

REQUEST, v. — humilíng, makiusap—paghangyo, pagpalihug — magpangabáy

REQUISITE, n. — kailangan — kinahanglanon — pagkinahanglan

RESCUE, v.—sagipín, iligtás — pagluwas — sagupón, luasón

RESEMBLE, v. — kawangis, kamukhâ — pagmay-ong, pagsama —kaanggid, nakawóng

RESEMBLANCE, n.—pagkakahawig, pagkakamukhâ, pagkakatulad — panagsama, panagmayong — pagkaanggid, pagkanawóng

RESENT, v.—magalit, magtampó —pagligutgot, pagbatok—magkaakig, magsunggod

RESENTFUL, adj.—galít na galít—maligutgoton, nasuko — naakig

RESENTMENT, n.—galit, pagtatampó — kaligutgot, kasuko — akíg, pagsunggod

175

RESERVATION, n.—reserbasyón, laán, paglalaán — tagana, inandam — reserbasyon, pagpanigana

RESERVE,—iriserba, ilaán, itagò—paglain, pagtagana — reserba, panigana

RESERVOIR, n.—imbakan ng tubig—tangke sa tubig—tiligan-an sang tubig

RESIDE, v.—manirahan, tumirá—pagpuyo—magpuyô

RESIDENCE, v.—táhanan, tírahan—puloy-anan, pinuy-anan — puy-an ukón puluy-an

RESIDUE, n.—latak—salin — salín

RESIGN, v.—magbitíw — pagluwat—maghalín

RESIGNATION, n.—pagbibitíw — ang pagluwat—paghalín

RESIGNED, adj. — nátatalagá sa mangyáyari—mokalawat sa dadangatan—nakahalín

RESIST, v.—labanan, pigilan — pagsukol—pamatukan, pamunggan

RESISTANCE, n.—paglaban, pagsawatâ—ang buhat sa pagsukol —pag-away, pagpamatuk

RESOLUTE, adj.—nakahandâ — andam, maandamon, tapát—nakahandà

RESOLVE, v.—pasyahán — pagtapat, pagbuot, pag-uyon — butan

RESORT, n.—bákasiyunan — lulinghayawan — balakasyonan

RESOURCE, n.—kakayahán, kuwarta—kabtangan, kahinguhaan —pagkabutáng, manggad

RESOURCEFUL, adj.—marunong, mabilís, maisip — mapaninguhaon, malugoton—mahibaló, maabtik, matandos

RESPECT, v.—igalang, pagpitaganan — pagtahud, pagmanggad—tahuron, pangalag-agán

RESPECTFUL, adj. — magalang, magpitagan — matinahuron — matinahuron

RESPECTFULLY, adj. — buóng galang—sa dakung katahuran—ang matinahuron

RESPECTIVE, adj.—ang ilán, tangì, tungkól — tinagsa, linain, iya-iya—ang pilá, pinasahî, tungód

RESPIRATION, n.—paghingá — ginhawa — pagginhawa

RESPIRE, v. — humingá — pagginhawa — magginhawa

RESPITE, n.—pagtigil — paglangay, kalangan — pagdulog

RESPLENDENT, adj.—maliwanag, makisláp—magilakon, makidlapon — masanag, masilí

REVENGEFUL, adj. — mapaghigantí — mapanimaslon — ma-
panghimalús

REVENUE, n.—kita, buwís — tubo sa buhis, kinitaan — buhís,
kinitaan

REVERBERATE, v.—umalingaw-
ngáw—pagdahunog, paglanog —
ñaglanóg, nanglakaak

REVERE, v.—igalang, pagpitaganan—pagmahal, pagtahud, pagmanggad—tahuron.

REVERENCE, n.—paggalang, pa-
mitagan — mahadlokong pagtahud, pagyukbo—pagtahud

REVEREND, adj. — kagalang-galang—talamdon, tinahud, talahuron — matinahuron

REVERIE, n.—panaginip, alaala—
damgo, handurawan — dalamgo-
hanon, handurawan

REVERSAL, n. — kabaligtarán —
kabalit-aran, pagkabali — kaba-
liskarán

REVERSE, v.—baligtarín — pag-
baliktad, pagbali, pagbalit-ad—
baliskarón

REVERT, v.—mabalík, masaulî —
pagbalik, pagsumbalik — íbalík,
iulì

REVIEW, n. — pag-uulit, parada,
balík-aral, ulitin—pagsubli, su-
bliay, pasunding — pagsulit, parada militar

REVIEW, v.—ulitin, sulitin—pag-
subli-subli, balik-balik—suliton,
liwatón

REVIEWER, n.—taga-basa, tagasulit — magsusubli — tagsulit,
tagliwát

REVISE, v.—palitán, baguhin —
pagtarung, pag-usab—islan, bag-
ohón

REVISION, n.—pagbabago — pa-
nagbag-o—pagbag-o

REVIVAL, n.—pagbubuhay—pagkabanhaw—pagbuhì

REVIVE, v.—buhayin — pagban-
haw—buhion

REVOKE, v.—baguhin, putulin —
pagbakwi—bag-ohón

REVOLT, n.—paghihimagsík, pag-
lalaban, labanán—Ragubut, pag-
alsa—ribúk, kinagubot

REVOLT, v.—maghimagsík, lumaban—paggubut, pag-alsa —
magribúk, magkinagubot

REVOLTING, adj.—nakasúsuká
—nagagubut, mangilngig — makatalaka

REVOLUTION, n.—pag-ikot, hí-
magsikan—kagubut, kaguliyang
—paglibot, rebolusyon

REVOLUTIONARY, adj. — ma-
panghimagsík, mapagbago —
mahatungod sa kagubut—mang-
riribuk

REVOLVER, n.—rebolbér —
bolber, luthang — rebolber

REVOLVING, v.—umiikot — nag-
tuyok-tuyok — lumibot
REVULSION, n.—pagkamuhî—suka, dugwa—pagbalhin
REWARD, n.—gantimpalà — balus, gantî—padyà, balos nga kinabubut-on
REWARD, v. — gantimpalaan —
pagbalus, pagganti — padyaán,
premyohán
RIB, n.—tadyáng—gusok—gusok
RIB, v.—tudyuhín — pagsikdo —
lamâlamaón
RIBBING, n.—panunudyó — - pa-
nikdo—paglamâlamâ
RIBBON, n.—liston, sintas, lasò—
liston, laso—liston, sintas, laso
RICE, n.—bigás, kanin, palay —
bugas, kan-on — bugás, kan-on,
humáy
RICH, n.—mayaman, saganà—dato, saplan, adunahan—manggaran, dagayà
RICHES, n.—kayamanan—bahan-
dî, kakabtangan—manggaranon
RID, v. — magpalayas, paalisín—
paglikay, pagpahilayo — pahalinón, hingabutón
RIDDLE, n.—bugtungan — tigmo
—paktakon
RIDDLE v.—punuín paputukán—
pagtusak-tusak, pabuthan—pun-
on, daskon
RIDE n.—pagsakáy, pamamasyál
—pangabayo, panakayan — pagsakáy

RIDE, v.—sumakáy—pagsakay —
sumakáy
RIDER, n.—tagasakáy, nakasakáy
—sumasakay—mananakay
RIDGE, n.—tugatog, palupo—ta-
gaytay, tagudtod, bungtod—ta-
ludtod
RIDICULE, n.—pagkutyâ—yubit,
biay-biay, pakaulaw—libák, hi-
kay
RIDICULE, v.—kutyaín—pagyubit, pagbiaybiay—libakón, hikayan
RIDICULOUS, adj. — nakatátawá
kataw-anan, salawayon—makahalam-ot
RIGGER, n.—tagaayos ng lubid,
layag—panimbang sa sakayan,
katig—tagtatap sing lubid, layag
RIGHT, adj.—tamà, kanan, wastô
—matarung, husto, tul-id — tamà, husto, igò
RIGID, adj.—matigás — magahi
—matigdas
RILE, v.—yamutín, pikahín—pagdaut, pagyubit—samongón, paakigon
RILL, n.—munting ilog, sapà —
sapa, anig-ig—diótay nga subâ,
sapâsapà
RIM, n.—tabíng-tabí, gilid—bang-
kawan, daplin, ngilit—kilid

RIME, n.—tugmâ—garay, binagay nga sinulat—sibù, nagahílituon

RING, n.—entablado ng boksíng, singsíng—singsing, boksingan — boksingan, singsing

RING, v.—magbatíng, tugtugín— pagbagting — bagtingón

RINGWORM, n.—buni—bun-i, sa-kit sa panit—empiene

RINSE, n.—banláw—pagwaswas, paghugas—bunlawán

RIOT, n.—pagkakaingáy, kagúlu-han—kagubut—pagkinagubot

RIOT, v.—manggulό—paggubut — manggubot

RIOTER, n. — manggugulό — manggugubut — manggugubot

RIP, v.—sirain, lapain—paggisi — gision, laplapón

RIP, n. — sirà, wasak — nagisi, —gisî, wasák

RIPE, adj.—hinόg—hinog, lumόy —lutò, tanáng

RIPEN, v.—mahinόg—pagpahinog —malutò, matanáng

RIPPLE, n.—maliít na alon — di-yutayng balud—diόtay nga ba-nul sang balúd

RISE, n.—pagtaás, pag-alsá—pag-pataas, pagbangon — pagbatak, pagtindog

RISE, v.—tumindíg, umalsá, mag-bangon—pagtindog — tumindog, bumangon

RISK, n.—panganib, peligro—ku-yaw, peligro—katalagman, peli-gro

RISK, v. — ipanganib, isubò — pagbutang sa kuyaw — pagta-gám, pag-andam

RISKY, adj.—mapanganib—maku-yaw—makatalagam

RIVAL, n.—kalaban, kaaway, la-banán—kaatbang, kaindig—ka-sumpong, ribál

RIVALRY, n.—paglalabanán—pa-nag-atbang — pagsumponganay, pagribalay

RIVER, n.—ilog—suba—subâ

RIVERSIDE, n. — tabíng-ilog — daplin sa suba—banas sa higád sang subâ

RIVERVIEW, n.—tánawin sa may ilog—talan-awon sa suba — ta-lan-awon sa subâ

ROAD, n.—daán, lansangan, kar-sada—dalan, karetera — dalan, kalsada

ROADSIDE, n.—tabí ng daán — daplin sa dalan—higád sang da-lan

ROAM, v.—lumaboy, gumala-galà —pagsuroy, paglibud — manu-roysuroy

ROAMING, n.—paglalakád, pag-paparoό't parito — libud-suroy, bagdoy—pagsuroysuroy, palihô-lihô

179

ROAR, n.—sigáw, ungal — dahunog, tiyabaw — ngurob

ROAR, v.—umungal, sumigáw — pagdahunog, pagtiyabaw—magngurob

ROARING, adj. — nagngángalit, nag-íinit—nagdahunog — naganngurob, nguroban

ROAST, n.—inihaw, nilitsón—inasal—inasál, linitson

ROAST v.—íihaw litsunín—pagasal—iasál, ilitson

ROB, v.—magnakaw — pagkawat, pagkiriw—magpangawat

ROBBER, n.—magnanakaw, tulisán—kawatan, kiriwan — makawat, tulisán

ROBE, n.—balabal, kasuutan—bata sa kaligo—kunóp

ROBIN, n.—ibong martines—langgam martinis—pispis martines

ROCK, n.—bató—batong lagi-it — bató

ROCK, v.—galawín, iduyan—pagduyan, pagtay-ug—uyogón, habugon, duyanon

ROCKY, adj.—mabató—bato-on—batohón

ROD, n.—baras, tungkód—tuod, sungkod, batota—bilugón, putik, sihigon

RODENT, n.—mga dagâ — ilága, ambaw—ilagâ

ROGUE, n.—salbahe, magdarayà —salbahis — salbahe, pilyo

ROLL n.—rolyo, lulon, ikot, tálaan—linukot, talaan—rolyo, pulón, linukotan

ROLL, v. — ibalumbón, umikot, ikutin, gumulong — paglukot, pagtuyok, pagligid—irolyo, ipulon, ilukot, ipaligid

ROLLICKING adj.—masayá, pabayâ—masadyaon, danghag — masadya, talayhà

ROLLING, adj.—pagulung-gulong —nagligid-ligid—pagligídligíd

ROMANCE, n.—romansa, pag-ibig —gugma, romansa — romansa, paghigugmaanay

ROMANCING, v. — nag-íibigán, nagsúsuyuán — naghigugmaay —higugmaanay, daluáy

ROOF, n.—bulungán, bubong — atop—bubongán, atúp

ROOM, n.—silíd, kuwarto—lawak —sulód, kwarto

ROOMMATE, n.—kakuwarto—kauban sa lawak — kaupod sa kwarto

ROOMY, adj.—maluwáng maaliwalas—maluag —' masangkad

ROOST, n.—hapunan — lumloman sa manok—haponán, hulonán

ROOT, n.—ugát, pinanggalingan—gamut—gamút, gingikanan

ROPE, n.—lubid—pisi—lubid, pisi
ROPE, v.—itali, lubirin—pagpisi, paggapus—ihigút, lubiron
ROSE,' n.—rosa, bulaklák na rosas —rosas—rosas
ROT, v.—mabulók, masira—pagkadunot—madunot, mapierde
ROTTEN, adj.—bulók, sirâ—dunot pagkadunot
ROUGH, adj. — magaspáng, bakubakô—masapnot, sagalsalon — mabahúl, batsehón
ROUND, adj.—mabilog, bilóg — malingin—bilóg, manipulon
ROUNDS, n.—ikot—mga paglibut —libut
ROUSE, v.—gisingin, pukawin — pagpukaw — pukawon
ROUSING, adj.—maingay — mabanha—magahud
ROWDY, adj.—maguló, maharót— paras-paras, samokan—magamó, magarút
ROYAL, adj.—marangál, ukol sa harì, maka-harì — harianon — dungganon, natungód, 'sa harì, harianon
ROYALTY, n.—ang mga harì, bayad—mga harì, kabayranan — mga harì, kabayarán
RUB, v.—haplusín, kuskusín — paghaplas, pagnusnos — haplosón, kuskusón

RUBBER, n.—pamburá, manghahaplús, goma—gom.., igpapanas —-goma, inogpanás
RUBBISH, n.—dumí, tirá, basura —sagbut, basura—sagbut, basura
RUDE, adj.—bastós, magaspáng— bastos, way-batasan—bastos, damuhál
RUDENESS, n.—kagaspangán — kabastos—kadamuhál
RUG, n.—alpombra, baníg—alpombra—alpombra
RUGGED, adj.—mabató, bakíl-bakíl—batoon—batohón, batsehón
RUINS, n.—pagkaguhò, pagkakagiba, pagkasira — kagusbatan, kagubaan — pagkagubâ, pagkarumpag
RUIN, v.—sirain, iguhò—pagguba, pagdaut, paglumpag — gub-on rumpagón
RUINOUS, adj.—nakasisirà—magubaon, malumpagon—gulub-on, rurumpagon
RULE, n. — batás, pamamálakad, panguluhan, paghaharì — baod, kamandoan—sulundan, kasugoán, pagharì ukón harian
RULE, v.—pagharian, magharì, sakupin, guhitan — pagmando, pagharì — dumalahan, reglahan

RULER, n.—regladór, punò, harì —sukod, magmamando—talaksan, punôpunò, harì

RUMBLING, adj. — dumadagundóng—nagdahunog—linagabong

RUMOR, n.—higing, bulung-bulungan, alingawngáw — hulonglhong — kutsokutso, huringhuring

RUMORED, v.—nabalità, kumalat —gihungihong, gibalita — ginakutsokutso, ginahuringhuring

RUN, v.—tumakbo, takbo—pagdagan—dalagan

RUNAWAY, n.—nagtatagò — ang layas—dumalagan

RUN OVER, v.—magulungan — pagkaligis, pagkadasmag—malatayan, maipít

RURAL, adj.—ukol sa parang o bukid—bukidnon, banikanhon—natungód sa kaumhan

RUSE, n.—lalang, patibóng—lansis—laláng, tugalbong

RUSH, adj.—madalian—dinalian—dalalian

RUSH, v.—magmadalí— pagdali, pag-liksi — magdalî

RUST, n. kalawang — tayá, taáy —tuktok

RUSTY, adj. kálawangín — taayon, tayáon—tuktukón

RUT, n.—butas, pagkakabaón — lungag-lungag—buslot, natibalug

— S —

SABBATH, n.—aráw ng pahingaláy—Adlaw sa pahulay, Domingo—Adlaw sa pagpahuway

SABLE, n.—balahibo ng hayop—itum, dagtum, balhibo sa manananap—malagtum, itúm, balahibo sang hayup

SACK, n.—sako, supot—sako, puyo—sako, puyópuyo

SACK, v.—halughugin, nakawan—pagkawat, pagtampalas—tampalason, kawatan

SABOTAGE, n.—paninirá, pagwasak—sabotahe, liput —sabotahe. pagbudhì

SACRED, adj.—banál, natatalagá sa Diyos—balaanon—balaanon pakasakit — balanusan, pag-antus—pagpaninghakul, pag-antus

SAD, adj.—malungkót, nakalulunos—masulob-on, mamingawon —masinulub-on, mamingawon

SADDLE, v. — isingkaw — paginggansa — silyahán

SADDLE, n. siyá ng kabayo — silya sa kabayo, montura—silya sang kabayo

SADNESS, n.—kalungkutan, kapighatían — kasub-anan, kamingawan—kasulub-on, kamingawan

SAFE, adj.—tiwasáy, ligtás—naiwas, gawas sa katalagman — hilway, luás

SAFE, n.—kabáng bakal — tipiganan sa salapi — talagoán-pilak, kaha

SAFETY, n.—katiwasayan, kaligtasan—kalwasan, pagkagawas sa katalagman—kahiwayan, kaluásan

SAGACIOUS, adj. — matalino—maalam—mainalamon

SAGE,, n.—marunong, dalubhasà —makinaadmanon sabyo — mangin-alamon, sampaton

SAIL, n.—layag—layag—lumayag

SAIL, v.—maglayág—paglawig — maglayag

SAILOR, n.—marinero, magdaragát — mananakay— marinero,

SAINT, n.—banál, santo—santos, matarung—santos

SAINTLY, adj.—masiyadong banál, lubháng banál—balaanon—balaanon

SALABLE, adj. — maipagbibili, mabilí—halinon—mabaligyà

SALAD, n.—ensalada — ensalada —ensalada

SALARY, n.—suweldo, sahod — suhol, sweldo — sweldo, suhol

SALE, n.—pagbibilí, pinagbilhán —baligya, tinda—baligyà, tinda —pagbaligyà

SALESMAN, n. — tagapagbilí—magbabaligya—manogbaligyà

SALESWOMAN, v. —babaing tagapagbilí—babayeng manininda —babaeng manogbaligyà, tindera

SALT, n. —asín—asin—asín

SALTINESS, n. —kaalatan —ang kaparat—kapaitán

SALTY, adj. —maalat — parat—maasín

SALUTATION, n. — bating panimulâ — timbaya—pangatahurán

SALUTE, v. magpugay, sumaludo—pagsaludo, pagtahud—magtahud, magsaludo

SALUTE, n. saludo, batì, pagpupugay — saludo katahuran — saludo, pagtahud

SALVATION, n.—kaligtasan—kaluwasan —katubosan

SAME, adj.—gayon din, pareho—sama, pariho—amó man, pareho

SAMPLE, n. —muwestra, patikim —pananglitan, tilaw—mwestra, patiláw

SAMPLED, v. pinili—tinilawan—tinilawán

SAND, n.—buhangin—balas, bonbon — balás

SANITARIUM, n. — pahingahan, pagalingan—tambalanan sa sugpaon — bululngan sa anunón

SANDY, adj.—mabuhangin, buhanginan—balason—mabalás, balasón

SANCTIFIED, v. gawing banál —pagbalaan — pagpabalaan

SANCTITY, n.—kabanalan — kabalaanon — kabalaanon

SAP, n.—dagtâ, katás, ulól—duga, kuwanggol—dagtà, dugâ

SARCASM, n. parunggít, pagpaparunggít — biaybiay — pagpanghikay, pagyubit

SARCASTIC, adj.—mapagparunggít—mabiaybiayon — manoghíkáy, manogyubít

SASH, n.—talì o sintás na pamigkís—bigkis sa hawak—wagkus, inogbugkos

SATIATE, v.—busugín —pagtagbaw — busgon

SATAN, n. demonyo — satanas, demonyo — demonyo, panuláy, yawà

SATANIC, adj. —maka-diyablo—demonyohon — panulayon, yawan-on

SATIN, n. — raso, satin — satin, usa ka panapton—satín

SATISFACTION, n. —kasiyahan —katagbawan—kaayawan

SATISFACTORY, n. —kasiyahan —makatagbaw — makapaayaw

SATISFY, v. — masiyahán busugín pagbusóg, pagtagbaw, pagbuhóng — naayawan, nabusóg

SATURDAY, n. —Sabado—Sabado —Sabadó

SAUCE, n.—salsa, sawsawan — salsa sarsa

SAUCER, n. — platito, maliit na pinggán — platito, pinggan mga gamay—platito

SAUCY, adj. —mapang-akit—malami—marimis, mananám

SAUSAGE, n.—langgonisa, soriso —longganisa, soriso — sausage, soriso

SAVAGE, n.—taong-gubat— luog irihis, taong-bukid

SAVAGE, adj.—mabangís — mapin-tas—malalimon

SAVE, v.—iligtás, mag-ipon, mag-impók—pagluwas, pagdaginot luasón, sagupón, magtipon

SAVOR, v.—lumalasa—págpalami —saborán, laliman

SAVORY, adj. — malinamnám—lamián—pagpalalim

SAW, n. lagarì—gabas —iagarì

SAW, v.—lagariin, nakita—paggabas, nakíta — lagaricn, nakitâ

SAY, n. sabi, diga, ppayó—sulti, pulong—siling, hambal, pulong

SAY, v.—sabihin, bigkasín—pagsulti, pagsaysay—silingón, ham-
balón, mitlangón

SAYING, n.—kasabihán—panultihon—hurubaton

SCALE, n. —timbangan, kaliskis-
timbangan, kalis, hagdan—timbangan, eskala

SCALE, v. akyatín—pagkatkat—
sakaon, eskalahon

SCALY, adj. —makaliskís kukhan
—mahimbison

SCAFFOLD, n. bibitayan — bitayán—bitayán

SCANDAL, n. — eskandalo, ali-
ngasngas—eskandalo, kaulawan
—eskandaló, kagarukán

SCANDALOUS, adj.—maalingas-
ngas, maguló—makauulaw—es-
kandaloso

SCARCE, adj. —bihirà, madalang
nihit, talagsaon — talagsa, malakâ

SCARCITY, n. kawalán, kakulangán —kanihit, kakulang— ka-
apinas, kaiwatón

SCARF, n.—kurbata, isang damit
na pambalot o panapín sa liíg
o balikat—panyo sa li-og—kurbata, panyò sa liug

SCATTER, v. — magkalat --- pagsabwag — laptahón

SCATTERING, n. —nagkakalát—
pagbulag-bulag, pagsabwag —
nagalinapta

SCENE, n. —bista, tánawin—talan-awon—talan-awon

SCHEME, n. — panukalà, paraan
—hunahuna, laraw, paagi—
panghunâhunà, pahitò

SCHEME, v. — magmanukalà. u-
misip —paglaraw — magpang-
hunâhunà, magpahitò

SCHEMING, adj. — mapaglaláng
—naglaraw — panghunâhunaon,
pahituon

SCHOLAR, n. — estudiante, nag-
aaral, dalubhasà — manggialamon, tinun-an—estudiante, pala-
tun-on

SCHOLARSHIP, n. — pag-papa-
aral—tanyag pagpatuon — pag-
papatuón

SCHOOL, v. turuan, sanayin —
pagtudlo, pagmatuto —tudloán,
buthoán

SCHOOL, n.—eskwelahán, páaralán — tunghaan — eskwelahan,
buluthoan

SCHOOLHOUSE, n. — bahay-pá-
aralan—balay tun-anan — ba-
láy-buluthoan

SCHOOL TEACHER, n. — maestra, titser, gurò — magtutudlo,
magtutuon—maestra, manunudlò

SCIENCE, n.—siyensa, aghám— kinaadman, siyensiya—siensya, kinaadman

SCIENTIFIC, adj. — maka-siyen-sya, maka-aghám — makinaadmanon, siyentipiko — sientipikó makinaadmanon

SCIENTIST, n. taong naalam sa siyensya, o aglám — tawong maalam, makinaadmanon—sientipikó, makinaadmanon

SCISSORS, n. — guntíng — gunting — gunting

SCOLD, v. murahin, pagsalitaán, kagalitan—pagbasaba, kasab-an —buyayawon, akigan

SCORE, n. —punto, biláng, guhit —tala, punto—puntos

SCORE, v.—iguhit, italâ—agtala —paghamak

SCORN, n.—paghamak — tamay, yubit — paghamak

SCORN, v.—hamakin—pagtamay, pagyubit — hamakon

SCOUT, n. — tagasubok, tagatuklás—iskawot, sundalo—maninilág

SCOUT, v. —manubok, magmatiyág—pagpangita, pagbulong — manilag

SCRAP, n.—mumo, maliit na piraso, tira-tirahan—momho, salín—momho salín

SCRAPE, v.—kayurin, kudkurin—pagkuskos, pagkagud — kudkurón, kagusón

SCRATCH, n.—kamot, galos —kison, kamusón

SCRATCH, v. —galusan, kamutin —pagkawot, paggaras — kaluton

SCRATCHY, adj.—makatí — maka—makatúl

SCREAM n. —tili—siyagit, tiyabaw—tiyabaw, siyagit pagsinggit — tumiyabaw, sumiyagit

SCREEN, n. — tabing, pangsalà tabil, sala-an—salaan, esena

SCREEN, v.—tabingan, salain — pagtabil, pagsala—esenahan, salaon

SCRUB, v. — maglampaso, magisís—paglampaso, pagnusnos — manglampaso

SCRUPULOUS, adj. —mabusisì—kilkilán—mabusisíon

SCRUPLES, n. —kabusisian—kinilkilan—kabusîsían

SCULPTOR, n. manlililok— magkukulit, eskultor—eskultor

SEA, n.—dagat—dagat, kadagatan—dagat

SEAL, n. — timbre, taták—patík, timbre — timbre, selyo, marka

SEAL, v.—tatakán, isará—pagpatik, timbrehan—timbrehán, selyohán, márkahán

SEAMAN, n.—magdaragát—marinero—mananagat

SEAMSTRESS, n. — babaing mánanahì—kustorera — manogwalis

SEARCH, v. —hanapin, halughugín, paghanapin—pagpangita—pangitaon

SEASON, adj. — paná-panahón —agad sa panahón—tigpanahón

SEASONAL, adj.—paná-panahón bahin sa tuig—panahón

SEASONING, n.—pantimplá—panimpla, pagpalami — panimpla

SEAT, n.—úpuan, luklukan—lingkoranan, bangkô—língkuran

SECEDE, n.—umurong—pagsibog —kumabós, lumip-ot

SECOND, n.—pangalawá—ikaduba, gutling—pangaduhá, ikaduhá

SECOND, v. — pangalawahán — pagdason — pumangaduhá

SECRET, n.—lihim — tinagoan— —likúm

SECRETARY, n.—kalihim, sekretaryo—kalihim — kuymi, sekretaryo

SECRETLY, adv. — palihím — sa tago — malikumon

SECTION, n.—bahagi, panig—bahin, tipík—bahin, tipík

SECTIONALISM, n.— pagkanyákanyahán—iya-iya, ako-ako — maiyaiyahon

SECURE, adj.—panatag — siguro, walay kuyaw — mabakud, wala'y katalagman

SECURE, v. —kumuha— pagkabut, pagbaton—magkuhà

SECURITY, n. — katiwasayán—kasigurohan, kaiwasan — kabakurán

SEE, v.—makita, mátanáw—pagkita, pagtan-aw—makità, lantawon

SEEM, v.—tila, warì — ingon sa daw — daw sa

SEEMINGLY, adv.—tilà, warì — daw mao—daw sa

SEIZE, v.—agawin, hawakan — pagsakmit; pag-agaw —agawon

SEIZURE, n.—pag-agaw, paghuliang inagaw, ang sinakmit — pagagaw

SELDOM, adv.—bihirà— talagsaon, tagsa ra—talagsa, malakâ

SELECT, v.—pinilì, piliin—pagpili pinili, pilion

SELECTION, n.—pagpilì—ang panilian—pagpili

SELECTIVE, adj. — mapamilì —pili-an—mapislì, mapill

SELF, n.—sarili—kaugalingon — kaugalingon.

SELFISH, adj.—makasarili, maramot, mapagsarilí—daló, hakogán makiugalingón, dalúk

SELFISHNESS, n.—karamutan— ang kadaló, kahakóg—kadalúk

SELL, v.—magbilí, ipagbilí—pagbaligya—magbaligyà, ibaligyà

SELLER, n.—nagbíbilí—magbabaligya — tagbaligyà, mamaligyà

SEMI, adj.—kalahatian — katunga—katungâ

SENATE, n.—senado, mataás na kapulungang mambabatás —senado—senado

SENATOR, n. —senadór—senador —senadór

SEND, v.—ipadalá, magpadalá —pagpadala — ipadalá, magpadalá

SEND-OFF, n.—parangál sa pagalís—pagpagikan — pagtulód

SENILE, adj.—nápakatandâ — tigulang—katigulangón

SENSE, n. — pandamdám, malay, ulirát—balatian—pamatyag

SENSATION, n. damdám— pagbati—pamatyagon

SENSIBILITY, n. pandamdám — pamalátian — balatyagon

SENSIBLE, adj. —may pakiramdám, matalino—babation, takus bation—mabinatyagon

SENSITIVE PLANT, n.—makahiyâ—tanum nga tukbihon, makahiya—huyâ-huyâ

SENSUOUS, adj.—mainit — mainiton, mabination — mainitón

SENTENCE, v.—hatulan—paghukom, pagsilot—pamatbatán

SENTENCE, n. —pangungusap — hunahuna, laray—dinalán

SENTIMENT, n. — damdamin— pagbati—balatyagon

SENTIMENTAL, adj.—punô ng damdamin—limbatianon, mamingawon—mabinatyagon

SEPARATE, v. ihiwalay, maghiwaláy — pagbulag, paglain — ibulág

SEPARATE, adj.— bukód — bulág, himulag—himulágon

SEPTEMBER, n.—Setyembre — Septiyembre—Septiembre

SERENE, adj.—mahinahon— malinawon, bugnawg buot—mapainumuron

SERIES, n.—kawíl, serye — sumpay-sumpay— serye, binangday bangday

SERIOUS, adj. — malubhâ, pormál, waláng bikô—grabe, maugdang — malisúd, grabe, maligdong pormal

SERIOUSLY, adv.—malubhâ, may kapormalán — sa kaugdang— kalubhaán, kagrabehón, kaligdongán

SERPENT, n.—ahas, serpyente — halas — serpente, man-ug

SERVANT, n. alilà, utusán, ali-
pin—binatonan, sulugoon — suluguón

SERVE, v.—maglingkód, ihain—
pag-alagad, pagdulot sud-an —
mag-alagád, maghandà

SERVICE, n. — paglilingkód —
alagad—pag-alagád

SERVICEABLE, adj.—pakikinabangan—makaalagad — maalaga-
rón

SET, v.—ilagáy, iupô, ilapat —
pagbutang paghan-ay—ibutáng,
ipahamtang

SET, n. — isáng huwego, isáng
kumpól — huwego—hwego

SETTING n.—tagpuan— himuta-
ngan—kilitaán, halamtangan

SETTLE, v.—yariin, tapusin, manirahan—paghusay, pagpahiluna
—husayon, tapuson, puy-an

SETTLEMENT, n.—pagtutuós, tírahan, bayan-bayanan—kaaabu-
tan, sityohan — pagkahusay,
pagkaminyò, puluy-anan

SETTLER, n. — ang nakatirá sa
isáng lugár—molupyo—mangluluntad

SEVEN, n. —pitó—pito—pitó
SEVENTEEN, n.—labimpitó—na-
pulog-pito—napulo'g pitó

SEVENTEENTH, adj.—ikalabim-
pitó—ikanapulog-pito, kapitoan
—ika-napulo'g pitó

SEVENTH, adj.—ikapitó—ikapito
—ikapitó

SEVENTY, n. —pitumpû— kapitoan—kapitoán

SEVER, v. — putulin o putlín—
pagputól—putlon, utdon

SEVERAL, adj. — marami, mga
ilán—pipila—kadamoan

SEVERANCE, n.—pagkaputol —
pagkaputól — pagkautód

SEVERE, adj.—mahigpít, latigás
—mapig-ut, magahi — madu-
milion, matigdas

SEW, v.—tahiín, manahí—pagtahi
tahión

SEX, n.—ang pagkalalaki o pagkababae—kinaiyanhon matang
sa tawo—pagkalalaki ukón pag-
kababáe

SHABBY, adj.—ayos na nakahíhiyâ, gusgusin — magkató nag-
kakidlay—hulagáñ, dagway nga
makahuluyà

SHACKLE, v.—itali, ikabít—pag-
posas—ihigút, iumang

SHADE, n.—lilim—landong—handongan

SHADOW, n.—anino — anino—
landong

SHADOWY, adj.—maanino —ani-
nohon — malandong, mahag-
bong

SHADY, adj.—malilim — **lando- ngan, malandong** — landongan, handongan

SHAFT, n.—panà, palasô —**paná** —**panâ**

SHAKE, v. — kalugín, alugín — pag-uyog—lûguón

SHAKY, adj.—maalóg, magaláw— **mâuyog, tay-ugón** — mauyogón

SHALL, v.—pandiwang panghiná- haráp—**panumong sa umalabut** —**paga-**

SHALLOW, adj. — mababaw — mabáw, matugkad — manabaw

SHALLOWNESS, n.—kababawan —**kamabáw—kabanawan**

SHAME, n.—kahihiyán, hiyâ—**ka- ulawan—kahuluy-an, huyâ**

SHAMEFUL, adj.—nakahíhiyâ — **makauulaw** —' makahuluyà

SHAMELESS, adj. —waláng-hiyâ **walay ulaw** — wala'y huyâ

SHAPE, n. — hugis, porma, hu- bog—**tabas, porma** — dagway, bayhon

SHARE, n.—bahagi, hatì, kapartí —**bahin, ambit** — bahin, parti, ambit

SHARE v.—bahaginan, hatiin — **pagbahin, pag-angay-angay** — bahinan, partihán, ambitán

SHAREHOLDER, n. — kahatì — **tag-iya sa bahin**—katuwang, ka- sosyo

SHARP, adj.—matalím, matulis— **talinis, mahait** — matalúm, ma- taliwis

SHARPEN, v.—ihasà, patalimín— **paghait, pagbaid** — bairon, pa- talumón

SHAVE, v. —mag-ahít, ahitan— **pagkagis, paghimungot** — ma- marbas

SHAVINGS, n.—pinagputulan, pi- nagkatamán — **ang kinagisan**— binarbasán

SHE, pron.—siyá (babae) — **siya** (babaye) — siá (babáe)

SHED, n. — dampâ, kuwadra — kwadra, diyutayng payag —pa- silongán, kwadra

SHED, v.—magbuhos, tumulò — pagtulo, pagaagay— ulaan, pa- tuloan

SHEAT, n. — bayna, lalagyán — sakuban, bayna—bahina, tagúb

SHEEP, n. — tupa, mga tupa — karnero—karnero

SHEEPISH, adj. — torpe, sutíl —karnerohon — torpe, sutíl

SHEET, n. — pansapín ng kama, pilas ng papél—**pílgo sa papel,** hapin sa katre — pinikás nga papél, hapín sa kama

SHELF, n.—pitak ng aparadór— **kahon, hunos** — hunosán sang lamisa ukón aparadór

SHELL, n.—kabibi, bala ng kanyón—bayanan, bala sa kanyor —tuwáy bala sang kanyon

SHELTER, n. — tírahan, kanlungan—salipdanan — bombahón bombardeyohon

SHEPHERD, n. — pastól, tagapagalagà ng tupa—magbalantay sa karnero—pastor, tagbantay-karnero

SHERIFF, n. — syerip, punò ng mga pulís—serip, mananakmit—seríp, punò sang mga polís

SHIELD, n. —kalasag, pananggá —sangga, kalasag—tamíng

SHIFT, n. pagpapalít—turno, panag-ilis-ilis — pagbaylo, pagilisáy

SHIFT, v. — lumipat, bumago — pagbalhin —sumaylo, bumalhin

SHINE, v. — lumiwanag, kumináng, sumikat—paghayag, pagsidlak—kumanaw

SHINY, adj.—maliwanag, masikat —masinaw, mahayag—makanaw

SHIP, n.—sasakyáng-bapór — bapor, sakayan-dagat — sakáyán, bapór

SHIP, v.—ilulan, ipadalá—pagluwan—ilulan, ipadalá

SHIPPING, adj.—ang magbabapór — bahin sa bapor—manogbapór

SHIRT, n.—barò, kamisadentro—kamisadentro — kamisadentro

SHIVER, n. — gináw — pangurog — mangligbos kíg—pagkurog — mangurog

SHIVER, v.—mangatóg, mangalig

SHOCK, n.—pagkabiglâ, pagkagulat—kakugang, kalit nga kalisang—pagkakibút

SHOCK, v. — gulatin, biglain—pagpakugang, paghadlok — kibutón, tikmaón

SHOE, n — sapatos —sapin — sapatos

SHOELESS, adj.—waláng sapatos walay-sapin—wala'y sapatos

SHOEMAKER, n.— manggagawà ng sapatos--mamumuhat sapin —sapatero, manogsapatós

SHOOT, n. supling, tubò — udlot, tubo—siwíl, tubò

SHOOT, v.—barilín, bumaríl, — pagluthang pagbaril — luthangón, sumiwíl

SHOP, n.—gáwaan, tindahan—buhatan, tindahan — tindahan

SHOP, v. — mamilí, maghanáp—pagpamalít, pagpangita — mamakál

SHORE, n.—pampáng, tabí ng dagat—baybayon, lapyahan — baybayon

SHORT, adj. — maigsí, putól — hamubo—malip-ot

SHORTAGE, n.— kakulangán — kakulangan, kanihit — kakulangán

SHORTY, n.—pandák — pandak, purukó—putót

SHOULD, v.—nárarapat — angay, kinahangian — nabagay

SHOULDER, n.—balikat — abaga —abaga

SHOULDER, v.—balikatin— pagabaga — abagahón

SHOUT, n.—sigáw—singgit, tiyabaw—singgit, tiyabaw

SHOUT, v:—sigawán — pagsiyagit, pagsinggit—suminggit, tumiyabaw

SHOVEL, n. —pala—pala — pala

SHOVEL, v.—palahin, linisin — pagpala—palahon

SHOW, n.—palabás, pakita— pasundayag — talan-awon, palaguaon

SHOW, v.—palabasín, ipakita — pagpakita, pagpasundayag—ipaguâ, ipakità

SHOWDOWN, n.—paghahayag — dayganay — pag-athagay

SHOWER, n. — ambón, paligò— alindahaw—dabúdabú, banyo

SHOWY, adj. — pasikat—tigpagawál, magawalón — paladayaw

SHREWD, adj.—tuso, magulang— mabintaka-on, limobongán—toso

SHRIEK, n.—tilî—imik, siyagit — tig-ik, siyagit

SHRIEK, v.—sumigáw, tumilî — pagsiyagit—tumig-ik, sumiyagit

SHRILL, adj.—ingay na nakasásakít ng tainga dahil sa katalasan—alingiis, mataliis—makalilisang

SHRUB, n.—kahoy na maliít — sagbut —kahoy nga magagmay

SHUFFLE, adj.—balasahin—pagsaksak — balasahon

SHUN, v.—layuán, kamuhián — paglikay, pagpahilayo — pahilayoán, likawán

SHUT, adj. —nakasará, nakapinid—linukban, sirado—nakasirá, nakatakúp

SHUT, v.—isará, ipiníd—paglukob, pagtak-op—isirá, itakúp

SHY, adj. — mahíhiyaín, kimì— manggiulawon — mahuluy-on, matahapon

SHYNESS, n.—kakimián—kamaulawon—pagkatahap, pagkahuyâ

SICK, v.—may-sakít — masakiton —nagabalatián

SICKLY, adj.—masakitin—balatianon—masakitón

SICKNESS, n. — sakít kamandaman—sakit, balatian—balatian

SIDE, n.—tabí, gilid, tagiliran— kiliran, kilid—higád, luyó, kilid

SIDE, v.—kumampí, kumatig — paglaban, paglampig — umapin

SIDEWALK, n. — bangketa, dáanan ng mga tao—asiras—bangketa, alagyan sang táo

SIDEWISE, adj.—nakatagilid — nagtakilid — nakatakilid

SIGH, n.—buntunghiningá—panghupaw—hibubun-ot

SIGH, v. — magbuntunghiningá—pagpanghupaw — maghibubunot

SIGHT, n.—tingín, paningín—panan-aw, talan-awon—tulok, panulok

SIGHT, v.—makita, matanáw—pagtan-aw—makità, malantawán

SIGN, n.—tandâ, pirmá, lagdâ—timaan ilhanan — tandà, pirma, lagdà

SIGN, v. — pirmahán, lagdaán—pagtimaan, pagpirma — pirmahán, lagdaán

SIGNAL, n.—tandâ, senyas—kidhat, sinyas—senyal, tandà

SIGNAL, v.—senyasán, hiwatigan—pagkidhat, senyalán—tandaán

SIGNATURE, n.—pirmá, lagdâ—pirma, timaan sa kamut—pirma lagdà

SILENCE, n. — katahimikan — kahilum — kahipos

SILENCE, v.—patahimikin —paghilum — pahipuson

SILENT, adj.—tahimik—mahilum —kahipos

SILENTLY, adv.—matahimik—sa kahilum—mahipos

SILK, n.—sutlâ, seda—sida, mahamis panapton—suklâ seda

SILKY, adj.—malasutlâ, malambót—sidahon, hamis — masuklaon

SILLYNESS, n.—kaululán—kahangál—kabuangán

SILVER, n.—pilak—pilak, salapî —pilak

SILVERY, adj. — maputî—pilaknon, maputî—mapilakon

SIMILAR, adj. — magkamukhâ, magkaparis, magkawangkî — amgid-amgid, magkamay-ong — magkaanggid, magkanawóng, magkamukhà

SIMILARITY, n.— pagkakawangkî, pagkakatulad — ang pagkaamgid —pagkaanggid, pagkanawóng, pagkamukhà

SIMILARLY, adv.—gayón din — sa mao gihapon—amó man

SIMPLE, adj.—yano, musmós — yano—simple, yano, pasagì

SIMPLICITY, n. — kayanuhan— ang kayano—kayonohan, kapasagì

SIN, n.—kasalanan —salá—kasalanan

SINCE, adv.—mulâ sa, yamang—sukad sa — sugod sang, kutob sang

SINCERE, adj.—tapát na loób—maugdang, mabination—tampad sing buót

SINCERELY YOURS, buóng katápatan — imong mabination—ang matinahuron

SING, v. — umawit, kumantá — pag-awit—umamba, kumanta

SINGULAR, n.—isahin—usa lang —isahón

SIR, n.—ginoó—ginoo—ginuo

SIRE, n.—amá—amaban, ginikanan — amáy

SKATE, n. — iskeit — iskit, puthawng bakya — eskeit

SKATE, v.—magpadusdós sa yelo na suót ang bakyáng bakal— —pagpadailos sa yelo—mag-eskeit

SKELETON, n. bungô, kalansáy —bukog, kalabera —bagúl, kalabera

SKILL, n.—kabihasnán, kaalaman —kabatid, kahanás —kasampaton, kaalam

SKILLFUL, adj.—bihasá, maalam at matulin—batid, hanás—sampaton, mangin-alamon

SKIM, v.— bawasan, hapawín — pagsangyad — hapawán, kalisón saplirón

SKIN, n. — balát, upak — panit pakpak — panit, upak

SKIP, v. — ilaktáw, laktawán—paglaktaw, paglukso—laktawán lumpatán

SKIRT, n.—saya, laylayan—saya saya

SKY, n.—langit—langit — langit

SKYROCKET, v. — pumailanláng —pagsulbong sa itaas—tumimbuok

SLAVE, n.—busabos—ulipon—esklabo, ulipon

SLANT, n hilís, palagáy—panabút, hirig—takilíd, likday

SISTER, n.—kapatíd na babae madre—igsoong babaye — utod nga babáe, utoron, madre

SIT, v.—umupô—paglingkod—lumingkod

SITE, n.—poók, dako; pagtatayuán—dapit, yutang tarokan—duóg, palatindogan

SITTING, n. — úpuan, pag-upô— —pagkalingkod, naglingkod — lingkurán

SITUATED, v.—nakalagáy, nároroón — nahimutang — nahamtang

SIX, n.—anim—unom—anum

SIXTEEN, n.—labíng-anim — napulog-unom—napulo'g anum

SIXTH, adj.—ikaanim—ika-unom —ikan-um

SIXTY, n.—animnapû—kan-uman—kan-umán

SIZE, n.—lakí, kalakihán, kalakhán—gidak-on—kadakû

SIZEABLE, adj.—malakí — dakumay gidak-on—masangkad, kadakuón

SLAY, v.—patayín — pagpatay, pagluha, pagbunó — patyon

SLAYER, n.—mámamatay-tao—ang nagpatay, mamumuno—manogpatay

SLED, n.—kareta, paragos — karetón—kareta

SLEEP, n. — pagtulog — katulog—pagtulog

SLEEP, v.—matulog — pagtulog—magtulog

SLEEP, adj. — nag-antók, antukín—katulgon, nagduká -- natuyó, matuluyhon

SLEEPINESS n. — pag-aantók—ang pagkakatulgon—pagkatuyó

SLEEVE, n.—manggás—manggas—pakû

SLEEVELESS, adj. — waláng manggás—walay manggas—wala'y pakû

SLENDER, adj.—payát, manipís—daut, niwangon, yagpis—maniwang, hayát

SLICE, n.—putol, hiwà—hiwa, adlip—hiniwâhiwà

SLICE, v.—hatiin, hiwain—pagbiwa, pag-adlip—hiwaon

SLIDE, n.—pagkadulás — dahilá—pagkadanlog

SLIDE, v.—magpadulás —pagdalin-as — magpadanlog

SLIGHT, adj. — muntî, maliít — diyutay — diótay

SLIGHT, v. — walaíng halagá, muntiín — pagdaut-daut— wala'y bilí, kadiotayón

SLIP, n.—piraso, pagkakamalî — pirasong papel, sayóp—piniraso, pagkasayúp

SLIP, n.—piraso, pagkakámalî — pagsayop, pagdakin-as—madanlog, magsayúp, makadalin- as

SLIPPER, n.—tsinelas—sinilas —sinelas

SLIPPERY, adj.—madulás —madanglog — kadanlogón

SLOPE, n. —gulód, libís—bakilid, hanayhay sa bukid — bäkulód, pukatód

SLOPPING, v. lumílibís—hanayhay—nagadulhog

SLOW, adj.—mabagal, makupad—mahinay—mahináy, makurì

SLOWLY, adj.—marahan—sa hinay—hinayhinay

SLOWNESS, n. — kabagalan—kahinay—kakurión, kahinay

SLUMBER, n.—pagkakatulog, idlíp—katulogon, himanok—pagkatulog, págkapisók

SLUMBER, v.—matulog, umidlíp —pagkatulog, paghinanok—matulog, mapisók

SLY, adj. — tuso, sinungaling— limbongán — toso, butigón

SLYLY, adv.—matuso, tuso — sa limbong—tosohon, katutigón

SMALL, adj.—maliít—gamay, diyutay, bulilit—diótay

SMALLNESS, n.—kaliitan — ang kagamay — kadiotayón

SMALLPOX, n.—bulutong — buti —butí

SMELL, n.—amóy, langháp—ang baho — bahò, haklù

SMELL, v.—amuyín, langhapín— pagsimhot —hakluón, singhotán

SMELLY, adj.—nangángamóy — nanimaho — mabahò

SMILE, n.—ngitî— pahiyum, yuhom—yuhóm

SMILE, v.—ngumitî—pagpahiyum, pagyuhom—yuhóm

SMILING, adj.—laging nakangitî —mapahiyumon — pirme nagayuhóm, mayuhomon

SMITH, n.—pandáy — panday na puthaw—panday sa salsalón

SMOKE, n. —asó—asó—asó

SMOKE, v.—paasuhán, humitít— pagpanabako,· pagpaasó — paasohán, manigarilyo

SMOKY, adj.—maasó, maasap — asohón—maasó

SMOOTH, adj.—pino, makinis, patag—mahamis, mahinlo—mapino, mahining, mahinlò

SMOOTHNESS, n. — kapinuhan, kaliñisan, kakinisan— kahamis, kapino—kahinloán, kahiningón

SMOOTHLY, adv.— mapino, mapanatag—sa kahamis—kapinohón

SNAIL, n.—susô—susó— taklong

SNAKE, n.—ahas, ulupóng—halas, bitin — man-ug, bitín

SNAP, n.—lagitík, lagutók—litik, labtik—linagatik, linagutok, latô

SNAP, v.—lagitikín, alisín—pagiitik, pagbuto— palagutokón, palatuón

SNAPPY, adj.—mabilís, maayos— madali, maliksi—madasig matalunsay

SNATCH, n.—pag-agaw — pag-agaw, pagsignit—pag-agaw

SNATCH, v.—agawin, saklutín— pag-agaw — agawon, sabnitón

SNARL, v.—umangil— pagyagubyob—sumambo

SNEEZE, n.—bahín—atsi, bahá— nanimaón

SNORE, n.—paghihilík—paghagok —paghuraguk

SNOW, n.—niyebe, tubig na naging yelo—yelo—niyebe, tubig nga nangin-yelo

196

SNOWY, adj.—punô ng yelo — púno sa yelo—punô sing yelo

SO, adv.—kayâ ngâ, totoó, gaya nitó—busa, ingon niini — ganì man

SOAP, n. —sabón — sabon— habón

SOAR, v.—lumipád pataás—pataas nga lupad—tumimbuok

SOARING, adj.—tumátaás—nagkataas—nagatimbuok

SOAP, adj.—mabulâ—sabonon — mahabón

SOBER, adj.— mahinahon, di-lasíng—dili hubog—masinulub-ón

SOCIAL, adj.—marunong makisama—makidaiton —maki-katipunán

SOCIETY, n.—lípunan, kasama — kapunongan, katilingban —katipuñan

SOCK, v.—buntalín — pagsombag —sumbagón

SOCK, n.—medyas ng lalaki — midyas sa lalaki—medyas

SOFT, adj.—malambót—mahumok —mahumok

SOFTEN, v.—palambutín—paghumok—pahumukon

SOFTLY, adj.—may kahinaan — mahinay—kahumukón

SOIL, n.—lupà — yuta, lapok — dutà, mahigkò

SOIL, v.—magdumí, dumhán — paglapok, pagbuling — higkoán, bulingán

SOILED, adj. — nadumhán, márumhán—lapokon, nabulingan—maghigkon, mabulingón

SOLDIER, n. kawal, sundalo — sundalo—soldado, hangawáy

SOLE, n.—kaisá-isá tálampakan, suwelas—bugton, swelas — swelas, lalapakán

SOLELY, adv. nag-íisá — nagusa—isahanon

SOLEMN, adj.—magalang, matahimik, kapitapitagan—solemne, maligdong—matinahuron, mahipos

SOLICIT, v.—maghanáp, manghingî—pagpangayo— magpangità

SOLID, adj.—tipî, matigás, buô—tibuok, magahi—matig-a

SOLITARY, adj.—nag-íisá—naginusara — isahanon

SOLUBLE, adj.—may kalutasan—mahimong tunawon—tulunawón

SOLVE, v. — lunasan, husayin, liwanagin—pagsulbad—husayan

SOME, ad-pron, — ilán—pipila—ibán

SOMEBODY, n. — isáng taong dî matiyák kung sino, ang isáng tao—usá ka tawo—si-sin-o

SOMEONE, n. — ang isáng tao, isáng bagay—usa ka tawo—ang isá ka táo

SOMETHING, n.—iláng bagay — usa⁰ ka butang—isá ka butáng

SOMETIME, adv.—kung minsan, sa ibáng panahón—usahay—kon kaisá, sa ibán nga adlaw

SOMEWHAT, adv.—halos tila — maorag—halos daw

SOMEWHERE, adv.—isáng lugár, sa isáng poók—sa usa ka dapit—bisán diín

SON, n.—anák na lalaki— anak nga lalaki—anák nga lalaki

SONG, n.—awit, kantá — awit, kanta, saloma—amba, kanta

SON-IN-LAW, n.— manugang na lalaki — umagad nga lalaki— umagad nga lalaki

SOON adj.—agád, madalî — sa madali—gilayón, madalî

SOONER, adv.—sa lalong madalî—sa labing madali — labíng madalî

SORE, n.—sugat—samad, nanuyó —pilás

SORROW, n. — kalungkutan, dalamhatî—kasakit, kasub-anan— kasulub-on

SORROW, adj.—nalúlungkót—nagasubó—masubô

SORROWFUL, adj. — lipós ng· lungkót — masulob-on — lubos sing kasubô

SOUL, n.–-káluluwá—kalag—kalág

SOULFULLY, adj.—nagtítika—sa kalagnon—mahinulsolon

SOUND, adj.—waláng-salá,—waláng sakít—walay-sala, maayog lawas — wala'y lidan

SOUND, n.—ingay, tunóg, ugong tingog, ugong, timik— gahud, tunóg, bagrong

SOUND, v.--tantiyahín, usisain— pagtingog, pag-usisa — tansyahón, bulobantaon

SOUP, n.—sabáw, sopas— sabaw, pospas—sabáw, sopas

SOUR, adj.—maasim—maaslum— maaslum

SOURCE. n. — pinagmulán, punô —ginikanan—gingikanan

SOUTH, n.—sur, timog, katimogan—habagatan — bagatnan

SOUTHWARD, adj.—patimog — tumong sa habagatan — pabagatnan

SOVEREIGN, n. — harî, pangulo pinakamataás — hari, labawng pamuno—harì, punôpunô

SOVEREIGNTY, n. — kaharián, kapangyarihan—kagahum, gingharian—ginharian, kagamhanan

SOW, v.—maghasík, magtaním — pagpugas — magsab-og, magpanggas

SOW, n.—baboy na babae—anay, landay—nayón

SPACE, n.—patláng, pagitan—wanang—lang-at

SPACIOUS, adj.— maluwág, maluwáng—maluag — masangkad, malang-aton

SPADE, n.--pala, espada sa baraha—pala, espada sa baraha —pala, espada sa baraha

SPARE, v.—magpatawad — pagsalin, pagpasalin —magpatawad

SPARINGLY, adj. —pambihirà — sa daginot — tumalagsahon

SPARK, n.—kisláp, kisáp —aligato, kidlap—kiráb, inggat

SPARKLE, n. maliít na kisláp—kipat-kipat — diótay ngà igpat

SPARKLING, adj.—kumíkisláp — nagpangidlap — nagakiráb, nagainggat

SPARROW, n. —maya —maya — maya

SPEAK, v.—magsalitâ — pagsulti, pagpamulong — maghambal

SPEAKER, n.—pangulo ng asamblea, tagasalitâ o tagatalumpatì—manunulti, pangulo sa Dalam—espiker

SPEAR, n. — sibát, v. sibatín— bangkaw, sapang—sibát, v. sibatón

SPEARHEAD, n.—nangúnguna — ang nag-una, tumoy sa bangkaw—nagapanguna

SPECIAL, adj.—tangì—tinuyo, es pisyal—pasahî

SPECIALTY, n. — katángian — tinuyong kabatid—kapasahî

SPECTACLE, n.—pánoorín salamín sa matá—talan-awon, salamin sa mata—antyohos

SPECTACULÁR, adj. — kahangahangà — masilakon — makadalayaw

SPEECH, n.—diskurso, talumpatì, pagsasalitâ — pakigpulong — diskurso, pamulongpulong

SPEECHLESS, adj.—di-makapagsalitâ—naamang, di-kasulti—dì makahambal

SPEED, n. — tulin, katulinan— katulin—dasig, kadasigón

SPEED, v.—tulinan—pagtulín — dasigon

SPEED MANIAC, n.—kaskasero —tigpatulin—kaskasero

SPEEDY, adj.—matulin—matulin — madasig

SPELL, n.—engkanto—diwaanong gahum, paglitok — batóbatohón, engkantohón

SPELLING, n.—pagbaybáy,—panlitok, pantitik — pagtigbató

SPEND, v.—gumugol—paggugol— manghinguyang

SPENDTHRIFT, adj. — bulagsák, pabayà — gastador — buhahâ

SPHERE, n.—lobo, mundó, poók na nasásakop—lingin — sinakupan, kalibutan

SPHERICAL, adj.—mabilog—malingin — mabilog

SPICE, n.—panahóg, panlasa, panimplá — panakot — panakut, panimpla

SPICY, adj—malasa—puno sa panakot, lamian — malalim

SPIDER, n.—gagambá — tambayawan, lawa-lawa—damáng

SPIN, n.—inog—tulilik, tuyok — pulon

SPIN, v.—painugín, uminog—pagtulilik, pagtuyok—pulondan

SPINNING, adj.—umíinog—nagatulilik—pinulonan

SPIRIT, n.—espíritú, diwà, káluluwá—diwa, kalag—espiritú, kalág

SPIRIT, v.—mawalâ — diwanhon —puno'y espiritú

SPIT, v.—lumurâ, magluwâ—pagluwa—dumuplà

SPITE, n.—samâ ng loób, magpasamâ ng loób—dumot — kalain sang buót

SPLENDID, adj.—kaayaaya, mainam—maayo dalaygon—matarung, maayo

SPLENDOR, n.—karilagán—ka hayag, katahum—kagayonan

SPLIT, v.—biyakín, biyák, hatiin —pagsiak, pagsip-ak — buk-en, himulagón

SPLIT n.—pagkakáhatì — siak, sip-ak—pagkabukâ, paghimulagay

SPOIL, v.—sirain, biguín — pagdaut, pagkadunot — pierdehón, parutón

SPOILAGE, n.—kasiraan — kadunotan — pagkaparút

SPOILED, adj.—nasirà, nabigô—dunot, baklag—napierde, naparút

SPONGE, n.—espongha—espongha—espongha

SPONGY, adj.—parang espongha, malaespongha—sama sa espongha—malaespongha

SPOON, n.—kutsara—kutsara — kutsara

SPORT, adj.—pareho — isport, himiste — alalangay

SPORT, n.—larô, líbangan—dula, panugnat sa. kusog — deportes, hampang

SPOT, n.—batík, mantsá, dako — dapit, buling — pintok, mantsa, buling

SPRAY n.—pandilíg, pansabog — bisibis, salibo — bunyag, inogbunyag, inogwisik

SPRAY, v.—diligín, wisikán—pag-bisibis, pagsalibo — bunyagán, wiskan

SPREAD, n.—pagkakalatag, pag-kakakalát—han-ay—paglinapta

SPREAD, v.—ikalat, ilatag—pag-han-ay, pagsabwag—laptahón

SPREADING, adj. — malapad — nagasabwag, nagakaylap — li-napta

SPRING, n.—bukál, bitag, buwán ng pagtubò—tingpamulak — tu-borán, primabera

SPRING, v. — tumalón, siluin — paglukso, pag-ambak—lumum-pat, siniúd

SPRINKLE, v.—wisikán, magwi-sík—pagsablig — wiskan, sabli-gán

SPRINKLING adj. — mangilán-ilán—pila-pila—mamilágpilág

SPY, n.—tiktik—tiktik, espiya — espiya

SPY, v.—maniktík, sundán—pag-paniktik, pangispiya—mangispi-ya

SQUANDER, v.—aksayahın—pag-usik-usik — uyangán

SQUARE, n.—kuadrado, plasa, pa-risukát — kuwadrado, hawan-lungsod—kwadrado, magkasilo

SQUARE, v.—magkaayos, mag-kásundô—nagkauyon, nagkaas-but—maghangpanay, maghisu-got

SQUIRE, n.—don, lalaking may dangál — tawong tinamud — may katarungan

SQUIRE, v.—ipasiyál, samahan —kinuyogan — ipasyar, buylo-gán

SQUASH, n.—kalabasa—kalabasa, —kalabasa

SQUIRREL, n.—ardilya, hayop na nanínirahan sa butas ng mga kahoy at kawangis ng koneho—ardilya, putiong mananap — ha-yup nga daw sa koneho

STABLE, adj.—panatag—maayong kabutang—pagkahamtang

STABLE, n.—silungán ng kabayo —kuwadra sa kabayo, alad — kwadra sang kabayo

STACK, n.—mandalà, salansán — panghaw — hinantalan

STACK, v.—punuín, itambák — pagtipig, pagtambak — pun-on, hantalán

STAFF, n.—tukod, tungkód, mga katulong — sungkod, mga sakop sa buhatan — tukód, mga ka-bulig

STAGE, n.—platáporma, entabla-do—entablado, tablado — pla-taporma, entablado

STAGE, v.—maglabás ng isáng dulà—pagpagula, pagpasunda-yag—magpauâ sa entablado

STAGEPEOPLE, n.—ang lumála-
bás o mga mandudulà, artista—
mga magdudula sa tablado —
gumuluà sa entablado, artista

STAGGER, v.—lupaypáy — pag-
sapinday, pagsarasay — lalóng,
lakát nga nagaisiisi

STAGGERING, adj.—nakapanlú-
lupaypáy — nagsusapinday —
mag-isiisi, magdunglaydunglay

STAIN, v. — mantsahán — pag-
mantsa — dagtaán, mantsahán

STAIR, n.—baitáng, hagdanan —
ang-ang sa hagdan — lintang

STAKE, n.—tayâ—taya, pusta —
pusta, tayâ

STAKE, v.—tumayâ, tulusan —
pagtaya, pagtisok ng lipak —
tumayâ, pumusta

STALK, n.—sangá o punò ng halaman—punoan sa tanum — sangá ukón punò sang talamnon

STALK, v.—lumakad nang may
kahambugán — minaut nga li-
naktan — maglakát sing pa-
hambog

STALL, n.—kakanan ng hayop—
puy-anan sa mananap — kalan-
an sang hayup sa kwadra

STALL, v.—mag-atubilì, humintô
— paglangay-langay — magdulog, mag-isul-duksol

STAMP, n.—selyo, taták, timbre –
patik, prangkiyo — selyo, timbre, marka

STAMP, v.—tatakán, selyuhán —
pagpatik, pagtimbre — markahán, selyohán

STAND, n. — panindigán, dako,
pagkatig — gibarugan, baruga-
nan — pagtindog, pag-akù

STAND, v.—tumayô, tindigán —
pagtindog, pagbarug — magtin-
dog, tindogán

STANDARD, n.—ulirán, parisan,
bandilà — sukdanan, panig-ingnan — istandard

STAR, n.—bituín — bitoon — bi-
tuon

STAR, v.—nanguna sa labás—pag-
kabitoon sa dula o lilas—nanguna sa guâ

STARCH, n.—almiról — amiról —
tayubong

STARCH, v.—mag-almirol, tigasán
—pag-amirol — mapangalmidól

STARCHY, adj.—malagkít — mahagkot — mapilít

STARE, v.—tumingín nang matagál, tumitig, titigan — pagtutok,
paglutok — tumulok sing madugay, naghimutad

STARE, n.—titig, tingín — tan-
aw, tutok — himutad, tulokon

STARRING, v — itinátampók—
inapilan — ginuaán

STARRY-EYED, adj. — pulos ng kasiyahan, waring nangangarap —mapangandoyon — mahandurawon

START, n.—pasimulâ — sugod, sinugdanan — sugod

START, v.—magsimulâ — pagsagod — sinugoran

STARTLE, v.—gulatin — pagkignat, pagkurat — kibutón

STARTLING, adj. — nakagugulat —makapakurat — makakilibot

STARVE, v.—gutumin, magutom —paggutum, gutmon—gutomon, magutom

STATE, n.—estado, kalágayan — kahimtang, bansa — estado, kahimtangan

STATE, v.—isaysáy, sabihin — pagsaysay, pag-asoy — isaysay, siiingón

STATELY, adj.—marilág, marangál — barugan, maambong — silingon, alasuyón

STATEMENT, n. — pagsasalitâ, ulat na nakasulat — pahayag, saysay — pagpangasoy

STATESMAN, n. — dalubhasà sa pagpapalakad ng pámahalaán — makinasud, estadista — estadista

STATION, n.—kalágayan, himpilan o hantungan—humongan, estasyonan — estasión

STATIONARY, n.—laging nakahimpíl—nagpuyo, way-lihok — unáy, dulogán

STATIONERY, n.—papél susulatán—papel-sulatan — papél nga sulutatan

STATUE, n.—estatua, rebulto — kinulit, estatwa — estatwá

STATUESQUE, adj.—mataas, matuwíd—taason, tarung — matayog, tadlong, bunghayon

STAY, n.—pamamalagì, pagtirá—pamuyo — pagpabilin, pagpahawid

STAY, v. — mamalagì,. pigilan — pag-abutan, pagpuyo — magpabilin, punggan ukón hawiran

STEADY, adj.—panáy, tapat, walang galaw—kanunay, makanunayon — lunsay, unáy

STEAK, n.—isáng hiwang karnéng baka—hiniwang unod sa baka — isá ka hiwâ sang karne sang baka

STEAL, v.—magnanakaw—pagpangawat — mangawat

STEATHILY, adj.—panakáw, dahan-dahan—hinay-hinay — pagpangawat, tiid

STEAM, n.—usok ng kumukulong tubig, singáw — alisngaw — usbong, hulás

STEAM, v. — pausukan, pasingawan—pagpabukal, pag-alisngaw —pahulasán, pausbongán

STEAMER, n.—sasakyáng pinalalakad ng singaw—bapor, barko sakayán nga ginapadalagan sang pahulás, sakayán-hulás

STEAMSHIP, n.—bapór — bapor, barko — bapór

STEEL, n.—patalím, asero — asiro — asero, patalúm

STEELY, adj.—matalím — asirohon—matalúm

STEEP, adj.—matarík — tuktok, matitip — tukaron, taklaron

STEEPLE, n.—torre, kampanaryo —anting, kampanaryo — torre, kampanaryo

STEER, n.—guyang toro — baka nga linghod — baka nga linghod

STEER, v.—akayin, ugitan—pagmaniho, paggiya — guyuron, lisoán

STEERAGE, n.—pag-ugit, sasakyán sa bapór ńa malapit sa mákiná—bahin sa bapor duol sa makina — lilisoán

STEM, n.—tangkáy—udlot — uyatán, paklang

STENOGRAPHER, n.—takígrapó —takigrapo — takigrapó

STEP, n.—hakbáng — lakang — tikáng

STEP, v.—humakbáng, bilisán — paglakang, pagtunob, pagtamak —tumikáng

STERILE, adj.—baog—dili makaanak—baóg

STERN, adj. — malupít — ulin, mapig-ut, isugan — madumilion, mapigoson

STERNLY, adv.—mabalasik — sakapig-ut—mahar-ang

STEW, v.—igisa, iprito—pagbukal, paglaga—igisá, iprito

STICK, n.—patpát, palito—tukog, pawo—lipák, palito

STICK, n.—patpát, palito—tukog, pawo—lipák, palito

STICK, v.—dumikit, mamalagi — pagdikit, pagpabilin — dumukót

STICKY, adj.—malagkít, madikit —pilit, mahagkot — mapilít

STIFF, adj.—matigás—magahi — matig-a, matiskug

STIFFNESS, n.—katigasán — kagahi — katiskusgán, katig-ahón

STILL, adj.—tahimik, walang galáw, waláng ímik, patahimikin— mahilum, walay-timik—matawhay, malinóng

STILLNESS, n.—katahimikan — kahilum, kamingaw — kalinongán

STING, v.—mákagát ng hayop na gaya ng putaktí—pagpahit — kutot

STING, n.—kirót, sakít—lala, sa-kit—busóg, hapdì

STINGY, adj.—maramot — inot, kuripot — dalúk, dingút

STINGINESS, n.—karamutan — kainot, pagkakuripot — kadalukán

STIR, v.—haluin, kalikawin, kálusin — pag-ukay, pagsugkay — lgayón

STITCH, v.—tahiin, sulsihán — pagtahi, pagsursi — tahión, sibtan

STITCHES, n.—mga sulsí o tagpî —mga sursi, sinursihan — inogtahì

STOCK, n.—natatagò, nakaimbák— — tinipigan, tinago — kapitál, naaman

STOCK, v.—magtaan, maglaán — pagtipig, pagtingub—mag-aman, magtigana

STOCKING, n.—medyas ng babae —midyas sa babaye — medyas sang baáe

STOLEN, adj.—ninakaw, inumít—kinawat — kinawat

STOMACH, n.—tiyán—tiyán, koto-koto—tiyán

STONE, n.—bató—bato — bató

STONE, v.—batuhín, pukulin — pagbato — batohón, habuyón

STONECUTTER, n.—mamumutol ng bató—maninipak ug bato — manog-utód-bató

STONY, adj.—mabato, waláng kibo—batoon — batohón

STOOL, n.—úpuan—banko—lingkuran

STOOL PIGEON, n. — espiyá — espiya — espiya

STOOP, v.—yumukô — pagyuko —dumukô, kumûkò

STOOPED, adj.—yukód, baluktót —baku, yuko — dukô, kûkò

STOP, n.—paghintô—hunonganan —dulog

STOP, v. — pahintuín, tumibil — paghunong — dumulog

STORE, n.—tindahan — tindahan —tindahan

STORE, v.—mag-imbák — pagpuno mga baligya — magtipon

STORAGE, n.—imbakan—bodega —tiliponán

STORM, n.—bagyó—bagyo, unos, urakan — bagyo, unós

STORMY, adj.—may bagyó, malakás ang hangin — bagyohon — mabagyohon

STORY, n.—kasaysayan, kuwento, lapág o piso ng bahay—sugilanon, audana — sugilanon, eskalón, panalgan

STOUT, adj. —siksik, matabá — supang, tambok — matambok

STOUTNESS, n.—katabaan, katibayan—katambok — katambokón

STOVE, n.—kalán, apuyan, pugón —pugon, lutoan — kalán, pugón

STOWAWAY, n—tagò—sumasakay sa tago (sa bapor)—tagò

STOWAWAY, v.—magtagò—pagsakay sa tago—magtagò

STRAIGHT, adj. — matuwíd, tulúy-tulóy — tul-id, tanus — tadlong

STRAIGHT FORWARD, adj.—tiyakan, tuwiran — lakturay, laktud—tadlongón, katadlongán

STRAIN, v. — salain, bistayín — pagsala, pag-ag-ag—salaon, ayagón

STRAIN, v. —salain, bistayín — tono, paningog, kalapóy — bugat, tingog

STRAIT, n.—makitíd na daanan ng tubig — sigpit wanang sa dagat — makitíd nga iligán sang tubig

STRANGE, adj.—náiibá, bago — kahibudnganan, lain — kamalámalahán

STRANGER, n.—taga ibáng lupà, taong bagong dating, taong di kilalá—dumoduong — dumuluong, ekstranhero

STRANGELY, adv. — kakatuwâ, kakaibá — sa kahibudnganan — makamalámalahán

STRAP, n.—sintás, panali—bakus, panagkus—wagkus, banda

STRAP, v.—itali, ikabít—pagsabit, pagbakus—ibanda, iwagkus

STRAW, n.—dayami, ginikan — dagami — dagami

STRAWBERRY, n.—presas, duhat —lomboy — istroberi, lumboy

STRAY, n.—pagkakaligáw—saag —pagkadaplis, dapyos

STRAY, v.—maligáw, umalís — pagkasaag, pagsalaag — madaplis, madapyos

STRAYED, adj.—sumama—nahisalaag — kadaplisán

STREAM, n.—agos, batis, ilog — sapa, agos—ilig, sapâ, subâ

STREAM, v.—umagos, tumakbó— pag-agos, pagdagayday — umilig

STREAMING, v.—umaagos—nagdaygay—nagailig

STREET, n.—kalye, daan—dalan —kalye, dalan

STRENGTH, n.—lakás, kalakasán —kusog--kusóg

STRENGTHEN, v.—palakasín — pagpakusog, pagligon — pakusgon

STRETCH, n.—unat, layò, paha-
bahin — gilay-on, dag-anan —
unat

STRETCH, v.—unatin, pahabain—
pag-inat — unaton

STRICT, adj. — estrikto, mahigpit
—mapig-uton, estrikto — estrikto, madumilion

STRICTLY, adv.—mahigpít — sa
kapig-ut—pagkamadumilion

STRICTNESS, n. — kahígpitan—
ang ka-estrikto—pagdumill

STRIDE, n.—mahabang hakbáng
—tag-as nga lakang—tumikáng,
nadanlog

STRIDE, v.—lumakad—paglakaw
—nakadanlog

STRIFE, n.—pakikiβag-alít, paki-
kipagbabág, pakikipaglaban —
pakigbisug, pakig-away — pag-
ilinaway

STRIKE, v.—humampás, pumalò,
umaklás—pagpukpok, pagwelga
—nagpaaloy, linamposán, hina-
plit

STRIKING, adj.—kapuna-puná —
mabihagon, madanihon —.maka-
salat-um

STRING, n.—pisì, sinulid, panalì,
kuwerdas—lubld, kuldas — higút, kwerdas

STRING, v.—sumunód, talian —
pagsunod, pagtagkos — kwerda-
sán, higtan

STRIP, n.—ano mang bagay na
mahabà at makitid—butsang
nga taas ug hiktin — bisán anó
nga malabà kag makitíd

STRIP, v.—hubarán, talupan —
paghubad, paghukas — ubahan,
panitan, upakan

STRIPE, n.—guhit, markang mahabà, gumuhit—badlis, badlit—
kurit, guráy-guráy

STRIVE, v.—magsikap, magpilit
—pagpaningkamut — maghimulat, maghimud-os

STROKE, n.—tamà, bugbág, hampás, kilos — hapak, linihokaŋ,
ataki sa sakit — tamà, sumbag,
bara

STRONG, adj.—malakás, matibay
—makusog, kusgan — barahon

STRONGLY, adv.—matigás na—sa
paaging kusog — makusog, mahunit

STRUGGLE, n. — pagpupunyagî,
paglaban—pakigbisug — matigdas, paghimud-os

STRUGGLE, v.—magpunyagî, ma-
kilaban—pagpakigbisug — maghimulat, maghimud-os

STUBBORN, adj.—maulit, matigás ang ulo—sukihan, gahig-ulo
—matigdas ang ulo, banihút

STUBBORNLY, adv.—matigás na
—sa paaging sukihan — pagka-
banihút

STUDENT n.—nag-aaral, estudyante — tinun-an — estudiante, bumuluthô

STUDIES, n.—pag-aaral — mga pagtuon, tulun-anan — pagtuón

STUDIOUS, adj.—mapag-arál, palaarál — makituon — palatuón

STUDY, v.—mag-aral—pagtuon — magtuón

STUFF, n.—bagay, kasangkapan —unsa dihang butang, kasangkapan—butáng kasangkapán

STUFF, v.—siksikan, punín—pagpuno—daskon, pun-on

STUMBLE, v.—mátisod, magkamalî—paghisukamud, pagkadagma—bumaliskad, nagsukamud

STUMBLING, adj.—waláng tiyák —walay siguro — wala'y pat-ud

STUMP, v.—kumanpaniya — pagkampanya — magkampanya

STUMPED, v.—nabigô, nápaudlót —wala makatingog, napaurong —napas-awán, nakaisul

STUMPY, adj—maliit at makapál—diyutay ug mabaga—diótay kag madamul

STUPEFIED, v.—magulumihanan —nahungog, nawad-ag isip—nahanusbô

STUPID, adj — hangál, mangmáng—hungog, burong — banihút sutíl

STUPIDITY, n.—kahangalán—kahungog—kahanusboán

STYLE, n.—uso, moda, pamagát—urog, moda—estilo

STYLE, v.—magpamagát — paghambug sa kaugalingan—mag-estilo

STYLISH, adj. — posturyoso — makiurog, makimoda — posturyoso

SUBDUE, v.—sumupil, magpasukô —pagpaampo, pagbuntog, paginpig—but-an, pasungkaón

SUBJECT, n.—paksâ, pinag-aaralan, nasasakop—ginsakopan, butang hilisgutan — tuluyuón, tulun-an

SUBJECT, v.—padaanin, pasukuin —pamugos nga pagpaampo — paagyon, payaubón

SUBJUGATION, n.—pagsakop — ang pagpangsakop sa lugos — pagkasakup

SUBMIT, v.—sumukô, pahinuhod, ipagkaloób—pag-ampo, pagduko —ipasakup

SUBMISSION, n.—pagsuko, kababaan—ang pag-ampo — pagyaúb pagpaubós

SUBMISSIVE, adj.—malambót na loób—masunoron, maampoon — mapainuboson

SUBSTANCE, n.—kalamnán, sustansya—sustansiya, unod—sustansia

SUBSTANTIAL, adj. — marami,
malamán — daghan, puno sa
sustansiya—masustansia

SUBSTITUTE, n.—panghalili, kahalili, kapalít—halili, ilis — ilis,
salili

SUBSTITUTE, v.—palít, ihalili—
paghalili—iilis, isalili

SUBSTITUTION, n. — pagpapalít
—ang paghalili — pag-ilis, pag-
salili

SUBTRACT, v. — restahin, alisín,
ibawas, bawasan—pagkunhod —
buhinan, pakubsan

SUBTRACTION, n.—pagbabawas
—ang kakunhoran — pagbuhin,
pakubsan

SUBWAY, n.—daán ng tren na ilalim ng lupà—dalan ilalum sa yuta—alagyan tren sa idalum-du-
tà

SUCCEED, v.—magwagí, humalili,
palitán—paglampus — magdaúg,
maghiagum

SUCCESS, n.—pagwawagí, tagumpáy—kalampusan, kadaugan —
kadalag-an

SUCCESSFUL, adj. — nagwagí,
mapagwagí — malampuson, madaugon—mahiagumon, madalagon

SUCH, adj.—ang ganyán, ang gayón o ang ganitó — kana, kini,
kadto — tagsubong sinâ

SUCK, v.—sipsipín, sumipsíp —
pagsupsop, pagsuso—supsupón,
suyopon

SUCKLING, n.—bíik — masuso—
idík

SUDDEN, adj.—biglâ, agad-agád
—kalit, hinanali — hinali

SUDDENLY, adv.—kaginsá-ginsá
—kalit, sa hinanali—kahinalián

SUFFER, v.—magtiís, tiisin—pag-
antus—magbatás, mag-antus

SUFFERING, adj.—naghíhirap —
ang kaantusan, nag-antus—pag-
antus

SUFFICE, v.—magkasya, sumapát
—pag-igo—magpaigôigò, magpa-
hilituon

SUFFICIENT, adj.—hustó, sapát
—igo, husto—nagakaigò, tuman

SUGAR, n.—asukal, matamís —
asukal, kamay — kalamay

SUGAR CANE, n.—tubó—tubo—
tubó

SUGGEST, v.—magpaalala, imung_
kahì—pagsugyot—magpanugyan

SUGGESTION, n.- panukalà, su-
hestiyón—sugyot — pagpanug-
yan

SUIT, n.—terno, asunto — trahe,
buruka — terno, asunto, kasa-
baón

SUIT, v.—ibagay — pag-angay,
pagbagay — iangay

209

SUITABLE, adj.—lapat, bagay —
angay, nahauyon—sibuon

SULLEN; adj.—kimî sa kapwà,
mayayamutin — makusmoron—
pagkatahap

SULTRY, adj. — maalinsangan —
maigang, mainit — matinahapon

SULTRINESS, n. — alinsangan—
kaigang—makalilisang

SUM, n.—suma, kabuuán—gidaghanon, kantidad — pagsuma,
pagbilóg

SUM, v.—pagsamahin — pagsuma,
paghugpong — sumahon, bilogón

SUMMARY, n.—kabuuán — kasu-
mahan, katibuk-an — kasuma-
hán, kabilogán

SUMMER, n.—tag-aráw — ting-
init, berano — tingadlaw

SUMMON, v.—tawagin, ipasundô,
pagtawag—pagtawag, pagsundo
—tawagon, ipasugat, ipatawág

SUN, n.—araw—Adlaw — adlaw

SUNDAY, n.—Linggó, Domingo —
Domingo — Domingo

SUNLIGHT, n.—liwanag ng araw
—siga o hayag sa Adlaw — sanag sang adlaw

SUNNY, adj.—maaraw, masayá—
mahayag—may adlaw, masadya

SUNSET, n.—paglubóg ng araw
—pagsalop sa Adlaw -- paghina-
lúp sang adlaw

SUNSHINE, n.—sikat ng araw —
silaw sa Adlaw—pagsilak sang
adlaw

SUPERINTENDENT, n. — superintendente, tagapamahalà —
superintendente — superintendente, tagdumala

SUPERIOR, n.—mataás, nakatá-
taás—labing maayo, hataas nga
punoan — mataas nga punoan

SUPERIOR, adj.—mataás ang urì,
mabuti — mataas ng matang —
mataas sing sarî

SUPERIORITY, n.—kahigtán —
ang gihabwon, ang pagkalabaw
—kasarián

SUPERVISION, n.—pamamahalà
—pagdumala—pagsayasat

SUPERVISOR, n. — tagasiyasat,
superbisór, tagamasíd — super-
bisor, magdudumala — superbi-
sor, tagsayasat

SUP, v.—maghapunan — pagkaon
sa gabii — magpanyapon

SUPPER; n.—pagkain sa gabi
panihapon — panyapon

SUPPLY, n.—kailangan — linum-
pong kagamitan — kinahanglanon

SUPPLY, v.—magbigáy ng kailangan—pagsangkap — maghatag
sing kinahanglan

SUPPORT, n.—sustento, alalay—hinabang — pagsakdag, pagtabang

SUPPORT, v.—sustentuhán, kandilihín—pagbulig, pagsustento—sakdagón, tabangan

SUPPOSE, v.—magpalagáy—pagpananglit — pananglitan, bulobantaon

SUPREME, adj. — kataasán sa kapangyarihan o pangungulo, mataás sa lahát — labing taas, kinatas-an—katasón sa tanán

SUPREMACY, n. —pamamayani, paghaharì—ang pagkataas, pagkalabaw sa ngatanan — pagkamataason sa tanán

SURE, adj.—tiyák—siguro — patud

SURELY, adv.—siyáng tunay — siguro gayud—kapat-urán

SURFACE, n.—mukhâ, balat, ibabaw—ibabaw—nawóng, dagway

SURGEON, n.—siruhano, -doktór na tumítistís—mananambal, siruhano — siruhano, doktor nga nagabusbos

SURGERY, n. — karunungan sa pagtistís—kinaadman sa panisdis — kiñaalam sa pagbusbos

SURGICAL, adj.—náuukol sa tistís—mahitungod sa panisdis — natungód sa pagbusbos

SURNAME, n.—apelyido, pangalang-angkán—bansagon — apelyido

SURPRISE, n.— pagkakamanghâ, pagkakagulat—kahitingala, kabingangha— pagkatingala, pagka-kibót

SURPRISE, v.—gulatin, biglaín—pagpakugang, paghingalit — kibutón

SURPRISING, adj.—katakataká, kamanghá-manghâ — katingalahan, kahibulongan — makatilingala, makapakibót

SURRENDER, n.— pagsukò—ang —pag-ampo—nagyanib

SURRENDER, v.—sumukò, ibigáy —ibigáy—pag-ampo—nagyanib

SURROUND, v. —paligiran, kubkubín—paglibut, paglikos—palibotan

SURROUNDING, n. — kapaligiran, paligid, painog — mga butang nanaglibot — sa palibot

SURVEY, n.—pagkasukat, pagmamasíd — panukod — pagtakús, pagtul-id

SURVEY, v.—sukatin, masdán — pagsukod, pagpaniid — takson, tul-irón

SUSPECT, n.—ang pinaghíhinalaan—gikatahapan — halan-an

SUSPECT, v.—paghinalaan—pagpanahap, pagtatap—han-an

211

SUSPEND, v.—pahintuín, pansa
mantalá — pagpaurong — sus
pendehón, pauntatón

SUSPENDER, n.—tirante — tirante — tirante

SUSTAIN, v.—umalalay, katigan
—pagpakaon, pag-agwanta —
sakdagón, sustenerón

SUSTENANCE, n.—sustento, pagkatig—sustento—sustento,
pagsagúd

SWALLOW, n. —langáy-langayan
—langgam sungko-langit — li-
gong-ligong

SWALLOW, v.—lunukín, lagukín
—pagtulon — tunlon, lumyon

SWAMP, n.—latian — kalasahan,
pilapilan—kanipaan, dalanawán

SWAMPY, adj.—maraming latian
—lasak-lasak—manipaon

SWAN, n.—tagák — langgam nga
putí—dugwak

SWAN SONG, n. — hulíng pag-
awit—katapusang awit— hingapusán ng amba

SWARM, n.— pulutóng ng mga
hayop—panon sa mga pak-an—
gubán sang mga hayup

SWARM, v.—pagdumugan — pag-
panugok — dulumugán

SWAY, n.—galáw, lakás, bigát—
tabyog — tabog

SWAY, v. — pakilusin, galawín,
iyugóy— pagtabyog — tabugon

SWEAR, v. — magtungayáw, sumumpâ — pagsumpa — mag-
sumpà

SWEAT, n.—pawis—singut—balbas

SWEAT, v.—pagpawisan — pag-
pagsingut — pabalhasán

SWEATY, adj.—pawisán — sing-
tanon, nagdusingut — pagpabal-
has

SWEEP, n.—palís, walís—silhig
—silhig

SWEEP, v.—magwalís, magpalis-
pagsilhig — silhigón

SWEEPING, adj.—lubós na pagpalís —nagasilhig, maharuson—
panilhigón

SWEET, n.—matamís — matam-
is—matam-is

SWEETEN, v. —patamisín— pag-
patam-is — patam-isón

SWEETLY, adv.—may katamisán
—may katam-is —katam-isón

SWELL, n. —pamamagâ— hubag,
hupong—palamanóg

SWELL, v. —mamagâ, palakihín
—paghubag, paghupong — ma-
manóg

SWIFT, adj.—matulin — matulin
—madasig

SWIFTLY, adv.—mabilís, matulin
—may katulin—kadasigón

SWIM, v.—lumangóy, maglangóy
—paglangoy—lumangóy

SWIMSUIT, n. —damít na panla-ngóy—sinina sa lángoy— sapút sa langóy

SWING, n.—duyan, suntók —duyan, suntok—duyan, habyog

SWING, v.— iduyan, isayáw na maharót—pagduyan, paglabyog—duyanon, ihabyog

SWITCH, n.—suwít, susì — suwit sa elektrisidad—swít, yabihán

SWITCHMAN, n.—ang nangánga-siwà ng elektrisidád—tig-ati-man sa suwit sa dagitab—ang tagtatap sang elektrisidád

SWORD, n.—tabák, ispada—es-pada — espada

SYMBOL, n.—sagisag, tandâ—ti-mailhan—timaan

SYMBOLIC, adj.—masagisag, ma-kahulugán — mahuloganon — mapatimaanon, may kahulogán

SYMBOLIZE, n.—nagsásagisag — pagtimaan — patimaanan

SYMPATHY, n.. — pakikiisáng damdamin, diwà ng pagdamay —pakigduyog sa kaguol —pag-buylog sa kabubut-on

SYNONYM, n.—singkahulugán — samag-kahulogan — kabaragu-bay, sibù-kahulogán

SYNTAX, n.—palaugnayan — sin-tax — balayán sang sinulatán ukon dinalán

SYRINGE, n. heringilya—hering-zilya — heringilya

SYSTEM, n.—sistema, paraán—paagi, sistema—sistema, paagi, pahitò

SYSTEMATIC, adj. — maparaán, maayos—subay sa paagi—mapa-hituon

— T —

TABLE, n. —mesa, dulang — ta-lad, kan-anan—lamisa, latuk

TABLET, n. — tableta, kuwader-nong tiklupin — tableta, papel-sulatan—tableta, kwaderno

TACK, r..—pakong espilé, pakò—lansang gagmay — lansang nga malapad ang ulo

TACTICAL, adj.—maparaán—pi-naagi — mapahituon

TACTICS, n.—paraán — mga pa-agi, taktika—paagi, pahitò

TAIL, n. —buntót—ikog — ikug

TAILOR, sastré, mánanahì—ma-nanahi — sastre, mananahi

TAILOR SHOP, n.— patahian — tahian—talahian, sastreriya

TAKE, v.—kumuha, kunin, dalhín —pagkuha — kumuhà, kuhaon, dalhon

213

TALE, adj.—may bakás — may tunob—may inagihan

TALE, n.—kwento, katháng salaysáy—kasaysayan, sugilon — sugilanon nga maragtason sa panaysayon

TALENT, n. — talento, likás na karunungan — kait-on, kahíbalo —talento, kinaadman

TALENTED, adj.—matalino—may kahíbalo, utokán — angin-alamon, makinaadmanon

TALISMAN, n.—antíng-antíng — anting-antíng — anting-antíng

TALK, n.—makipag-usap—pakigsulti, pagsulti—hambal

TALKATIVE, adj. — masalitâ—matabi, sabaan — palahambal

TALL, adj.—mataás, matangkád, matayog — mataas, malayog—mataas, lantyog

TAMARIND, n.—sampalok—sambag—sambag

TAME, maamò, paamuin — anad —mahagúp

TAN, adj.—kayumanggí — tabunon — kayumanggì, kaki

TANK, n. — tangké — tangke — tangke

TANNER. n. — mangkakatad — magtitina — kurtidór

TAP, n. — tuktók, kalabít—tuktok, dagpi — pikpik

TAP, v. — tuktukín, kalabitín—

pagdagpi—pikpikón

TAR, n.—alketrán—alkitran—alketrán

TARDY, adj.—hulí, náhulí, mabagal—naulahi — ulihi, mabundol

TARDINESS, n.—kabagalan—ang kaulahi — kabundulón

TASK, n.—gáwain, trabaho—buluhaton — buluhatón, trabaho

TASTE, n.—lasa, lasáp—lami, tilaw—lalim

TASTE, v.—lasahin—pagtilaw — lalimán

TASTEFUL, adj.—malasa — lami-an—malalimon

TASTELESS, adj. — waláng lasa —walay lami — wala'y lalim

TASTY, adj.—masaráp, may mabuting lasa—malami-an—manamit, marimis

TAVERN, n.—bahay-túluyan, kárihan—balay-abutan, imnaman—baláy dalayonán

TAX, n.—buwís, mag-atang ng buwís—buhis — buhís

TAX, v.—pabuwisin—pagbuhis — buhisán

TEA, n.—tsa—tsa—tsa

TEACH, n.—magturò, turuan — pagtudlo, pagtuon — tudlò tudluán

TEACHER, n.— tagapagturò, guró, maestro—magtutudlo, magtutuon — manunudlò, maestro ukón maestra

TEACHING, n. —turò—magatudlo —pagtudlò

TEAM, n.—pareha ng kabayo, koponàn, magkakasama — tim, pundok sa magdudula — hugnatan, kampihan

TEAM. v.—magsama, magtulong —pag-uban — maghugnatan, magkampihan

TEAR, n. — luhà, punit — luha luhà, gisî

TEAR, v.—punitin, kaltasín—pagisi—gision

TEARFUL, adj. — umíiyák, luhaan—maluhaon, nagaluha—luhaon

TEASE, n.—panunuksó tuksó—sungog, tiaw, sulog-sulog—tuksò, sunlog

TEASE, v.—tuksuhín—pagsungog, pagtiaw—tuksuón, sunlogón

TEDIOUS, adj.—nakaíiníp—malaay — makatalaka

TELEGRAM, n. —telegrama, hatíd-kawad — hatudkawat, telegrama —: telegrama, hatudulós

TELEPHONE, v.—tawagan—pagtelepono—teleponohán

TELEPHONE, n.—teléponó—telepono—teleponó

TELL, v. — sabihin, salaysayín, isaysáy— pagsulti, pagtug-an—silingón, singganón

TELLER, n.— tagasabi, tagasalitâ, empleado sa bangko—ang nagsulti, tigbayad sa bangko—tagbayad ukón tagkubra sa bangko

TEMPER, n.—init ng ulo—kinaiya sa ulo—kainit sang ulo

TEMPER, v.—ilagáy sa ayos — pagpahimutang sa husto — ibutáng sa naigoan

TEMPERAMENTAL, adj—pabagubago, biglâ-biglâ — saputón, tukbilon —- pagbag-obag-o, padasûdasû

TEMPERATE, adj. — katamtaman, mahinahon—kasarangan—kasarangan

TEMPERATURE, n. — lagáy ng panahón, timplá o init ng katawán — kainiton-kabugnawon sa panahon — kahimtangan sang panahón, kainitón sang lawas

TEMPEST, n. — bagyó, sigwá—dakung unos, bagyo — bagyo, unós

TEMPESTUOUS, adj. —mapusók, —bagyohon — masupok

TEMPLE, n.—templo, simbahan—templo, alampoanan — templo, simbahan

TEMPT, v.—tuksuhín, tumuksó—

pagtintal —tuksuón, tumuksó

TEMPTATION, n.—tuksó, pang-
akit—tintal—makatuluksò, ma-
kasululay

TEN, n.—sampû— napulo — napulò

TENANCY, n.—pangungupahan—
pana-op—pagpangagsa

TENANT, n.—ang bumúbuwís,
nangúngupahan—sa-op — agsa-
dór

TEND, v.—mag-ingat, tumanod—
paghilig, pagpaingon — maghalong, magbantáy, mag-andam

TENDER, adj.—malambót, maselan, maalók maghandóg —
mahumok, pagtanyag — mahumok

TENEMENT, n. — bahay na ipi-
nagpápaupá o bahay na páupa-
hán—balay-paabangan— baláy-
hinakayán

TENSE, adj.—banát, pigil—hugót, magahi—santing

TENSE, n.—kapanahunan — panahon sa berbo—kapanahonan

TENT, n.—dampâ, tolda—tulda—
tolda

TENTATIVE, adj.—pansamantalá
—dili-dayon—tililawan

TERM, n. takdáng panahón, ka-
yarian, isáng panahón—gidugayon, tagal sa panahon—pinat-ud
nga panahón

TERMITE, n.—anay—anay—anay

TERMINATION, n. — katapusán,
hanggáhan — katapusan — pa-
lat-uron, kahingapusán

TERRIBLE, adj —kakilá-kilabot,
nakapangíngilabot — makalilisang, makapakitbi — makahaladlok, makangilidlis

TERRITORY, n. — poók, distrito,
lupaíng sakop—yutang-sakóp—
puók, distrito, teritoryo

TERROR, n. — sindák, malakíng
takot—kalisang—kahadlok, kugmat

TERRORISM, n. — maninindák,
pananakot — panghulga, pagli-
sang — makakulugmat

TERSE, adj. —maiklî at galít—
iinis pagkasulat—malip-ot kag
akíg

TEST, n.—subok, examen, pagsusulit—pasulit — tiláw, eksamin,
salawsaw

TEST, v.—subukin, sulitin —pagsulay, pagpasulit— tilawán, salawsawón

TESTIFY; v. —sumaksí—pagsaksi
—sumaksi

TESTIMONY, n.— patotoó, saksí
—pahayag sa saksi— pamatuod

TETHER, v.—italì, ikabít —pag-
higot, pagsab-it — ihigút, igaid

TEXT, n.—lamán, nilálamán—
mga sinulat nga pulong—teks-
to

216

TEXTILE, n.—habì, kayo, tela — panapton — bayuón, tela

THAN, conj.—kaysa — kay sa— sángsa

THANK, v. — magpasalamat — pagpasalamat — pasalamatán

THANKFUL, kumilala ng utang na loob—mapasalamaton —mapasalamaton

THANKLESS, adj. — waláng mapapalâ—walay-mapaabut — wala'y pasalamat

THANKS, n. —salamat, pasasalamat—salamat, pasalamat — salamat

THANKSGIVING DAY, n.—Araw ng Pagpapasalamat — Adlaw sa Pasalamat — Adlaw sa Pagpasalamat

THAT, pron.—yoón iyán —kana, kadto — inâ, ató

THAT, adv.—na, upang — aron— nâ, agúd

THE, art.—ang—ang mga — ang

THEATRE, n. — teatro, dulaan— dulaan, sinehan — teatro, sinehán

THEATRICAL, adj. — mapalabas —bahin sa tiyatro— palaguaon

THEIR, pron.—kanilá, nilá — ila, ilang—ila, nila

THEM, pron.—sa kanilá— kanila —silá man, ila man

THEMSELVES, pron. — silá rin, kanila rín—sila usab—kon amó

THEN, adj. — kung gayón, sakâ, noon—kon mao, unya, kaniadto —sugod karón, tungód siní

THENCE, pron.—mulâ ngayon sa dahiláng itó, mulà noón—sukad karon, sukad niadto — sugod karón, tungód siní

THERE, adv.—diyán, doón — diha, didto — dirâ, didto

THEREBY, adv.—sa pamamagitan nitó, dahil dito — tungod —niana, tungod niini — sa kalalangan siní, bangód siní

THEREFORE, adv. — kayâ, anopá't kung magkagayón —busa, gumikan niini—ganì

THEREOF, adj — ng bagay na iyán o itó, mulâ sa bagay na iyán o itó—gikan niadto — butáng nga inâ

THEREUPON, adj.— sa gayón— sa ingon niadto—sa amó inâ

THESE, pron.—ang mga itó—kini, kining — inf

THEY, pron. —silá—sila—silá

THICK, adj. — masinsín, makapál, malapot—mabagá, dasók — madámul, malapuyot

THICKET, n. —kasukalan sa gubat, mababang punungkahoy — dasók nga kakahoyan — talon

THICKNESS, n. — lapot, sinsin, kapál—gibag-on, kabaga, kadasók—lapuyot, damul

THIEF, n.—magnanakaw — kawatan, kiriwan—kawatán

THIGH, n.—pigî,— tipik sa paa, paa—hitâ

THIMBLE, n.—didál — didal — didál

THIN, adj. — manipís, payát—manipis, maniwang, daut —manipís, maniwang

THING, n. bagay — butang — butáng, bagay

THINK, v.— isipin, mag-isip — paghunahuna — isipon, hunâhunaon

THINKING, adj.—mapag-isip — naghunahuna, mahunahunaon—mahunâhunaon

THIRD, adj.—ikatló, ikatatló — ikatolo —ikatlo

THIRST, n. —uhaw — uhaw — uháw

THIRSTY, adj. — nauuhaw—giuhaw — nauhaw

THIRTEENTH, adj.—ikalabintatlô—napulog-tolo—napulo'g tatlo

THIRTY, n.— tatlumpû—katloan —katloán

THIS, pron.—itó—kini—iní.

THORN, n.—tiník—tunok—tunók

THORNY, adj.—matiník — tunokon—matunok

THOROUGH, adj.—ganáp—hingpit —bug-os

THOUGH, adj. — bagamán, ka himan—bisan, maskin — wala'y sapayán

THOUSAND, n.—iisáng libo o sanlibo—usa ka libo—sanglibo

THREAD, n.—sinulid, hiblá—hilo —hilo

THREAT, n.—pagbabalà, pananakot—hulga—pagpamahug, pagpamahug, pagpahodlok

THREATEN, v.—takutin, manakot— paghulga, paghadlok—pahugon, hadlokón

THREE, n.—tatló—tolo, totolo— tatlo

THRESH, v.—giikín—paggiyak—linason

THRESHING MACHINE, adj. — pangiik—giyakan — panglinas nga makiná

THRICE, n. —makaitló, makatatló—makatolo—makatlo

THRILL, n.—kaagtingán — hi—nam — kakulunyag

THRILLING, adj.— maagtûng — mahinamon — makakulunyag

THRIVE, v.—mamuhay ng masaganà—pagtubo nga mauswagon —maghimulat

THROAT, n.— lalamunan — tutonlan—tûtunlan

THRONE, n.— trono, luklukang-hari—trono — trono, lingkuran sang harì

THRONG, n.—buntón ng tao, sa-ma-sama, karamihan — hut-ong sa katawhan — gubán, hubón

THRONG, v.—magbuntón — pag-panon — maggubán, maghubón

THROUGH, adv. — sa, sa buóng, sa pamamagitan ng — pinaagi sa labus sa — sa bug-os, sa ka-lalangan sang

THROW, v.—itapon, ihagis, ipu-kól — paglabay, pagbuno- -iha-bóy, ipilák

THROW, n.—pukól, tapon —labay, buno—pilák, habóy

THRUST, v.—itulak, dumaluhong —pagtulod, pagtukmod—itulak, idusô

THRUST, n.—daluhong, sundót—tulod, tukmod—tulód, ousô

THUM, n.—hinlalakí — kumag-ko—kumalagkò

THUMB, v. piliin, isá-isabín — kumagko—pilian, kusiparon

THUNDER, n. — kulóg—dalugdog —daguob

THUNDEROUS, adj.—nakagúgu lat—makapakugang — madagu-obon

THURSDAY, n.—Huwebes — Hu-webes — Huebes

THUS, (adj.)— ganitó, gaya nitó —sa ingon niini — amó inâ, su-bóng siní

THY, pron.—iyó, mo—imo, imo-ha, imong — imo, mo

TICK, n.—tik-tak ng orasán, pur-gás, hanip — pulgas, tik-tak sa relo—tik-tak sang orasán, bi-tík, dapaw

TICKET, n.—bilyete, tiket — ti-ket, papelita — bilyete, tiket

TICKLE, v.—kilitiín— pagkiliktí —itikon

TICKLISH, adj.—makilití — tan-dugon, tukbilon — makalamon

TIDE, n.—laki't kati ng tubig—taub-hunas sa dagat — taub

TIE, n.—buhól, patas korbata — baligtos, higot, korbata — pa-tas, balû, kurbata

TIE, v.—talian, gapusin— pagba-ligtos, paggapus — balighutón, baluón

TIGER, n.—tigre—tigre — tigre

TIGHT, adj.—banát, unát, mahig-pít—hugót, mapig-ton — hugót, sanfing

TILE, n.—tisà, laryó, baldosa — tisa, baldosa — tisà

TILL, adv.—hanggáng sa — hangtud sa — tubtob sa

TILT, n.—labanán, páligsahan —
sangka, indigay — paindisay

TILT, v.—itagilid, itabini — pag-
takilid. paghiwi — patakiliron,
palikión

TIMBER, n. kahoy na malalaki,
troso—troso sa kahoy — troso

TIME, n.—oras, panahón— panahon — oras, tinión

TIMELY, adj.—nápapanahón, ta-
mang-tamá—tukma sa panahon
—sibú sa oras

TIMID, adj. — mahihíyain, madalíng matakot — maulawon, ma-
likayon — mahuluy-on matahapon

TIMIDITY, n.—kakimlán, pagka-
mahihiyain — ang kamaulawon,
kahadlokan — kamahuluy-on,
kamatinabapon

TIN, n. —lata—lata—lata

TINSMITH, n. —latero —latiro,
—latero

TINT, n.—bahagyáng kulay —tina, bulok—malus-aw nga duág

TINT, v.—kulayan — pagbulok—
duagán lugumon

TINY, adj.—muntíng-muntí —gamay kaayo — diótay kaayo

TIP. n.—dulo, pabuyà, — tumoy,
porpina — ukbong punta, pabuya

TIP, v. — magpabuyà, ipaalam—
paghatag kasayuran — magpa-
buya, magpasuhot

TIPTOE, n.—patingkayád, o pa-
tiyád—pagkinto—tihín

TIRE, n. — goma ng auto—goma
sa awto—goma sang awto

TIRE, v.—pagurin — pagkapoy,
paglapoy — kapoyon

TIRESOME, adj. — nakapápagod
—makalapoy, makapoyon—ma-
kapoy

TITLE, n. — tituló, pamagát —
ulohan,—tituló

TO, adv. — sa, kay, upáng — sa,
alang aron, — sa, kay, agúd

TOAD, n.—palakâ—baki — pakâ

TOAST, n. — sinangág, inihaw—
ginanggang — sinanlag, tinosta, kalukalu

TOAST, v. — magsangág, mag-
tustá — paggang-gang—suman-
lag tinosta, magkalukalu

TODAY, adv.—ngayón, ngayóng
araw na itó—karon, karong ad-
lawa — karón nga aldaw

TOE, n.—daliri ng paá—tudlo sa
tiil — tudlô sang tiil

TOGETHER, adv. — sama-sama
—uban-ubañ, nagkaipon — ulo-
lupod

TOILET, n.—pag-aayos ng katawán, kasilyas, pálikuran — kahimanan sa lawas, pansayan —
paghipid sa lawas, kasilyas

TOKEN, n. — tandâ, alaala — timaan, handumanan — tandà, pahahumdum

TOLERATE, v.- pabayaan, paraanin—patnugot lamang, pasagdan — pabayaan, paligaron

TOLERATION, n. — pagbibigáy — pagpatugot — pagpaligad, pagpaumod

TOLL, n.—gawâ, pagod, bayad — bayranan, talaan sa patay — buhat kapóy, bayad

TOLL, v.—kalampagín — pagtugtog, pagbagting—bagtingón

TOMATO, n. kamatis — kamatis —kamatis

TOMB, n. líbingan — lubuganan —lulubngan

TOMORROW, n. —bukas—ugma —buás

TON, n.—tonelada—tonilada—tonelada

TONE, n. — tinig, tono—tingog, tono, nota sa musika —tonóg, tono

TONE, v.—tonohán, bawasan — pagpatono— tonohan, bahohan

TONGUE, n. —dilà—dila—dilà

TONGUE-TIED, adj. — di-maka-pagsalitâ, umíd—amáng, di-makasulti — apâ

TONIGHT, n. —ngayóng gabí, sa gabíng itó—karong gabii, ning gabhiona—karón nga gab-i

TOO, adv.—nápaká, din o rin — hilabihan, usab — man ukón na man

TOOL, n.—kasangkapan — galamiton — kasangkapan

TOOTH, n.—ngipin—ngipon—ngipon

TOOTHLESS, adj.—waláng ngipin — pangag, hingo — wala'y ngipon

TOP, n.—ibabaw, turumpó, trumpó—ibabaw, kinaibabwan — ibabaw, trompo

TOP, v.—mangibabaw—paglabaw mangibabaw

TOPIC, n.—paksâ, úsapan—sultihonon—halambalan, tuluyuón

TORCH. n.—sulô—sulô—sulû

TORMENT, n.—pahirap—kasakit, kaguol — pagpaantus

TORMENT, v. — magpahirap — pagsakit, pagpaantus — magpaantus

TORTURE, n.—pahirap — pagsakit, pagdagmal — paantusón

TORTUROUS, adj. — mahirap — malisud — maantuson

TOSS v.—ihagis ng kamáy—pagitsa — tagay

TOSS, n.—sápalarán— antogán— pagtagay

TOTAL, n.—kabuuán—taman, tibuok—kabilogán

TOUCH, n.—hipò, dampí—paghikap, paghimil—kamlut

TOUGH, adj.—magayót, matigás, maganít—magahi, malig-on, hunít — mauganot, matigdas

TOUGHNESS, n.—katigasán, kaganitán—kagabi, kahunít, kalig-on—katigdasón

TOWARD, adv.—sa gawíng, patungo sa— padulong sa unahan, paduol—padulong sa

TOWEL, n.—tuwalya—tualya, pahiran—twalya

TOWER, n.—tore, moóg, — panting, balayng habug—torre

TOWN, n.—bayan—lungsod—banwa

TOWNMATE, n. — kababayan—katigilungsod — kasimanwa

TOY, n.—laruán—dulaan — hampanganan

TRACE, n.—bakás, guhit—subay, badlit, tunog—inagihan

TRACE, v.—bakasín, guhitan — pagsubay, pagbadlis — sundon, kuritan

TRACK, v. tuntunín, bakasán—agianan, lumbaan, riles—magsunód

TRACT, n.—pitak ng lupà—tipik nga yuta — isá ka pahát nga dutà

TRACTLESS, adj.—waláng bakás walay tunob— wala'y inagihan

TRADE, n.—kalakal— patigayon —balaligyaon

TRADE, v. — makipagkálakalán, magpalít—pagpatigayon— magbaligyaay

TRADEMARK, n. —taták—timaan, marka—marka

TRADER, n. — mángangalakál—magpapatigayon — mamaligyà

TRADING, adj.—poók ng kalakal —nakigpatigayon — duóg sang balaligyaon

TRADITIONAL, adj. — palagian, lagi—nabatasan, naandan — kinabatasan

TRAFFIC, n.—kalakal, pag-aayos ng mga daán—patigayon, trapiko — kinabun-agán

TRAFFIC, v.—kalakalin— pagpamatigayon—baliligyaon, trapikó

TRAGEDY, n.—sakunâ, pangyayaring nakakíkilabot—masulob-on, dugoong hitabo—ipamaligyà

TRAGIC, adj.—malungkót, nakalúlunos — masulob-on, makapakitbi—masinulub-on nga hitabò

TRAIL, n.—landás, bakás—agianan, gamayng dalan—mahinuklugon

TRAIL, v.—bakasín, tuntunín — pagsubay—banas, inagihan

TRAIN, n.--tren, buntót—tren—tren

TRAIN, v. — turuan, sanayin—pagbansay, pagtudlo — tudloán hanason

222

TRAITOR, n.—lilò, taksíl — mabudhion — mabudhì

TRAITOROUS, adj.—mapagtaksíl
—maluibon, mabudhion — mabudhion

TRAMP, n.—palaboy, hampás-lu-
pà — libud-suroy, bagdoy — ti-
yógtiyóg

TRAMP, v. — lumabuy-laboy —
pagbagdoy — nagtiyógtiyóg

TRAMFLE, v.—yurakan —pagyatak—lapakan, tumbanán

TRANSFER, n.—paglipat — bal-
hin — pagsaylo, pagliton

TRANSFER, v.—maglipát, magsalin sa ibá—pagbalhin — isaylo
iliton

TRANSFERABLE, adj. — maá-
aring ilipat — mahimong ibal-
hin—mahimò iliton

TRANSLATE, v.—magsalin, mag-
hulog, sa ibáng wikà—paghubad
pagbadbad — huarón, lubarón

TRANSLATION, n. —pagsasalin-
wikà—hubad — paglubád

TRANSPORT, n.—bapór na transporte — bapor ighahakot —
transporte

TRANSPORT, v.—ilipat —pagha-
kot, paghatud—ipaalinton

TRANSPORTATION, n.— paglili-
pat, sasakyán — salakyanan,
trasnportasyon — salakyan, pa-
laalintonan

TRANSIENT, n.— di-palagian —
lumalabay — dî-unáy

TRANSITION, n.—pagpapalít —
kabalhinan, kalainan —pagbaylo

TRANSITORY, adj. — maáaring
lamipas — mihimong lumabay—
mahimò, magligad

TRAP, n.—hibò, salò, bitag, sala-
káb — lit-ag, bitik, pasgong—
siúd tugalbong

TRAP, v.—siluin, hulihin — pag-
lit-ag, pagbitik — sid-on, tugal-
bongón

TRAVEL, n.—paglalakbáy — panaw — pagpanakayon

TRAVEL, v.—maglalakbay —pag-
panaw, pagbaktas — magpana-
kayon

TRAVELER, n.—biyahero, man.
lalakbáy — magpapanaw, mag-
babaktas — biyahero, mamalig-
yaon

TRAVELING, adj. — naglálakbáy
—nagpanaw, nagbaktas —nags-
panakayon

TREAD, n.—yapak—tunob, lakra
—lapak, tumban

TREAD, v.—yurakan, tapakan —
pagyatak— lapakan, tumbanán

TREASON, n.—pagkakánulò, pag-
tatraidor, pagtataksíl — saláng
pagbudhi — pagbudhì

223

TREASONABLE, adj. — mapag-taksíl — budhianon — mabud-hion

TREASURE, n. kayamanan—ba-hándi—manggad

TREASURER, n. — ingat-yaman, tesorero—mamahandi — kuymi, tesorero

TREASURY, n. —taguán ng sala-pí, kaban-yaman—tipiganan sa bahandi—kuymihan, tilipigán-pilak

TREAT, v.— gamutín, pagpasun-dán — pagtambal, pagatiman—buingon, inakupón

TREATMENT, n.—pagpapasunód, kagámutan — pagdumala, pag-alima —pagkasugtanay, pagbu-lóng

TREATY, n.— kasunduan, pinag-káyarián — kasabutan sa mga nasud — kasugtanan, ginkasug-tan

TREBLE, v.—tatlóng ulit— tolo-hon — tatlo ka sulit

TREE, n.—punungkahoy— kahoy —kahoy

TRELLIS, n.—balag — kapvotan sa tanum — palapala

TREMBLE, v.—manginíg, manga-ligkíg, matakot — pagkurog, pagkuray — magpalangurog

TREMBLING, n.—panginginíg — nagakurog, kurog-kurog —pag-palangurog

TRIAL, n.—paghuhukóm, pagsu-bók — husay sa hukmanan — pagkitá (sa kasabà)

TRIBE, n.—tribu, lipì—banay, tri-bu—tribu, kaliwatan

TRIBUTARY, n. — sangá, namú-musan — sanga, nagbayad bu-his—salangatán, buwisán

TRIBUTE, n.—buwís, handóg — buhis — buwís, handóg

TRICK, n.—dayà, salamangka — bitik, limbong — dayà, sala-mangka

TRICK, v.—dayain, linlangín — paglimbong, pagbitik — dayaon, liputón

TRICKY, adj. — mapaglinláng—malimbungon — maliputon

TRIFLE, n. — muntíng bagay — way-biling butang —diótay nga butáng

TRIFLE, v.—paglaruán — pagti-aw-tiaw — hampangán

TRIFLING, adj.—napaglálaruán — katiaw-tiawan — halampa-ngan

TRIM, v.—putulin, maghandâ — pagputol, paghapsay — utdon, kortehán, kaponón

224

TRIMMING, n.—pagputol, gayák —pinutol, hininlo — pag-utód, pagkorte

TRIP n.— pagbibiyahe, biyahe, paglalakbáy —panaw, biyahe — byahe, panakayon

TRIUMPH, n.—pagwawagí, pananalo — pagdaug, kadaugan — pagdaug

TRIUMPH, v.—magwagí, manalo —pagdaug, paglampus — magdaúg

TROLLEY, n. trole, trambiyá — trambiya — trambya

TROOP, n.—tropa ng mga kawal, hukbó — tropang kasundalohan —tropa sang mga soldado

TROT, n.—lakad, luksó —daganlukso, pag-ikid-ikid — lak-ang, liktin

TROT, v.—lumakad nang parcho, tumakbó nang paluksó —pagdagan, kaguol— lak-angón, liktinón

TROUBLE, n.—sakunâ, abala — kasamok, kaguol — gamó

TROUBLE, v.—abalahin, guluhín —pagsamok, paggubut — gamohón

TROUBLESOME, adj. — maguló, malikót — samokan, magubtanon — magamó

TROUSER, n. — salawál, pantalón—kalsonis — sarwal, pantalón

TRUCK, n.—trak, kotse — trak trak

TRUCK GARDEN, n. — tániman ng mga gulay — tanaman sa utanón — talamnan sing utanón

TRUE, adj.—fotoó, tapát—tinuod minatuód

TRULY, adv.—matapat — tinud- —anon — matuoron

TRUMPET, n.—trumpeta, turutot —trumpeta, budyong — trumpeta, budyong

TRUNK, n.— punô, baúl, kabán —punoan sa kahoy, baul, kabas —punò sang kahoy, kabán

TRUST, n. —tiwalà — ang pagsalig — salig

TRUST, v.—magtiwalà — pagsalig, paglaum — magsalig

TRUSTWORTHY, adj.—mapagkákatiwalaan — kasaligan, kapiyalan — masaligon

TRUTH, n. —katotohanan —ang matuod, kamatuoran — kamatuoran

TRUTHFUL, adj.—tapát, di-sinungaling — matud-anon, di-bakakon — tampad, d,-butigón

TRY, v, —subukin — pagsulay— tilawán

TUB, n. —batyâ —dulang, timba- —batyà

TUBE, n.—tubo, padaluyan ng tubig — tubo — tubo, iligán-tubig

TUESDAY, n.—Martés — Martes
—Martes

TUG-O-WAR, n. — batakán, hila-
hán—binutaray — butongáy

TUMBLE, n. —pagkabuwál, pag-
kabaligtád — paghísukamod,
pagbutalid — pagkapukan, pag-
kabansuli

TUMOR, n.—bukol— hubag way-
buthanan, grano — bukól

TUNE, n.—tono, tinig—paningog,
tono—tono, tunóg

TUNE, v. — itono, iayos —pag-
angay sa kuldas — itono, itu-
nóg, ibagay

TUNEFUL, adj.—mahimig — ha-
lim pamation — malulû nga
lanton

TURKEY, n.—pabo—pabo — pabo

TURN, n.—pihit, palít, likô—liko,
tokab, ukab — baliswà, baliskarón

TURN, v.—pagpihit, pumihit, lu-
mikô—pagliko, pag-ukab, pagtuyok — binaliskad, binaliswa

TURTLE, n. — pagóng, pawikan
—ba-o, pawikan—baó, pawikan

TWELFTH, adj.— ikalabindalawá
—ikanapulogduha —ikinapulo'g
duhá

TWELVE, n.—labindalawá — napulog-duha — napulog duhá

TWENTIETH, adj.—ikadalawam-
pû—ika-kawhaan—ika-duhá ka
pulò

TWENTY, n.—dalawampû —kaw-
haan—duhá ka pulò

TWICE, adv.—makálawá —kaduha, makaduha—makaduhá

TWIG, n. —suplíng, maliít na sangá — gamitoyng sangá — si-
ngíl, siwíl

TWILIGHT, n. — takipsilim—sa
wumsom, kilom-kilom — kasi-
sidmon

TWIN, n.—kambál — kaluha —
kapid

TWINE, n.—pisì, hiblá — pisì,
lubid, binubod — pisì, lubid

TWINE, v.—ipulupot, italì—pag-
bubod, pagpisi — lubiron

TWINKLE, n.—kisláp, kuráp —
kipat, kidlap, gilaw-gilaw — ig-
pat-igpat, kisápkisáp

TWINKLING, adj.— makuráp —
pagpamilok, pagkipat-kipat —
maigpaton

TWIST, v. — ikirin, tirintasín —
paglubag, pagtuis — lubiron

TWOSOME, adj.—dálawahan—tagurhaay — tigduhá

TYPE, n. titik, anyô, urì — titik, tipo, matáng—tipo, dagway,
sarî

TYPEWRITER, n. — makinilya—
makinilya — makinilya

TYPIST, n.—ang nagmámakinilya —tagmakinilya — manogmakinilya

TYPHOID FEVER, n.—tipus—tipus—tipos

TYPHOON, n. — bagyó —bagyo, urakán—bagyo

TYRANNY, n.—kalupitán, panggagahís—panglupig, panaugdaug —kabangisán, pagpanglupig

TYRANT, n.—manlulupig— manlulupig, madaugdaugon — manlulupig

— U —

UGLY, adj.—pangit, waláng ayos —mangil-ad, malaksot — malaw-ay

ULCER, n.—pigsâ — hubág ulsira — hubág

ULCEROUS, adj. — namamagâ, pigsahin — nana-on, naghubág —mahubagon

ULTIMATE, adj.—pantapos, hulihán — katapusan — pahingapós, pangulihi

ULTIMATUM, n. —ultimatum — katapusang pasayud — ultimatum, kahingapusán

UMBRELLA, n.—payong — payong — payong

UMPIRE,n. —tagahatol (sa larô), reperi — kuyme, tigbukóni — reperí, tagapamatbat sa hampang

UNABLE, v.—waláng kaya, hindî maáarì — di-makahimo, di-takus — wala'y ikasaráng, dî-mahimò

UNACCUSTOMED, adj.—di-gawî nabábaguhan — di-anád, nabagohán—dî-batasan, namag-ohán

UNALLOYED, adj.—waláng halò, dalisay — lunsay, way-sagol — wala'y sakút, dalisay, puraw

UNANIMOUS adj.—pinagkáisamán—inuyonan sa tanan—ginugyonán, wala'y kasumpong

UNARMED, adj.—waláng sandata —walay armas—wala'y hinganiban

UNAVOIDABLE, adj.—di-maiwasan—dili-kapugngan — dî-malikawán

UNAWARE, adj.—di-handâ— wala-makabantay — dî-handà

UNBENDING, adj. —matigás — dilî-malubay — matig-a, dî-mabawod

UNBIND, v. — kalagán—pagbadbad—hubaran

UNBORN, adj. dî pa iniáanák — wala pa mahimugso— dipa-inanák

UNBROKEN, adj.—di-baság, waláng pagkaputol — wala-mabu-ak—dí-buóng, dí-mautód

UNCERTAIN, adj.-- hindí tiyak —way seguro—dí-pat-ud

UNCLAD, adj.—hubád — hukás, hubó — hubò

UNCLE, n.—amaín, tiyó — uyoan tiyò

UNCLEAN, adj.—marumí — mahugaw — mahigkò

UNCLOTHE, v.—maghubád, magalís ng damít—paghubad, paghubo — huboan, ubahan

UNCOMMON, adj.—di-karaniwan —talagsaon — dí-tumalagsahon

UNCONCERNED, adj. — waláng pagkabahalà — way-labut—wala'y hakilabtanan

UNCONDITIONAL, adj.—waláng pasubali — way-kinutoban — wala'y kahimoan

UNCONSCIOUS, waláng malaytao— napunawan, gipanlimutan —wala'y hinalung-ong

UNCONSTITUTIONAL, adj.— labág sa saligáng batás — supak sa batakan-balaod — batok sa kasugoán

UNCORK, v. alisán ng tapón — pagbukás sa songsong —kuhaan takúp

UNCOUNTED, adj.—di-biláng — wala maihap — dí-naisip

UNCOVER, v.—mátuklasán, buksán — pagtukás, pagbukás — buksan

UNDER, prep.—sa ilalim, silong —sa ubos, ilawon—sa idalum

UNDERGO, v.—dumaán, paraanín —pag-agi, pag-antus — umagi, paagyon

UNDERLINE, v.—lagyán ng guhit— pag-ubos-badlis —kuritan sa idalum

UNDERNEATH, prep.—sa ilalim —sa ilalum — sa kaidadalman

UNDERSHIRT, n. — kamiseta-kamisín — kamiseta

UNDERSTAND, v.—unawain, intindihín — pagsabut, pagkasabut — hangpon

UNDERTAKE, n.— tagapangasiwà ng punerarya — tig-alagad sa patáy — tagtatap-punerarya

UNDERWENT, v.—sumailalim — miagi, miantus — nagpaidalum

UNDERWRITER, n. — agente ng siguro — ahente sa seguro — ahente sa seguro

UNDRESS, v. —maghubád, magalís ng damít — paghubo, paghukas — ubahan

UNDULATION, n. galáw, pagalon — balúd-balód, sagalsalon —paghublag, pagbalúd

UNDYING, adj.—waláng kamátayan — walay-kamatayon, malungtaron — wala'y kamatayon

UNEASY, adj. — di-mápalagáy— —magil-ason, naghiwaos — di-mahamtang

UNEVEN, adj. — bukúl-bukól, di-pantáy, di-patag — sagalsalon, hagis — dî-talaid

UNEXPECTED, adj.—dî akalain, hindî hiníhintáy — tuháw, talahaw — dî-ginapaabót

UNFAITHFUL, adj. — taksíl, ditapát — maluibon, masalaypon —mabudhî, dî-tampad

UNFIT, adj.—di-bagay, di-kaya— dilî takus — dî-bagay, di-makasaráng

UNFOLD, v.—iladlád — pagladlad, paghikyad—iladlad, ihumlad

UNFORGETTABLE, adj.—di-malimot — halandumón — di-malimutan

UNFORTUNATE, adj. — waláng kapalaran, di-mapalad — walay palad — wala'y kapalaran

UNFOUNDED, adj. — waláng katotohanan — bakak — wala'y kamatuoran

UNFRIENDLY, adj.— di-malapít —mabatokon, maawuyon— dî-maabyanon

UNFURNISHED, adj. — waláng kasangkapan — dili sangkap — wala'y kasangkapan

UNHAND, v.—bitiwan —buhian, pagbuhi — buy-an

UNHAPPY, adj.—malungkót, dimasayá — masub-anon, magulanon — masinulub-on

UNIFORM, n. — uniporme, paréparehong damít — uniporme— talaid, alalangay.

UNIFORM, adj.—magkakaanyô— managsama, pariho —mag-alalangay

UNIFORMITY, n.—pagkakátulad —ang panagsama — pag-alalangay

UNHEALTHY, adj. —masasakitín —masakiton, mahugaw— masakitón

UNION, n.—pagkakáisá, pag-íisá —ang paghiusa, panagtipon — paghilusa, pagtilingob

UNIQUE, adj.— waláng kapareho —talagsaon uyamot, way-tumbas — wala'y katulad

UNITE, v.—magkáisá, pag-ísahín —paghiusa, pagtipon — maghiliusa, magtilingob

UNITED STATES, n. — Estados Unidos — Tinipong Bansa sa Amerika — Estados Unidos

UNIVERSAL, adj. — náuukol sa sansinukob, para sa lahát —tibuok kalibutan, ngatanan —natungód sa kalibutan, sangatanán

UNIVERSE, n.—sansinukob—ang kalibutan — sangatanán

UNIVERSITY, n. unibersidád, pámantasan — unibersidad — unibersidad

UNJUST, adj. — waláng katarungan, hindî matuwíd—dili matarung, hiwî — wala'y katarungan

UNKEMPT, adj.—gusgusin—nagkató, kalkagon — mabahúl

UNKIND, adj.—malupít, waláng awà — way-kalooy, bangis — mabangís, wala'y kaluoy

UNKNOWN, adj.—di-kilalá—dala hiilhi — dî-nakilala

UNLAWFUL, adj—labág sa batás — supak sa balaod — batok sa kasugoán

UNLESS, prep.—máliban sa—kon dili, kawas kon — luás sa

UNLETTERED, adj — di-marunong, mangmáng — way-hibangkaagan — dî-maalam, mangô

UNLIKE, v.—di-gaya, di-kamukhâ —dili-ingon — dî-subong sang, dî-kanawóng sang

UNLOAD, v.—diskargahín, ibisán —paghaw-as—diskargahán

UNLUCKY, adj.—waláng suwerte —walay palad — wala'y kapalaran

UNMISTAKABLE, adj.—di-maipagkakamalí — walay pagkasayóp — dî-masaypan

UNNECESSARY, adj. — di-kailangan — walay kapuslanan, wala kinahanglana — dî-kinahang lan

UNPALATABLE, adj. — di-masaráp, di-makain—way-lamí, way katailas — dî-manamit

UNQUALIFIED, adj.—di-bagay walay katakus — dî-bagay

UNQUESTIONABLE, adj. — dimatátawaran — dili malalis, dili matuki — dî-mabaisan

UNREASONABLE, adj.—waláng katwiran — way-katarungan — wala'y katarungan

UNREST, n.—waláng kasiyahán —kaguliyang, way kalinaw— wala'y kaayawan

UNRIPE, adj.—hiláw — hilaw — —hiláw, bagnas

UNRUFFLED, adj.—di-nabábalino —wala masamok—dî-matandog

UNRULY, adj—maguló — langasán, si aw—magamó

UNSAFE, adj.—mapanganib—makuyáw—makatalagam

UNSEEN, adj.—di-nákikita—dili makita — dî-makit-an

UNSOPHISTICATED, adj. — dibihasá — dili tigpagawál — dî-anád

UNSPOTTED, adj.—waláng batík —walay buling — wala'y dagtâ

UNSTEADY, adj.—di-matatág — mabalhinon, dili kanunay — dî-mabakud

UNTHINKING, adj.—di-nagiisíp—walay paghunahuna, tanga—di-maisipón

UNTIE, v.—kalagán — pagtangtang, paghubad — hubaran

UNTIL, conj.—hanggáng — hangtud — tubtob

UNTIMELY, adj. — di-kapanahunan — sayó ra, ahát — dî-kapanahonan

UNTO, prep.—hanggáng sa, sa — ngadto sa, nganha — tubtob sa, sa

UNTRUE, adj.—waláng katotohanan — bakák — wala'y kamatuorán

UNUSUAL, adj.—di-karaniwan — tagsa-on — dî-tumalagsahon

UNWILLING, adj.—di-sang-ayon —dili buút, dili mosugót — dî-sugót

UNWORTHY, adj. — di-karapatdapat — dili angay — dî-bagay

UNWRAP, v.—alisán ng balot — pagbukhad — kuhaan putós

UP, prep.—sa itaás — sa itaas — sa ibabaw

UPBRAID, v.—kagalitan — pagsuway, pagkasaba — kaakigón

UPHOLD, v.—ayunan — paglaban, pagbulig — pasugtan, pasundan

UPLIFT, v. — itaás, itanyág — pagpataas, pagkiwing—batakon, ipahayag

UPPER, adj.—sa gawíng itaás—sa ibabaw, sa itaas — sa ibabaw nayon

UPRIGHT, adj. — matuwíd, banál — matarung, maligdong — matarung, balaan

UPON, adj.—sa, sa ibabaw — sa ibabaw — sa, sa ibabaw sang

UPRISING, n.—paghihimagsík — dinaghan nga pagsukol, kagubut —pagkinagubot

UPROAR, n.—kaingayan, pagkakaguló — kabanha, kasamok — kagahud

UPSET, v.—itaób, biguín — pagkulób, pagyabó — ipakulób, pakulbon

UPSHOT, n.—kinahinatnán — gisangputan, sa katapusan — maguaán

UPSTAIRS, n.—sa itaás ng hagdán, sa bahay — sa itaas sa balay — sa ibabaw sang hagdan ukón baláy

UPWARD, adv.—pasa itaás — paingen sa itaas, paibabaw — paíbabaw

URGE, v.—pilitin, himukin — pagagda, pagdasig — piliton

URGENT, adj.—kailangan, mádalian — dinalián — kinahanglan

URGING, n.—paghimok, pagpipilit — mga pag-agda — pagpamilit

URINE, n.—ihí — ihi — ihi

US, pron.—(sa) amin, (sa) atin — kita, kanato — (sa) amon, (sa) aton

USE, n.—paggamit, kagamitan — gamit, gawi — paggamit

USE, v. -- gamitin — paggamit, paggawi -- gamiton

USEFUL, adj.—makabuluhán, magágamit — mapuslanon, magpulós — magamit, mapuslanon

USELESS, adj. — waláng kabuluhán, di-magamit — walay kapuslanan—wala'y kapuslanan

USHER, n.—tagasama, tagaħatíd —tigtultol sa lingkoranan —

tag-ubáy, tubtob sa lingkoran

USHER, v.—iharáp, ipasok—pagtultol—ipaatubang, dalhon, ubayán

USUALLY, adv.—ang karaniwan —sa nandan — naandan

USUAL, adj.—kinágawián — na andan, nabatasan — kinaandan

USURER, n.—usurero, mapagpatubò—tigpatubo, usorero — usurero

USURP, v.—angkinín — pagagaw — angkunón

UTILITY, n.—kagamitán.— kagamitan — kagamitán, palatindugon

UTMOST, v.—kataás-taasan, kaduluduluhan, buóng kakayahán —labing halayó, kinatas-an — kataasón, kaukbongán, ikasaráng

UTTER, v.—bumigkás, magbadyá —paglitok, pagsulti — nagmitlang, naghambal, nagpautwas

UTTERANCE, n.—sinabi, binigkás —ang sinulti, lititák — hinambal, minitlang, pinautwas

UTTERLY, adv.—ganáp na ganáp —labing hingpit — sibù gid kaayo

— V —

VACANCY, n.—kawaláng-lamán— ang kawalay-sulod — wala'y suludlan

VACANT, adj.—bakante, waláng lamán — bakante, way-sulód — bakante, wala'y unód ukón suludlan

VACATION, n.—bakasyón, pagliliwaliw, pagpapahingá — lulinghayaw, bakasyon — bakasyon, pagpaliwáliwa

VACCINATE, v. — bakunahan, magbakuna — pagbakuna—bakonahan, magbakona

VACCINATION, n.—pagbabakuna, bakuna — bakuna — pagpamakona

VAIN, adj.—waláng bunga, hambúg—pakyas, tighambug—wala'y bunga, hambog

VALE, n.—mababang lupà — walóg — nalupyakán nga dutà

VALLEY, n.—kapatagang lupà sa tabí ng bundók, lambák—kawalogan — kunsarán nga dutà sa luyó sang bukid

VALID, adj.—maáarì, ayon-sa-batás— dunay-bili, may gibug-aton —mabaton

VALISE, n.—maleta — maleta — maleta

VALUABLE, adj. — mahalagá — mahál, bilihon — malahalon

VALUE, n.—halagá — bili — bilí

VALVE, n.—barbulá — gawang, balbúla—balbolá

VANISH, v.—maparam, mawalâ—pagkawalá, pagkahanaw — madulà, mapalà

VANITY, n.—kapalaluan, pagkawaláng kabuluhán — mga pagawál — kabugalón, wala'y ikasaráng

VANQUISH, v. — talunin, matalo —pagbuntog, pagparot — lutoson

VARIABLE, adj.—paibá-ibá—balhin-balhin, palain-lain — sarí-sarí, patuhaytuhay

VARIED, adj.—sari-sari — kalasadrakas, sari-sari — sarí-sarí

VARIETY, n.—pagkakáibá't ibá—nagkalain-lain — pagkatuhaytuhay

VARIOUS, adj.—ibá't ibá, sari-sa. rì — panaglahi-lahi — sarí-sarì

VARY, v.—magbago — pag-usab, pagbag-o — bag-ohón

VAST, adj.—malakí, malawak — daku, halapad — masangkad, manayuknayuk

VASTNESS, n. — kalawakan — ang kadaku. ang kalapdon—kahanayuhayukan

VAULT, n.—arkong binubungán, pagluksó — tipiganang puthaw —arko nga balayán, halín

VAULT, v.—lumuksó—pagluksó—lumukso, lumumpat, humalín

VEAL, n.—karnéng malambót — unód sa bakang nati — karne nga mahumok, kaundan

VEGETABLE, n.—gulay — utanón, lagutmon — utanón

VEHICLE, n.—sasakyán sa dálatan — salakyanan — salakyan sa dalan

VEIL, n.—belo, talukbóng, tabing —taptap, tabón, belo, pandong—mantò

VEILED, adj.—nakatagò — tinaptan, binilohan — natagò

VEIN, n.—ugát — ugát—ugát

VELVET, n.—gamusa — tersiyopilo, sidahon — gamosa

VELVETY, adj.—malambót—mahumok, malumó — kahumok

VELOCITY, n.—bilís, kabilisán — katulin—kadasigón

VENDETTA, n.—higantí — dugoong pinatyanay — himalús

VENERABLE, adj.—kagalang-galang, marangál — halangdon, talahuron — talahuron

VENERATE, v.—igalang — pagtahud, pagtamud — tahuron

VENERATION, n. — pagsambá, paggalang — ang pagmahal — pagtahud

VENGEANCE, n.—paghihigantí—panimalus — pagtimalús, paghingabút

VENGEFUL, adj—mapaghigantí —mapanimaslon — mahingabuton, mahimalusón

VENOM, n.—lason—hiló — hilô

VENOMOUS, adj.—punô ng lason, nakamámatáy — makahilo, makamátay—makahililò

VENT, n.—butás, bukás — lungág, gul-anán—buhò, buslot

VENTILATE, v. — pahanginan — pagpahangin, paghayahay — pahanginan

VENTILATION, n. — pagpapahangin — pahayahay — pagpabangínhangín

VERACITY, n. — katotohanan — pagkatinuod, katinuoran — kamatuoran

VERB, n.—pandiwà — berbo, panglihok

VERBAL, adj.—pasalitâ — binabá—palihokon, palahambal

VERBALLY, adv.—sa salitâ — sa binabá—sa hambal

VERBAL NOUN, n.—pangngalang makadiwà — binabá nga berbo —pangalan-panglihok

VERDANT, adj.—luńtian — labas, malangsob — buloberdehon

VENTURE, v.—mangahás — pagpangahás, pagpatugá — mangahás

VENDOR, n.—tagapagbilí — mamaligya — mamaligyà

VERIFICATION, n.—katotohanan —ang kamatuoran — kamatuoran

VERIFY, v.—patotohanan — pagmatuod — pamatud-an

VERY, adv.—totoóng tunay — labi gayud, tinud, kaayo—matudo gid

VERSE, n.—berso, tulâ — balak, bagay — berso, binalaybay

VESSEL, n.—sasakyán, sisidlán— sakayán—sakayán, suludlan

VEST, n. — tsaleko — tsaliko — tsoleko

VEST, v.—pagkalooban, ipagkaloób — paghatag gahúm — hatagan

VERSUS, prep.—laban sa — batok sa—batuk sa

VETERAN, n.—beterano — beterano, sinati, salin — beterano

VETO, n. — beto, pagpapawaláng halagá — beto — pamalabagan, dî-kilalahon

VETO, v.—betuhan, waláng halagá — pagbeto, betohan — balabagayn, sikwayón

VEX, v.—magpainit ng ulo, pagalitin — paglangas, pag-alingasa —pasilabuon, paakigon

VEXATION, n.—galit, yamót—kalangas, kasamok — akíg, mahanusbò

VIA, n.—sa pamamagitan — pinaagi sa, hapit sa — sa kalalangan sang

VIAND, n.—ulam—sud-an—ikaon

VICE, n.—bisyo, kahalili, bise — kahilay-an, halili, lugpit — bisyo, tal-us

VICINITY, n.—sa paligid—kasilinganan — sa palibot

VICTIM, n —bíktimá, ang nasawi —biktima, sinakit—biktima, himalaut

VICTOR, n.—nagwagí, nanalo — mananaog mamumontog—nagdaúg, mananaóg

VICTORIOUS, adj. — mapagwagí —madaugon — madaugon

VICTORY, n.—ang pananalo, ang pagwawagí — nagdaúg, kadaugán — pagpandaóg

VIE, v.—makipagpaligsahan — pakigtakus, pakigdiga — makigtusay, makigtakús

VIEW, n.—tánawin, pagtingín — talan-awon, panan-awón — talan-awon

VIEW, v. — tingnán, tanawín — pagtan-aw, pagsid-ing — tanawón

VIGIL, n.—pagtatanod — pagbantay sa hinaya — pagbantay

VIGILANCE, n. — pagbabantáy nang lubós — ang pagbantay maigmaton — bantayán maayo

VIGOR, n.—lakás, siglá — kusóg, kabaskug — kusóg, pagsik, gahúm

VIGOROUS, adj.—maalakás — mabaskugon, aktik — mapagsik, makusog

VILE, adj. — hamak, marumí — ubós, talamayon, mahugaw — kubós, mahigkò

VILLAGE, n.—nayon.— balangay —duóg, kunsarán

VILLAIN, n.—masamáng tao, kontrabida—dautang tawo, kontrabida—malaut nga táo

VILLAINOUS, adj. — nápakasamá, mámamatay — dautan, talamayon — ma'auton

VIM, n.—lakás, siglá — kusóg — kusóg, pagsik

VINE, n.—halamang gumágapang na baging gaya ng ubas — balagón, makapyotong tanúm — balagon

VINEGAR, n.—sukà — suka — langgaw

VIOLATE, v, — lumabág, pumasláng — paglapas, pagsupak — lumapas

VIOLATION, n.—paglabág — kalapasan — pagpanglabag, paglapas

VIOLENCE, n. — ahg paglabág, ang pamamasláng, dahás—panglugos, paniapas—pagpanglabag, pagpanglapas

VIOLENT, adj.—marahás — maharuson, mainiton — makàhas

VIOLIN, n.—biyolín — biyolin — byolín

VIRGIN, n.—birhen, babaing waláng bahid dungis sa kalinisan ng pagkababae — putli, ulay, birhen — birhen, ulay

VIRGINITY, n.—kalinisan ng pagkababae — ang kaulay, ang kaputli — pagkaulay

VIRTUE, n.—kabanalan, bisà — hiyas sa kabuotan kaligdong — kaulay

VIRTUOUS, adj.—banál, malinis—boutan, malinis, maligdong — belaan, ulay

VISIBLE, adj.—pagdalaw, dumalaw, natátanáw — makita, dayág—makit-an

VISION, n.—pangitain, malas — panan-aw, handurawan — talanawon

VISIONARY, adj.—mapangitain—handurawnon, talidamgo — mahandurawon

VISIT, n.—pagdalaw — duaw, pakigkita — duaw

VISIT, v.—dumalaw, dalawin — pagduaw — magduaw, duawon

VISITOR, n.—bisita, panauhin — dumoduaw — bisita, dumuluaw

VITAL, adj.—kailangan, mahalagá —gikinahanglan uyamot — kinahanglanon, malahalon

VITALITY, n.—kalakasán — ang Kakusóg — kapagsikón

VIVACIOUS, adj.—masiglá—lagsik, abtikón, ngayá—mapagsik

VOCABULARY, n.—talásálitaan-pulonglaan, kapulongan — bokabularyo, tigkapulongan

VOCALIST, n. — máng-aawit — mag-aawit — manog-amba, mangangamba

VOCATION, n.—hilig, gawî, gáwain — pangita, buhat — trahabo, hilikutón

VOCATIONAL, adj.—ukol sa mga gáwain — mahatungod sa buhat —natungód sa hilikutón

VOGUE, n.—moda, uso—urog — moda, uso, binag-o

VOICE, n.—ihayag—tingog — tingog, pahayag

VOICE, v.—ipagtapát — pagpadayág sa hunahuna — ipahayag

VOID, adj.—walâng lamán, waláng halagá o bisà — walay bili —wala'y unód, wala'y bili ukón gahúm

VOID, n.—kawaláng-lamán — kawalay suíod, basiyo — pagkawala'y unód

VOLUBLE, adj.—masalitâ — mausabon, daling maligid — palahambal

VOLUME, n.—aklát, tomo — anib, tomo sa basahón — binahin, tomo

VOLUMINOUS, adj.—makapál — mabagá, daghang anib — madamul

VOLUNTARY, adj.—kusang-loób —kinaugalingon — hungód

VOMIT, v.—sumuka — pagsuka, pagdugwa — sumuka

VOTE, n.—boto, halál — boto, suprahiyo — toto, pili

VOTE, v.—bumoto, humalál—pagboto, pagpili — bumoto, pumili

VOW, v.—sumumpâ — pagsumpa —manaad

VOW, n. — tandâ ng paggalang, sumpa — panaad sa Dios—pagpanaad

VOWEL, n. — patinig, (titik ng abakada) — paningog, mga bokál—patunóg (sa abakada)

VOYAGE, n.—paglalayág, pagda-
ragát — panaw sa dagat — pagpanakayon, pagpanagát
VULGAR, adj.—magaspáng—ma-

hilas, law-ay — mabahúl
VULNERABLE, adj. — mahiná,
masásalakay — mahuyáng —
maluya, saráng masalakay

— W —

WADE, v.—maglunoy — pag-ubog
—mag-ubog

WAG, v.—igaláw, ipaspás — pag-
kitíw — palibutliboton, pakiay-
kiayon

WAGE, n.—kita, sahod — suhol —
kinitaan, suhol

WAGER, v.—pumustá — pagpus-
ta, pagkasado — pumusta

WAGER, n. — pumustá — pusta,
kasado — magpusta

WAGE WAR, v.—makipagdigma-
an — pagpakiggubat — makig-
awayón

WAGON, n.—bagól—kareton, ka-
romata — bagón

WAIL, v.—manangis, managhóy—
pagminatay, pagsubó, pagbakho
—manganduhoy, managhoy

WAILING, n. — pananangis, panaghóy — minatay, bakbo —
pagpanangis, pagpanganduhoy

WAIST, n.—baywang—hawak —
hawak

WAISTCOAT, n.—tsaleko — sa-
liko — tsaleko

WAIT, v.—maghintáy — paghulat
—maghulát

WAITING ROOM, n. — hintayan,
páhingahan — lawak-hulataan
—hululatan

WAITER, n. — tagapaglingkód —
maninilbi sa kan-anan — serbi-
dór

WAITING, n.—paghihintáy — na-
gahulat — paghulát

WAIVE, v.—pabayaan — pagbiyá,
pag-iway — pabayaan

WAKE, v.—gumising, gisingin —
pagmata, pagpukaw — pukawon

WALK, v.—lumakad — paglakat,
paglakaw — lumakát

WALL, n. — padér — bungbong,
paril — padér

WALLET, n.—pitaka — pitaka —
pitaka

WALLOW, v.—maglubalób—pag-
lunang, pagtona — magligídligíd

WANDER, v.—gumalà, lumaboy—
paglibud, paglaag — manghu-
longhulong, magtangâtangà

WANDERINGS, n.—paggagalâ — mga paglibud-libod, pamagdoy— pagtangátangà

WAN, adj—maputlâ — luspad, lusparon — malapsì

WANT, n.—pangangailangan—kinahanglanon — kinahanglanon

WANT, v.—mangailangan — pagkinahanglan — magkinahanglan

WANTING, adj.—kulang, nangángailangan — kulang, nagkinahanglan — nagakinahanglan

WAR, n.—digmaan, gera, gulò — gubat — inaway, gera

WARBLER, n. —pipít — magaawit, langgam tig-awit tamsi-amba sang pispis

WARD, n.—alagà, silid sa ospitál, kanlungan — tig-alima sa tambalanan — tatapán, hulót sa ospitál

WARDEN, n.—tagapangasiwà ng bilángguan — alkayde, punoan sa karsel — àlkaide

WARDROBE, n.—aparadór ng damít — aparador sa mga sapút —aparadór sang panapton

WARE, n.—panindá, pang-akit — mga tinda, baligya — balaligyà

WARM, v.—initin, painitin — mainit, maigang, alimuot — maalabaab

WARMLY, adv. — may kainitan, buóng-pusò — mainiton — may kaalabaab

WARN, v.—bigyán ng babalâ — pagpasidaan, pagpabantay — magpatundà

WARNING, n.—babalâ — pasidaan — patundà

WARRANT, n.—patotoó, patunay —pasalig, sugo sa pagdakop — pamatuod, sugò sang hukóm

WARRIOR, n. — mandirigmâ — mangugubat — mangangawáy

WASH, n.—lábahan — labhonón— kalunggo — kalunggo

WASH, n.—labahan — labhonón— lalabhan, bulunakán

WASH, v.—labhán, linisin — paglaba — labhan, bunakan

WASHER, n,—manlalabá, lábaban —manlalaba — manglalaba

WASHOUT, adj.—lipás — tawós na — hinugasan

WASTE, v.—sayangin — pag-usik, hugaw — usikan

WASTEFUL, adj. — bulaksák — mausikon — buhahâ

WATCH, n.—orasáng maliít, bantáy — gamay nga taknaan, relos — orsán nga diótay, bantay

WATCH, v.—magbantáy — pagbantay — magbantay

WATCHDOG, n.—bantáy — tigbantay — bantay-idû

WATCHFUL, adj.—mapagbantáy —mabinantayón — mabinantayon

WATCHMAN, n. — bantáy, tanod —sirino, magbalantay — bantay, sereno

WATER, n.—tubig — tubig — tubig

WATER, v. — tubigan, diligín — pagtubig, pagbasá — tubigan, bunyagán

WATERMELON, n. — pakwán — pakwan, sandiya — sandiya

WATERPROOF, adj.—di-tatagusán — dili dutlag tubig — dîmabasa

WATERY, adj.—matubig — tubigon — tubigon

WAVE, n.—alon, panahón — bálud, kulong — balúd

WAVE, v.—iwasiwas, kumawáy — pagkayab — iparagpag

WAVY, adj.—magaláw — mabahid kulóngon — mahulág

WAX, n.—pagkít, tutulí — talo— atutuli, waks

WAXEN adj.—namúmutî—namutî—mamutî

WAY, n—daán, páraán — aginan, dalan, paagi — nagapalamutî

WAYLAY, v.—harangin, abatan — pag-atáng, pagbanhig — dalan, paagi

WAYWARD, adj. — waláng tuto, pabayâ — danghág, way-tumóng —dalamhak

WE, pron.—kamí, tayo, kitá — kami, kitá — kamí, kitá.

WEAK, adj.—mahinà, marupók — maluya, maluyahon — maluya, matapók

WEAK-KNEED, adj.—mahinà ang loób — hinayg-tuhod, lulid — maluya ang tuhod

WEAKNESS, n.—kahinahan, karupukán — kahinayan, kamaluyahon — kaluyahón, katapók

WEALTH, n.—kasaganaan, kayamanan — bahandi, katigayonan —manggad

WEALTHY, adj.—mayaman, saganà — dato, sapian, adunahan — manggaranon

WEAN, v.—awatin, ilayô — pagbuwag, pagpalayó — bulagón

WEAPON, n. — kasangkapan, armás, sandata — hinagiban — hinganiban, armas

WEAR, n.—kasuutan — mga sulobon, sapút—panapton

WEAR, v.—magsuót, gumamit — pagsul-ob, paggamit — magpanapuót

WEARINESS, n. — kapaguran — kaluya, kalapóy — kakapoyán

WEARY, adj.—pagód — gikapóy, naluya — kapóy

WEATHER, n.—lagáy ng panahón —kahimtang sa panahon — panahón

WEATHER, v.—batahín — pagsagubang — sulayon

WEAVE, v.—maglala, humabi — paghabol, paghablon — lalahon, maglala, maghabúl

WEAVE n.—pagkakahabi, habi — hinabol, hináblon — paghabúl paglala

WEAVER, n.—manlalala, tagalala, manghahabi—maghahabol—manghahabúl, manoglala

WEB, n.—bahay-gagambá — baláy sa lawá-lawá—lawà

WEBBY, adj.—sali-salimuót — lawa-lawaón—malawaon

WED, v. — ikasál, pakasalán — pagkasál, pagminyo — ikasál, kasalon

WEDDING, n.—kasál — kasál—kasál

WEDDING BELLS n.—tunóg ng kampanang pangkasál — lingkanay sa kasál — linigganay sa kasál

WEDGE, n.—kalang — bahi, saról, ighahapák—pitalâ

WEDNESDAY, n.—Miyérkolés — Miyerkoles — Mierkolés

WEED, n.—masamáng damó, yagít — sagbut — barit

WEED, v.—linisin, alisán ng damó pagiinis — baritan, kuhaan barit

WEEK, n.—linggó — semana — simana, pitoadlaw

WEEKLY, adj.—lingguhan — sinimaná — pitoadlawan, simanál

WEEP, v. — umiyák, lumuhà — paghilak, pagbakho — humibî, nanangis

WEEPING, n.—pagluhà — nagahilak, nagaluha — pagpanangis, paghibî

WEEVIL, n.—bukbók — bokbok—bukbok

WEIGH, v.—timbangín — pagtimbang -- timbangón

WEIGHT, n. — timbáng — timbang, gibug-aton — timbang

WEIGHTY, adj. — matimbáng — bug-at — matimbangón

WEIRD adj.—nakatátakot — makahadlok — makahaladlok

WELCOME, n.—maligayang pagdating, pagsalubong—maayong pag-abut — pagtamyaw, pagpadungóg sa pag-abót

WELCOME, v.—sumalubong nang magiliw — pagsugat, pagdawat —tumamyaw sing malipayon

WELD, v.—paghinangin—pagsulda — soldahón

WELL, n.—balón—atabay — bubón

WELL, adj.—mabuti, magaling — maayo — maayo

WELFARE, n. — kaginhawahan, ikabúbutĩ — kaayohan, kahamugaway — kaayohan

WELT, v.—paluin — pagpalo, mohón — hampakón, papaón

WEST, n.—kanluran — kaṣadpan —katundan

WESTERN, adj.—gawíng kanluran — ḍapít sa kasadpan — nayon sa katundan, katundanon

WESTWARD, adj. — papúntáng kanluran — patumóng kasadpan —pakatundan

WET, adj.—basâ—basá, tumóg — basâ

WET, v.—basaín — pagbasá, paghumód — bas-on

WET BLANKET. n. — pampawaláng-siglâ — bínasang habol — wala'y ginkasugtan

WHALE, n. — isdáng balyena — balyena, ambuhotan — balyena

WHARF, n.—pantalán — pantalán, landíganan — pantalán, dungkaan

WHAT, pron.—anó — unsa, unsay (?)—anó

WHAT, interj. –. anó — ha unsa (?)—anó, ngaa

WHATEVER, n.—kahit ano — bisan unsa — bisán anó

WHEAT, n.—trigo — trigo—trigo

WHEEL, n.—gulóng — ligid, kareton — rweda, ariring

WHEEL, v.—bumuwelta, pagulungin, paikutini — pagliko, pagpaligid — bumalík, patiyogon

WHEN, adv. — kailán — anus-a, kanus-a (?) — kasan-o

WHENEVER, adv.—kailanmán — bisan anus-a — kutob san-o

WHERE, adv.—saán — hain, diin, asa — diín

WHEREBY, adj. — sa pamamagitan nitó — sa paagi nga — amó man

WHEREFORE, adv. — kayâ ngâ, dahil dito — tungod niini — ganì man, tungód siní

WHEREIN, adv.—na doón — sa diin — diín

WHEREVER, adv. — saán man — bisan diini — bisán diín

WHET, v.—ihasà — pagbaid, paghait — bairon

WHETHER, v.—kahit — maskin, kon — bisán

WHICH, pron.—alin, na—hain sa, nga — diín sinâ

WHILE, adv. — samantala—samtang — samtang

WHILE, n. — sandalî — kadiyut nga panahon -- tinión

WHILE, v.—aksayahín — pagpalabay — nakaligad

WHINE, v.—umigít, humuni — pag-agulo, pagngulob — umigot, naghuní

WHIP, n.—látikó, pamalò—latús, pamalo — latigó, putik

WHIP, v.—paluin—paglatús, pagpalo — putikon, latigohón

WHIRL, n.—ikot — tuyok, liko, tulibong — budyong, tuyob

WHIRL, v.—paikutin—pagtuyok, pagtulilik — pabudyongón, patuyobon

WHISPER, n. — bulóng — honghong, hagawhaw — hutík

WHISPER, v.—ibulóng, bumulóng .—paghonghong, paghagawhaw—hutikán

WHISTLE, n.—pasyók, sutsót, pito—taghoy, tihol, pito — pito, panihól

WHISTLE, v.—sumipol — pagtaghoy, pagtihol — pítohan, paniholán

WHISTLING, adj. — sumísipol—nagtaghoy — nanihoól

WHITE, n.—putî, maputî — putî, mapute — putî, maputî

WHITE ANT, n.—anay — anay—anay

WHITHER, adv.—saán — sa diing dapit—diín?

WHO, pron.—sino, na—kinsa, nga —sin-o

WHOEVER, pron.—sínumán—bisan kinsa — bisán sin-o

WHOLE, n.—buô, lahát, waláng sirà, waláng kulang — tibuók, tanán—bugos, tanán

WHOLESALE, n. — pakyawan—pinakyaw, pinisán — pakyawan

WHOLESOME, adj. — magalíng, pampalakás — makaayo sa lawas, lamian — kabug-osán

WHOLLY, adv.—buô, lahát at lahát — tibuók, tanán-tanán—binug-os, tanántanán

WHOM, pron.—na—nga kinsa—kay sin-on

WHOSE pron.—kanino, sino ang may-arì — kang kinsa—sin-o ang tag-iya

WHY, n.—bakit — ngano (?) — ngaa?

WICKED, adj.—masamâ, makasalanan—lampingasan, dautan — malain, makasasalà, makangililad

WIDE, adj.—malapad, maluwáng —halapad, haluag—masangkad

WIDOW, n. balong babae, biyuda, balo — babayeng balo, biyuda — balo nga babáe

WIDOWER, n.—balong lalaki, biyudo—lalaking balo, biyudo — balo nga lalaki

WIDTH, n.—kalaparan — gilapdon—kalapad

WIFE, n.—asawa (babae), may-bahay — asawa — asawa

WILD, adj.—ligáw, mabangís, ma-iláp—luóg, ihalas—mailá, ilahas

WILDERNESS, n.—ilán — kala-sángan, kasiutan — banlas, desierto

WILL, n.—kalooban, loobin — ka-bubut-on, tugon — kabubut-on, but-on

WILL, v.—ipagkaloób, ipamana—paghatag kabilin—ihátag, idulot

WIN, v.—manalo, magwagí, mag-tagumpáy — pagdaúg, paglam-pus — magdaúg

WINCE, v.—mamaluktót, masak-tán — pag-urong, pagkusnot —mabarikutot, masakitán

WIND, n.—hangin — hangin — hangin

WIND, v. kidkirín, linisin, umi-nog — pagliso — barubonan

WINDMILL, n.—mákiná na pina-tátakbó ng hangin — galingan ginatuyok sa hangin — makina sa hangin

WINDOW, n.—bintaná, dúrunga-wán — tamboan, tamboanan bintaná, gawahán

WINDY, adj.—mahangin —maha-nginon — mahangin

WINE, n.—alak — alak, bino — alak, bino

WING, n.—pakpák — pakó, kapáy —pakpak

WING, v.—lumipád — paglupád, pagkapáy — lumupád

WINK, n.—kindát — kidhat, kiló, pamilok — mangiláy

WINNINGS, n.—kapanalunan, pa-ralunan—mga dinuúgan—pag-daúg

WINTER, n.—tagginaw, taglamíg —tingtugnaw — tigtulugnaw

WIPE, v.—magpahid, magpunas, lipulin — pagpahid, paglinis—pahiram

WIRE, n.—alambre, kawad — ka-wad, alambre — alambre, dulós

WIRE, v.—telegramahán, padal-hán ng pahatíd-kawad — pagte-legrama — telegramahan, ha-tudulosán

WISDOM, n.—kaalaman, karunu-ngan—kaalam, kahibalo — ki-naalam

WISE, adj.—maalam — maalam, manggialamon — maalam

WISH, n. — nais, ñasà, pita, kahí-lingan — pangandoy, paningnha —handum, humon, bukò

WISH, v.—naisin, pitahin hilingín —pagpangandoy, pagpaninguha handumón, humunon, bukuon

WIT, n.—kaisipan, katulinan sa pag-unawà — salabutan, mahait, panabút — kaabtikón, kahapós maghangúp

WITCH, n.—mangkukulam—ungo balbal, abát—manghihiwit

WITCHERY, n.—pang-akit, pangkulam — pangabát, pamalbal—pagpanghiwít

WITH, prep.—patí, kasama, kalukob — uban, apil sa, dungan—sa

WITHDRAW, v.—umurong, alisín, bumawì, lumayô—pagbiya, pagsibug—ûmisul, lumayô

WITHDRAWAL, n. — pag-urong, pagbawì, pagkuha — ang pagbiya, ang pagsibug — nag-isul, nagpahilayô

WITHER, v. — matuyô, malantá, maluóy — pagkalaya, pagkalawos — malanta, malayà

WITHIN, prep.—sa loób — sa sulód, sulód — sa sulód

WITHOUT, adv.—sa labás, kung walâ — sa gawás, sa gulá—sa guâ, kon walâ

WITHSTAND, v.—matagalán, matiis—pagdugay, pag-agwanta—makapadugay, makugi

WITNESS, n. — saksí, testigo—saksi, testigos — saksi, testigo

WITNESS, v.—saksihán — saksihan — saksihán

WITTY, adj.—matalino — masabtunon — mangin-alamon

WOE, n. — sa abâ, sakit, hirap—kaguól, kasubó — huól, kalisúd

WOLF, n.—lobo, halimaw — lobo —lobo

WOMAN, n.—babae, ale — babaye — babáe, tyâ

WON, v.—nanalo, nagwagí — midaúg, nakadaúg — dag-on

WONDER, n.—kagitlá-gitlâ, pagtataká—katingalahan, kahibudnganan — katingalahán

WONDER, v.—magtaká, mámanghâ—pagtingala, paghibulong — magkatingala

WONDERFUL, adj.—kahanga-hangà, kagilá-gilalás — kahibulongan, katingalahan — katingalahán

WONDROUS, adj.—katakataká nakamámanghâ—makahingangha — katingalahán

WOOD, n.—kahoy na putól o pinutol — kahoy, tabla—tapî, kakahoyan

WOOD CARVER, n.—mang-uukit ng kahoy—magkukulit—mangbabanhay sa kahoy

WOOL, n.—lana, balahibo — lana, balhiho sa karnero — lana

WORD, n. — salitâ — pulong — hambal

WORK, n.—trabaho, gawâ — buhat, trabaho — trabaho, hikut

WORD, v.—gumawâ, magtrabaho —pagbuhat, paggamá — magtrabaho, maghikut

WORKER, n. — manggagawà — magbubuhat, maggagamá—niamumugón

WORKMAN, n.—manggagawà — magbubuhat, maggagama—mamumugón, hornal

WORLD, n.—mundó, sanlibután—kalibutan — kalibutan

WORM, n.—uod — ulod — ulod

WORRY, n. — pag-aalapaáp, pagaalaala — kayugót, kabalaka — pagkabalaka

WORRY, v.—pag-alahanin, magalaala — pagkayugót, pagbalaka — kabalak-an

WORSHIP, v.—sambahín, sumambá — pagsimba, pagmahál — pangamuyoan

WORST, adj.—pinakamasamâ, ang kasama-samaán — pinakadautan, labing ngil-ad — labíng malain

WORTH, n.—halagá — bili—malahalon, bilí

WORTHLESS, adj.—waláng halagá, waláng silbí — walay bili, walay pulós — wala'y bilí, wala'y pulós

WORTHY, n.—kahálagahan—malahalon—malahalon

WOUND, n. — sugat — samád—pilás

WOUND, v. — sugatan — pagsamad — pilasan

WRAP, v. — balutin, ibalabal — pagputós — putson, kunopan

WRAP, n.—balabal — tapis, patadyong — tapis, patadyong

WRATH, n. — poót, galit—kasukó kaligutgot, kapikál — aligutgot

WREATH, n.—koronang bulaklák, pulutóng ng mga dahon at bulaklák—lukóng sa mga bulak —pagkabará, pagkagubâ

WRECK, n. — pagkabagbág, pagkasirà, pagkawasak — gubá gun-ob, mga gusbat—pagkagubâ, pagkawasák

WRECK, v.—sirain wasakin, mábanggâ — paggubá, paggun-ob, paggusbat, pagkalunod — gubon, wasakón

WRESTLE, v. — ibunô — pagdumog — lubagon, detsohón

WRETCH, n. — kawawà, abâ — makaluluoy, alaut—makaluluoy

WRETCHED, adj.--kawawà, hamak—hinimong alaut, timawa—kinulabos

WRINKLE, n.—kulubót, kunót — kunót, gum-os — kumurinut

WRINKLE, v.—gusutin — pagkunót, paggum-os — lunsay kurinút

WRINKLED, adj.—punô ng kulubót—kunotón, gum-osón—punô sing kurinút

WRIST, n.—kasu-kasuan sa punò ng kamáy — puso — punyos, bulutkonan

WRIST WATCH, n.—relos na pamulsó—reló sa pulso — relo de pulso, taknaan sa bayóbayo

WRITE, v.—sumulat, lumiham — pagsulát — sumulát

WRITER, n.—mánunulat, autor, mánunulat ng mga aklát—tag-sulát, magsusulat — manunulat, tagsulát

WRITHE, v.—mamilipit — paglubag, pagbalikó — maghiyod

WRITINGS, n.—ang mga isinulat, akdâ — mga sinulát—sinulatán

WRONG, v.—salbahihin, tampalasanin, pagtaksilán—sayóp, kasaypanan — basulon, budhián

— Y —

YAM, n.—ubi — ubi — ubi

YANK, n.—hila, pilipit — butad, bulibod — torse, lubag

YANK, v.—hilahin, pilipitin—pagbutad, pagbulibod — torsehón, lubagon

YAP, n. — tahól, satsát — tabí, yawyaw, lamlam — taghol, katâkatà

YAP, v. —.sumatsát, tumahól—pagtabi, pagyayaw, paglamlam —tumaghol, nagkatâkatà

YARD, n.—bakuran, yarda—yarda, tugkaran, bara—yarda, lagwertahan

YARN, n.—kuwento — sugilanan, sugid, lubid — manugilanon

YATCH, n.—maliít na bapór o sasakyán, yate — yate, sakayán

lulinghayawan — yate, diótay nga sakayán

YAWN, n.—paghihigáb — huy-ab —panguy-ab

YAWNING, adj.—naghíhigáb, ma.tatarík — nanghuy-ab — pagpanguy-ab, tukarón

YEAR, n.—taón — tuig — tuig

YEARLY, ad.—taún-taón, táunan — tinuig, tuig-tuig, panuig — tuigtuig, tuigan

YEARN, v.—manabík — pagpangandoy — hidlawón

YEARNINGS, n. — pananabík — mga pangandoy — pagkahidlaw

YEARNY, adj.—nakapanánabík — mapangandoyan — kahidlawón

YEAST, n.—lebadura, pampaalsá —buwá nga maaslum, libadura —lebadora

247

YELL, n.—pagkantiyáw — suli-
yaw, singgít — siyagit

YELL, v.—sumigáw—pagsuliyaw,
pagsinggit — sumiyagit

YELLOW, n.—diláw — madalág,
talawán—dalág,. kanaryo

YELLOWISH, adj. — madiláw —
madalág-lalág, madalagon—ma-
dalagdalag

YELLOWING, v.—maniláw—ang
pagpangdalag — nagadalág

YFLP. n.—biglâng sigáw — pag-
hut, hulhol, uwáng sa iró—hinalì, suminggit

YES, n.—oo, opò—oo, pagtangdo
—huo, huod

YESTERDAY, n. — kahapon —
gahapcn, kagahapon — kahopon

YESTERNIGHT, n. — kagabí —
kagabii — kagab-i

YET, adv.—pa, sa kabilâ noón—
bisán, apán, ugaling—pa, sa pi-
hák sinâ, apang

YIELD, n.—bunga, ani — bunga,
ani abút—pagpamunga, pagsugót, paghiuyon

YIELD, v.—pumayag, magbunga
—pag-uyon, pagpamunga—mag-
pamunga, magpasugot, magpa-
hiuyon

YIELDING, adj.—pumápayag, malambót — namunga, sumosugót
—pagpasugót, paghiuyon

YOKE, n.—pambatok, singkáw—
yugo, tangkol — tuwangtuwa-
ngán

YOLK, n.—pulá ng itlóg — pug-
hak sa itlog — batog

YONDER, adv.—nároón, doón, diyán — sa unáhan, didto sa layó
—dirâ, didto nayon

YOU, pron.—ikáw, kayó — ikáw,
kámó—ikáw, kamó

YOUNG, adj.—batà—batanon —
kabataón, kalamharon

YOUNGEST, adj.—pinakabatà —
labíng bata, kinamanghuran —
lamíng bataón

YOUNGISH, adj.—batá-batâ—bo-
batan-on — bataón, lamharon

YOUR, pron. — ang inyóng, mo,
ninyó — ang imong, ang inyong
imo, inyo

YOURS, pron.—inyó, iyó — imo,
inyo — sa inyo, sa imo

YOURSELF, pron.—ang sarili mo
—ikáw gayúd, imong kaugalingon—ang kaugalingon mo

YOUTH, n.—kabataan — pagkabata, kabatan-onan — pagkaba-
taón

YOUTHFUL, adj.—parang binatà
—batan-on, may pagkabata —
lamharon

— Z —

ZEAL, n. — kainitan sa paggawâ ng anó mang bagay — kainit, kadasig sa tinguha — handum sa paghumán sang bisán anó nga butáng

ZEALOUS, adj. — masigasig, mapagwaláng pagod — masingkamuton, maluguton — mahimulaton, wala'y pagkatakà

ZEBRA, n. — kabayo na guhitán ang balát—kabayong may badlis-badlis sa lawas—kabayo nga guráyguráy ang balahibo, sebra

ZENITH, n.—katuktukán — tuktokán, kinatúktokán — putokputokán

ZERO, n. — sero, walâ — sero wala—sero, walâ

ZEST, n.—kasiglahán — kaabtik —kapagsikón

ZESTFUL, adj. — masiglâ—maabtikon—mapagsik

ZINC, n. —yero — sin alang sa atóp — sin

ZONE, n.—sona, poók, sakop, isá sa limáng bahagi ng mundó ayon sa init at lamíg—walog, purok, binahin nga dapit—sona, puók, sinakpan, isá sang limá ka bahin sang kalibutan sunô sa init kag kabugnaw

ZONIFICATION, n. — pagbahatì ng poók—pagkabahin-bahin sa usa ka dapit—pagdulon sang isá ka poók

ZOO, n.—álagaán ng mga hayop —pasundayagán sa mga mananáp—alaypan hayup, tangkalan

ZOOM, v.—pumailanláng — pagsulbong, pagpaitaas — tumimbuok